THE GREATER WAR 1912–1923

General Editor

ROBERT GERWARTH

The Italian Empire and the Great War

VANDA WILCOX

Great Clarendon Street, Oxford, OX2 6DP,
United Kingdom

Oxford University Press is a department of the University of Oxford.
It furthers the University's objective of excellence in research, scholarship,
and education by publishing worldwide. Oxford is a registered trade mark of
Oxford University Press in the UK and in certain other countries

First Edition published in 2021

Impression: 1

Published in the United States of America by Oxford University Press
198 Madison Avenue, New York, NY 10016, United States of America

British Library Cataloguing in Publication Data

Data available

Library of Congress Control Number: 2021931246

ISBN 978–0–19–882294–3

DOI: 10.1093/oso/9780198822943.001.0001

Printed and bound by
CPI Group (UK) Ltd, Croydon, CR0 4YY

In Loving Memory of

Philippa Nicholls
(1952–2017)

Acknowledgements

At Oxford University Press, I would like to thank the editors who have steered the manuscript through the process of commissioning and publication: Robert Faber, Stephanie Ireland, Cathryn Steele, and Henry Clarke, as well as the production team. I am grateful to Series Editor Robert Gerwarth for giving me the opportunity to contribute this volume, and I also thank the anonymous reviewers, both of the original proposal and of the finished text, whose suggestions helped me immensely.

I had the immeasurable fortune of living for many years in the same city as my archival sources; nevertheless, without the expert assistance of the staff of the Archivio Centrale dello Stato, the Archivio del Ufficio Storico dello Stato Maggiore dell'Esercito, and the Archivio Storico del Ministero degli Affari Esteri, as well as the Biblioteca di Storia Moderna e Contemporanea and the Biblioteca Centrale Nazionale in Rome, this book could never have been possible. In Paris I thank the Bibliothèque Nationale Française and in Oxford the staff of the Bodleian Library.

Sections of this research were presented at conferences and seminars hosted by the Universities of Leeds and Wolverhampton, Penn State University, the Freie Universität Berlin, the Stato Maggiore della Difesa, the Association for the Study of Modern Italy, and the International Society for First World War Studies; I thank all the organizers who invited me and all those participants who offered feedback and asked tough questions. John Cabot University's faculty development funds supported my travel to some of these conferences for which I am most grateful. I owe a huge debt to Adrian Gregory for twenty years of support and encouragement. I benefited greatly from discussing ideas with many people, whether in person or on Twitter, including Nir Arielli, Jonathan Boff, Selena Daly, John Gooch, Dónal Hassett, Franziska Heimburger, John Horne, Oliver Janz, MacGregor Knox, Alan Kramer, Nicola Labanca, Stefano Marcuzzi, Roberto Mazza, Marco Mondini, Emanuele Sica, Hew Strachan, Mesut Uyar, the late Bruce Vandervort, and Jay Winter, who was also immensely hospitable to me and my family in Paris. James Halstead chased down an errant reference and Andrew Pfannkuche helped with the index. David Brown and Sabina Donati were kind enough to share unpublished work with me. Pierre Purseigle, Jenny Macleod, Jessica Meyer, Chris Kempshall, Edward Madigan, Michael Neiberg, Martina Salvante, Julia Ribiero, and other friends in the International Society for First World War Studies have all helped me in many ways over almost twenty years of the society's activities. In this field we are blessed with many superlative women scholars, like Michelle Moyd, Heather Perry, Jennifer Keene, and Sophie de Schaepdrijver, who have been inspirational role models. Colleagues at John Cabot University and Trinity College, Rome Campus have provided much in the way of friendship, support, and encouragement over the years; Luca De Caprariis also shared his expertise on fascist foreign policy. I am happy to thank my talented undergraduate research assistants at John Cabot University, Demetrio Iannone and Quinlan Davenport, whose enthusiasm and dedication were a great assistance and who made valuable contributions to the research process. Demetrio went above and beyond the call of duty to track down obscure articles in various inaccessible libraries. NYU Paris, where I taught for a semester, also provided invaluable library access during the Covid-19 pandemic.

It turns out that having already written one monograph doesn't make the second significantly easier; the musical cliché of the difficult second album applies here too. I was fortunate to have the expert support and guidance of Dr Jane Jones, writing coach and editor extraordinaire, without whom I would have greatly struggled to get the book done.

I have no research grant or funding body to acknowledge, alas. Much of this book was written in Paris, during what I have called my 'self-funded sabbatical'. After twelve years as an adjunct, and having never held a permanent job, there is no other kind. I was lucky enough to get work writing a commercial TV documentary series entitled 'The Cost of War'. This—combined with my husband's job—paid enough for me to sit in my local co-working space eating unlimited madeleines and writing this book for a year. Most contingent faculty don't get this type of break and I want to acknowledge my good fortune. To all other precariously employed academics out there, still trying to research and write, goes my endless admiration.

Between originally writing a book proposal in 2014 and finishing the manuscript, my progress was slowed by many things: rashly editing two books in the same year, a 5/5 teaching load, bereavement, an international move, a global pandemic, breaking my foot; but above all by the arrival of my daughter Elena, the best of all possible distractions. The support of my wider family was therefore essential to the completion of this book, especially Nonna, Granet, and Uncle Patrick who cheerfully travelled abroad to help out: I owe them all so much. Writing is solitary work which takes a supportive team behind the scenes. Above all my thanks go to my husband Terry without whom none of this would have been possible. He spent many long days of solo child-wrangling while I was in the archives. Despite his firm belief as an agency journalist that no story needs more than 1000 words—and ideally fewer than 650—he has supported every stage of this long process with great patience, and he deserves my infinite love and gratitude.

Contents

Note on Translation and Transliteration

All translations from the Italian are mine unless otherwise stated.

I have used contemporary place names throughout, rather than Italian or historic versions, with exceptions only for places whose older names are more appropriate in the historical context (Constantinople, Smyrna, Fiume rather than Istanbul, Izmir, Rijeka). For Arabic personal names and terms, I have followed the transliteration stylesheet of the International Journal of Middle East Studies.

List of Abbreviations

ACS	Archivio Centrale dello Stato
ANI	Italian Nationalist Association
ASMAE	Archivio Storico del Ministero degli Affari Esteri
BSMC	Biblioteca di Storia Moderna e Contemporanea
CGdL	Confederazione Generale del Lavoro
CGE	Commissariato Generale dell'Emigrazione
DDI	Documenti Diplomatici Italiani
EEF	Egyptian Expeditionary Force
ICI	Istituto Coloniale Italiano
IOH	Italian Official History: Ufficio Storico, Corpo di stato maggiore, ed. *L'esercito italiano nella Grande Guerra, 1915–1918*, 7 vols (Rome: Provveditorato generale dello stato libreria, 1927–)
ITO	Ufficio Informazioni Truppe Operanti
JMIS	*Journal of Modern Italian Studies*
PPI	Partito Popolare Italiano
PSI	Partito Socialista Italiano
RMI	*Rivista Militare Italiana*
SAI	Società Africana d'Italia
TAIF	Truppe Ausiliarie Italiane in Francia
UCEI	Italian Union of Jewish Communities

Maps

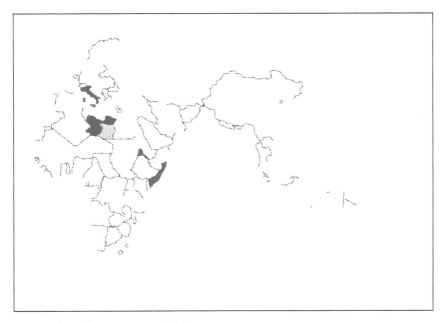

Map 1 The Italian Empire in 1914

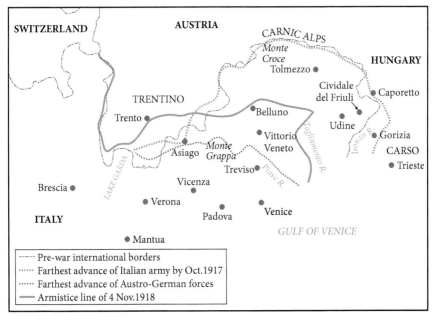

SWITZERLAND

AUSTRIA

CARNIC ALPS

Monte Croce

Tolmezzo ●

HUNGARY

Cividale del Friuli ●

● Caporetto

TRENTINO

Trento ●

● Belluno

Udine ●

● Gorizia

● Vittorio Veneto

Isonzo R.

CARSO

Monte Grappa

● Asiago

Treviso ●

● Trieste

Tagliamento R.

Piave R.

Vicenza ●

Brescia ●

● Verona

LAKE GARDA

ITALY

Padova ●

Venice ●

● Mantua

GULF OF VENICE

----- Pre-war international borders
...... Farthest advance of Italian army by Oct.1917
...... Farthest advance of Austro-German forces
——— Armistice line of 4 Nov.1918

Map 2 The Italo-Austrian Front

Map 3 The Macedonian and Albanian theatre

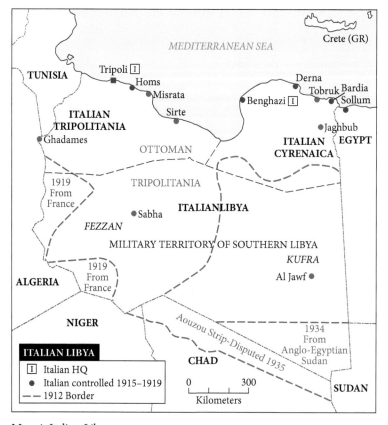

Map 4 Italian Libya

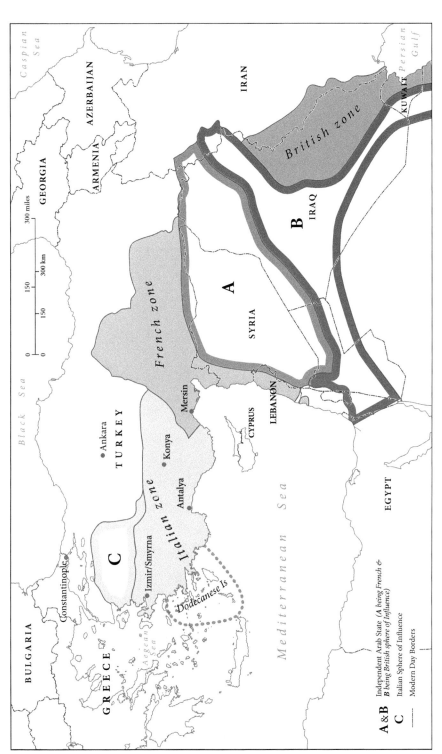

Map 5 The Saint Jean de Maurienne Agreement for partitioning the Ottoman Empire

A & B   Independent Arab State (*A being French & B being British sphere of Influence*)
C   Italian Sphere of Influence
------   Modern Day Borders

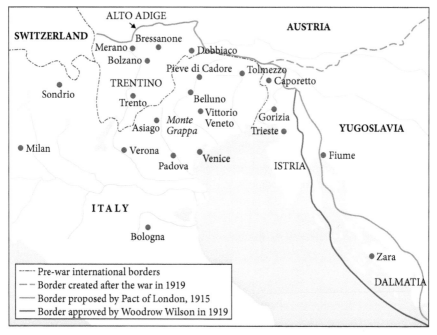

Map 6 Post-war borders in the Adriatic

1

Introduction

On 4 November 2018, over a thousand soldiers stood to attention in Trieste's main square, the evocatively named Piazza Unità d'Italia, as a parade of troops in First World War replica uniforms marched past. Overhead, Italy's aerial display team, the Frecce Tricolore, completed a flyover, while the parade was greeted by a 21-gun salute from two warships present in the port, before President of the Republic Sergio Mattarella addressed the watching crowds. Italy was celebrating the centenary of the end of the First World War: precisely one hundred years earlier, the armistice with Austria-Hungary had ended forty-one months of brutal fighting along the countries' borders. Mattarella's speech invoked thankfulness, peace, and European solidarity, but the event itself was distinctly militarized—and triumphant. Commemoration of the war mingled with honouring Italy's contemporary military: the anniversary is now known as the 'Day of National Unity and the Armed Forces'. The centenary event was a powerful celebration of military victory; equally significant was the emphasis on territorial gain, specifically the city of Trieste, and the close link between this expansion and the unity of Italy.[1]

To remember the First World War in terms of triumph and territorial acquisition is unusual: other combatant nations have very different shared narratives. But in the Italian case, the conquest of new lands was the driving force of intervention into the war and dominated its post-war diplomacy. Its claims rested on two bases: some areas, known as the *terre irredente*, were defined as rightfully Italian national territories, inhabited by Italians who had to be 'redeemed' from foreign rule, while others were necessary to the state on the grounds of security, stability, or prestige. The war was thus intended to complete national unification, and simultaneously to both achieve and demonstrate Italy's rightful status as a European great power. Territorial expansion was intrinsic to both objectives. But while the national element is now celebrated as central to the Italian experience of the war, the second aim—the quest for security and prestige—is largely absent from collective memory. However, it was an integral part of Italian decision-making and policy before, during, and after the war, and it was manifested chiefly in the form of imperialism. Rather than simply the 'Fourth War of

---

[1] For a general assessment of the Italian commemorations, see Bracco, Barbara: 'Centenary (Italy)', in: *1914–1918 online. International Encyclopedia of the First World War*, ed. by Ute Daniel, Peter Gatrell, Oliver Janz, Heather Jones, Jennifer Keene, Alan Kramer, and Bill Nasson, issued by Freie Universität Berlin, Berlin 2019-09-26. https://encyclopedia.1914-1918-online.net/article/centenary_italy.

The Italian Empire and the Great War. Vanda Wilcox, Oxford University Press (2021). © Vanda Wilcox.
DOI: 10.1093/oso/9780198822943.003.0001

the Risorgimento', as it was often termed at the time and as official narratives today choose to celebrate, Italy's First World War was also an imperialist, colonialist adventure. If Trento and Trieste were needed to finally make Italy a complete nation, it was empire—in Africa, the Balkans, and Asia Minor—which was to make it a great power. In the competitive arena of great power politics, the *terre irredente* might win Italy a place in the championship, but only an overseas empire would allow it to challenge for honours. Without considering both these dimensions of the conflict it is impossible to understand Italy's conduct of the war or its position at the Paris Peace Conference.

1.1 How Imperial Was Italy's War?

In what ways was the Italian experience of the First World War imperial? Most obvious, and perhaps most important, were the explicitly imperial and colonial war aims embraced by Italian politicians, diplomats, and pressure groups during and after the conflict, along with the diplomatic and military actions undertaken in pursuit of these goals in Africa, the Middle East, and beyond. Building on several decades of imperial ambitions, and most directly on the Italo-Turkish War of 1911–12, the Italian ruling classes actively pursued expansionist objectives in the First World War. These could be clearly identified as early as August 1914 but would increase considerably in scope and ambition in 1916–17. In 1919–20, imperial and colonial projects acquired a special importance as Italians struggled with disappointments at the war's end. Another crucial feature is the contribution of the Italian colonies to the war effort. Under this heading may be analysed both the formal colonies under direct rule in Africa and the informal colonies of Italian emigrants around the world, in the USA, Canada, Latin America, and Australia as well as Egypt, Tunisia, and France. To ignore the manpower and resources which Italy mobilized from beyond its national territories is to miss out an important part of the war experience; it is also to fundamentally misunderstand how many contemporary Italians viewed their place in the wider world. In early twentieth-century Italy there was considerable slippage between the national and the imperial, whether centred on formal colonies or on a global network of 'little Italies' (or both). The war was intended to 'make Italy' not only by conquering new territory but also by 'making Italians'. The nationalization of the masses was arguably as important to the process of unification as the completion of the country's 'natural' borders. The lives and loyalties of Italian citizens wherever they found themselves are thus an intrinsic part of the story. Importantly, in post-war Italy, this process of Italianization included the new minority populations which the war had brought into the nation.

To approach the war from this angle adds new texture to many stories. In October 1916, a train was transporting reserves of the 56th infantry unit towards the front; many of the men were singing—and slightly drunk—when a shout came up from the soldier sat by the window, 33-year-old Domenico De Santolo. 'Down with the war! Long live Austria!' he cried. The rest of the compartment ignored him, including his sergeant (who was apparently too depressed at leaving home to bother reprimanding him). Later, when a disciplinary inquiry was held, De Santolo described his background. Born in Alexandria in Egypt, home to a sizeable Italian population, he had been living in Trieste when the war began. He left the city two days before the war began, crossing into Italy to join up along with his brother, a military policeman. Although born and permanently resident outside Italy, his orientation and identity were firmly Italian, and he had even joined the Italian National League, making him part of that overseas community of Italians which constituted the 'informal' empire of emigrant families. His time in Trieste had led him to embrace the irredentist movement, and he had chosen to move to Italy to join up (or, perhaps, to avoid serving in the Austrian army). Under interrogation after his 'seditious utterances', he gave this account of his personal history which highlighted his free choice to serve in the Italian army and was designed to demonstrate his *italianità*.[2] Did he perhaps regret his decision? How did his life history influence his identity—and how did the presence of men like De Santolo influence the conduct and sentiments of the Italian army? A framework which incorporates the varied and complex ways in which ideas of a 'Greater Italy' operated in this period allows us to better understand the diverse experiences of many Italian soldiers, such as those born in Tunisia who served and died in Albania, or who came from America only to die in Macedonia.

1.2   The Libyan Theatre?

Beyond simply widening our framework for analysis of familiar events, to consider the war in an imperial context also opens up an important new topic: war in the colonies. Throughout 1914–15, while Italy was still neutral, it was engaged in a brutal counter-insurgency war in Libyan territory, which continued and indeed escalated during the Great War, spreading from Tripolitania to Cyrenaica as the indigenous population sensed new opportunities to undermine the precarious Italian colonial regime. This conflict has not traditionally been considered as an element of the First World War but simply as an internal Italian matter. However, Simona Berhe argues convincingly that, on the contrary, Libya was a theatre of the wider war. In fact, for the Central Powers, all Italy's colonies were considered as terrain for pursuing the war; in East Africa this met with almost complete failure, but in the two Libyan provinces of Tripolitania and Cyrenaica the war against Italy

---

[2] Archivio dell'Ufficio Storico dello Stato Maggiore dell'Esercito (AUSSME), Fondo E2:50, Comando 56° Reg. Fant., N. 429 Prot. R, 30/10/1916.

was prosecuted with considerable success.[3] Where Berhe considers Libya as Italy's 'southern front', Stefano Marcuzzi has instead described it as a 'parallel war' which he nonetheless terms 'the Libyan front of World War I', while Roberta Pergher has written that 'for Italy, the war meant a two-front engagement'.[4]

This analysis is supported on two core grounds. Firstly, in Libya two major European combatant powers—Italy and the Ottoman Empire—were directly engaged, with considerable support from their allies on both sides. As Lisa Anderson notes in her 1983 study of the Tripolitanian Republic, 'the struggle was undertaken by the Imperial Ottoman government [and by] Ottoman army officers acting on their own'.[5] When Italy declared war on Turkey in August 1915, the Sublime Porte repudiated the Treaty of Ouchy, signed in 1912. Consequently, it considered the territories of Italian Libya to be illegitimately occupied Turkish lands. This was the legal and strategic justification for Turkish operations there throughout the following years, and in this sense the idea that the war in Libya was a part of the First World War seems unarguable. The fact that Turkey operated chiefly though the proxy of indigenous troops who had their own goals in the conflict does not alter the fact that Turkish officers led Arab forces against the Italians, with Turkish, German, and Austro-Hungarian financial and material support. The Italian authorities at the time also perceived Libya as a theatre of the war: more than 3,000 men who died on active service there between 1915 and 1918, whether in combat or from service-related illness, were recorded in the official honour rolls as casualties of the Great War.[6]

Secondly, a similar interpretation emerges if we consider the conflict in Libya from the perspective of the indigenous anti-colonial movements. Arab and Berber insurgents in Tripolitania and Sanusi fighters in Cyrenaica saw themselves as engaging in a wider struggle which operated in the context of a global war. As Amal Ghazal writes, 'In the eyes of North Africans, WWI was a second chapter of a war that had already begun in 1911 and had galvanized them.' The Italian invasion of 1911 had helped to create a new anti-colonial, pan-Maghribi form of

[3] Simona Berhe, 'Il fronte meridionale della Grande guerra: la Libia come teatro del primo conflitto mondiale', *Nuova Rivista Storica* 101, no. 3 (2017): 797–828.

[4] Stefano Marcuzzi, 'Italy's "Parallel War" in Libya: A Forgotten Front of World War I (1914–1922)', in *Africa and the First World War: Remembrance, Memories and Representations after 100 Years*, ed. De-Valera N.Y.M. Botchway and Kwame Osei Kwarteng (Newcastle: Cambridge Scholars Publishing, 2018), 164–87; Roberta Pergher, *Fascist Borderlands: Nation, Empire and Italy's Settlement Program, 1922–1943* (New York: Cambridge University Press, 2017), 40. I am grateful to John Horne for the observation that in fact the nature of fighting of Libya precludes the use of the term 'front' here; 'theatre' is more accurate.

[5] Lisa Anderson, 'The Tripoli Republic, 1918–1922', in *Social & Economic Development of Libya*, ed. E. George H. Joffé and Keith Stanley McLachlan (Wisbech: Middle East & North African Studies Press, 1982), 43.

[6] Italia: Ministero della Guerra, *Militari caduti nella guerra nazionale 1915–1918: Albo d' Oro*, 28 vols (Rome: Istituto Poligrafico dello Stato Libreria, 1926).

pro-Ottomanism which tied the two conflicts together.[7] Along with Pan-Islamicism, ties forged from linked and intersecting anti-colonial struggles operated within the French and British colonies and between widely separated Muslim colonies.[8] The Libyan independence movement(s) of 1911–23 can also be read in the light of these transnational anti-colonial campaigns. For Angelo Del Boca, the war cannot be separated from internal events in Libya: 'it is clear that the outbreak of the First World War, with the return of the Turks to Libya, contributed to the "great Arab revolt"' along with 'other contributing factors, foremost among them the acts of brutality' including deportations and the 'relentless use of the gallows'.[9] Not all analysts agree: Jason Pack considers that only the Cyrenaican theatre should be considered as part of the First World War. He argues that the ongoing indigenous resistance to Italian colonization of Libya was not part of the First World War but a simultaneous yet separate conflict. This is because these anti-colonial struggles antedated the global conflict and were not catalysed by it, nor—he suggests—were they understood as a separate front in the First World War by any of the major participants. He sees the Anglo-Sanusi confrontation in Egypt's Western Desert from 1915 to 1917 as fundamentally different: it was catalysed by the First World War, it was not a direct continuation of a pre-war conflict, and it was understood by both the Central and the Entente Powers as representing the opening up of a novel front in the global conflict.[10] However, there is good evidence that both the Central Powers and Italy saw wartime events in Tripolitania too as intrinsically linked to the wider war in a variety of ways, as argued in Chapter 6 below. Michelle Moyd has made a powerful argument for 'centring the sideshows' of the African campaigns as an integral part of creating a truly global history of the First World War. The war was critically important to the lives of Africans, including those living in lands claimed or occupied by Italy in North and East Africa. She rightly observes that 'During these years of sustained violence, Africa mattered to Europe, and Europe mattered to Africa.'[11] This book restores Italy's African colonies to their place in the narrative of the Italian war effort.

In addition to Italy's imperialist and colonialist war aims, the contribution of the colonies to the war effort, and the fighting which took place in the colonies itself, this book identifies a fourth 'imperial' element of the war experience: a

[7] Amal Ghazal, 'Counter-Currents: Mzabi Independence, Pan-Ottomanism and WWI in the Maghrib', *First World War Studies* 7, no. 1 (2016): 87.
[8] On this dynamic, see Erin O'Halloran, '"A Tempest in a British Tea Pot": The Arab Question in Cairo and Delhi', in *1916 in Global Context: An Anti-Imperial Moment*, ed. Enrico Dal Lago, Róisín Healy, and Gearóid Barry (Abingdon: Routledge, 2018), 107.
[9] Angelo Del Boca, *Mohamed Fekini and the Fight to Free Libya* (New York: Palgrave Macmillan, 2011), 49.
[10] Jason Pack, 'The Antecedents and Implications of the So-Called Anglo-Sanussi War 1915–1917', in *The First World War and Its Aftermath* (London: Gingko, 2015), 41.
[11] Michelle Moyd, 'Centring a Sideshow: Local Experiences of the First World War in Africa', *First World War Studies* 7, no. 2 (2016): 111–30, DOI: https://doi.org/10.1080/19475020.2016.1174591.

culture of racialized thinking, which produced racist colonialist policies and practices during the war. Italians perceived themselves, their colonial subjects, and their enemies through a racialized lens, which deeply influenced wartime and post-war treatment of minorities. This was particularly important given that the war brought new minorities under Italian rule. As Roberta Pergher observes, Italy had to manage the 'central conundrum facing all radical nationalists wishing to enlarge state territory while reinforcing national cohesion, namely, how to square that national cohesion with rule over non-Italian lands and peoples'.[12] The problem presented by non-Italian Others, who were conceived in racial as well as cultural terms, was significant. Racial thinking was widespread in the armed forces, and cultures of violence in occupied areas were shaped by this 'coloniality' in important ways. Even in supposedly national territories, then, imperial and colonial discourse was a key part of the war experience. These four themes—war aims, the global war effort, the colonial theatre, and racial thinking—together constitute my argument for understanding the First World War in Italy within an imperial framework.

My purpose here is to analyse the imperial and colonial dimensions of Italy's First World War, focusing chiefly on Italian political and military decision-making, and on the cultures which underpinned these choices. The sources used are largely Italian official documents supplemented by journalism and cultural sources where appropriate. This book is not, therefore, a study of the Italian colonies or colonized peoples in wartime, though such a project is definitely needed. Nonetheless, the agency and views of Italy's colonial subjects—and those whom Italians sought to colonize—are an important strand in the story. The gulf between aspirations and achievements, between rhetoric and reality is one of the core themes of the book, and one important reason why Italy was unable to fulfil its imperial dreams was the effective resistance of its prospective subjects from Libya to Anatolia or Albania. This reality was minimized by contemporaries and has often been underplayed by historians; instead, attention has focused on Italy's position relative to other major powers, as though these alone were responsible for thwarting Italian plans. Without denying the influence of French, British, or American policy, I hope to better balance this picture as well as highlighting the ways in which domestic political and economic problems also determined the overall outcome of the wider Italian war effort. Domestic dissent and the great diversity of viewpoints within Italy itself acted to limit possibilities of Italian expansionism as, of course, did the crucial factor of military contingency.

---

[12] Pergher, *Fascist Borderlands*, 2.

1.3 History, Memory, and Historiography

It is no longer fair to say that the history of Italian colonialism has been neglected by scholars. Both within Italy and internationally it has become a thriving field, and approaches from allied disciplines—literature, film studies, travel writing, gender, anthropology—have greatly enriched our understanding of Italian colonial policy, principles, and practices in recent decades.[13] Today, the historiography on the colonialism of the liberal era has been transformed; yet public perceptions and indeed awareness of this history still lag very far behind. On 5 July 2019, Manlio Di Stefano, a member of the Five Star Movement and Undersecretary of State for Foreign Affairs made a startling statement on Facebook: 'we [Italy] have no skeletons in our closet, we have no colonial tradition, we've never unleashed bombs on anyone and we've never put our boot on any economy's throat. We are Italy and we are Italians', he concluded, as though this very statement of nationality precluded any link to a colonial tradition.[14] His remarks were greeted with a chorus of public derision—but as military historian Nicola Labanca observed more than twenty-five years ago, if even Fascist Italy's imperial adventures are neglected in Italian collective memory, there seemed little hope of incorporating the Liberal State's participation in the Scramble for Africa into national discourse.[15] Within scholarly circles, however, it is precisely the relationship between fascist imperialism and the earlier period which has attracted a considerable debate. In 1932, Benito Mussolini wrote that 'all peoples which are rising are imperialist', inextricably linking empire-building and national status at the heart of the fascist ideology.[16] In the words of postcolonial scholar Neelam Srivastava, 'colonialism [w]as a historical *precursor* of fascism, its necessary precondition'.[17] Pergher's important work on fascist borderlands shows that empire was central to Italian nationalism under fascism, and that imperial and national sovereignty were inseperable.[18] Given the earlier emphasis on colonial conquest by Liberal statesmen as part of the nation-building project, does an imperial

---

[13] Some key works include Nicola Labanca, *Oltremare: storia dell'espansione coloniale italiana* (Bologna: Il Mulino, 2002); Jacqueline Andall, ed., 'Italian Colonialism: Historical Perspectives Introduction', *JMIS* 8, no. 3 (1 January 2003): 370–4, DOI: https://doi.org/10.1080/09585170320000113734; Ruth Ben-Ghiat and Mia Fuller, eds, *Italian Colonialism* (Basingstoke: Palgrave Macmillan, 2008); Ruth Ben-Ghiat and Stephanie Malia Hom, eds, *Italian Mobilities* (London and New York: Routledge, 2015).

[14] Manlio Di Stefano, 5 July 2019, Facebook.com personal post. https://www.facebook.com/ManlioDiStefano/posts/2593496807375096?comment_tracking=%7B%22tn%22%3A%22O%22%7D [accessed 6/10/2020].

[15] Nicola Labanca, *In marcia verso Adua* (Turin: Einaudi, 1993), Introduction.

[16] Benito Mussolini, *The Doctrine of Fascism* (Florence: Vallecchi, 1935).

[17] Neelam Francesca Rashmi Srivastava, *Italian Colonialism and Resistances to Empire, 1930–1970* (London: Palgrave Macmillan, 2018), 17.

[18] Pergher, *Fascist Borderlands*.

reading of the First World War indicate a continuity from liberalism to fascism in terms of attitudes to empire?

The debate over the extent to which fascism was a genuinely new phenomenon or grew from and retained many elements from the liberal state is extensive and ongoing. Since the great liberal historian Benedetto Croce began to study the Liberal era, Italian historiography has been divided over the qualities and weaknesses of the pre-1915 state, and over the extent to which its failures would contribute to the rise of fascism. For Croce, Liberal Italy was a functioning and democratizing state which, despite its problems, could bear comparison with its European peers; for Antonio Gramsci and successive generations of Marxist historians it was a fundamentally flawed structure, reflecting incomplete nation-building, an inadequate political class, and weak economic and social development. This 'anti-Liberal' narrative proposed that fascism was the outcome of this catalogue of failures. By contrast, Croce's followers (like William Salomone, who memorably described pre-war Italy as a 'democracy in the making') offered a more positive view, particularly of Giolittian Italy.[19] Accordingly, fascism was read merely as a 'parenthesis', to use Croce's famous phrase: an aberration in the successful development of a functioning democratic nation state. However, much recent historiography has emphasized the sometimes surprising effectiveness of many aspects of the Liberal state and the considerable progress in the creation of national sentiment even before the First World War, despite tracing some of the roots of fascism back to the late nineteenth century.[20] As a result, the 'Italian Sonderweg' thesis has been generally discarded in favour of a more nuanced analysis of the Liberal state, acknowledging both strengths and weaknesses—and its relationship to fascism is therefore necessarily more complex and involved. However, as Pergher has recently noted, 'many of the larger arguments made about the origins of Fascism, even those apparently reflecting on the relationship between war and Fascism, in fact tell us relatively little about the war itself'.[21]

Debates over the relationship between fascist Italy and its predecessor state have been particularly intense in the field of imperialism and foreign policy, though again without necessarily revealing much about the First World War.[22] Richard Bosworth, for instance, has consistently argued that the difference

[19] A. William Salomone, *Italy in the Giolittian Era: Italian Democracy in the Making, 1900–1914* (Philadelphia: University of Pennsylvania Press, 1960).
[20] For a comprehensive analysis of the historiography, the best guide is in Nick Carter, *Modern Italy in Historical Perspective* (London: Bloomsbury Academic, 2010), http://www.bloomsbury.com/uk/modern-italy-in-historical-perspective-9781849663335/.
[21] Roberta Pergher, 'An Italian War? War and Nation in the Italian Historiography of the First World War', *Journal of Modern History* 90, no. 4 (December 2018): 863–99, DOI: https://doi.org/10.1086/700561, p. 884.
[22] For some older analyses of the debate, see Alan Cassels, 'Was There a Fascist Foreign Policy? Tradition and Novelty', *The International History Review* 5, no. 2 (1983): 255–68. Stephen Corrado Azzi, 'The Historiography of Fascist Foreign Policy', *The Historical Journal* 36, no. 1 (1993): 187–203.

between liberal and fascist foreign policy was chiefly of means rather than aims.[23] Mussolini's intensive propaganda campaigns identified familiar targets—the Mediterranean basin and the East—but presented them with a new urgency and a new rhetorical style. A clear preference for military means characterized the fascist regime while the liberal state also embraced diplomacy as a tool, yet the quest for prestige dominated the thinking of Antonino di Sangiuliano and Antonio Salandra as much as of Mussolini. Renzo De Felice saw Mussolini's foreign policy as 'realist' rather than ideologically motivated, whereas McGregor Knox has highlighted the intensely ideological approach which it adopted from the mid-1920s onwards. Further, Mussolini's embrace of militarism in the 1930s closely echoed Futurist thinking on the purifying, revivifying effects of war on Italian society.[24] Studies of colonial society have also emphasized continuity between the liberal and the early fascist periods.[25] The radical new ideological orientation which fascism gave to its colonialism and the new forms and messages of the regime's representations of empire are perhaps its most distinctive features. In this view, the true turning point in Italian foreign policy lies in 1943, with the downfall of fascism and the end of Italy's politics of grandeur. In analysing more fully the scope, nature, and limits of imperial ambitions within late Liberal society and government, this book will offer a useful supplement to the debate over the roots and origins of fascist imperialism.[26]

The general failure to recognize fully the imperialist dimensions of Italy's war is odd given that the central fact of Italy's frustrated claims to Fiume and Dalmatia—leading to the post-war myth of the so-called mutilated victory—is well known. The 'mutilated victory' has rarely been analysed in an imperial framework by historians, though recognition of the extent to which imperial concerns and realities shaped the Italian Great War has perhaps been more common among Italianists working outside Italy than within the country. Richard Bosworth and Giuseppe Finaldi wrote unequivocally in their 2014 essay, 'Italy's version of the First World War was to prove as imperial as that of the greater powers, but imperial in its own manner, fluctuating between the (weak) reality of boots on

---

[23] Richard J. B. Bosworth, *Italy, the Least of the Great Powers: Italian Foreign Policy before the First World War* (Cambridge: Cambridge University Press, 1979); Richard J. Bosworth and Sergio Romano, *La politica estera italiana* (Bologna: Il Mulino, 1991).

[24] MacGregor Knox, *Mussolini Unleashed 1939–1941: Politics and Strategy in Fascist Italy's Last War* (Cambridge and New York: Cambridge University Press, 1986); for a critical analysis of De Felice's view, see Knox, MacGregor. 'The Fascist Regime, Its Foreign Policy and Its Wars: An "Anti-Anti-Fascist" Orthodoxy?' *Contemporary European History* 4, no. 3 (1995): 347–65, https://jstor.org/stable/20081559.

[25] For instance Barbara Sorgoni, *Parole e corpi. Antropologia, discorso giuridico e politiche sessuali interrazziali nella colonia Eritrea* (Naples: Liguori, 1998).

[26] For a historiographical analysis of the relationship between liberal and fascist imperialism, see R. J. B. Bosworth, *The Italian Dictatorship: Problems and Perspectives in the Interpretation of Mussolini and Fascism* (London and New York: Bloomsbury Academic, 1998).

African ground and (hugely powerful) myth.'[27] In the Italian historiography, both the fascist era and the first twenty years of the Italian Republic were marked chiefly by what Marco Mondini has described as the 'patriotic paradigm' which largely accepted a Risorgimento, liberal-national analysis of the war.[28] The subsequent turns to social and cultural history focused on the marginalized and dissident voices within Italy but paid scant attention to imperial concerns—and still framed the war in exclusively national terms. However, since 2000 the growth of scholarly attention to imperial dimensions of the war effort has also been accompanied in some cases by a new analysis which increasingly highlights the imperialist, expansionist aspects of the intervention in 1915 and of Italy's evolving war aims. Signs of this important shift can be found not only in cultural histories but in military and diplomatic histories too, which have sometimes taken longer to move beyond the patriotic paradigm. Military historian Giovanni Cecini, in a monograph published by the Official Army Historical Office—hardly a hotbed of radical revisionism—even writes that 'The Great War with its poorly concealed imperialist and colonial objectives encouraged ambitious Italy towards significant portions of Asia Minor.'[29] Yet this framework is still far from common in the wider historiography (let alone in public discourse).[30] In reality, the quasi-hegemonic interpretation established by the late twentieth century—which is rooted in analysis of coercion, illiberalism, and repression within the army and society—might be usefully refreshed by a wider horizon which includes the theoretical and practical fields of colonial history, which have much to offer on the mechanics of repression and social control. In a recent historiographical essay on Italy and the war, published during the centenary, Roberta Pergher questioned the usefulness of the exclusively national framework in which many histories of the conflict are still conceived, given that 'many of the national combatants were themselves empires, and their war efforts involved the mobilization, exploitation, and often political awakening of colonial populations and imperial subjects'. She rightly challenges narratives of Italian exceptionalism even while noting that, 'there continue to be many compelling reasons for writing about the war in

[27] Richard Bosworth and Giuseppe Finaldi, 'The Italian Empire', in *Empires at War*, ed. Robert Gerwarth and Erez Manela (Oxford: Oxford University Press, 2014), 35, DOI: https://doi.org/10.1093/acprof:oso/9780198702511.003.0003. An extremely important new contribution to the historiography, which fully acknowledges the imperial framework of the Italian war effort, is Stefano Marcuzzi, *Britain and Italy in the Era of the First World War. Defending and Forging Empires* (Cambridge: Cambridge University Press, 2020)

[28] Marco Mondini, 'L'historiographie italienne face à la Grande Guerre: saisons et ruptures', *HISTOIRE@POLITIQUE* 22, no. jan–avr (2014), http://www.histoire-politique.fr/index.php?numero=22&rub=dossier&item=208.

[29] Giovanni Cecini, *Il Corpo di spedizione italiano in Anatolia: 1919–1922* (Rome: Stato Maggiore dell'Esercito, Ufficio Storico, 2010), 467.

[30] An important exhibition was organized on this topic in 2017 by the Archivio dello Stato in Rome: Eugenio Lo Sardo et al., *La Grande Guerra: l'Italia e il Levante*, Cataloghi 4 (Rome: De Luca Editori d'Arte, 2017). The exhibition achieved high visitor numbers and some media coverage, but the word 'imperialism' was only rarely to be found in any press reports.

national terms' when it comes to Italy.[31] Despite Pergher's observation that to divide 'nations' from 'empires' in the context of the First World War is a false binary, her historiographical review contains no analysis of Italy as a colonial empire—because so little has been published in this field. It is to be hoped that the move to incorporate colonial and imperial histories into the study of the First World War more generally—of which the *Greater War* book series with Oxford University Press is one key indicator—will filter through into the Italian scholarship and help to rectify this omission.

However, histories of imperialism and the First World War have so far tended to ignore Italy. No single volume history of the Italian empire in the war has yet been published, and—with the notable exception of Robert Gerwarth and Erez Manela's *Empires at War*—even the best collected works on imperial dimensions of the war tend to omit Italy entirely. John Morrow's huge and influential imperial history of the war mentions Italy and its colonies only in passing.[32] Perhaps one reason why Italy is rarely considered as an empire in the Great War is because the Italian empire was in many ways unusual. By the standards of the world's largest empires—France and Britain— it was small, weak, and scarcely populated. But this was equally true of most colonial empires in 1914: Belgium, Portugal, Japan, even Germany could not directly compete with the two Entente powers. It may be more useful, consequently, to compare the Italian imperial experience to these other European colonizers rather than to the anomalous pair who between them dominated the world. Only if we take the French and British experience as normative does the Italian empire seem so strange.

Limited in size and wealth, the Italian empire in the First World War was also very new—in the case of Libya it had been scarcely conquered at all. But the most distinctive feature of Italy's empire was away from its own formal colonies, in the form of emigrant participation in other forms of settler colonialism around the world. By 1914, '870,000 Italians [had] left the country, ironically constructing, outside the nation state, an informal empire of the Italies, which was and would remain much more extensive as well as more economically and culturally productive than any conquered by Italy.'[33] This

---

[31] Pergher, 'An Italian War?', 864, 899.

[32] Robert Gerwarth and Erez Manela, eds, *Empires at War: 1911–1923* (Oxford: Oxford University Press, 2014); John Morrow, *The Great War: An Imperial History* (London and New York: Routledge, 2004). Important recent edited volumes on empire include Santanu Das, *Race, Empire and First World War Writing* (Cambridge: Cambridge University Press, 2011); Andrew Jarboe and Richard Fogarty, eds, *Empires in World War I: Shifting Frontiers and Imperial Dynamics in a Global Conflict* (London: I. B. Tauris, 2013); Julie d'Andurain and Colette Zytnicki, eds, *Les Empires dans la Grande Guerre*, Special Issue, *Outre-Mers. Revue d'histoire* 390–391, 2016; Dónal Hassett and Michelle Moyd, eds, *First World War Studies* Special Issue: *Colonial Veterans of World War I*, 10, no. 1 (2019); none includes the Italian empire.

[33] Bosworth and Finaldi, 'The Italian Empire', 36. For the history of Italian emigration and the importance of the diaspora to Italian history, see Donna Gabaccia, 'Italian History and gli italiani nel

'informal empire of Italies' was an important strand in the story of Italy in the First World War, as shall become clear in chapters 2 and 3. It also significantly complicates the analysis of how colonial thought operated, as Srivastava has noted: it 'shakes up conventional understandings of hegemonic versus subaltern relationships in postcolonial studies, as it does not distinguish neatly between colonization and diaspora'.[34] However just as historians have only slowly understood the importance of these communities for Italian history (rather than as a part of the history of their destination societies), as yet few First World War historians have considered these emigrants as an integral part of the story of Italy in the war.[35] Nonetheless, as this book will show, not only were Italians overseas an essential part of the war effort but their role was understood within a colonial framework.

The war's impact on Italy's formal colonies is more generally ignored for several reasons. First, these all bordered onto Entente-governed lands (such as Tunisia, Egypt, Sudan, Djibouti, Somaliland) which meant that Italian territories were unlikely to become the scene of battle with Central Powers armies. Disappointingly, from the Italian perspective, this also ruled out the possibility of directly conquering German lands in Africa. As a result, historians of the Great War in Africa have generally been relatively uninterested in Italy.[36] Secondly, the support which Italian colonies were able to offer was insignificant compared to that offered by French and British overseas possessions to their respective war efforts. The sophisticated and long-standing extractive mechanisms by which France and Britain obtained wealth and manpower from their colonies had no counterpart in Italy. Nonetheless, the topic deserves to be examined on its own terms. As Simona Berhe notes, the war arguably forged stronger bonds between metropole and colonies in the case of these two great empires but had the opposite effect in Italy.[37] Just as the imperial and colonial dimensions of the First World War ought not to be ignored, so too should this conflict be better incorporated into the history of Italian colonialism (which too often skips directly from the war of 1911–12 through to the advent of fascism).

mondo, Part I', *JMIS* 2, no. 1 (1 March 1997): 45–66, DOI: https://doi.org/10.1080/13545719708454939 and Donna Gabaccia, 'Italian History and gli italiani nel mondo, Part II', *JMIS* 3, no. 1 (1 March 1998): 73–97, DOI: https://doi.org/10.1080/13545719808454967.

[34] Srivastava, *Italian Colonialism and Resistances to Empire*, 2.

[35] Emilio Faldella and Selena Daly are two notable exceptions.

[36] See for instance, the classic study by Hew Strachan, *The First World War in Africa* (Oxford: Oxford University Press, 2004) which barely mentions Italy. A noteworthy exception to this tradition is a recent collection edited by two leading Ghanaian scholars: De-Valera N.Y.M. Botchway and Kwame Osei Kwarteng, eds, *Africa and the First World War: Remembrance, Memories and Representations after 100 Years* (Newcastle: Cambridge Scholars Publishing, 2018).

[37] Berhe, 'Il fronte meridionale della Grande guerra', 797.

1.4 War Beyond War: Italy 1911–23

The story of Italy and the First World War begins in 1911 with the war against the Ottoman Empire. If we broaden our understanding of the First World War in Italy to place imperial concerns front and centre, we must also of necessity broaden the chronological framework in which the war is placed. This dovetails neatly with a current trend in the international historiography to examine what John Horne and others have termed 'the Greater War', which is a logical conse- quence of dethroning the Western Front, and the states which fought there, from their position of pre-eminence in scholarly understandings.[38] One way to do this is with an increased focus on what William Mulligan, Andreas Rose, and Dominik Geppert, in their 2015 edited volume, termed 'The Wars before the Great War'.[39] The Italo-Turkish War of 1911–12 and the two Balkan Wars of 1912–13 are integral to an understanding of how the First World War began but also many aspects of how it was fought. It was the succession of defeats suffered by the Ottomans in North Africa and the Balkans which began the process of destabil- izing the precarious European balance of power. Yet some scholars go further: Elena Chiti, cultural historian of the Ottoman Empire, in her essay 'Et si la Grande Guerre commençait en 1911?' suggests that within the Ottoman lands the war may be said to begin with the Italian invasion of Tripolitania.[40] War did not end in Turkey until the Treaty of Lausanne in 1923; while by convention we have described the Ottoman Empire's wars between 1911 and 1923 as a series of distinct episodes, we might equally see these as simply multiple facets of one larger, more complex event. Italy, too, experienced more than a decade of conflict of one kind or another—from 1911 through to 1923–4, when the final exped- itionary forces in the Mediterranean were withdrawn and the last territorial adjustments arising from the war were completed.

In arguing the importance of the Italo-Turkish War of 1911–12 for a proper understanding of Italy's First World War, it is worth considering the comparable arguments about the relationship between Fascist Italy's imperial and European wars. Eminent military historian Giorgio Rochat has persuasively argued that the

---

[38] Robert Gerwarth and John Horne, eds, *War in Peace: Paramilitary Violence in Europe after the Great War* (Oxford: Oxford University Press, 2012); François Lagrange, Christophe Bertrand, Carine Lachèvre, Emmanuel Ranvoisy, and Musée de l'armée (France), eds, *À l'Est, La Guerre sans Fin, 1918–1923* (Paris: Gallimard: Musée de l'Armée, 2018). On the importance of the 'Greater War' paradigm specifically in the context of imperial history, see Richard S. Fogarty, 'La «Plus Grande Guerre». Les colonies, la race et l'armée française (1906–1916)', *Mil neuf cent. Revue d'histoire intellectuelle* no. 33 (7 March 2016): 97–112.

[39] William Mulligan, Andreas Rose, and Dominik Geppert, eds, *The Wars before the Great War. Conflict and International Politics before the Outbreak of the First World War* (Cambridge: Cambridge University Press, 2015).

[40] Elena Chiti, 'Et si la Grande Guerre commençait en 1911? L'entrée en guerre vue d'Alexandrie', *Revue des mondes musulmans et de la Méditerranée* no. 141 (15 June 2017): 153–71, DOI: https://doi. org/10.4000/remmm.9900.

war in Ethiopia (1935–6) was an essential precursor to Italy's intervention in the Second World War in 1940. More generally Rochat highlights the continuity behind a series of aggressive, expansionist interventions, from Ethiopia to Spain, Albania, France, Britain, Yugoslavia, Greece, and beyond.[41] Without eliding the specificity of fascism's colonial project, he argues it is wrong to artificially separate these generally expansionist conflicts from one another, and invites us to consider the links between imperial and great power wars. Clearly, Liberal Italy lacked the ideological fixation on militarism and empire which its successor saw as foundational, yet in this book I propose that the necessity of examining a (largely) European war in the light of its immediate colonial predecessor still applies. The social and political mobilization for war in 1911–12 left important legacies which shaped both the war of 1915–18 and its immediate aftermath.

While the 'official' dates of Italy's war effort are 1915–18, this book therefore argues that only through examining the wider era 1911–23 can the war be fully understood. To rely simply on formal declarations of hostilities or their cessation is to risk ignoring the realities of conflict. After all, peace is not simply the absence of interstate war. It is well known that there was no peace at home in Italy between 1919 and 1922: paramilitary violence and social unrest wracked the country throughout the death-throes of the Liberal state. An attentive examination of foreign and imperial policy shows that for Italy peace had not yet broken out abroad either, whether in Libya, Albania, or Anatolia.

Italy must therefore be incorporated into the wider historiographical analysis of the Greater War in the Mediterranean and south-eastern Europe. This approach also usefully problematizes the traditional Italian turning point of 1922, the year of the March on Rome. It is impossible to end an examination of the messy aftermath of the war with Mussolini's seizure of power; during his first 12–18 months in office events and approaches set in train in 1918–19 were still well under way. By exploring Italian political, diplomatic, and military moves across the decade, illuminating similarities and differences begin to emerge. Some of the problems which Italy would experience in 1915–18 were already identifiable in 1911–12, as John Gooch has observed: 'Italy's first colonial war was both the product and the expression of two features that characterised her exercises in arms before, during and after her participation in the Great War: political ambitions that outran military capabilities, and military actions that all too readily threw caution to the winds.'[42] In other respects, Italian policies and practices evolved notably over time, as political aspirations waxed and waned, and successive governments and military leaders showed greater or lesser awareness of the limitations of their resources.

---

[41] Giorgio Rochat, *Le guerre italiane 1935–1943* (Turin: G. Einaudi, 2005).
[42] John Gooch, *The Italian Army and the First World War* (Cambridge: Cambridge University Press, 2014), 17.

Italy's territorial ambitions have generally been treated with scant sympathy internationally, and Italian conduct during both the period of neutrality and at the Peace Conference has been much vilified by contemporaries and historians alike. The events of the Second World War have served to give further weight to the popular depiction of Italy as a greedy and self-seeking turncoat, above all in the anglosphere. Diametrically opposed to this narrative, a strongly patriotic—not to say openly nationalist—strain of historiography within Italy has sought to depict the decision for war in 1915 as a logical, natural, and even necessary one, and Italy's fate at the Peace Conference simply the result of its allies' fickleness and mistreatment. This position is hard to sustain with any balanced analysis: Italy's goals were undeniably expansionist and imperialist throughout the period 1911–19 (and beyond). But we need not endorse the traditional British (and French) view of Italy as uniquely opportunistic or grasping, either. Perhaps Italy's worst crime, in many eyes, was its inability to achieve its ambitions. What might have been perceived as legitimate arrogance on the part of a successful conqueror was read as insufferable presumption when allied to military, financial, and political weakness. As René Albrecht-Carrié astutely noted in his 1936 study of Italy at the Peace Conference, and as many postcolonial critics have concurred, Italian policy did not much differ from the traditional approach of Britain or the other great powers; the difference lay rather in the observers' assumptions about Italy. 'Real Politik is not an application of Christian morality,' he wrote, 'and no nation likes to be dealt with by others as it has dealt with them, least of all by a nation which it has been wont to think of as of an inferior status.'[43] For many critics, then and now, Italy's true offence lay in not knowing its place.

The year 1911 was an important one for Italy, as it celebrated its fiftieth anniversary. It was a momentous occasion, marked by the inauguration of the enormous *Vittoriano*, the Victor Emanuel monument, in Rome, to honour the nation's founding monarch. The jubilee year witnessed the first government discussions of extending the franchise to all adult males, a critical moment in the democratization of the country. It was no coincidence that this year also witnessed the final realization of a long-held ambition, the acquisition of a colony on the north African shore. Chapter 2 explores the history of this objective and its position within the wider framework of Italian imperialism. Equally pressing, as the young country sought to mark its maturity, was the still unresolved issue of completing national unification through the incorporation of the 'unredeemed' lands in the north and east. Trento, Trieste, and their surrounding regions still lay in Austrian hands but were understood by Italian nationalists to be intrinsically Italian in population and character. Imperialism and irredentism were two distinct yet compatible strands of expansionist thought in the years before the First

---

[43] Albrecht-Carrié, *Italy at the Paris Peace Conference* (New York: Columbia University Press, 1938), 17.

World War, which combined to dramatic effect in 1914–15 to lead Italy into war, as Chapter 3 illustrates.

Italy's main war effort was fought on the front with Austria-Hungary along its northern and eastern borders. Here the great majority of its forces would be deployed, the highest number of casualties suffered, and the main struggle for victory focused, as Chapter 4 shows. The war effort relied on the contributions of men and women in Italy and around the world—the 'Italians overseas'. Emigrants and colonies were potential sources of manpower and materials; Italy fought the war as an empire, not merely a nation, and called on all its resources for the conflict. While Chapter 4 explores the military side of mobilization, in Chapter 5 we see the financial, industrial, and social mobilization of Italians for the bloody but ultimately victorious war against Austria. Where Chapters 4 and 5 highlight the imperial and global aspects of the national war, in Chapters 6 and 7 we see the Italian dimensions of the imperial and global war. First, Chapter 6 analyses events in the North African colonies, where Italy waged war against the Ottoman Empire and its allies, the anti-colonial forces in Tripolitania and Cyrenaica. Chapter 7 explores Italy's war(s) beyond its own lands, as fought by its expeditionary forces in Albania, Macedonia, the Middle East, France, and Russia. The political and diplomatic story of ever-increasing engagement in the global conflict shows the way Italian war aims evolved over time; the (generally) national objectives at the heart of the 1915 interventionist movement were increasingly flanked by openly imperialist aspirations. Despite the gulf between political aims and military means, Italian military engagement beyond its own borders was significant.

Underpinning the military and political events of the war was a deep-seated cultural and ideological framework of racial theories and coloniality. In the early twentieth century, Italians increasingly understood their identity and place in the world through a racialized framework. Ideas about race and culture underpinned the colonial project and the global network of Italians overseas, but also shaped ideas about domestic social reform. At a time when citizenship itself was undergoing important changes—with the arrival of manhood suffrage on the eve of the war—overseas expansion posed questions about belonging and its limits. The relationship between nation and empire was not merely a question of foreign policy but also one of race and citizenship, as Chapter 8 demonstrates.

Italians' understandings of their place in the world were to come into sharp conflict with the harsh realities of the post-war climate. The Paris Peace Conference was a critical moment, often seen as a disaster for Italian policymakers and a key milestone in the path towards fascism. Here Chapter 9 analyses Italian priorities and performance at the conference, in light of both its domestic political situation and augmented war aims, and of the rapidly changing circumstances which limited the scope of Italian action in 1919 such as the roles of the USA, Yugoslavia, and Greece. Chapter 10 explores the impact of decisions in Paris and Rome on Italian borders in the north and east, and in the Adriatic and Balkans.

The relationship between national goals—Trento and Trieste—and more ill-defined expansionism in the Adriatic region became increasingly complex in 1919–20 as Gabriele D'Annunzio's seizure of Fiume would highlight. Even in the supposedly 'national' territories which had been 'liberated' a range of remarkably colonial policies would be implemented by the post-war occupations, as shown here. Elsewhere in the Adriatic region, Italian ambitions would be thwarted.

Further afield military operations continued for several years. Chapter 11 analyses Italy's expeditionary force in Anatolia, an attempt to construct an informal empire in the Eastern Mediterranean. This effort lasted until 1923, when the creation of the Turkish Republic marked the final defeat of Italian ambitions in the region—though the Dodecanese Islands remained Italian throughout the fascist era. In Africa too there were a series of Italian disappointments, along with some major adjustments to the colonial order due to the war and the new ideas it had helped to generate in the realms of citizenship and identity.

Ultimately, what outwardly appeared to be Liberal Italy's moment of triumph—victories in colonial and European wars—instead proved its swansong. The Liberal State failed to convince all sectors of Italian society or the other great powers at Versailles of either the necessity of its expansionist vision or its ability to live up to its ambitions. The imperial and colonial aspect of the war for the new Italy was unsuccessful. The repressiveness of wartime government, including the suspension of normal parliamentary processes, also played a critical role in undermining the fledgling democracy. The new fascist state would build on these experiences and policies even as it denounced the failures and weaknesses of its predecessor.

2

Imperialism and Irredentism in Liberal Italy

The Kingdom of Italy was officially unified in 1861 but in fact this was only one step in a long, drawn-out process lasting from 1848 to 1919. As a result, throughout the Liberal period, Italy was always quite consciously a work-in-progress. The completion of the national territory, the propagation of national identity, and the acquisition of great power status were all interconnected, making Italy a project as much as a reality.

2.1 Nationalism, Nation-building, and Completing Italy

Most nationalists agreed that the kingdom created by the three nineteenth-century wars of the Risorgimento (1848, 1859–60, 1866) was incomplete. Even after the incorporation of Rome as the new national capital (1870), many Italian nationalists embraced the position known as irredentism—the desire to 'redeem' the largely Italian-inhabited cities of Trento and Trieste, with their respective hinterlands, from Austrian rule. Between 1870 and 1914 no progress was made towards this goal, but other forms of nation-building were still possible. In the famous and probably apocryphal words attributed to Massimo d'Azeglio, having made Italy, it was now necessary to make Italians. The project of nationalizing the masses would also be a long, slow process, heavily reliant on state education (above all primary schools) and the army.[1] It was rendered more problematic by the papal ban on participation in Italian politics which meant that, at least in theory, devout Catholics could neither vote nor join parties. Not repealed until 1904, this ban—known as the 'Non Expedit'—prevented the formation of a strong conservative party which could appeal to a cross-section of classes. This created a gulf between Catholics—a majority of the population—and the state, limited the possibility of a religious-patriotic nexus of loyalty centred on the monarchy (as

---

[1] On education and nation-building, see Simonetta Soldani and Gabriele Turi, *Fare gli italiani: scuola e cultura nell'Italia contemporanea* (Bologna: Il Mulino, 1993); in wartime, see Andrea Fava, 'War, "national Education" and the Italian Primary School, 1915–1918', in *State, Society and Mobilization in Europe during the First World War*, ed. John Horne (Cambridge: Cambridge University Press, 1997), 53–69; on military service, see Marco Rovinello, *Fra servitù e servizio: storia della leva in Italia dall'Unità alla Grande Guerra* (Rome: Viella, 2020).

The Italian Empire and the Great War. Vanda Wilcox, Oxford University Press (2021). © Vanda Wilcox.
DOI: 10.1093/oso/9780198822943.003.0002

compared, for instance, to the Habsburg Empire), and thus undermined the nation-building project.[2] In the eyes of many nationalists and, later, the fascist regime, it was only with the First World War that this process would really be completed.[3]

The process of the Risorgimento suggested that further territorial gains at Austria's expense were unlikely to come about through peaceful means: only war could force the Habsburg Empire to relinquish any of its lands, and any appeal to the principle of nationality was unlikely to carry weight with a multi-national empire dedicated to suppressing this concept at all costs. But the decision in 1882 to join the Triple Alliance rendered this prospect unfeasible for the foreseeable future. As a new power Italy found itself in need of allies for its security and to bolster its status; rivalry with France over trade, naval supremacy, and Mediterranean prestige made Germany an attractive partner, as did Germany's military reputation. Alliance with Austria-Hungary was the price to be paid for this desirable agreement, and so to the disappointment of irredentist Italians living within the Dual Monarchy, the two powers came together with Germany to forge a long-lasting defensive agreement (it was renewed in 1912, on its thirtieth anniversary). By this time many Italian moderates agreed that a strong Austria was inherently desirable, securing stability in central Europe; some even hoped for a negotiated transfer of the *terre irredente*, with Austria taking compensation elsewhere at the expense of the Ottoman Empire (as article 7 of the Triple Alliance, on the Balkans, implied). The Triple Alliance, while difficult to reconcile with what we now consider to be the key goals of irredentism, was perfectly compatible with another, forgotten irredentism to the west. Savoy—the ancestral home of the Italian monarchy—and Nice—birthplace of Garibaldi—had been reluctantly ceded to France only during the Risorgimento. War alongside Germany and Austria against France offered the pleasing prospect of reclaiming them (and even perhaps Corsica too).[4] Thus in one way or another, for the first fifty years of its existence Italy was firmly dedicated to the goal of territorial expansion as an essential step in achieving its rightful place in the world; the completion of national territory was postponed, not abandoned, and the widely shared perception of incompleteness was crucial to the shaping of Italian political culture.

[2] See John Neylon Molony, *The Emergence of Political Catholicism in Italy: Partito Popolare 1919–1926* (London: C. Helm, 1977), 17–20; on the monarchy, see Andrea Ungari, *La guerra del re: monarchia, sistema politico e forze armate nella Grande Guerra* (Milan: Luni editrice, 2018).

[3] A classic example of this argument is in Adolfo Omodeo, *Momenti della vita di guerra. Dai diari e dalle lettere dei caduti, 1915–1918* (Turin: G. Einaudi, 1968 [1934]). On the history of the debate, see Emilio Gentile, *La grande Italia. Il mito della nazione nel XX secolo* (Rome: Laterza, 2011).

[4] Federico Chabod, *Storia della politica estera italiana: dal 1870 al 1896* (Bari: Laterza, 1962) is dated but still fundamentally important. See also Bosworth, *Italy, the Least of the Great Powers*; Rinaldo Petrignani, *Neutralità e alleanza. Le scelte di politica estera dell'Italia dopo l'Unità* (Bologna: Il Mulino, 1987).

Equally significant, and closely linked to this focus on expansion, was an ongoing sense of anxiety about Italian status. Italian governments of left and right were both aware of Italy's position on the periphery of great power politics, and there was a clear agreement that the core goal of foreign policy was to improve Italian standing within Europe so as to be fully acknowledged as a great power. This led Italy to adopt positions which came into tension with its Risorgimento-based embrace of the principle of nationality: the compromise with the multi-national Austrian Empire was one, the occupation of the Dodecanese in 1912—clearly Greek in national terms—was another. The rhetoric of national liberation continued, but the reality of Italian foreign policy frequently belied it. Ironically, the First World War—presented as a national war par excellence—would actually undermine the internal cohesion of the nation, both by exacerbating class and political divides and by incorporating huge numbers of non-Italians within the borders of the newly enlarged national territory.

2.2   Nineteenth-century Colonialism

If after 1882 it was not possible to seize the Italian borderlands—and indeed there was little popular focus on irredentism in this period—there were territories further afield to which nationalists might turn their eyes. The origins of Italian colonial expansion can be found as early as 1869, even before the seizure of Rome. In this year, a missionary from the Order of St Lazarus named Giuseppe Sapeto, who had lived and worked extensively in the Horn of Africa, acted as an agent for the private acquisition of the port of Assab in Eritrea. The creation of an Italian colonial empire formally began in 1882, when Assab passed from private owner-ship into the hands of the state. This was followed by the formal seizure of all Eritrea in 1890, while Italian Somalia was created as a protectorate in 1889 and became an official colony in 1908. But empire-building was not merely a substitute for nation-building, rather the acquisition of an empire was a direct extension of the original Risorgimento project. In the words of military historian Bruce Vandervort, 'it was an article of faith that the birth of the "New Italy" signalled at one and the same time the rebirth of the Roman Empire'.[5] Indeed, so central was colonialism to the nation-building project that Angelo Del Boca, the pre-eminent historian of Italian colonialism, includes on his list of Italy's colonial wars the fight against brigandage conducted by the newly unified state in 1861–85. Here the nexus between imperialism and national completion was at its clearest (and the link between colonial conquest and racist/orientalist attitudes to

[5] Bruce Vandervort, 'A Military History of the Turco-Italian War (1911–1912) for Libya and Its Impact on Italy's Entry into the First World War', in *Italy in the Era of the Great War*, ed. Vanda Wilcox (Leiden: Brill, 2018), 15, DOI: https://doi.org/10.1163/9789004363724_003.

conquered peoples can also be seen in action).[6] In 1926 the Italian Communist Party, in their analysis of nineteenth-century Italian colonialism, also observed that 'Italy's colonial expansion originate[d] from the political need to seek out all the elements that could help to create a *consciousness of the unified state* within the metropole.'[7] The Liberal State saw colonial expansion as an important goal for domestic political and economic reasons, as well as making it an important element in foreign policy. And Italian colonialism was very much a State project, centrally directed, in common with other 'late imperialists' like Germany, rather than following a more 'organic', capitalist, French or British model. But this is not to say that there was no wider social participation: the Italian Nationalist Association (ANI), founded in 1910 by Enrico Corradini, was a broad umbrella institution which united 'liberal imperialists' with radical nationalists and irredentists, and incorporated both gradualists and advocates of war. By the early twentieth century, irredentism and imperialism were not alternatives but complementary, interconnected ideals which might alternate as priorities depending on circumstance. Irredentism and colonialism were but two different facets of a wide-ranging expansionist policy.[8]

Italy's desire to demonstrate its great power status also led it to look further afield: its military participation in the European expedition to China to crush the Boxer Rebellion led to the creation of the Italian concession at Tianjin (then known as Tientsin) in 1901. This was by most standards a complete failure, achieving nothing more than the construction of a pleasant neighbourhood of charming Italian villas, today a popular leisure destination for locals and tourists. Already by 1921 its streets were resonantly named for key sites of nation and empire: Via Roma was joined by Via Trento, Via Trieste, and Via Tripoli.[9] A tiny area of the city, bounded by the Austrian and Russian concessions on the north bank of the Hai river, the Tianjin concession was a clear example of the 'wishful thinking' underpinning Italian visions of global power projection in this era.[10] Government efforts to sell off the land and encourage investment were humiliatingly unsuccessful: there was almost no interest at all from either Italian or Chinese investors, and by 1908 the tiny colony was almost bankrupt. The foreign ministry committed considerable effort, if only limited funding, to upholding the concession in order to protect 'Italian dignity and prestige in the Far East'.[11] Such

[6] Angelo Del Boca, *Italiani, brava gente?* (Vicenza: Neri Pozza, 2011), 57–70.
[7] Emphasis in original; cited in Srivastava, *Italian Colonialism and Resistances to Empire*, 36–7.
[8] Aristotle Kallis, *Fascist Ideology: Territory and Expansionism in Italy and Germany, 1922–1945* (London: Routledge, 2000), 15–18.
[9] Vincenzo Fileti, *La concessione italiana di Tien-Tsin* (Genoa: Barabino e Graeve, 1921).
[10] Maurizio Marinelli, 'The Genesis of the Italian Concession in Tianjin: A Combination of Wishful Thinking and Realpolitik', *JMIS* 15, no. 4 (2010): 536–56, DOI: http://dx.doi.org/10.1080/1354571X.2010.501975.
[11] Aglaia De Angeli, 'Italian Land Auctions in Tianjin: Italian Colonialism in Early Twentieth-Century China', *JMIS* 15, no. 4 (2010): 568, DOI: http://dx.doi.org/10.1080/1354571X.2010.501976.

a capital-intensive form of colonial project was never likely to succeed in Italy, though the Tianjin concession continued to act as a sphere of informal empire (or informal imperial aspirations) well into the Fascist period. In the words of Maurizio Marinelli, it 'reveal[s] a distinctive feature of the foreign policy of the newly unified Italian state: the dichotomy between the frustrated desire for self-assertion on the international scene on the one hand, and the problematic localization of the national interests on the other'.[12] A similar assessment might well be made of Italian aspirations in several other places, before and after the First World War.

2.3 The Growth of an Imperial Culture

A vigorous colonial imaginary was thriving in Italian print culture even before the first formal steps into colonialism: travel writing, geographical and geological studies, popular romances, economic analyses, magazines, and journals of all kinds brought Africa to Italy long before Italy came to Africa.[13] Giuseppe Finaldi has convincingly shown that this culture of colonialism was both abundant and flourishing in late nineteenth-century Italy. From primary schools to theatre to the popular media, cultural institutions heavily promoted colonialism in the 1880s and 1890s; the middle and upper classes participated fully in this culture, as we can see from sources as diverse as funeral orations and puppet shows, and evidence suggests that significant inroads were made into popular culture too.[14] Contemporary imperialists often disagreed: continual laments about the weakness of Italian colonial mentalities and the inadequacy of colonial sensibilities among the masses were a commonplace of this very culture.[15] However, Finaldi has argued consistently that in this respect late nineteenth-century Italy can indeed be meaningfully compared to contemporary France or Britain, and that further-more the overseas acquisition of colonies was intimately connected to the creation of post-Unification patriotism.[16] The image of the new Italian—citizen of a modern, outward-looking, national state—was built upon the exploration and conquest of Africa as well as Risorgimento heroism. Already by the late nineteenth century, the myth of ancient Rome was widely used to underpin both colonialism and patriotism. Prime Minister Francesco Crispi (1887–91; 1893–6) believed that

[12] Marinelli, 'The Genesis of the Italian Concession in Tianjin', 538.

[13] Antonio Schiavulli, *La guerra lirica: il dibattito dei letterati italiani sull'impresa di Libia (1911–1912)* (Ravenna: Fernandel, 2009), 9–11.

[14] Giuseppe Finaldi, *Italian National Identity in the Scramble for Africa: Italy's African Wars in the Era of Nation-Building, 1870–1900* (New York: Peter Lang, 2009).

[15] Giampaolo Calchi Novati, 'Studi e politica ai convegni coloniali del primo e del secondo dopoguerra', *Il Politico* 55, no. 3 (155) (1990): 487–514.

[16] See also Gaia Giuliani, *Race, Nation and Gender in Modern Italy: Intersectional Representations in Visual Culture* (London: Palgrave Macmillan, 2018), 43–4.

only colonial expansion could generate the patriotic national spirit which Italy desperately needed.[17]

In 1896 the Italians suffered an international humiliation at Adwa: Ethiopia successfully prevented an Italian invasion from neighbouring Eritrea, inflicting a resounding and unprecedented defeat which had a profound effect on both countries.[18] This failure caused a brief halt in the growth of Italian colonial culture, but within the decade expansionism returned to the political agenda. Civil society organizations dedicated to exploration and commercial expansion proliferated in Italy; cartographic and geographical expeditions abounded.[19] In Milan, the Società Italiana di Esplorazioni Geografiche e Commerciali (Italian Society for Geographical and Commercial Exploration) published a monthly bulletin and was influential in building economic ties to North Africa; the Istituto Agricolo Coloniale Italiano, founded in Florence in 1904 with links to the university there, focused on agriculture in tropical regions. Along with many others, these bodies surveyed physical and human geography, produced maps for sale in Italy, and encouraged entrepreneurs and investors to look to Africa (and to a lesser extent Asia and the Far East) for future industrial and commercial opportunities.[20] Anthropologists, archaeologists, and art historians were also among the scholarly enthusiasts for colonial empire. The Società Italiana per il Progresso delle Scienze (Italian Society for the Advancement of the Sciences), for example, strongly supported the invasion of Libya and the Dodecanese on scholarly grounds. By 'Othering' local inhabitants as barbarous and unable to properly care for the artistic and cultural heritage of these areas, which were presented as part of a larger 'Italian' inheritance, they argued that Italy held a 'duty of care' and a moral obligation to look beyond its own borders in defence of classical and Byzantine cultural legacies.[21] But the most important pro-colonial organization was undoubtedly the Istituto Coloniale Italiano (Italian Colonial Institute, ICI) which was founded in Rome in 1906 with a broad vision of promoting all forms of imperial and colonial expansion. The ICI acted as an umbrella organization which could coordinate other patriotic bodies and endeavours, working closely with the Dante Alighieri Society, one of Italy's most important cultural institutions, and the Lega Navale (Naval League) among others. It published

[17] See Christopher Duggan, *Francesco Crispi, 1818–1901: From Nation to Nationalism* (Oxford and New York: Oxford University Press, 2002).

[18] On the legacies and memory of Adwa within Ethiopia, see Maimire Mennasemay, 'Adwa: A Dialogue between the Past and the Present', *Northeast African Studies* 4, no. 2 (1997): 43–89, DOI: https://doi.org/10.1353/nas.1997.0008.

[19] Maria Carazzi, *La Società Geografica Italiana e l'esplorazione coloniale in Africa (1867–1900)* (Florence: La Nuova Italia, 1972).

[20] Anna Milanini Kemény, *La Società d'esplorazione commerciale in Africa e la politica coloniale: (1879–1914)* (Florence: La Nuova Italia, 1973).

[21] Simona Troilo, '"A Gust of Cleansing Wind": Italian Archaeology on Rhodes and in Libya in the Early Years of Occupation (1911–1914)', *JMIS* 17, no. 1 (2012): 48–53, DOI: https://doi.org/10.1080/1354571X.2012.628103.

(semi-)scholarly monographic studies and a monthly bulletin, hosted major national congresses and generally propagandized among the intellectual, commercial, and administrative ruling classes.[22]

Colonialism was pursued in partnership between public and private actors. Despite the rhetoric of a settler-led popular movement, the reality of Italian colonial expansion was generally one of capital-heavy investment. The economic sectors which backed foreign and colonial policy—banking and investment, steel, shipbuilding, and armaments—received special support from the state, including favourable tax, tariff, and subsidy conditions along with special treatment in cases of financial difficulty, in the form of emergency rescue packages.[23] This distorted the domestic economy in certain damaging ways—including the proliferation of clientelism and corruption—and is thus indicative of the extent to which the state was committed to its projection of great power status in this era. The army was the chief agent of Italian colonialism, through both conquest and administration of new territory; this was not accidental but by design, in the effort to refute lingering doubts about Italian military capability left by the less than glorious wars of the Risorgimento. Since one of the chief purposes of colonial expansion was that of asserting great power status, it was perfectly logical that military supremacy ought to be demonstrated at the same time. As a result, the administration of the new colonies remained in military hands for prolonged periods (in Eritrea, it was not until 1897 that Ferdinando Martini, later minister of the Colonies 1914–16, became the first civilian governor). Thus Italian colonialism was given a distinctly military imprint from early on.

How did Italian culture represent and conceive of its own imperial expansion? Did Italy embrace a 'white man's burden', or seek 'a place in the sun'?[24] The most important narrative of Italian colonialism, one to which many Italians were deeply wedded, was the idea of *italiani brava gente*—Italians are good people. This concept, which was particularly applied to soldiers, would recur as a major trope in Italian interpretation and memory of the Second World War; in both cases, it was an implicitly comparative assessment. Italian colonizers were nicer than British or French colonizers; Italian fascists were nicer than Nazis. (Neither comparison seems especially worthy of celebration.) In its early, imperial incarnation, this idea translated into the apparently sincere belief that most 'inferior'

[22] On the role of these organizations in late Giolittian Italy, see Alberto Acquarone. 'Politica estera e organizzazione del consenso nell'età giolittiana: il Congresso dell'Asmara e la fondazione dell'Istituto coloniale italiano', *Storia contemporanea* VIII (1977): 57–119; Giancarlo Monina, *Il Consenso Coloniale: Le Società Geografiche e l'Istituto Coloniale Italiano: 1896–1914* (Rome: Carocci, 2002).

[23] Douglas J. Forsyth, 'Monetary and Financial Policy and the Crisis of Liberal Italy, 1914–22', in *Italy in the Era of the Great War*, ed. Vanda Wilcox (Leiden: Brill, 2018), DOI: https://doi.org/10.1163/9789004363724_016 calls this sector 'too strategic to fail' (p. 290).

[24] Mussolini would invoke a 'place in the sun' in his speech announcing the invasion of Ethiopia in October 1935. Benito Mussolini, *Opera omnia di Benito Mussolini*, ed. Edoardo Susmel and Duilio Susmel, 35 vols (Florence: La Fenice, 1951), Vol. 27, 158–60.

races would recognize Italian benevolence. The historiography of this myth is extensive and countless examples of it might be cited.[25] To give just one, in 1909 the military newspaper *La Preparazione* wrote: 'Italians never leave hateful memories behind them anyway, because of all the superior races ours is the least rapacious, the least over-bearing, the most equal towards the inferior or subject races.'[26] These sentiments are remarkably similar to those expressed by Manlio Di Stefano in 2019 (see Chapter 1—7–8). The author proceeded to assert—without any evidence—that the subject peoples of the Ottoman Empire would greatly prefer Italian rule to French or British colonialism. Italian imperialists never made clear just how they thought the average Arab or Ethiopian was supposed to have learned about Italian values, nor why these prospective colonial subjects were supposed to be so impressed. Perhaps imperialists were confident that Italian governance was globally renowned, and its cultural superiority self-evident, but this seems a major gap in the belief-system. Nonetheless, the belief in Italian imperial benevolence, and its acceptance among non-European peoples, was commonplace in both civilian and military circles; Italian colonial culture thus meant not only enthusiasm for colonialism but also this specific understanding of expansion as moderate and welcome. In fact, it was not uncommon to find explicitly Risorgimento-style rhetoric of 'liberation' from foreign or oppressive rule in Italian colonial discourse. Whether it was Ottoman rule in Libya or the supposedly backwards system of the Ethiopian Empire, Italian colonial invasion was presented as a liberating force which would bring good governance and benevolence to the subject peoples.[27] These narratives recurred frequently in the abundant publications and activities of the pro-colonial civil society organizations which proliferated before 1914.

2.4 Emigration and Imperialism

We can see, then, that geopolitical expansion was a core part of Italian thinking and aspirations in the Liberal Era. But this was not the only area of expansionism at play: alongside geopolitics was a biopolitical vision (though interestingly the concept of biopolitics would not be named until during the war, in 1916). In the words of Rhiannon Noel Welch, this entailed a government focus on the 'national

---

[25] On the pervasive cultural ideal of Italian soldiers as essentially good-natured, following the title of Giuseppe De Santis's 1965 Second World War film, see Del Boca, *Italiani, brava gente?*, especially chapter 1.

[26] *La preparazione: trisettimanale politico-militare*, 1 July 1909.

[27] Nicola Labanca, 'Discorsi coloniali in uniforme militare, da Assab via Adua verso Tripoli', in *Guerra e pace*, ed. Walter Barberis, I, Storia d'Italia, Annali 18 (Turin: Einaudi, 2002), 518–19, 534.

population, whose borders and numbers must expand, enveloping new territories and reproducing itself, in order to survive'.[28]

Italian imperial culture grew simultaneously with the rise of emigration. In fact, the key period of emigration (1880–1914) precisely overlaps with that of the birth of the colonial empire. This was no coincidence: the two phenomena were linked in a complex inter-relationship, highlighted by the dual meaning of the term *colonie*—which described Italian communities overseas as well as the dispersed territorial possessions of the state. A 'colony' was not a function of political sovereignty but derived simply from the presence of Italian nationals, language, and culture. This understanding, which prioritized people over territory, shared roots with the ideas of irredentism. Two key ideas can be identified in this distinctively Italian formulation: firstly, emigrant communities were a type of informal empire, both a proxy and a vector for global influence. Secondly, the creation of formal empire was a response to mass emigration—the establishment of settler colonies would allow the migratory flux to be redirected into channels more directly beneficial to Italy. At least in the imagination of its proponents, all Italian colonialism was to be settler colonialism, in that Italy's problem was not a labour shortage requiring indigenous labour (or soldiers) but on the contrary a surplus of labour, which led to emigration and thus to loss of income (and military manpower). But we should note that the peasant-focused settler colonial vision of enthusiasts like Baron Leopoldo Franchetti, or indeed of the later fascist regime, required that African lands would be empty and ripe for claiming—whether as a result of famine and drought, or of forced displacement and in some cases 'nomadification' of indigenous populations.[29] Agricultural settler colonialism, while less ostensibly violent than conquest, was not a benevolent project.

Scholars of Italian emigration have persuasively argued that in the late nineteenth and early twentieth century Italy embraced a two-pronged imperial strategy, in which emigrant communities would operate alongside formal colonial expansion in the projection of global power.[30] If the French and British approaches to imperialism are taken as normative, this may seem bizarre, but by analysing Italian political culture on its own terms it becomes clear that this

---

[28] Rhiannon Noel Welch, *Vital Subjects: Race and Biopolitics in Italy 1860–1920* (Liverpool: Liverpool University Press, 2016), 4–5.

[29] Lorenzo Veracini, 'Italian Colonialism through a Settler Colonial Studies Lens', *Journal of Colonialism and Colonial History* 19, no. 3 (15 December 2018), DOI: https://doi.org/10.1353/cch. 2018.0023.

[30] Ruth Ben-Ghiat and Stephanie Malia Hom observe that the inter-relation of these phenomena is critical and needs further investigation. See 'Introduction' in Ruth Ben-Ghiat and Stephanie Malia Hom, eds, *Italian Mobilities* (London and New York: Routledge, 2015). Recent work in the field includes Stefano Pelaggi, *Il colonialismo popolare: L'emigrazione e la tentazione espansionistica italiana in America latina* (Rome: Nuova Cultura, 2015); on emigration and social mobility, see Francesca Fauri, 'Italians in Africa (1870s–1914), or How to Escape Poverty and Become a Landowner', *The International History Review* 27, no. 2 (2015): 325–41, DOI: https://doi.org/10. 1080/07075332.2014.904811.

was a core strand in Italian imperial thinking from the 1870s through to the era of the First World War, only ending decisively in the 1920s with the rise of fascism (and changing international attitudes to migration).[31] Emigration was not simply an uncontrolled mass phenomena, initiated spontaneously by the populace; on the contrary, Italy actively encouraged, managed, and directed emigration in this period, since 'the Italian emigrant constituted an instrument for the projection of strength across the world'.[32] Mark Choate has analysed the 'ethnographic' empire which was built upon the global Italian diaspora—as the state sought to re-conceptualize a weakness (mass emigration) into a strength (global status).[33] Catherine Dewhirst's research on 'diaspora colonialism' highlights that although the state's vision of global power projection might not match up with migrants' own values or priorities, some migrant communities abroad did deliberately cultivate *italianità* and actively further these imperial ambitions.[34] This model highlights the appeal which alternative forms of expansionism could hold beyond conservative nationalist circles. Many Italian liberals embraced a vision of a peaceful, modern colonialism of people and goods, rather than conquest and control, most notably the economist Luigi Einaudi (later to serve as President of the Republic) in his 1900 work *Un principe mercante*.[35] For the young Einaudi, rather than wasting money in costly and dangerous military enterprises (such as Adwa) it was more practical to undertake a 'soft' imperialism of emigrant settler colonies; just as importantly, this form of expansionism was not in conflict with the core principles of the Risorgimento. Einaudi identified Argentina (and Latin American more generally) as being of critical importance to this project, since they offered more social mobility to Italian immigrants. Compared to the USA, Italians in Argentina suffered less racism and were less likely to see their identity eroded by an over-powerful national culture, he argued.

There across the Atlantic, on the banks of the Plata, a new Italy is growing, a new people is forming . . . which will prove to the world that the imperialist ideal is not destined to remain solely an Anglo-Saxon ideal. On the contrary, we are showing

[31] Pergher argues convincingly that Italian settler colonialism under fascism was driven not by the need to accommodate surplus population but to Italianize contested territories and consolidate imperial control; *Fascist Borderlands*.

[32] Marco Soresina, 'Italian Emigration Policy during the Great Migration Age, 1888–1919: The Interaction of Emigration and Foreign Policy', *JMIS* 21, no. 5 (2016): 723–46, DOI: https://doi.org/10.1080/1354571X.2016.1242260; 725.

[33] Mark I. Choate, 'From Territorial to Ethnographic Colonies and Back Again: The Politics of Italian Expansion, 1890–1912', *Modern Italy* 8, no. 1 (2003): 65–75, DOI: https://doi.org/10.1080/1353294032000074089; Choate, *Emigrant Nation: The Making of Italy Abroad* (Cambridge, MA: Harvard University Press, 2008).

[34] Catherine Dewhirst, 'Colonising Italians: Italian Imperialism and Agricultural "Colonies" in Australia, 1881–1914', *The Journal of Imperial and Commonwealth History* 44, no. 1 (2016): 23–47.

[35] Luigi Einaudi, *Un principe mercante: studio sulla espansione coloniale italiana* (Turin: Fratelli Bocca, 1900). See analysis in Choate, 'From Territorial to Ethnographic Colonies'.

the world that Italy is capable of creating a type of colonisation more perfect, more evolved than the Anglo-Saxon type.[36]

Italian settlers in Argentina were thus building a Greater Italy even as they remodelled traditional conceptions of empire. Even in Australia, where fewer than ten thousand Italians were present, Dewhirst identifies Italian imperialism in action via an 'economic and imperial strategy that would operate under the direct administration of its colonies and, more indirectly, across the scattered diasporic communities'.[37] Here too the state specifically envisaged agricultural settlement as the means for achieving its goal.

Italian citizenship laws, based on blood not birthplace, meant that new generations born to these emigrants retained all the rights and obligations—including military service—of their emigrant forebears; the state continued to provide services to these dispersed citizens, through language schools, chambers of commerce, cultural institutions, and banking services.[38] Legal measures, such as banking reform, were introduced to protect the interests of emigrants and tie them closely to the motherland. State institutions, such as the Regia Marina (navy), as well as the diplomatic service, formed essential elements in the network of ties which kept emigrants Italian. The Dante Alighieri Society played a crucial role in educating young second-generation emigrants in the language and culture of their forefathers, building a sense of Italian national identity in the face of competing national cultures. And the civil society institutions which most eagerly promoted colonial expansion were also involved. The Società Geografica Italiana was a keen proponent of emigration to Latin America in the late nineteenth century. The ICI aimed to encourage the development of both 'direct domination' colonies and the diaspora communities, hosting major congresses dedicated to 'Italians Overseas' in 1908 and 1911. These twin strands of Italian overseas expansion were circulating in the military world too: an article published just a few months before the Libyan war began in the *Rivista Militare Italiana* showed the military version of these ideas. Infantry captain Achille Vaccarisi (who would eventually become a general in the colonial army) argued for a rethinking of army structure and organization to consider the impact both of emigration and of the drive to acquire formal colonies, two aspects of the Italian political landscape which he expected to endure and which required a careful military response.[39]

[36] Einaudi, *Un principe mercante*, 12–13.

[37] Dewhirst, 'Colonising Italians: Italian Imperialism and Agricultural "Colonies" in Australia', 28.

[38] The state's efforts to tie people to *italianità* continued for many years: as a child in the UK in the 1980s, I received free Italian tuition as the descendent of a 'migrant worker'—namely my Milanese grandmother, despite the fact she was at no time active in the labour force—who married my English grandfather and moved with him to Manchester.

[39] Achille Vaccarisi, 'L'importanza dell'odierna espansione coloniale', *RMI* 56, no. 8 (1911): 1685–1702.

Finally, there were also economic incentives. The emigrant 'colonies' of the Americas had an enormously positive impact on the Italian economy via remittance payments, while the spread of Italian culture helped create new markets for Italian exports, especially food. Unsurprisingly therefore, the Italian commercial and shipping sectors, especially the major firms operating out of Genoa, also vigorously supported emigration as a form of expansionism.[40]

Right through the era of the First World War, Italian emigrants were clearly conceived of as a core part of the national community and of the nascent empire. Italians in French- or British-ruled North Africa lived at a particularly interesting intersection of the two forms of colonialism: more than 30,000 Italians lived in Algeria and a similar number in Egypt, along with 88,000 in Tunisia and a small number in Morocco, for a total of around 168,000 Italian citizens in 1911. Many North African Italians, particularly among the social and economic elite, were firmly committed to the nation-building process but also saw their presence on the continent as a key source of legitimacy for formal colonial aspirations.[41] Emigrants elsewhere also supported formal colonialism, suggesting that the two models might be intertwined—for instance during the war for Libya, new nationalist bodies were created within the Italian communities in Brazil and Argentina to carry out patriotic activities and emphasize support for Italy's imperial endeavour.[42] At the same time, as Antonio Bechelloni has perceptively observed, the two types of expansionism fed upon one another's perceived weaknesses: just as military failures encouraged Einaudi and his supporters to promote emigrant colonies, the lack of clear advantages these provided was used to support arguments in favour of conquest and formal imperialism. There was never true consensus as to whether many 'Little Italies' could ever add up to a 'greater Italy': for some nationalists, like Corradini, mass emigration to other sovereign lands could only ever be a sign of weakness.[43] But even for this party, the emigrant problem was an inseparable part of the imperial question. As such, emigrants' many forms of participation in the war effort—or their failures to do so—are important elements in reconceiving the Italian experience of the First World War in an imperial framework.

[40] Pelaggi, *Il colonialismo popolare*.

[41] Gabriele Montalbano, 'The Italian Community of Tunisia: From Libyan Colonial Ambitions to the First World War', in *The First World War from Tripoli to Addis Ababa (1911–1924)*, ed. Shiferaw Bekele et al. (Addis Abbeba: Centre français des études éthiopiennes, 2018), DOI: https://doi.org/10.4000/books.cfee.1532.

[42] Emilio Franzina, 'La guerra lontana. Il primo conflitto mondiale e gli italiani d'Argentina', *Estudios Migratorios Latinoamericanos* 15, no. 44 (2000): 69.

[43] Antonio Bechelloni, 'De Petites Italies au service d'une Plus Grande Italie?', in *Les petites Italies dans le monde*, ed. Marie-Claude Blanc-Chaléard et al. (Rennes: Presses Univ. de Rennes, 2007), 344–7.

2.5 Mare Nostrum: Libya and the Mediterranean

By the early twentieth century the troubles of the Ottoman Empire appeared to offer a prime opportunity for Italian expansion. Here the secondary, but none-theless significant, strand of colonial discourse was to emerge: that of ancient rights. Across the Mediterranean and Asia Minor, Italy was presented as the rightful inheritor of the classical Roman Empire. Italian claims were thus legitim-ate, lawful, and historically unchallengeable. Imperialists looked to the classical heritage of Rome to justify both the scope and the specific geographical focus of their interests: North Africa, Asia Minor, and the Middle East all fell under this acquisitive gaze. Long before Mussolini propounded his vision of a new Rome, the lands of the glorious imperial past were perceived as a legitimate and desirable objective by many nationalists and colonial activists. As Italy recovered from the economic recession of 1907, an increasing number of Italian activities were launched within the Ottoman lands, ranging from numerous Catholic schools and missionary foundations, to railway building using Italian engineers and specialist labour, and the export of luxury goods such as silk or rose oil. Trading companies and investors saw southern Anatolia and the Levant as particularly fertile areas for future expansion. Religion was another sphere through which Italy sought to project power into the region, managing in 1905 to achieve the right to protect Italian-run Catholic institutions in the Levant (previously the responsibil-ity of France). Catholics became increasingly interested in and supportive of imperial expansion in this period, and leading Catholic newspapers such as *La Civiltà Cattolica* were among the earliest proponents of expansion into North Africa.[44] Meanwhile from 1907 the Banco di Roma undertook extensive commer-cial and industrial investments in Libya, both preparing the way for Italian penetration on the ground and promoting the idea that the region could be economically highly profitable. This bank formed a critical link between industrial and financial elites and government circles—but was also extremely close to the Vatican, one of its major shareholders. The Banco di Roma's president Ernesto Pacelli was personal financial adviser to successive popes as well as first cousin to then apostolic nuncio Eugenio Pacelli, who would later be named Pope Pius XII.[45]

A foundational principle propounded by Italian nationalists and imperialists was that 'the sea unites, it does not divide' (borrowing, perhaps, from Alexander

---

[44] Eileen Ryan, *Religion as Resistance: Negotiating Authority in Italian Libya* (New York: Oxford University Press, 2018), 57–63.

[45] Ruggiero Romano and Corrado Vivanti, eds, *Storia d'Italia. Vol. 4, t. 3: Dall'Unità a oggi* (Turin: Einaudi, 1976), 1946–7. On Pacelli, and the bank's relations to the Vatican, see John F. Pollard, *Money and the Rise of the Modern Papacy: Financing the Vatican, 1850-1950* (Cambridge: Cambridge University Press, 2009), 69–75, 103–7.

Pope's line in *Windsor Forest*: 'seas but join the regions they divide').[46] Thus Italy was logically joined by the Mediterranean to North Africa, just as the Adriatic joined it to the Dalmatian coast; by this logic, the Aegean would 'unite' Anatolia to the Dodecanese (and, even more optimistically, the Red Sea should link Yemen to Eritrea). This understanding also underpinned the description of North Africa as the 'fourth shore'—the first three were those parts of the Italian mainland bathed by the Adriatic, Tyrrhenian, and Ionian seas. The Mediterranean was now to become the centre of the new Italian physical and cultural space.[47] Originally the imagined 'fourth shore' was that of Tunisia, which boasted a large population, including many wealthy Italians, and the thriving port of Tunis with all its economic advantages. An added attraction lay in the fact that this was Carthage of old, and thus a most fitting target for conquest by the new Rome, which could thus formalize the relationship with the informal emigrant colony there. But when French strength made it clear that Tunisia was off limits, Corradini and his supporters had turned their eyes to the neighbouring provinces which still lay in Ottoman hands.[48]

2.5.1 Libya

Even to name Italy's projected territory as Libya was an inherently colonial act: while the term was not unknown to inhabitants, it represented neither the extant administrative reality nor the psychogeography of the area, which was divided firstly into three major regions—Tripolitania, Cyrenaica, and Fezzan—and then further subdivided into many smaller provinces. Nor were there truly 'Libyans', but a diversity of religious and ethnic communities, connected or divided by tribe, dialect, and locality. Libya, then, was a project rather than an extant reality.[49] In fact, Libya and the Mediterranean space were the object of two, competing geo-political imaginaries, in that Ottomanism as much as Italian colonialism was a projection of imperial nationalism.[50] Libya was also an object of fantasy and

---

[46] A principle clearly propounded by the Italian Colonial Institute, under Ernesto Artom, at its 1911 congress in Florence, see Istituto Coloniale Italiano. *Atti del secondo congresso degli Italiani all'Estero (11–20 giugno 1911)* (Rome: Tipografia Editrice Nazionale, 1911).

[47] On the long history of the Mediterranean as a colonial and colonized space, see Manuel Borutta and Sakis Gekas, 'A Colonial Sea: The Mediterranean, 1798–1956', *European Review of History: Revue Européenne d'histoire* 19, no. 1 (1 February 2012): 1–13, DOI: https://doi.org/10.1080/13507486.2012.643609.

[48] Enrico Corradini, *Sopra le vie del nuovo impero: dall' emigrazione di Tunisi alla guerra nell'Egeo* (Milan: Fratelli Treves, 1912) made the link explicit.

[49] See Nicola Labanca in Gabriele Bassi, Nicola Labanca, and Enrico Sturani, *Libia. Una guerra coloniale italiana* (Rovereto (TN): Museo Storico Italiano della Guerra, 2011), 8–9.

[50] Jonathan McCollum, 'Reimagining Mediterranean Spaces: Libya and the Italo-Turkish War, 1911–1912', *Diacronie. Studi di Storia Contemporanea* 23, no. 3 (2015), DOI: https://doi.org/10.4000/diacronie.2356.

Orientalist desire for Italians, rather than practical planning: contemporary articles waxed lyrical about the probable Tripolitanian location of the garden of the Hesperides and lamented the lack of lion hunting.[51] Nonetheless, through the first decade of the twentieth century, it would become the major focus of imperialists' attention, culminating in war against the Ottoman Empire. One of the most important elements in this process was 'peaceful penetration' by economic means, chiefly via the operations of the Banco di Roma. This bank acquired significant holdings in Ottoman lands, and later became a key agent in pressing for military intervention in 1911. But the conquest of Tripolitania and Cyrenaica, and their incorporation into the Italian Empire under the name of Libya, were not simply a matter of financial interests: indeed, they were such a major theme of both the popular and intellectual press in this period that Mario Isnenghi, Italy's leading cultural historian of war, writes 'one may say that the Libyan enterprise was evoked, invoked, imposed by and through the press itself'.[52] Not only the usual suspects, such as Corradini and his *L'Idea Nazionale*, but moderate Liberal newspapers such as *La Stampa* and *La Tribuna* were campaigning vigorously for war; along with supposed economic motives, both nakedly nationalist ambitions and the desire to cancel the shameful memories of Adwa were clear. Even the previously sceptical liberal Luigi Albertini, editor of the influential *Corriere della Sera*, was convinced to support the endeavour. Catholic public opinion too was rapidly mobilized, with much of the episcopate openly supporting a crusading interpretation of the war (to the extent that the pope, Pius X, even felt the need to distance himself from the most outspoken clerical positions).[53] The vigorous interventionism of the Banco di Roma, known for its proximity to the pope, made Pius' position the more awkward. Nonetheless, this was a critical moment for the integration of Catholics into Italian national politics, thanks both to religious and political-economic media representations; the bank's ability to unite financial, industrial, and Catholic interests was important. Highly optimistic agricultural and geographical studies of the region proliferated, and misinformation of every kind circulated suggesting that the two provinces would simply and rapidly be transformed into fertile, prosperous, easy-living lands which would absorb the mass of Italian emigration. Only the socialists held back from this unprecedented national mobilization; there could be no colonial 'union sacrée'. The Partito Socialista Italiano (PSI) called out a general strike on 27 September, though adherence was patchy in many cities; a number of local party sections limited themselves to issuing formal condemnations of militarism

---

[51] Adolfo Orsini, 'Tripoli e Pentapoli', *RMI* 56, no. 12 (1911): 2589–604.

[52] Mario Isnenghi, *Le Guerre degli italiani: parole, immagini, ricordi 1848–1945* (Bologna: Il Mulino, 2005), 176.

[53] Giovanni Sale, *Libia 1911: i cattolici, la Santa Sede e l'impresa coloniale italiana* (Milan: Jaca book, 2011).

and colonialism.[54] Left-wing southern historian Gaetano Salvemini was particularly fierce in his denunciation of the war, and felt that the PSI should be doing even more to oppose it. Libya, he famously proclaimed in his new weekly *L'Unità*, was nothing but 'a box of sand', whose riches existed only on the pages of the Italian mainstream press.[55] But the successful pro-war campaign was highly suggestive as an example of the mobilizing power of the media, even in a country not yet fully literate; a telling example of the 'productive power of the word [...] which can materialize into political action'.[56] The word was flanked with posters, poetry, and postcards which enabled it to reach an unprecedently broad cross-section of Italian society.

Despite this intensive press attention to the so-called 'Libyan question' from spring 1911 onwards, the Italian declaration of war against the Ottoman Empire on 29 September was nonetheless a surprise to many. The ultimatum which had been delivered to the Sublime Porte the previous day was simply a matter of form and offered little real justification for hostilities: Giovanni Giolitti's government was already determined on war.[57] The fact that Giolitti—long considered a highly cautious and equivocal figure—was so personally committed to the war shows the extent to which colonial fever had gripped the ruling class. Symbolically falling on the fiftieth anniversary of unification, the invasion of Tripolitania and Cyrenaica was perhaps Italy's first truly national moment: enthusiasm for the war transcended political boundaries, with liberals and Catholics alike united in support for this seizure of the 'Fourth Shore'.[58] Significantly, community leaders of Italians overseas were also galvanized: the Italian-language press of Argentina and Brazil shared in this general acclamation of the war and even the (remote) possibility of future migration to a Libyan settler colony, reversing the emigrant communities' traditional diffidence towards formal colonialism.[59] However, it was not popular pressure but the international situation which had really prompted the final decision for war. The Agadir Crisis of July 1911 had raised fears that France might be further expanding in North Africa without any corresponding Italian advance, and provided a concrete opportunity not to be missed, given that it would be hard for the French or British to directly oppose Italian action at this

[54] Leonardo Saviano, 'Il Partito Socialista Italiano e la guerra di Libia (1911–1912). I.', *Aevum* 48, no. 1/2 (1974): 102–30. https://.jstor.org/stable/25821263.

[55] Gaetano Salvemini, *Come siamo andati in Libia e altri scritti dal 1900 al 1915*, ed. Augusto Torre, 3 vols, v. 1 (Milan: Feltrinelli, 1973).

[56] Schiavulli, *La guerra lirica*, 29.

[57] Angelo Del Boca, *Tripoli bel suol d'amore, 1860–1922*, vol. 1, *Gli italiani in Libia* (Bari: Laterza, 1986), 74–5. See also Vandervort, 'A Military History of the Turco-Italian War', 244–51.

[58] Isabella Nardi and Sandro Gentili, eds, *La grande illusione: opinione pubblica e mass media al tempo della guerra di Libia* (Perugia: Morlacchi, 2009). Luca Micheletta and Andrea Ungari, eds, *L'Italia e la guerra di Libia cent'anni dopo* (Rome: Edizioni Studium, 2013).

[59] Federica Bertagna, 'Nazionalismo da esportazione: la guerra di Libia sulla stampa italiana in Argentina e Brasile – A.S.E.I.', *A.S.E.I. ARCHIVIO STORICO DELL'EMIGRAZIONE ITALIANA*, 2012, https://www.asei.eu/it/2012/03/nazionalismo-da-esportazione-la-guerra-di-libia-sulla-stampa-italiana-in-argentina-e-brasile/.

time. By contrast, Italy tried to avoid any meaningful consultation with its Triple Alliance partners, owing to their close ties to the Ottoman Empire. Tripolitania and Cyrenaica were now the last 'unclaimed' areas in North Africa from the Italian point of view; the Moroccan Crisis created both a sense of urgency and a window of opportunity in which Giolitti at last felt able to act.

Military preparation for the war was poor. Mobilization was ordered on 19 September, but it was a relatively bureaucratic and slow process, with troops not ready to disembark in Tripolitania until early October. The delay between the declaration of war and the beginning of the bombardment of Tripoli on 3 October allowed the Turks precious time to organize their defences. The expeditionary force was placed under the command of 66-year-old General Carlo Caneva, who had begun his career in the Austrian army and even fought against Italy in 1866, before transferring his allegiance once his hometown (Udine) became part of the kingdom. Initially given just two divisions—around 20,000 men—Caneva was expected to conquer Tripolitania and Cyrenaica with ease and speed. Simultaneous strikes on Tripoli and Homs by the army and navy were to be followed by a rapid advance into the interior. Within the first three weeks, key ports and coastal towns were indeed captured: Tripoli, Tobruk, Derna, Benghazi, and finally Homs were seized. Additional troops were soon landed to bolster Caneva's numbers, while the Ottoman forces numbered only a few thousand men.

But on 23 October, a serious miscalculation in Italian thinking was revealed. Given that regular Turkish troops were numerically few, the only major force likely to resist the Italian conquest was that of the native Arab and Berber population. Pre-war popular assessments of the local people had, however, been largely upbeat, sometimes speculating that they would welcome their 'liberation' from the oppressive yoke of Ottomanism—a Risorgimento-inspired reading of the war. A more dependable source of pro-Italian sentiment was identified by government intelligence: the Arab social and commercial elite, especially in the Tripoli area, who were generally Westernized and many of whom had close working ties to the Banco di Roma, which had made itself the pre-eminent source of investment in the region.[60] The head of the consulate in Tripoli, Carlo Galli, believed that any tribespeople who might have some loyalty to the Ottomans were all 'poor, unarmed, or too distant to present any real threat'.[61] But these interpretations of Arab and Berber sentiment were wildly optimistic; in reality, the Turkish regulars began to organize native guerrilla units as soon as the war began.

This was the backdrop to the assault which was launched at the oasis of Sciara Sciatt, on the outskirts of Tripoli, by a combined force of Arab irregulars and Turkish troops on 23 October 1911. The Italians found themselves surrounded

---

[60] Francesco Malgeri, *La guerra libica (1911–1912)* (Rome: Edizioni di storia e letteratura, 1970), 177–80.
[61] Cited in Del Boca, *Mohamed Fekini and the Fight to Free Libya*, 16.

and outnumbered; the irregular forces took no prisoners, instead massacring them all, including a number of wounded men, for a total of 21 officers and 482 other ranks killed. Wild atrocity stories soon circulated, alleging torture, crucifixion, and the mutilation of slain Italians; these evoked the memory of the defeat at Adwa in 1896, where Eritrean *ascari* had indeed been mutilated while rumours of similar atrocities against white men had spread. These lurid allegations were mobilized to help justify the brutal Italian response, which involved severe reprisals (400 women and 4,000 men executed or simply slaughtered) and the internment of thousands of Tripolitanians both within Libya and in concentration camps in Ustica (Sicily) and Caserta.[62] Giolitti's decision to deport 'arrested rioters' to Italy highlights the policy of internment of colonial convicts—or untried 'undesirables'—within the metropole, a highly unusual feature of imperial governance which had begun in Eritrea in in the 1880s and which would endure throughout the history of the Italian Empire.[63] If anything, this practice reversed the more common European policy of deporting metropolitan criminals to be interned in the colonies.[64] Meanwhile the massacre at Sciara Sciatt led to an escalation of the Italian war effort and a hardening of attitudes towards the local population—with terrible long-term consequences. The indigenous population—originally described as good-natured, peaceful, and friendly—was now depicted in the Italian media as treacherous, savage, violent, and devious. More troops were hastily dispatched from Italy, eventually bringing numbers up to around 100,000; the small force initially deployed might have sufficed for a conventional war strictly against the Turkish regulars but was hopelessly outnumbered by this unanticipated enemy. Sciara Sciatt also offered Giolitti an excuse to proceed to the next phase of operations politically: on 5 November 1911 the Italian government formally declared the annexation of both Tripolitania and Cyrenaica under the name of Libya. At the time, Italian forces occupied only a tiny fraction of this area, but this effectively ensured that no easy resolution to the crisis could be achieved (such as the idea, sometimes discussed, of an Egypt-style protectorate which maintained nominal Ottoman suzerainty).

A disastrous gulf soon opened between the government's understanding of the conflict and the military realities on the ground. Civilians imagined the enemy as a weak and racially inferior force which modern European organization and

[62] For a concise description, see Del Boca, *Mohamed Fekini and the Fight to Free Libya*, 19–29. The massacres were greeted by international outrage but were denounced in Italy only by some socialists, e.g. Paolo Valera, 'Le giornate di sciarasciat fotografate', supplement to *La Folla*, 1912, reproduced in Schiavulli, *La guerra lirica*, 147–64.
[63] Francesca Di Pasquale, 'The "Other" at Home: Deportation and Transportation of Libyans to Italy During the Colonial Era (1911–1943)', *International Review of Social History* 63, Special Issue: *Transportation, Deportation and Exile: Perspectives from the Colonies in the Nineteenth and Twentieth Centuries* (2018): 211–31, DOI: https://doi.org/10.1017/S0020859018000299.
[64] France also interned some high-profile political prisoners from the colonies within metropolitan prisons.

weaponry ought to be able to easily sweep aside. Instead Caneva found himself facing a highly committed opponent, supported by the local population, able to rely on deep knowledge of the challenging terrain and to use flexible guerrilla tactics against which the poorly trained Italian conscripts had little real response. Giolitti urged an offensive deep into the desert to destroy the enemy's strongholds; Caneva rightly identified that lacking any quality maps, the basic equipment for desert warfare, or any training in irregular combat, this could only lead to disaster. Hopes of a decisive victory on the battlefield quickly faded. For all that the Italians could use aerial reconnaissance and radio communications, modern technology did not resolve the impasse. The events at Sciara Sciatt had further embedded 'Adwa Syndrome' into Italian officership, making leadership tentative and uncertain, whereas Turkish leadership boasted such decisive characters as Mustafa Kemal, known to posterity as Atatürk, and Enver Bey who, as Enver Pasha, would later serve as the Ottoman Minister for War during the First World War.

2.5.2 The Dodecanese and the Eastern Mediterranean

It would take the Italian expansion of the conflict into the Eastern Mediterranean to bring about a decisive conclusion. The domestic press made much of Turkish reprisals carried out against Italian 'colonies' in Anatolia, presenting the extension of operations into the Eastern Mediterranean as an essential step in protecting the people of Greater Italy.[65] In February 1912 the navy sent two cruisers to attack Ottoman targets off the coast of Beirut, and later attacks were made around Samos and Lemnos. Selecting its targets carefully to avoid provoking any other great powers with interests in the area, Italy launched a series of attacks in the Aegean. In late April and early May, Italian forces under General Giovanni Ameglio landed on Rhodes and other islands of the southern Sporades group, gradually seizing the archipelago known as the Dodecanese. In July the navy made a brief show of force at the Dardanelles, largely for effect. Naval operations also took place in the Red Sea, against that portion of the Ottoman fleet based off the Arabian coast, and Italy shipped arms to support an Arab insurrection in Yemen (where it nurtured vague hopes of creating a sphere of influence).

None of these was in itself a decisive blow to the Ottoman Empire, but the expansion of the war into these new theatres threatened to place an ever-greater burden on imperial finance. Far more pressing concerns were taking up the Sublime Porte's attention: the Balkan powers were looking to take advantage of Turkish distraction, and if a new war broke out there while the conflict with Italy

[65] Valerie McGuire, 'An Imperial Education for Times of Transition: Italian Conquest, Occupation and Civil Administration of the Southeast Aegean, 1912–23', in *Italy in the Era of the Great War*, ed. Vanda Wilcox (Leiden: Brill, 2018), DOI: https://doi.org/10.1163/9789004363724_009, 151.

was still ongoing, Turkey risked significant difficulties in shipping its troops to the front through Italian naval attacks. Peace talks consequently began in July and August 1912, involving the ubiquitous Giuseppe Volpi whose extensive financial and industrial interests in Turkey had given him a network of informal connections there.[66] War in the Balkans began on 8 October and eventually on 18 October a peace agreement was signed at Ouchy, a suburb of Lausanne, just as Serbia, Bulgaria, and Greece had all declared war on Turkey. The Sultan retained his spiritual role in Libya, and the Italian occupation of the Dodecanese was agreed to be temporary only, but in practical terms Italy had won, despite all its difficulties. These residual measures of Ottoman influence would be abolished after the First World War, confirming Italy in all its gains including the Dodecanese islands.

2.5.3 Legacies of the Italo-Turkish War

What was the effect of the war? If on the one hand Italy's great power status seemed bolstered with the acquisition of an undeniably important colony, international public opinion had been implacably hostile to the conduct of the war, with denunciations of the Italian atrocities against the local population published widely in the international press.[67] In military terms, the war had scarcely demonstrated the might of Italian arms, while it left a serious hole in the state's finances, with grave consequences for its ability to prepare effectively for the far greater war yet to come.[68] Meanwhile the legacy of Sciara Sciatt—the new Adwa— also endured, a memory which was transmitted within the army to new recruits during the First World War, propagating colonial memories through the metropolitan army. Mussolini's vice-squadron leader, who was present at Sciara Sciatt, 'often tells me about it', he noted in his diary on the fourth anniversary of the massacre, 23 October 1915.[69] The event consolidated commanders' mistrust of enemy civilians, with important implications for their future conduct. At the same time, the war was celebrated as a key sign of Italian modernity: visual and literary depictions celebrated the artillery and machine guns, modern naval power, and the use of a wide range of machinery. The radio was much praised, and Marconi himself was photographed in Libya with his invention, accompanying the Italian troops; other technologies such as the diffusion of modern hygiene methods were also depicted in propaganda materials. Above all the deployment of aircraft in

---

[66] On Volpi and the intersection of finance capital with colonialism, see Sergio Romano, *Giuseppe Volpi et l'Italie moderne. Finance, industrie et État de l'ère giolitienne à la deuxième Guerre mondiale* (Rome: École Française de Rome, 1982).

[67] See for instance the French critiques reproduced in Bassi, Labanca, and Sturani, *Libia*.

[68] See Douglas J Forsyth, *The Crisis of Liberal Italy: Monetary and Financial Policy, 1914–1922* (New York: Cambridge University Press, 1993), chapter 2.

[69] Benito Mussolini, *Il mio diario di guerra (1915–1917) con 10 illustrazioni fuori testo* (Milan: Imperia, 1923), 70.

combat—a true global first—seemed to demonstrate that Italy had achieved modernity through warfare. In the words of one former artilleryman, 'the roar of the artillery [...] demonstrated the powerful means through which modern civilization can proudly redeem a coarse and uncivilised people'.[70] Empire, war, and modernity were thus rhetorically linked in the cultural imagination.[71]

In geopolitical terms the war was also critically important, shifting Italian priorities in the Mediterranean, where the 'Dodecanese islands provided a strategic pivot for Italy's larger imperial ambitions.'[72] Luigi Federzoni, co-founder of the Italian Nationalist Association, wrote a popular account of the invasion in 1913 which even raised the spectre of claims to Constantinople—however fantastical this seemed even at the time.[73] In the aftermath of the war against Turkey, the Eastern Mediterranean had become a major priority for Italian foreign policy.[74] The urgent need for coal—there are no coal deposits in mainland Italy—encouraged investors to seek access to the important coalfields at the Zonguldak-Heraclea basin, with the backing and encouragement of the state. Italian credit institutions were heavily engaged in financing new industrial and commercial projects within the Ottoman Empire in 1912–14 and poorly defined but nonetheless significant ideas circulated about Italian spheres of economic interest (chambers of commerce were created in both Constantinople and Smyrna). The ambassador to the Sublime Porte, Camillo Garroni, had been personally selected by Giolitti for the position, despite his entire lack of diplomatic experience; he was a Genoese lawyer with strong ties to his home city's shipping industries and to the Banca Commerciale Italiana. Railway construction, as ever, lay at the heart of these colonialist projects: with Garroni's support, Italian investors were interested in building spur to connect Antalya—where they had special interests—to the main Istanbul–Baghdad line.[75] The new Governor of Rhodes and the Dodecanese, General Giovanni Ameglio, also hoped to use the local population of the islands as a source of cheap labour for the Italian-backed Marmaris–Aiden railway, showing the link between formal colonialism, labour emigration, and the informal penetration of Anatolia.[76]

The conquest of Libya not only shifted Italian foreign policy but also changed public attitudes towards empire, with an increasing embrace of direct settler

---

[70] Cited in Nicola Labanca, ed., *Posti al sole. Diari e memorie di vita e di lavoro dalle colonie d'Africa* (Rovereto (TN): Museo Storico Italiano della Guerra, 2001), 90.

[71] On the wider links between modernity and colonialism, see Ruth Ben-Ghiat, 'Modernity Is Just Over There', *Interventions* 8, no. 3 (1 November 2006): 380–93, DOI: https://doi.org/10.1080/13698010600955883.

[72] McGuire, 'An Imperial Education for Times of Transition', 146.

[73] Luigi Federzoni, *L'Italia nel Egeo* (Rome: Garzoni-Provenzani, 1913), cited in McGuire, 'An Imperial Education for Times of Transition', 145.

[74] Marta Petricioli, *L'Italia in Asia Minore. Equilibrio mediterraneo e ambizioni imperialiste alla vigilia della prima guerra mondiale* (Florence: Sansoni, 1983).

[75] Cecini, *Il Corpo di spedizione italiano in Anatolia*, 22.

[76] McGuire, 'An Imperial Education for Times of Transition', 156.

colonialism rather than the emigrant model. One of the clearest evocations of this ideal can be found in a speech delivered in November 1911 by Giovanni Pascoli (1855–1912), a great luminary of Italian nineteenth-century poetry and university professor of classics. Declaring that 'the Great Proletariat has made a move', he lamented that previously Italy 'sent elsewhere those workers who were too many and worked for too little' and that these workers had always taken on the dirtiest, toughest, least prestigious jobs. They were mistreated and abused, he complained; they had become like 'i negri, in America'. Tellingly, along with this racialized analysis, Pascoli cited three national humiliations in particular: illiteracy, criminality, and the defeat to Ethiopia. But now—in Libya—'the Great Proletariat has found its own place' where they will be 'farmers in their own right, on the soil of the Fatherland…always seeing above them, fluttering in the immense breeze of our sea, our own tricolor'. The key transformation at the heart of his vision is from humiliation to pride—from cultural, economic, and racial inferiority to (white) supremacy.[77]

Perhaps the most important legacy of the Italo-Turkish war was the experience of unprecedented, cross-party national mobilization. This both demonstrated the new power of the media and mass culture to shape public opinion and indicated that the process of 'creating Italians' was well under way. Fatally, however, the experience taught that the shared causes around which Italians could coalesce were expansionism and war. This had important ramifications in 1915, and again in 1919.

2.6 The Balkans

Somewhere between the openly colonial aspirations in North Africa and the rhetoric of national liberation in the borderlands lay Italy's goals in the Balkans. The eastern shores of the Adriatic and their hinterlands had long been areas of interest: strategically, they held the key to security in the Adriatic Sea, while the legacies of Venetian rule there offered tempting justifications for claiming new territory. The 'slow but inexorable decline of the Ottoman Empire' had created 'opportunities and dangers for many years'.[78] These opportunities were also scented by the emerging Balkan powers themselves, where Serbia and Bulgaria in particular nurtured ambitions which went beyond the new organizing principle of nationality but also disregarded the more traditional model of a balance of power. The Balkan wars of 1912–13 highlighted the scale of these conflicting ambitions in the region, and also the awkwardness of Italy's position. Italy wanted

---

[77] Giovanni Pascoli, 'Il Grande Proletariato si è mossa', reproduced in Schiavulli, *La guerra lirica*, 43–54.
[78] Francesco Caccamo, 'Italy, the Adriatic and the Balkans: From the Great War to the Eve of the Peace Conference', in *Italy in the Era of the Great War*, ed. Vanda Wilcox (Leiden: Brill, 2018), 122, DOI: https://doi.org/10.1163/9789004363724_008.

to avoid the emergence of any strong new power in the region, without wishing to see any strengthening of the two rival great powers with existing interests there, Austria and Turkey. The Dual Monarchy had also shared Italy's desire to keep the Balkans out of the Italo-Turkish war, and while the two allies' aspirations were by no means the same both sought to maintain stability there as much as possible. Austria and Italy collaborated in support of the creation of an independent Albania against the expansionist (in their view) interests of Serbia, Montenegro, and Greece: with its vital position at the mouth of the Adriatic, it could not be left in the hands of potentially aggressive rivals. The strategically important port city of Vlorë (Valona)—capital of the newly independent state—quickly became an Italian objective in itself. Arguably an 'Albanian Question' existed in Italy even before Albanian independence; in 1908, the government seriously considered sending an occupying force there during the Austrian occupation of Bosnia-Herzogovina, to protect as yet undefined Italian strategic interests.[79]

Meanwhile, as the strength of the Habsburg state waned, the relationships between Italians and South Slavs also began to degenerate; from coexisting as two equally oppressed minorities, a new dynamic of national and ethnic rivalry began to emerge. While protests of Risorgimento-style sympathy for the oppressed might still be uttered on behalf of the Slavs, by the eve of the war Italy increasingly saw the Balkan peoples as rivals rather than potential allies, while the extension of political, economic, and cultural interest into the region was an ever more attractive prospect. Expansionists did not precisely imagine a colony across the Adriatic so much as a sphere of influence: Italian policy was to encourage the promotion of a series of small, weak yet viable Balkan nations while maximizing its own formal and informal control. Italian investment into the region had increased dramatically during the decade before the First World War, beginning with small private investors and soon followed by major commercial and financial interests. From 1908 there was an ambitious project for a trans-Balkan train line which would link Italy to Romania—and various schemes for control of strategic infrastructure such as ports and raw materials were developed. But despite the economic justifications with which Balkan ambitions were dressed up, the region was a source of expenses rather than profits, and in reality prestige and power projection underlay Italy's Balkan hopes.[80] It would be the chaos and confusion of war which opened a window to turn these hopes into concrete actions. If the Balkan Wars of 1912–13 suggested that new spheres of influence might be up for grabs, the July Crisis of 1914 blew all earlier calculations out of the water.

[79] Massimo Borgogni, *Tra continuità e incertezza: Italia e Albania (1914–1939). La strategia politico-militare dell'Italia in Albania fino all'operazione 'Oltre Mare Tirana'* (Milan: FrancoAngeli, 2007), 13–14.
[80] Alessandro Vagnini, *L'Italia e i Balcani nella Grande Guerra: ambizioni e realtà dell'imperialismo italiano* (Rome: Carocci editore, 2016), 16–25. See also Richard A. Webster, *Industrial Imperialism in Italy, 1908–1915* (Berkeley: University of California Press, 1975).

3

From Neutrality to Intervention, 1914–15

When Archduke Franz Ferdinand was assassinated on 28 June 1914, few Italians could imagine just what enormous events lay around the corner for their homeland. The public's attention was much more focused on domestic problems. The government was still recovering from the dramatic events of 'Red Week' in early June, when a major popular insurrection in the Marche, Tuscany, and Emilia-Romagna regions had threatened national stability and led to the calling of a general strike. Although the movement did not lead to the national revolution for which its supporters had hoped, and was ended relatively peacefully, it was a clear sign of the strength of socialism within the country. The Italian Socialist Party reiterated its commitment to democratic means, but the episode seriously alarmed many conservatives.

3.1 The July Crisis

The July Crisis in 1914 caught Italy at a bad moment. Military operations were ongoing in Libya, continuing to devour resources both human and material; the aftershocks of Red Week were still being felt. More generally, the political landscape had shifted rapidly in the previous two years: in May 1912 the loyalty of the masses in supporting the Libyan adventure had been rewarded with universal male suffrage (over age 30), and the first national elections under this new system had been held in November 1913. Though the Liberal Party had won a resounding victory, this innovation had increased the potential political influence of both socialists—who gained eleven new parliamentary seats at the election—and Catholics. Since the 1904 election, when the papal decree against participation in Italian politics had been tacitly lifted in the hope of preventing the spread of socialism, Catholics had become an increasingly important part of political life and were willing to collaborate informally with Giolittian Liberals.[1] The informal 'Gentiloni Pact', which bound Catholics and Liberals together in 1913 to fight against socialism, meant that the traditionally anti-clerical liberals were

---

[1] Romano and Vivanti, eds, *Storia d'Italia*. Vol. 4, t. 3, pp. 1936–7.

The Italian Empire and the Great War. Vanda Wilcox, Oxford University Press (2021). © Vanda Wilcox.
DOI: 10.1093/oso/9780198822943.003.0003

now committed to supporting Church education, among other measures; even wily old Giolitti could not keep these strange bedfellows united, and he was forced to stand down in March 1914. With experienced political players still re-orientating themselves to this new environment, a new government was formed by the conservative Antonio Salandra, an experienced and ambitious statesman and law professor from Puglia who had several times served as minister for finance. When the July Crisis began, Salandra was still busily engaged in consolidating his power, shoring up social order, and moving the Liberal party considerably to the right. The well-being of Italy's ally Austria-Hungary was not a top priority.[2]

Under Article 5 of the Triple Alliance, as renewed in 1912, the signatory powers were required to 'take counsel together in ample time as to the military measures to be taken with a view to eventual cooperation'. But as the month of July unfolded, while Austria immediately communicated with Germany over the question of how to respond to the assassination, no contact was made with the Italian government. In fact, it was simply assumed that Italy would play its part in the case of war—even though the alliance was strictly defensive, and no *casus foederis* therefore arose. This assumption was not wholly unfounded; the Italian chief of staff since 1908, General Alberto Pollio, was a committed 'triplicist', with marked German sympathies and an Austrian wife.[3] He was more than ready to join his allies in a war—but it was not to be; Pollio died suddenly on 1 July 1914 (leading to some conspiracy theorists to allege that this was a political murder). Now, in this hour of international crisis, Italy was without its chief of general staff. Not until 27 July would a new appointment be made, leaving the Italian army without a head at this critical juncture. The new man in charge, chosen somewhat to his own surprise, was Luigi Cadorna (already passed over for the job in 1908). Aristocratic, pig-headed, reactionary, and arrogant, Cadorna was nonetheless the best available option at the time; he was undoubtedly hard-working, dedicated, intelligent, and determined. It was unfortunate, however, that he had never held any operational command. More damaging yet was his innate inability to delegate or to work well with others, of whatever rank, and his almost pathological refusal to admit to any mistakes.[4] When he took the reins, Cadorna still expected to be ordered to join the Central Powers—and the very next day, Austria-Hungary declared war on Serbia. Instead, within less than a week, Italy would proclaim its neutrality.

---

[2] The best introduction is still Bruno Vigezzi, ed., *Da Giolitti a Salandra* (Florence: Vallechi, 1969).

[3] On Pollio and his strategic thought, see John Gooch, 'Inevitable War, Improbable War? General Alberto Pollio and the Likelihood of War in 1914', in *L'Italia Neutrale 1914–1915*, ed. Andrea Ungari and Giovanni Orsina (Rome: Rodrigo editore, 2016), 258–69.

[4] Indisputably the best biographical study is Marco Mondini, *Il capo. La grande guerra del generale Cadorna* (Bologna: Il Mulino, 2017).

3.2 The Outbreak of War

As a historical problem, far less attention has been paid to Italy's declaration of neutrality on 3 August 1914, the very day of the German invasion of France, than to its subsequent declaration of war in 1915. Implicitly this suggests that neutrality was the obvious, natural choice, and it is rather the decision for war which must be explained. But the Italian position in summer 1914 was by no means uncontroversial domestically, and it deserves investigation. If war alongside Austria was not necessarily in Italy's interests, the kingdom held no brief for the Entente powers either, and a range of conservative opinion—from nationalists to Catholics—remained pro-Triple Alliance. As foreign minister Antonino di Sangiuliano commented on 12 September, 'for us it would be ideal if on the one side Austria and on the other side France were both to be beaten'.[5] Anti-French sentiment was strong and widespread, and many nationalists would have been willing to place their austrophobia on hold in favour of war against this hated neighbour. Far from exclusively focusing on Trento and Trieste, in late July and early August 1914 Italian nationalists were imagining extending their power in the Mediterranean, where France not only held Nice but was a rival in both trade and colonial matters. The prospect of an anti-Slavic crusade against Serbia was also attractive, offering to open up new Italian opportunities in the Balkans.[6] There was even the remote possibility that within the framework of the Triple Alliance Italy might receive the *terre irredente* as a form of territorial compensation from Austria, in return for support in Austria's war. However, while war against France and Serbia was a not unattractive prospect, war against Britain was another kettle of fish: Italy was heavily dependent on Britain for essential raw materials, chiefly coal, and relied on British financial networks for credit. Critically, the strength of the Royal Navy in the Mediterranean directly threatened both the Italian coasts and all connections with the hard-won colonies; without continued support from the Italian mainland, Libya might very well be lost. From an imperial and colonial perspective, good relations with Britain were essential. From the time of the first Moroccan Crisis onward it was clear that the Triple Alliance could hold only within Europe itself, and once across the Mediterranean it was unsustainable. Was it worth going to war alongside Austria but losing the empire in the process?[7] The Entente victory on the Marne was perhaps the deathblow to the idea of Italy joining the Central Powers as a belligerent. Instead, neutrality was supported by most of the

    [5] Olindo Malagodi, *Conversazioni di guerra* (Milan: Riccardo Ricciardi, 1960), 20.
    [6] Brunello Vigezzi, 'L'Italia del 1914–'15 e la crisi del sistema liberale', in *L'Italia neutrale 1914–1915*, ed. Giovanni Orsina and Andrea Ungari (Rome: Rodorigo editore, 2016), 16–19.
    [7] Stefano Marcuzzi, 'A Machiavellian Ally? Italy in the Entente (1914–1918)', in *Italy in the Era of the Great War*, ed. Vanda Wilcox (Leiden: Brill, 2018), 103–4, DOI: https://doi.org/10.1163/9789004363724_007.

mass parties, as well as the most virulent austrophobes who had embraced it from the start.

On the other hand, the prospect of a complete reversal of pre-war foreign policy was also raised very rapidly. On the left, the origins of democratic interventionism—the idea of the fourth war of the Risorgimento—can be traced back to the very first days of the war.[8] At the diplomatic level, an expansionist interventionism can also be identified in this period, with a clearly discernible imperialist character. The new European landscape opened by the July Crisis and the outbreak of the war raised for the first time the prospect of actually implementing concrete policies in pursuit of some long-nurtured imperialist fantasies.[9] Discussions with the British government over Italian aspirations in Turkey began soon after the outbreak of the war, and long before the Ottomans themselves joined the conflict. As early as 11 August 1914, the Italian foreign minister Antonino di Sangiuliano secretly raised the possibility of war alongside the Entente with the ambassador in London, Guglielmo Imperiali. The scope of his thinking is indicated by the fact that his telegram included provisions about potential Italian spheres of influence in Turkey, 'among those provinces bathed by the Mediterranean', should the Ottoman Empire break up to the benefit of the other powers. He also asserted the need for protection of Italian interests in Antalya and environs. Considering that neither Italy nor the Ottomans were involved in the war in August 1914—and indeed on the contrary both were to a greater or lesser extent aligned with Germany at this point—these claims are perhaps rather startling. On the other hand, it was clear that Turkey was funding the ongoing war in Libya, and rumours had even circulated there was an Ottoman plot against the king; Italy had also managed to entangle itself in a Greco-Turkish row in spring 1914 which had further increased Italo-Turkish tensions.[10] Di Sangiuliano further instructed Imperiali to suggest that Vlorë be allocated to Italy and the rest of Albania divided up, with neutralized coasts under an 'internationalized' regime comparable to that in Tangiers. When Imperiali met with the British foreign secretary two days later, Sir Edward Grey informed him that Britain hoped to avoid the disintegration of the Ottoman Empire if at all possible, since it was 'the only remaining independent Muslim state'.[11] The ambassador replied that it was also in Italy's best interest 'to keep it alive and facilitate the economic development of the Asian provinces with our capital'. Clearly, Italian aspirations in Asia Minor were already well developed and

[8] Vigezzi, 'L'Italia del 1914–'15 e la crisi del sistema liberale', 19.
[9] Vagnini, *L'Italia e i Balcani nella Grande Guerra*, 10.
[10] Archivio Centrale dello Stato [hereafter ACS] Archivio Salandra fasc. 17: di Sangiuliano to Imperiali, 11 August 1914, Urgente n. 892. Interestingly, in this message, San Giuliano also conceded that 'Dalmazia è fuori dei confine geografici d'Italia'. On Ottoman action in this period, see Gooch, 'Inevitable War, Improbable War?', 266–7.
[11] For British strategy in the region, see Robert Johnson, *The Great War & the Middle East: A Strategic Study* (Oxford: Oxford University Press, 2016).

communicated to the British at this early stage; an informal sphere of influence was gently hinted at. Britain tried to use Italian interests in the Eastern Mediterranean as an incentive to encourage Italy to abandon the Triple Alliance and support the Entente. Grey warned Imperiali on 18 August that should the 'bellicose, megalomaniac currents, encouraged by Germany, prevail within Turkey' leading them to enter the war, the Young Turks would immediately seek to recover their lost North African provinces, starting with Egypt. Under these circumstances, argued Grey, Italy would be obliged to enter the war to defend its Libyan possessions. The populations of Tripolitania and Cyrenaica had never fully accepted Italian conquest in 1912 and several of the tribes in the interior were openly at war with Italy; this vulnerability would be much greater should the Ottomans also seek to intervene in the region once more. Britain even held out tantalizing, if implausible, prospects for future acquisitions at Ottoman expense. Imperiali reported to his government on 28 August that in a private meeting with Winston Churchill, the First Lord of the Admiralty had suggested that Britain might look favourably upon an Italian presence in the Dardanelles were they to enter the conflict as a British ally.[12] In mid-August the Russian foreign minister, Sergii Sazonov, also showed himself keen to redistribute other countries' lands, apparently offering Trento, Trieste, the whole of Dalmatia including Zara, and even Vlorë as an incentive for Italy to join the Entente (at least according to the Italian delegation in St Petersburg).[13] In the immediate term, none of these discussions had any discernible impact on Italian policy: di Sangiuliano saw no reason to abandon neutrality and serious talks over joining the Entente did not begin until early the following year. Nonetheless, we can see that irredentism was not the only focus of these August debates. It is significant both that Imperiali raised the topic of the Eastern Mediterranean so early on in discussions, and that the British government considered that it was a useful carrot to dangle before the Italians, while mentions of Albania and Dalmatia show that Italian aspirations there were well known.[14]

Historians have generally contrasted the more moderate so-called 'sensible imperialism' of di Sangiuliano with the more extreme 'idiot imperialism' of his successor Sidney Sonnino; as Francesco Caccamo notes, this ignores the fact both men's policy positions violated the principle of nationalities and would have created legacies of rancour in the Balkans.[15] It is revealing of Italian priorities and debates in this era that even the supposedly moderate position was inherently imperialist (and likely unrealistic). But di Sangiuliano's cautious policy was in any

---

[12] ACS Archivio Salandra f. 17: Imperiali to Gabinetto, 28 August 1914, n. 322.
[13] Ministero degli Affari Esteri, *I documenti diplomatici italiani*. [hereafter DDI] *Quinta Serie, 1914–1918*, XI vols (Rome: Istituto Poligrafico e Zecca dello Stato, n.d.). Docs 179 & 194.
[14] ACS Archivio Salandra fasc. 17, August 1914 papers.
[15] Caccamo, 'Italy, the Adriatic and the Balkans', 128–9.

case soon to be abandoned. His long battle with gout had made him increasingly immobile—he was by now actually living inside the foreign ministry building, the Palazzo della Consulta—and he died aged 71 on 16 October 1914. Had he remained in office it is unlikely that he would have kept Italy out of the war—but he certainly would have shaped Italian war aims in a different direction. He was soon replaced by Sonnino, the leading figure in the nationalist-conservative opposition during the Giolittian era, who would finally to be able to pursue some long-cherished dreams.

Sidney Sonnino was an interesting figure: his father was descended from a Jewish banking family based in Egypt, while his mother was Welsh. She named him Sidney after her father and raised him as an Anglican, making him something of an oddity in Italian political circles. A conservative liberal— or perhaps a liberal conservative—Sonnino was a strong supporter of royal prerogative and a committed 'meridionalist' who embraced Italian colonial projects in the hope that they would provide a valuable outlet for southern emigration and improve the lot of the southern peasantry. In many ways extremely reactionary, he was almost as suspicious of Catholics—a growing force in national politics—as he was of socialists.[16] In character he was ener- getic, determined, honest, and intelligent, with a reputation for integrity; on the other hand, he was also cynical, humourless, judgemental, and viewed inter- national relations as a dog-eat-dog zero-sum game. He would make few friends in Paris in 1919: David Lloyd George, for whom charm was perhaps overly important, found him 'dour, rigid and intractable'.[17] In Sonnino's view, if Italy were to risk going to war, it should do so for some truly worthwhile aims—which led to an escalation of territorial demands, including the ambi- tious new imperialist goal of 'Adriatic supremacy'. This led to the seizure of Vlorë in December 1914, and to much more extensive claims in Dalmatia—though this was also a response to the evolving ambitions of the Serbian government. The clearest articulation of these views, complete with open mistrust of Serbia, can be found in Sonnino's so-called 'Long Telegram' to Imperiali in London, on 16 February 1915.[18] This offered an extensive list of demands, including the lands up to the Alpine watershed, Istria, much of Dalmatia, and a substantial hinterland around Vlorë. Fiume, however, was excluded, as were more extravagant claims such as Dubrovnik (sometimes invoked by more ambitious colonial campaigners). Meanwhile, the Entente attack on the Dardanelles had important implications for Italian policy in the

---

[16]   Romano and Vivanti, eds, *Storia d'Italia*. Vol. 4, t. 3, p. 1939.
[17]   David Lloyd George, *The Truth about the Peace Treaties*, 2 vols (London: Victor Gollancz, 1938), vol. 1, p. 406, cited in Margaret Macmillan, *Paris 1919: Six Months That Changed the World* (New York: Random House, 2002), 281.
[18]   Caccamo, 'Italy, the Adriatic and the Balkans', 131–2.

Near East. On 1 March 1915 Sonnino wrote privately to Salandra, noting that if the Allies were to take Constantinople, 'the questions of Asia Minor will in some ways overtake those of the Adriatic for us'. In particular, he feared the possibility of Russian entry to the Mediterranean. By 20 March Tommaso Tittoni wrote from Paris that the Entente's failure in the Dardanelles was good news for Italy, as it should force the Entente to make greater concessions in their anxiety to secure Italian entry to the war.[19]

The feverish diplomatic negotiations which characterized the period of neutrality were not the only impact of the wider European war on Italy: the economy was affected almost immediately, as major trading relationships underwent seismic shifts, and Italian access to credit on the London market was rapidly limited.[20] The press was immediately and understandably full of war news: the great battles of the Western Front made for gripping copy and dramatic illustrations in dailies and weeklies alike, while the fate of Italian citizens of Austria-Hungary was also a major concern.[21] The extent to which the Libyan war had been a media event encouraged and normalized this highly active and influential press culture of generally positive depictions of warfare. Italian seasonal migrant workers in France and Belgium flooded back to Italy while officer training courses were hastily expanded. And while Italy was not yet officially at war, nor was it at peace either: as Simona Berhe has noted, it was engaged in combat operations in Libya throughout the period of neutrality.[22] Italians were also at war as volunteers in multiple armies. Most famously, the grandsons of Giuseppe Garibaldi recruited a 'legion' of volunteers who went to France to serve on the Western Front in 1914—to the great irritation of French and Italian governments alike, since they were undisciplined and demanding. But others also were keen to fight: members of the Italian community in Salonika joined the Serbian army while some in Britain tried to volunteer for that country's forces.[23] In short, across military, economic, social, and cultural dimensions, the First World War began for Italy in 1914.

[19] ACS Archivio Salandra. f. 17: Periodo della neutralità. See Tittoni in Paris to Gabinetto, 20 March 1918 n. 490.

[20] Forsyth, 'Monetary and Financial Policy and the Crisis of Liberal Italy'. On the local economic and social implications of neutrality, see Sean Brady, 'From Peacetime to Wartime: The Sicilian Province of Catania and Italian Intervention in the Great War, June 1914–September 1915', in *Other Combatants, Other Fronts: Competing Histories of the First World War*, ed. Alisa Miller, Laura Rowe, and James Kitchen (Newcastle: Cambridge Scholars, 2011).

[21] Marco Mondini, *La guerra italiana: partire, raccontare, tornare: 1914–18* (Bologna: Il Mulino, 2014), 18.

[22] Simona Berhe, 'Neutralità in Italia e guerra in colonia: il primo conflitto mondiale in Libia (1914-1915)', in *L'Italia neutrale 1914-1915*, ed. Giovanni Orsina and Andrea Ungari (Rome: Rodorigo editore, 2016).

[23] ACS Presidenza del Consiglio dei Ministri [PCM] Guerra Europea [GE] 1915-1918, busta 25, fasc. 17.1.11, Arruolamento Volontario dei cittadini italiani residenti all'estero e in Italia.

3.3 Neutralists

Once Italy had joined the war, neutralism was quickly rewritten as cowardice or inadequate patriotism. But throughout the period from August 1914 to May 1915 it was clearly the majority position among the Italian public, and much of its political class too. In parliament, neutralism was above all represented by Giovanni Giolitti, already four-times prime minister, elder statesman of the left-wing strand of Liberalism, and one of the great masters of political management. Giolitti had only resigned as prime minister five months before—it is interesting to speculate as to what might have happened if he had still been in office—and he commanded a solid parliamentary majority. His view was that participating in the war would not be in Italy's best interests. Its army was unprepared—not least owing to the huge depletion incurred in 1911–12—and he hoped to achieve '*parecchio*' (quite a lot) for Italy even without entering the war. Crudely, Italy could sell its neutrality to the highest bidder. That said, he was no pacifist; on the contrary, having led the country to war against the Ottomans, he was the more convinced that war was a tool to be used with caution when opportune, and so he did not a priori exclude fighting if it seemed likely to produce real advantages. His views, however, held little weight with Salandra or the nationalists, however much influence he held in parliament. More generally, the influence of parliament in decision-making relating to foreign affairs was limited at any time—and parliament was not in session at all from 5 July to 3 December 1914 (and after 12 December did not meet again until mid-February).[24]

In February 1915 the government set out to investigate public sentiment, inviting prefects from up and down the peninsula to respond to a kind of survey, outlining the views of the local population. The responses to this initiative displayed such overwhelming lack of enthusiasm for the prospect of war that the government hastily cancelled it before all the reports had been submitted.[25] Most implacably opposed to the war were two important constituencies: socialists and Catholics. Socialist faith in the international solidarity of the proletariat, or the ability of the Third International to broker a European peace, had already been shattered in August 1914; the decision of French, British, and German socialists to support their national war effort left the Italian socialist party with a relatively limited range of options. Catholics found themselves divided. Many of the middle- and upper-class laity had adopted nationalist positions during the Libyan war. Enjoined by the Church to support and obey the legitimate authorities of the state,

---

[24] For a complete record of parliamentary sittings throughout the war, consult the official website of the Chamber of Deputies. 'XXIV Legislatura del regno d'Italia / Lavori / Camera dei Deputati – Portale Storico', accessed 31 October 2019, https://storia.camera.it/lavori/regno-d-italia/leg-regno-XXIV/.
[25] Brunello Vigezzi, 'Un'inchiesta sullo stato pubblico alla vigilia dell'intervento', in *Da Giolitti a Salandra*, ed. Brunello Vigezzi (Florence: Vallecchi, 1969).

they were at best able to offer a 'conditional opposition to the war'.[26] Millenarian interpretations of the war as a form of divine punishment did not necessarily convince believers that it was just or necessary. The peasantry in particular adopted widespread neutralist positions based on a pacifist reading of the Gospel and a strongly left-wing form of popular Catholicism prevalent in some rural areas.[27] Neutralists of all stripes did not simply resign themselves to their fates but campaigned locally and nationally to stay out of the war, whether as pacifists, feminists, workers' rights advocates, politically engaged priests, devout laity, or reluctant soldiers.[28] However little the government or even parliament were moved to support them, many Italians made their opposition to the war known publicly. Yet the very diversity of neutralism—which took many different forms from north to south, town to country—mitigated against the emergence of a coherent movement which might have decisively shaped the nation's destiny.[29]

Once it was clear that Italy would not immediately declare war on the Entente, the German government dedicated considerable effort to persuading it to at least remain within the Triple Alliance and adhere to a benevolent neutrality. To this end it deployed the Italophile former Chancellor, prince Bernhard von Bülow, who had lived with his aristocratic Italian wife for many years in a luxurious villa on the Pincio in Rome, where the couple were at the centre of an important cultural and political circle. Germany strongly encouraged Austria to accommodate Italian desires for Trento and Trieste, while von Bülow tried to persuade Italy to accept a more modest compensation than nationalists were invoking; but neither party was convinced by this far from disinterested mediation. Giolitti had hoped that this might be a viable path, but in reality, at no time did the Austrian government remotely contemplate accepting any such proposal. At most they might have conceded Trento, but the economic and strategic importance of Trieste as a port doomed von Bülow's best efforts to failure. German-funded propaganda pamphlets also promised that once France and Britain were defeated, their Mediterranean colonies might form the basis of a new Italian empire—a prospect which foreshadowed the dreams of Fascist Italy twenty-five years later.[30]

[26]   Claudia Baldoli, 'Catholic Neutralism and the Peasant Protest against War, 1914–1918', in *Italy in the Era of the Great War*, ed. Vanda Wilcox (Leiden: Brill, 2018), 210–31, DOI: https://doi.org/10.1163/9789004363724_012, p. 215.

[27]   On Catholic neutralism, see Guido Formigoni, 'Il neutralismo dei cattolici', in *Abbasso la guerra!: neutralisti in piazza alla vigilia della prima guerra mondiale in Italia*, ed. Fulvio Cammarano (Florence: Le Monnier, 2015). For peasant and Catholic activism throughout the conflict, see Baldoli, 'Catholic Neutralism and the Peasant Protest against War'.

[28]   Fulvio Cammarano, ed., *Abbasso la guerra!: neutralisti in piazza alla vigilia della Prima Guerra Mondiale in Italia* (Florence: Le Monnier, 2015) identifies more than 1,000 public anti-war events or demonstrations during the period of neutrality.

[29]   The best study of Italian socialism during the period of neutrality is still Leo Valiani, *Il Partito socialista italiano nel periodo della neutralità* (Milan: Feltrinelli, 1963).

[30]   William A. Renzi, *In the Shadow of the Sword: Italy's Neutrality and Entrance into the Great War* (New York: Peter Lang, 1983), 165.

Von Bülow's assurances of support for Italian interests in Antalya and the Eastern Mediterranean would never have been enough to outweigh the lack of Trieste.[31] The British ambassador Sir James Rennell Rodd and his French counterpart Camille Barrère fought an equally vigorous campaign, financing pro-intervention media and working to uphold the British blockade against the Central Powers in ways which seriously threatened Italian business.

3.4 Interventionists

Italian intervention was the outcome of an intensive domestic struggle: a war of public speeches and private backroom deals which determined the fate of Italian neutrality. Irredentist austrophobia, which revived old Risorgimento-era tropes, was linked to Italy's wider aspirations in the Mediterranean but also to the nationalist embrace of war for its own sake, as a demonstration of power. The leading public faces of interventionism were the celebrity poet and playwright Gabriele D'Annunzio—aviator, debtor, scandal-brewer, journalist, orator, fashionista, nationalist, daredevil—and his unlikely ally Cesare Battisti, a sober, serious lawyer and geographer, socialist deputy in the Austrian parliament for the Italian province of Trento. D'Annunzio's nationalism was a matter of lofty rhetoric and militaristic populism; Battisti's was rooted in a secular, radical, Mazzinian tradition. As a socialist and an irredentist, Battisti was an awkward figure; his socialism was embarrassing to the many irredentists who were right-wing nationalists, while his support for war was anathema to his fellow socialists. As an elected and sworn deputy of the Habsburg parliament, his decision to volunteer for the Italian army was clearly treason (he would be executed in Trento in 1916 after his capture by Austrian forces), which could hardly be endorsed by the forces of law and order. Nevertheless, he became a political star in this period, alongside the already-legendary D'Annunzio. Both men travelled the length of Italy throughout the period of neutrality, delivering endless addresses in theatres, piazzas, cafés, and assembly rooms, to ever-growing audiences of excitable supporters. Their speeches were reprinted in the nationalist press, where they were joined by enthusiastic interventionist articles from the newly converted Benito Mussolini as well as long-standing nationalists like Corradini. Crucially, most of the daily press—including Luigi Albertini's *Corriere della Sera* and its illustrated weekly *La Domenica del Corriere*, as well as *Il Giornale d'Italia* and *Il Secolo*, and the leading regional newspapers—adopted anti-Triple Alliance views which soon shaded into open interventionism. The illustrated press was particularly important in reaching a broad sector of the public beyond the

---

[31] DDI, Quinta Serie, Vol. 3, Doc. 366, Salandra to Sonnino, 17 April 1915.

educated upper-middle classes, across the divide of semi-literacy, and Salandra himself acknowledged the role of the media as crucial in enabling the abandonment of neutrality.[32] Futurist interventionists and artists added to a burgeoning, if complex, intellectual war culture.[33] Meanwhile on the left, a small but committed group of social democrats and syndicalists embraced what they termed 'democratic interventionism', led by the fiercely anti-colonial Salvemini and the reformist socialist Leonida Bissolati (who, by contrast, had failed to oppose the Libyan war). An unlikely coalition of pro-war forces emerged, loosely uniting arch-conservative monarchists keen to bring lustre to the House of Savoy, young radical intellectuals embracing Filippo Marinetti's vision of purifying war, earnest democratic republicans from Emilia-Romagna who sought to complete Mazzini's Italy, and committed imperialists and nationalists like Corradini.

Behind the scenes, meanwhile, prime minister Antonio Salandra and his foreign minister Sidney Sonnino were manoeuvring and bargaining with both sides to see where Italy's best interests might lie. On 18 October 1914 Salandra had delivered his famous 'sacro egoismo' speech—stating that the national interest alone, or 'sacred egoism', would determine his government's actions. Moral concerns, historical friendships, binding treaties—none could compete with the 'sacred egoism' the nation demanded in this hour. The decision for war was not taken hastily: while both statesmen were determined to extract the maximum advantage from the situation it was not clear even by January or February 1915 that this would necessarily demand war against the Central Powers.[34] Not until March would the final choice be made, and even then it remained secret for some time. These two forces—public hysteria and secret diplomacy—converged slowly but inexorably in the events known as *maggio radioso*, Radiant May.

3.5 The Treaty of London and Italy's Expansionist War Aims

Finally signed on 26 April 1915, the Treaty of London reveals that Italy's war aims were inherently expansionist right from the outset. In Marco Mondini's formulation, 'Italy's paradoxical war' was presented as the last campaign of the Risorgimento, yet Salandra and Sonnino demanded the cession of Bolzano (Bozen)—home to a quarter of a million German Austrians—while ignoring Fiume, a majority Italian town.[35] Given that even the most ardent optimist did not, in 1915, predict the total collapse of Austria-Hungary, Italy's claims were made in the expectation that any post-war settlement would have to be hammered

---

[32] Mondini, *La guerra italiana*, 36–48.
[33] See Selena Daly, *Italian Futurism and the First World War* (University of Toronto Press, 2016).
[34] Vigezzi, 'L'Italia del 1914–'15 e la crisi del sistema liberale', 22–3.
[35] Mondini, *La guerra italiana*, 7.

out in the face of continuing Habsburg power. It seemed better, therefore, to embark on the war with grandiose claims which would leave some room for manoeuvre. Equally importantly, post-war Italy would have to survive without the comforting support of the Triple Alliance, within which it had operated for decades; it would therefore be forced to take on significant new security challenges.[36] While the acquisition of Italy's (debatably) 'national territories' from Austria formed the main focus of the new Entente agreement, just as they had come to dominate the national conversation about intervention in the preceding months, the Treaty also incorporated extensive claims in northern Dalmatia, which—like Bolzano—could not be justified according to any Risorgimento-style principle of nationality, as well as Vlorë in Albania which had in fact been occupied in December 1914 (illustrating once again the inherent opportunism of Sonnino's vision of the war). The agreements concluded were based largely on Sonnino's 'Long Telegram', but with modifications reflecting Serbian and Russian interests. In the Balkans, Serbia and Montenegro would be granted access to the Adriatic with most of northern Albania in their hands. Italy would gain full sovereignty around Vlorë, a sphere of influence over the rump independent Muslim state in central Albania—including the right to represent it in negotiations with foreign powers—and neutralization of the southern coasts.

Further afield, the Pact displayed that Italy's war aims were, from the start, not only expansionist but overtly imperialist. It confirmed Italian sovereignty over the Dodecanese islands—hitherto simply under military occupation but still considered Turkish—and offered a vague prospect of future gains in Asia Minor. According to Article 9 of the treaty, France, Great Britain, and Russia,

> recognise that Italy is interested in the maintenance of the balance of power in the Mediterranean and that, in the event of the total or partial partition of Turkey in Asia, she ought to obtain a just share of the Mediterranean region adjacent to the province of Antalya, where Italy has already acquired rights and interests.[37]

Significantly, preliminary discussions with the other powers had described this future possession as a 'settlement in Antalya', suggesting that the control of emigration flows towards settler colonies was already at the heart of this plan in March 1915.[38] By this date Sonnino had developed a very specific idea of Italy's proposed share of Turkey:

---

[36] Brunello Vigezzi, *I problemi della neutralità e della guerra nel Carteggio Salandra- Sonnino (1914–1917)* (Milan: Albrighi, Segati e C., 1962).

[37] *Agreement between France, Russia, Great Britain and Italy. Signed in London April 26, 1915* (London: His Majesty's Stationery Office, 1915).

[38] DDI, Quinta Serie, Vol. 3, Doc. 139; Tittoni, ambassador in Paris, to foreign minister Sonnino, 19 March 1915.

My preference is for the zone east of Antalya as far as Mersina and Adana included, with the vilayet of Konya as a hinterland, but excluding Alexandretta. The project of Smyrna with its connected area in the vilayet of Aidin, however appealing, raises the disadvantage of possible conflicts with English interests.[39]

The latter concession suggests that Sonnino was keen to put forward what he saw as a realistic claim which the Allies might accept rather than simply shooting for the moon—however exaggerated his ambitions might have seemed to others at the time. In the event, however, such detailed plans would not find their way into the final treaty, owing to French and British concerns about their own interests; meanwhile it was not such a priority to Italy as to be worth delaying significantly over at this stage.[40] Instead, the precise parameters of the Italian sphere of influence were to 'be delimited, at the proper time, due account being taken of the existing interests of France and Great Britain'. Equally, should the Ottoman Empire unaccountably fail to collapse, and 'alterations be made in the zones of interest of the Powers', Italy was still to be considered in any territorial settlement. Nor was this the only reference to extra-European lands: Article 13 made similar provisions for Africa, where 'if France and Britain increase their possessions at Germany's expense, the powers agree that Italy shall request fair compensation particularly with reference to the borders of the Italian colonies in Eritrea, Somalia and Libya and the nearby French and British colonies'.[41] France had already expressed reservations over any wartime renegotiation of colonial borders in Africa, so this agreement could only be very general.[42]

The contrast between these vague promises in the colonial sphere and the careful precision with which new national borders were described and Adriatic possessions specified in Articles 4 and 5 makes it clear that the primary focus of Antonio Salandra's government in 1915 was the irredentist cause, with Italy's strategically vital Balkan interests in second place—yet colonial expansion was certainly envisaged as a potential benefit of intervention. Moreover, as Richard Bosworth and Giuseppe Finaldi astutely note, 'even for the grander empires, during the "world war", "Europe" mattered more than "Africa"'.[43] The reality of Italian focus on irredentism cannot be taken as proof that its war was not imperial, just as much as the French and British wars were. In fact, the interests which emerged in 1914–15 were well established. The desire to amend the borders of Italian colonies in Africa was a long-standing one, and was particularly focused on

---

[39] DDI, Quinta Serie, Vol. 3, Doc 183; Sonnino to the ambassadors in Paris, London, and St Petersburg, 24 March 1915.

[40] DDI, Quinta Serie, Vol. 3, Doc. 378: Imperiali to Sonnino, 18 April 1915; Doc. 402: Sonnino to ambassadors in Paris, London, and St Petersburg, 21 April 1915.

[41] *Agreement between France, Russia, Great Britain and Italy. Signed in London April 26, 1915.*

[42] Renzi, *In the Shadow of the Sword*, 204.

[43] Bosworth and Finaldi, 'The Italian Empire', 40.

the 'completion' of Libya with small portions of disputed Egyptian and Tunisian land. Meanwhile, in discussions with the French, the Italian ambassador had emphasized that 'any accord for Asia Minor which did not include Italy would have the same effect on future Italian foreign policy as the French *coup de main* in Tunisia', which had damaged Franco-Italian relations for decades after 1881. This declaration placed the Eastern Mediterranean on the same level of importance as the 'fourth shore'.[44] Colonial compensation in Africa and Italian interests in the Eastern Mediterranean were sufficiently important issues to warrant their inclusion in the initial treaty and indeed for Italy to push her prospective allies hard over; as the war proved longer, deadlier, and more globally significant than initially anticipated, Italian ambitions began to increase, both in government circles and beyond. But as the Treaty was negotiated in secret, it was still possible to present the war as 'our war', a Risorgimento endeavour. News that Italy would join the Entente was presented as a fait accompli to the parliament a week after signing without the full details of the pact being made public. Not until the Bolshevik revolution in 1917 would the precise details of the agreement become widely known. For the first few years of the war therefore, Italian war culture would mobilize chiefly around Risorgimento rhetoric of liberatory nationalism, belying the more complex reality of the Treaty.

The interventionism of Radiant May was limited in its scope and appeal. So strong was parliamentary opposition to the decision for war—supported by the Crown and Salandra's minority government, along with a noisy and violent public fringe—that a constitutional crisis briefly threatened. Salandra resigned on 13 May, a performative manoeuvre which inspired the radical interventionists to threaten violence against Giolitti and the parliament itself. Giolitti, presented with the fait accompli of the Treaty, withdrew to Piedmont, and the king, who considered his own and Italy's honour to be now committed to the Entente, reappointed Salandra and thus 'restored order'. This was seen by some at the time (and since) as a form of coup: certainly, the way Italy entered the war highlighted division rather than unity, 'the people' against 'the establishment', and the threat of violence rather than the democratic process. In the words of historian Antonio Gibelli, 'Italy had set off on the slippery slope that would lead it towards fascism.'[45]

Parliamentary opposition to the war had the important consequence that the executive began to adopt an increasingly open anti-parliamentary attitude. Significant legislative powers were transferred from parliament to the executive in the 'state of exception' which rapidly developed; laws passed by the parliament in March and May 1915 granted the King (and his ministers) extraordinary powers which would be used extensively during the war to circumvent parliament's

---

[44] DDI, Quinta Serie, Vol. 3, Doc. 68, Tittoni to Sonnino, 9 March 1915.
[45] Antonio Gibelli, *La Grande Guerra degli italiani, 1915–1918* (Milan: Sansoni, 1998).

powers of scrutiny. The executive was thereby authorized to act unilaterally in three circumstances: in defence of the state, to uphold public order or to meet the exigencies of the war effort. These criteria were sufficiently broadly defined as to allow more or less any action which the government chose to undertake in wartime. Parliament could also be prorogued by the King, and indeed regularly was during the war; by 1919 it had been side-lined so often that its status and dignity were gravely compromised, a process which originated in the heated debates over intervention in 1915.[46] The long-term consequences of these measures would be devastating.

Pro-war sentiment was never a majority position in the early months of 1915. Yet once war had been declared, patriotic enthusiasm spread beyond narrow circles. The long months of neutrality had allowed a war culture to begin to develop ahead of war itself; the mobilization of the nation was already well under way before the declaration of war against Austria-Hungary (though not Germany) on 24 May 1915. On 2 June Salandra gave a speech in response to the denunciation of Italy by German Chancellor Theobald von Bethmann Hollweg. Speaking at the Campidoglio in Rome—a resonant location at the heart of the ancient capital as well as the modern city—he declared that,

> In defence of the oldest and highest aspirations, the most vital interests of our Country, we have entered a war greater than any other known to history, a war which overwhelms and sweeps away with its engine not only the combatants but all who remain at home also. [. . .] All hearts must remain high, ready for the most intense joy and for the most atrocious pain, ready for anything and believing in the final victory; for the cause which moves us is a just one and our war is a holy war.[47]

Peppering the speech with superlatives, he denied that Italy had committed any betrayal and instead discussed not only the two 'Italian Provinces' under Austrian rule (Trento and Trieste) but also the rivalry between Italy and Austria in the Balkans and the Eastern Mediterranean; he even harshly attacked supposed Austrian obstructionism during Italy's conquest of Libya. Colonial questions were thus intimately connected to Italy's declaration of war, even though they were never its principal justification.

Copies of Salandra's speech were circulated widely both nationally and internationally, receiving an extremely positive public reaction even beyond those who had participated in the 'agitations' of Radiant May. Enthusiastic personal notes

---

[46] Carlotta Latini, 'I pieni poteri in Italia durante la prima guerra mondiale', in *Un paese in guerra: la mobilitazione civile in Italia, 1914–1918*, ed. Daniele Menozzi, Giovanna Procacci, and Simonetta Soldani (Milan: Unicopli, 2010), 87–104.

[47] Il discorso del campidoglio, 2 June 1915, in Antonio Salandra, *I discorsi della guerra con alcune note* (Milan: Fratelli Treves, 1922), 31–66.

flooded into the prime minister's office: fulsome praise came from Italians over-seas, in France, Switzerland, Egypt, and the USA—one excited New York Italian addressed his postcard to 'Salandra, Father of the Nation'. Support came not only from predictable sources such as politicians and generals but also from aristocrats and all kinds of middle-class professionals. One Neapolitan lawyer called Salandra 'The Nation's God', and described his address as 'magnificent, sublime, masterly', concluding that 'after 40 years of horse-dealing and lowness we at last hear the first words of a truly Italian heart!' Hundreds of letters also came from local officials, teachers, musicians, journalists, and a number of women, especially mothers. Several of Salandra's correspondents were moved to compose sonnets in honour of the occasion and the rector of S. Bernadino in Novi Ligure sent a congratulatory message entirely in Latin. Understandings of the war's scope varied: one citizen looked forward to the day that 'the tricolour would fly from Trento down to the Bocche of Cattaro'—a clearly imperialist vision—while another invoked the memory of Cavour. A 79-year-old factory worker from Ancona celebrated Italy's 'just and holy war', while a mother wrote from Venice that she was proud to send her five sons to serve in the army.[48] Political enthu-siasm for intervention may have been limited but, once war was announced, patriotic adherence to the cause was widespread amid the middle classes.

Of course, the neutralist cause had not vanished overnight, but in the new climate of enforced patriotism, it became progressively harder to express anti-war sentiment in public. But many of those caught up in the moment of patriotic excitement might lose their enthusiasm quickly, once the harsh military realities of the war began to emerge on the Italo-Austrian front.

[48] All in ACS Archivio Antonio Salandra, busta 10, fasc. 5.

4

Italians on the Battlefield

The heart of the Italian war effort was the war against Austria: Trento and Trieste were to be captured and redeemed. To fight this war, millions of men would be mobilized into the army, in a complex process which starkly revealed the strengths and weaknesses of the Liberal State. The country's efforts to best use its manpower resources, including those found outside the kingdom's own borders, met with mixed results. Ultimately, almost 6 million men would serve, enabling Italy to sustain a brutal and bloody conflict on its north-eastern borders for three and a half years.

4.1 Military Mobilization

Given the fraught circumstances of intervention, and the generally weakened condition of the armed forces following the war against the Ottoman Empire in 1911–12, a rapid victory was highly desirable. But events on the Western Front had already suggested to the more acute observer that the war was unlikely to be short or straightforward, and Italian military attachés had been dutifully reporting back with great accuracy and detail.[1] How, then, did Italy prepare for war? And how did the Italian army interpret the decisions of the government?

As Austria-Hungary had been Italy's ally for more than thirty years, and given its superior levels of manpower and resources, military planning for war against the Dual Monarchy before 1914 had been almost exclusively defensive. Now the new chief of general staff had to develop an entirely new approach to fighting this old rival. Both political necessity and Cadorna's own preferences required an offensive strategy, and he drafted an initial operational plan by late August 1914. It set out an ambitious thrust into Austro-Hungarian territory in Friuli, heading towards Trieste and Gorizia. Despite the political importance of the Alpine city of Trento, this could only be a secondary objective in military terms, owing to the extreme difficulty of conducting major offensive operations in the mountains, and the improbability of achieving a strategically decisive battle there (especially in the face of Austria's extensive fortifications in the region). Instead,

---

[1] Andrea Ungari and Francesco Anghelone, *Addetti militari italiani alla vigilia della Grande Guerra 1914–1915* (Rome: Rodorigo Editore, 2015).

The Italian Empire and the Great War. Vanda Wilcox, Oxford University Press (2021). © Vanda Wilcox.
DOI: 10.1093/oso/9780198822943.003.0004

the bulk of the army would be concentrated along the eastern border between Monte Maggiore and the sea, roughly following the line of the Isonzo river, where concentrated firepower and manpower would hope to smash through the Austrian positions, ideally in coordination with Russian and Serbian offensives on other fronts.[2] If this was strategically sensible, it was also unsurprising, and Cadorna's counterpart in the Dual Monarchy, Franz Conrad von Hotzendorf, was easily able to anticipate the main focus of the Italian attack and organize his forces accordingly. And while the strategic choice of front was reasonable, Cadorna's initial operational plans were pure fantasy: after seizing Krainberg and Ljubljana, as well as Tarvisio and Villach and then Klagenfurt, he intended to advance rapidly on Vienna.

However, Salandra ignored Cadorna's urgent request to join the war as rapidly as possible in summer 1914, and instead the delicate negotiations of the neutral period were launched. Through the remainder of the year and the first months of 1915, therefore, Cadorna and his staff undertook the herculean task of preparing the Italian army for war as best they could. The political authorities were reluctant to order full mobilization during the early period of neutrality, since it would force them show their hand at a time when they still were busy bluffing both sides; instead, the process of preparing to mobilize the troops would be spread over a number of months, bringing the army up to an unprecedented strength. Inadequate planning for general mobilization made the task an enormous one. The standing army was based on conscripts performing their mandatory two-year military service, while those who had previously completed this service consti- tuted the permanent reserve. As early as 6 August 1914 the government blocked the emigration of all reservists (though the implementation of this ban was not always scrupulous, and even during the war some Italians managed to emigrate).[3] But hundreds of thousands of men had been exempted from service in peacetime who might well be needed to serve in wartime; they were, however, untrained. Many were emigrants and were spread throughout Europe or across the Atlantic. To effectively exploit these pools of manpower was challenging and complex. The question of how to draft emigrants entailed both a legal-political difficulty—would they return? Could they be forced to do so?—and logistical problems—were enough ships available? Could they sail freely and safely across the Atlantic? Was there funding to cover all these transport costs? And how were all these untrained men, whether within Italy or overseas, to be adequately prepared for the front?

---

[2] Massimo Mazzetti, 'I piani di guerra contro l'Austria dal 1866 alla Prima Guerra Mondiale', in *L'esercito italiano dall'Unità alla Grande Guerra*, ed. Ufficio Storico, Stato Maggiore dell'Esercito (Rome: Stato Maggiore dell'Esercito, 1980).
[3] Patrizia Salvetti, 'Il movimento migratorio italiano durante la Prima Guerra Mondiale', *Studi Emigrazione* 87 (1987): 287.

Another critical problem was a shortage of officers: though in August 1914 the army had 45,000 officers in service, only around one third were permanent regular officers and the remainder were reservists or members of the territorial militia. These categories had received less training and were poorly regarded by the army authorities. Already in March 1914 the war office had estimated that there was a shortfall of 7,500 regular officers; with war looming, that crisis became more severe, and urgent measures to recruit and promote more junior officers were undertaken. The result, though, was over-hasty commissioning of young men who had not been fully trained. The shortage of non-commissioned officers was also acute, as many had been killed or disabled in Libya and had not yet been replaced. The army urgently needed hundreds of thousands of uniforms and boots, while medical services were totally unprepared for a major war. Meanwhile, although Italian military spending had been among the highest in Europe in the immediate pre-war years, poor procurement policies and endless internal debates over development strategy had left Italy's artillery and weapons stocks inadequate in both quality and quantity.[4] Combined with tactical and strategic flaws in Cadorna's thinking, these problems would lead to an ongoing stalemate on the main fighting front between Austria and Italy which was very similar to that which had already emerged on the Western front.

By May 1915 some 400,000 troops were ready to fight on the borders. Cadorna had already realized that the war would not be short and had begun to plan for the manpower and resources which would be needed in 1916. All in all, the transformation achieved during the period of neutrality was remarkable: from fewer than 300,000 men (including officers) in August 1914, Italy had some 900,000 men under arms by the following May and by the time full mobilization was completed later in the summer there were more than 1.1 million men at the front supported by another 500,000 in the interior.[5] Whatever the many weaknesses of his leadership, Cadorna's enormous achievement in this regard should be acknowledged. It was particularly difficult to ready the army for war when mobilization was by no means universally supported or even accepted: on the contrary, both formal protests and anti-conscription riots broke out in several parts of the country, especially areas like Tuscany and Emilia-Romagna where socialist and pacifist traditions were strongest. Both men and women were involved in these demonstrations of anti-war feeling during spring 1915, but by the time the war began they had mostly died down (or been repressed by police action). Nonetheless, men's departure to the front was not universally marked by the cheering patriotic crowds and flower-wielding young ladies of classic international imagery; often the moment of parting was sombre, even disheartening.[6] The

[4] Gooch, *The Italian Army*, 50–1; 65–9.   [5] Mondini, *La guerra italiana*, 59–60.
[6] Mondini, *La guerra italiana*, 113–22.

widespread support for neutrality and the lack of real national consensus for war in 1915 and 1916 was a real obstacle towards creating high morale among the mass of the troops, who were mainly grumbling but obedient, rather than enthusiastic or fully committed to the war effort.

Ultimately, around 5.9 million men would be called up during the war—one-sixth of the entire pre-war population—of whom 4.25 million would serve in the army and another 600,000 in the territorial militia, with most of the remainder working in war industries. More than 2.5 million conscripts were peasant farmers; unsurprisingly this had devastating consequences for food production in the country. Many industrial workers also served but they were more likely than peasants to be mobilized into war manufacturing. Throughout the Liberal period, the Italian army had been recruited and organized on national rather than regional lines. This meant that the young conscript would be sent to some far-off military depot to perform his mandatory service in the company of an assortment of fellow soldiers drawn from a multitude of towns and villages across the nation; only the elite mountain units, the Alpini, were recruited and served locally. The military flaws of this system are easily apparent: it was slow, inefficient, costly, and owing to the prevalence of strong local identities and mutually unintelligible local dialects mitigated against the easy formation of a solid primary group identity within units. The sole purpose of this system was political: the army was to be the crucible of the nation, serving to forge Italians from the raw material of Milanese, Neapolitans, Pugliesi, or Venetians. Conscripts were to learn standard Italian, loyalty to the king, and the habit of obedience, a socio-political programme which left acquiring military skills as the least of priorities. And indeed, training was generally poor: infantrymen's shooting abilities and artillerymen's target location alike were inadequate and remained so throughout 1914 and 1915.[7] The army was conceived of not only as a tool of national policy but as a fundamental element in the formation, perpetuation, and development of the nation itself. Rather than a nation-in-arms where the nation constituted the army, it was the army that constituted the nation. As the war went on, it became increasingly impractical to retain this nationalized system of recruitment, and so locally organized units began to be created, though they continued to be a minority. The tension between political and military needs revealed in the organization of the army reflects a wider failure to fully integrate military and civilian decision-making, a phenomenon which would become increasingly clear under wartime conditions.

[7] For more on this issue, see Vanda Wilcox, 'Training, Morale and Battlefield Performance in the Italian Army, 1914–1917', in *The Greater War: Other Combatants and Other Fronts, 1914–1918*, ed. Jonathan Krause (London: Palgrave Macmillan, 2014), 177–94.

4.2 The Fighting Fronts, 1915–16

The reality of life at war hit home very soon for the inhabitants of the Adriatic coastal towns. On 23 May 1915 the city of Ancona was briefly attacked by an Austrian destroyer. Next day the Austrian fleet at Pola, including three dreadnoughts and eight pre-dreadnoughts, launched a major bombardment against the port and its surroundings. At least sixty-three people were killed in Ancona, of whom several dozen were civilians, including children and babies. Shipyards, warehouses, hospitals, the orphanage, and the cathedral were all damaged. Airports and hangars were attacked, while further down the coast at Senigallia a train, railway tracks, and an important bridge were all destroyed. Even Venice was bombed.[8] The Austrian intent was not merely to target important military and industrial installations, but to damage civilian morale precisely in that area where socialist, neutralist, and anti-war sentiments were highest (and where less than a year previously the events of Red Week had been most intensely concentrated). But it was soon clear that the naval war in the Adriatic would be of secondary importance, marked by caution and inaction: it was on land, immediately to the north, that the theatre's main front would emerge.

Italy's first major attacks would not be launched until a month after the declaration of war, on 23 June 1915. This delay, arising from incomplete preparation, allowed the Dual Monarchy a vital breathing space in which to make its own preparations, transporting troops to the Italian front and building up its defences along the line of the river Isonzo. By the time the offensive began, the Austrian defenders had already constructed complex entrenchments with multiple lines of barbed wire and mined protective zones. In line with Cadorna's ambitious strategic plan, the Italian army launched its offensives against Gorizia and the Carso plateau, in what became known as the First Battle of the Isonzo (23 June–7 July). This was soon to be followed by the Second (18 July–3 August), Third (18 October–4 November), and Fourth (10 November–2 December) of that name; ultimately eleven battles of the Isonzo would be fought by autumn 1917. This numerical proliferation poorly concealed the reality of repeated and repetitive fighting over the same difficult ground. Despite the confident tone of Cadorna's tactical preparations, above all as laid out in his February 1915 manual *Attacco Frontale*, the front quickly settled down into an attritional slugging match every bit as static and deadly as the Western Front. Italian casualties were very heavy—over 110,000 by the end of the year—and only Austria's numerical inferiority on the front, owing to their greater commitment in the east, prevented

[8] Marco Gemignani, 'Il bombardamento di Ancona del 24 maggio 1915', *Bollettino d'Archivio dell'Ufficio Storico della Marina Militare* December (2002).

them from inflicting a strategic defeat on the Italians.[9] Meanwhile the secondary front which had been opened in the Alps was also turning into a brutal bloodbath, conducted at high altitude in the face of snow and freezing temperatures, and on the steepest of mountain slopes. Despite the great bravery shown by troops on both sides, the inadequacy of both essential equipment and of tactics and training meant that the Alpine front was also marked by stalemate throughout 1915. Shortages of light and medium artillery and howitzers made offensive break-throughs almost impossible, and Cadorna soon ordered defensive measures which drew heavily on French regulations for trench warfare.[10]

In 1916 the overall strategic picture began to change, as Russia's struggles on. the Eastern Front meant that Austria-Hungary was at last able to move beyond the defensive in its war with Italy. As more artillery of better quality became available to the Habsburg armies, more guns and elite units were deployed to the Italian theatre and Conrad began to prepare an attack in the Tyrol. This was nicknamed the *Strafexpedition*, or punishment expedition: Conrad hoped that Italy's treacherous betrayal of the Triple Alliance would at last earn its dues. As these offensive preparations became clear, Cadorna called off the unproductive Italian attack on the Isonzo (the Fifth Battle, 9–15 March 1916), undertaken principally in response to French and British pressure after the Chantilly conference of December 1915. On 15 May 1916 the long-planned Austrian attack at last began with a huge artillery bombardment on the Asiago plateau; it met with immediate tactical success as the Dual Monarchy's infantry advanced some 12 miles into Italian territory. However, it was much harder to consolidate these gains than Conrad had anticipated, and soon the attack was floundering; once the Brusilov offensive began on the Eastern Front in early June 1916, placing huge pressure on Austrian reserves, it was impossible to continue the *Strafexpedition*. More than 76,000 Italian casualties had been inflicted; the poorly conceived Italian counterattack which followed caused a further 70,000 losses. The aftermath of this fiasco led to the fall of Salandra's government and his replacement by Paolo Boselli, a relative political non-entity, at the head of a non-partisan technical government.

With the Alpine sector quietening down, Cadorna returned his attention to the Isonzo front where the Sixth Battle of the Isonzo began on 6 August (lasting until 17 August), soon becoming known as the Battle of Gorizia. It was the first of the Isonzo battles which had achieved an objective worthy of being named after. Fierce fighting at Podgora, Oslavia, and Sabotino, with dramatically reformed and improved assault tactics, saw the Italians seize the critical high ground west of the border town of Gorizia, before on 8 August the first Italian troops entered the

[9] Vanda Wilcox, 'Italian Front', *1914–1918-Online International Encyclopedia of the First World War*, 2014, DOI: https://doi.org/10.15463/ie1418.10220.
[10] Fabio Cappellano, 'The Evolution of Tactical Regulations in the Italian Army in the Great War', in *Italy in the Era of the Great War*, ed. Vanda Wilcox, (Leiden: Brill, 2018), 30–54, pp. 34–6.

town, whose fine medieval castle and fourteenth-century cathedral had been largely destroyed by the intense preliminary bombardment. The battle gave a great boost to civilian and military morale; it also established an essential first bridgehead across the Isonzo, a promising sign for the future. Further south, at San Michele, Italian forces also gained a vital foothold on the Carso plateau, making the Sixth battle by far the most successful so far in military and political terms.

On 27 August 1916 Italy at last declared war on Germany. Its refusal to do so earlier had created an irreparable breach, particularly with France, and led to Italian exclusion from many Franco-British discussions (including the Sykes–Picot agreement). But in reality, the two countries had already been engaged in hostilities with one another—German U-boats were operating in the Adriatic under Austrian flags and supporting the anti-Italian resistance in Libya. In practical terms, little seemed to change. On the contrary, on the Isonzo front it was soon business as usual: the Seventh (14–17 September), Eighth (10–12 October), and Ninth (1–4 November) battles were largely inconclusive, a resumption of Cadorna's attritional 'shoulder nudges' (*spallate*). At a tactical level these attacks did display the continued evolution of Italian military thinking, being much more tightly focused battles with specific, limited objectives and making use of concentrated heavy artillery bombardments against the Austrians' dug-in positions on the high ground above the river. But their impact was broadly the same as the battles of 1915: very high casualties for minimal observable gain.

In the face of such high losses, infantry doctrine began to evolve to focus on minimising casualties. At the same time, the army was continually seeking to expand its ranks and to mobilize its manpower as effectively as possible. This meant looking beyond the borders of the kingdom itself to the colonies, both formal and informal, though with very different results in each case.

4.3 Military Service Among Emigrants

By 1914, an estimated 13 million Italians had left the country to form a global diaspora spread though North and South America, Europe, and North Africa and even during the war emigration was not entirely halted. These communities, known in Italian as *colonie*, were made up not only of emigrants but also their second- or even third-generation descendants who, in this period, received Italian citizenship automatically (though after 1912 they were also free to renounce it upon reaching their majority). These citizens were part of the 'greater Italy' which the war itself was so keen to expand.

Military service was a core constituent of (male) citizenship and thus was an obligation of all Italian men wherever they found themselves in the world; nonetheless, in peacetime, it was generally accepted that most emigrants would not perform it. Men were still required to report to their local consulate for a medical exam and to be classified according to fitness for service. Those suitable to serve were placed into Category I, while Categories II and III—fit but with various family obligations—were not required to serve in peacetime, and those with chronic conditions received exemptions. However most overseas men were not actually returned to Italy and instead were treated as reservists, even if placed into Category I. For example, in 1911, when the class of 1891 was called up, 29,643 men overseas responded to the draft and attended their local consulate. Of these only 11,613 were placed into Category I (out of 158,927, i.e. around 7 per cent of all Cat. I men were overseas), but more than 2,000 of them were then granted exemptions and did not return to Italy. Several thousand more did not even present themselves at all.[11] Draft evasion of emigrants, especially in the Americas, was tacitly accepted, and regular amnesties issued.[12]

In wartime however, the army required all physically able men (Categories I, II and III and anyone who had not already been categorised) to report for duty, wherever in the world they might be. In 1915, there were at least 1.2 million citizens of military age resident outside Italy, perhaps more; the 1911 census had identified fully 5 million Italian citizens living overseas, and the true figure was likely higher.[13] More than 700,000 men were called up. Failure to answer the call was an offence, and in the course of the war the army's military tribunals indeed issued no fewer than 370,000 charges of draft evasion to men who had legally emigrated.[14] The Commissariato Generale dell'Emigrazione (CGE), the state agency for managing emigration, founded in 1901, took on responsibility for organizing a census of emigrants liable to serve and arranging for the repatriation of draftees.[15] But the Italian state lacked the coercive mechanisms to enforce its writ overseas, although it did make some effort to do so, by threatening negative consequences for citizens who failed to return (as well as the positive incentive of offering an amnesty to anyone who had originally emigrated to avoid military service). However, the largest group of emigrants, in the US, was assured of its safety from the Italian law: already in August 1914 Secretary of State William Jennings Bryan had declared that the US would not compel any foreign-born residents to return to their homelands for military service.[16] Oddly, the Australian government—which never conscripted its own people—fully supported the process of conscription for resident Italians, and agreed to use its own civil police

[11] 'Statistica sulla leva della classe del 1891', *RMI* 59, no. 7–8 (1914): 2290–2300, 2468–78; 2295, 2471–2.
[12] Emilio Franzina, 'Militari italiani e Grande Guerra', *Zibaldone. Estudios italianos* 3, no. 1 (2015): 78–103; 85.
[13] Franzina, 'Militari italiani e Grande Guerra', 88.
[14] Giorgio Mortara, *Dati sulla giustizia e disciplina militare* (Rome: Provveditore generale dello stato, 1929), 14–17.
[15] Soresina, 'Italian emigration policy', 738.   [16] Ventresco, 'Loyalty and Dissent', 95.

force to arrest evaders.[17] In general though, returnees have been regarded as more or less willing participants, since overseas evaders could not be arrested or incarcerated for their failure to report. This is not to say there were no negative consequences for emigrants who evaded the draft: penalties might be applied if and when they ever sought to return to Italy in the future, with obvious consequences for them and their families. Returnees were not quite, therefore, 'volunteers'; rather, they were conscripts for whom draft evasion was a very easy option should they choose to take it.

How many men returned to fight? Most estimates suggest that around 103,000 returned from North America, 52,000 from South America, and around 128,000 from other parts of Europe. Nearly 20,000 returned from Africa (most from the large communities in Tunisia—at least 15,000—and Egypt) and much smaller numbers from more far-flung outposts (around 360 each from central America and Australia, a few dozen from Asia). In total there were some 304,000 emigrants who came home to fight, likely more since a few thousand may have returned privately rather than through official channels, of whom 51 per cent came across the Atlantic.[18] At the start of the war, returnees for military service were just one part of a greater flow of European repatriation: 500,000 Italians—men, women, and children—returned to Italy between 15 August and 30 September 1914 alone. Some of these arrived as refugees—young men working in the mines or heavy industries of northern France and Belgium who had fled the German invasion of 1914. Others were repatriated from Germany, especially Alsace-Lorraine, or from Austria-Hungary and Switzerland, as changing political, economic, and social situation made their circumstances untenable (Italian neutrality led to generalized mistrust).[19] The rate of repatriation was not constant through the war, nor did attitudes to service remain the same. In 1915, crowds gathered on docksides from Buenos Aires to Alexandria to cheer the departing steamships, filled with young returnees, as they set off to Italy. As time went on, and most of those willing to return had already done so in the first six months of the war, enthusiasm diminished. Nonetheless, if we consider that in total some 4.25 million Italians served in the army, this means that 7 per cent were returned emigrants—a figure which, as Selena Daly observes, is directly comparable to the contribution of Dominion troops in the British army or of colonial soldiers in the French

[17] I am grateful to Dr David Brown of Farnborough College who kindly shared material with me on this point.

[18] Franzina, 'La guerra lontana'; See also Italia, *L'Emigrazione italiana. Relaziona presentata a S. E. il Ministro degli-affari esteri dal Commissario generale dell'emigrazione* (Rome: Commissariato generale dell'emigrazione, n.d.).

[19] Matteo Ermacora, 'Assistance and Surveillance: War Refugees in Italy, 1914–1918', *Contemporary European History* 16, no. 4 (2007): 446, DOI: https://doi.org/10.1017/S0960777307004110; Douki, 'Les Italiens de Glasgow', 244–45.

army.[20] Returned emigrants were not organized into designated units but were rather summoned to the military district of their birth (or their father's birth, for second-generation returnees), though given the patterns of chain migration this still meant that many men were called up to the same location in Italy (e.g. a large number of Italian Jews in Tunisia originated from Livorno, and many ended up serving alongside one another).[21]

However, if on the one hand the number of those who willingly returned to serve is impressive, on the other it is inescapable that far more emigrants did not return. At most a quarter of eligible emigrants answered their call-up—and only around 13 per cent in the United States. Emilio Franzina estimates that at least 800,000 draft evaders remained in the Americas.[22] There were many reasons to stay at home—from the economic to the familial to the political. Some emigrants were pacifists or socialists, or were swayed by the determined anti-war campaigns of these groups; some were newly-wed, or had ageing or vulnerable dependents. Private letters from family in Italy urged men not to return, especially after Caporetto; a few of these were publicly circulated in thousands of copies.[23] Others feared the economic consequences of exchanging well-paid work in the USA for the meagre pittance of army pay, with its accompanying threat of poverty for family members left behind. Separation allowances were of course calibrated to the costs of living in Italy (and were scarcely generous even there). In 1915 a wife and child would receive just $5.12 per week, when—according to a local assistance committee—to rent even a single slum room in New York City would cost $6 a week.[24] The fear of leaving one's family in financial hardship was clearly a huge disincentive to compliance with the draft. By contrast, rising wages in the USA made staying on a much more attractive prospect, perhaps finding new employment in a war-related industry.

There were other problems too: it would be impossible to return home to convalesce if lightly wounded, or on leave for family or religious holidays. When the war began, the ministry of war had determined that overseas residents could return home only if granted a convalescent leave of more than six months, clearly fearing that men might not return (or might not be able to do so). In 1916 it was agreed that soldiers resident in France or Tunisia might go home if they were granted two months' leave, but this was still a rare occurrence and only for serious

---

[20] Selena Daly, 'Emigrant Draft Evasion in the First World War: Decision-Making and Emotional Consequences in the Transatlantic Italian Family', *European History Quarterly*, Vol. 51, April 2021 (forthcoming).
[21] Montalbano, 'The Italian Community of Tunisia', section 21.
[22] Franzina, 'La guerra lontana', 65–6.
[23] Some are reproduced in Giovanna Procacci, *Soldati e prigionieri italiani nella Grande guerra* (Turin: Bollati Boringhieri, 2000). See also Ventresco, 'Loyalty and Dissent', 107–8.
[24] ACS PCM GE 1915–1918, busta 72/19.1.72, New York.

illnesses or wounds.[25] After nearly three years, one Jewish soldier from Egypt grew so despondent about his inability to spend Passover with his family at home that he wrote to ask whether he could spend it with the Chief Rabbi of Rome and his family instead.[26] Emigrants were also unsure as to whether at war's end they would be able to return home, especially if they needed a costly transatlantic crossing: the army covered the costs of sending them to Italy to fight, but would it also pay their passage back home afterwards? After the initial enthusiasm—or compliance—of 1915, the numbers of returnees began to fall off considerably in 1916 and 1917. Around 200,000 men (two-thirds of the total) returned between May and December 1915, after which a further 100,000 young conscripts arrived as their classes were called up between 1916 and 1918.[27] To those who had seen Italians overseas as patriotic colonists, implanting tiny Italies across the globe, this was a terrible disappointment. Arguably this was a decisive blow to the Liberal 'emigrant empire' model. Yet if we consider the lack of war enthusiasm within Italy, and the many disincentives to service, it seems remarkable that as many as 300,000 men returned to Italy to fight.

Many returnees do seem to have motivated by patriotism, though it can be hard to distinguish genuine commitment from propagandist declarations. In December 1917, American monthly *The Century Magazine* published a letter 'From an Italian Reservist', which waxed lyrical over the strange experience of crossing the Atlantic and seeing Italy for the first time. Describing himself as a New Yorker, the author praised Italy's 'military discipline, about which I am nothing short of enthusiastic as medicine for a race permeated with ultra-individualism like mine. We are unruly bronchos, bound to make ideal horses if broken by a hand that will not yield.'[28] For other returnees, the motivation was extremely personal: Fausto Filzi, brother of the irredentist hero Fabio, who was captured with Cesare Battisti in 1916 and executed by the Austrians, was an emigrant to Argentina. After he heard the news of his brother's death he returned to Italy in order to avenge his brother's death (he was killed at Monte Zebio the following year).[29] Others returned less enthusiastically, sometimes only at the persuasion of their families. Italian-resident conscripts might find the emigrants' choice to return praiseworthy or bizarre depending on their own political preferences. In his war diary, Mussolini described fighting alongside a young man born in Constantinople, whose parents had stayed there (under the protection of the US

---

[25] Italia. *Atti del Parlamento Italiano—Discussioni della Camera dei Deputati, XXIV Legislatura—Sessione 1913–1916* (13/03/1916–16/04/1916), Vol. IX, I Sessione (Rome: Tip. Camera dei Deputati, 1916): 10137–88, https://storia.camera.it/lavori/regno-d-italia/leg-regno-XXIV/1916/11-aprile; 10145.

[26] Unione delle Comunità Ebraiche Italiane (UCEI), Centro Bibliografico, Archivio Consorzio (AC), busta 27, fasc. 152 Corr. Varia di militari.

[27] Douki, 'Les Italiens de Glasgow'.

[28] '"A Letter from an Italian Reservist", The Century Magazine, December 1917', 285–94; accessed 23 July 2015, http://www.unz.org/Pub/Century-1917dec-00285.

[29] Franzina, 'Militari italiani e Grande Guerra', 92.

consulate), but who had 'returned voluntarily to Italy for the war'. His platoon had nicknamed him 'little Arab' and teased him as 'an adjunct to Italy' until, enraged, he 'burst out proclaiming himself Italian by race and sentiment'. It is worth noting that the debate over *italianità* was framed in racial terms. At the same time, Mussolini described with approval the brother of another man in his platoon who had chosen to serve with the Canadian forces—the diary terms him 'an Italo-English volunteer'.[30] Returning was considered by army authorities as a sign of good character and devotion to duty. When a small revolt broke out in the 22nd infantry regiment at Christmas 1916, accusations against one particular soldier were immediately dismissed by his officers on the grounds that 'he was an excellent soldier who had come voluntarily from America at the outbreak of the war'.[31]

Not all Italian emigrants who fought in the war did so in the Italian armed forces, of course. Many preferred instead to serve their new homeland, especially Italian-Americans for whom the war was an important opportunity to demonstrate a new identity and a new loyalty. One estimate suggests that around 90,000 Italians, mostly from southern Italy or Sicily, served with the US army. Overall nearly half a million immigrants—18 per cent of the entire armed forces—were drafted there.[32] While this was an important stage in the Americanization of foreign-born citizens, the US military deliberately adopted policies which enabled the development of a dual identity and which could thus allow a sense of *italianità* to endure even while serving under the Stars and Stripes. Since many immigrants still did not speak English when they were drafted, many foreign-born conscripts in the US army were grouped together in ethnic units commanded by bilingual officers of their own heritage. From outside the army, community-based organizations—such as Italian-American body the Knights of Columbus—worked to offer support, socialization, and educational and leisure activities during the period of training, thus further reinforcing these troops' links to their original homeland. A concerted campaign was also made to limit anti-Italian racism, especially as manifested in derogatory terminology—though some newspapers suggested that the performance of Italians in the war was already having this effect.[33] *The Italian*, an Edmund Vance Cooke poem syndicated by the Newspaper Enterprise Association in 1918, addressed the topic directly:

> Do you see that brisk chap going over the top?
> You call him a 'guinea', a 'dago', a 'wop.'

[30]   Mussolini, *Il mio diario di guerra*, 131, 137.
[31]   AUSSME Fondo E2:50, Comando della 1a Divisione di Cavalleria, n.253, 25/12/1916.
[32]   Nancy Gentile Ford, '"Mindful of the Traditions of His Race": Dual Identity and Foreign-Born Soldiers in the First World War American Army', *Journal of American Ethnic History* 16, no. 2 (1997): 36–7.
[33]   See *The Evening News* (San José), 18 December 1918, p. 4; *The Athens Messenger*, 2 July 1919, p. 4; both in Chronicling America database, Library of Congress.

Instead, the poet offered, 'he might be a Rafael, Dante or Verdi', framing Italian worth in primarily artistic terms. Physical energy and hardiness were also emphasized: the adjective brisk contrasted with stereotypes of Italian laziness; and moreover, the verse continued, 'He conquered the Infinite snows / Of the Alps'. It was military service and above all the sacrifice of death which made anti-Italian racism outdated:

> He has come as a comfort, a stay and a prop.
> In the death that he dies
> With his brother allies
> Do you dub him a 'guinea,' a 'dago,' a 'wop'?[34]

It might not have won any literary prizes, but this verse suggests that Italians' position within American society might change as a result of their military efforts. The US War Department even suggested to the Committee of Public Information—which governed wartime news and propaganda—that they ought to emphasize Italy's importance to the Allied war effort, in the face of the negative stereotypes about immigrants which dominated the wartime popular press. Thus while on the one hand, the Italian presence in the American army was a sign of assimilation, not least because many of those serving had deliberately avoided answering their Italian call-up, it did not preclude an ongoing sense of *italianità* and of loyalty to their original home. By contrast, within civilian society a repressive push for Americanization and conformity was underway.[35]

Wartime arrangements sought to regularize the position of men who served in an Allied army, so as to avoid accusations of draft evasion, but these took a long time to organize: in December 1917 Arthur Balfour and Italian ambassador Imperiali at last signed an agreement that British and Italian men of military age residing in the other country were obliged to perform service in that country's army if they did not return home to serve in their own. Any emigrant who did not present himself to his consular authorities within sixty days would be obliged to serve in the army of his country of residence, receiving the same pay, pension, and leave entitlement as his fellows in arms.[36] A comparable agreement was made with France, but no such deal was struck with the USA, leaving many Italian-Americans in the awkward situation of being draft evaders even as they served in the US army. Not until August 1918 was the agreement signed (and finally

[34] *The Muskogee Times-Democrat*, 29 April 1918, p. 4; Chronicling America database, Library of Congress.
[35] Ford, '"Mindful of the Traditions of His Race": Dual Identity and Foreign-Born Soldiers', 48–50.
[36] ACS PCM GE 1915–1918, busta 85, fasc. 19.3.1 sf. 14, Accordi pel servizio militare con la Francia, l'Inghilterra e gli Stati Uniti.

ratified, unhelpfully, on 12 November 1918).[37] Long before these agreements on military service, however, France had been pressurizing the Italian government to grant service exemptions to Italian workers resident in France, especially those engaged in war-related industries. By November 1916, 3,400 Italians had been exempted on these grounds and in the end at least 57,000 Italian emigrants are estimated to have contributed to the Allied effort by working in France.[38] After the war, a broader view prevailed: more than 1,000 Italians who died while fighting in the US forces are recorded in the national roll of honour, published from 1926 onwards, along with several dozen who fell serving in the British, Canadian, or French forces.[39]

4.4 Colonial Troops

Italians overseas were not the only potential source of new soldiers: the formal colonies also offered a wealth of manpower. In the 1880s the Italian occupying forces in Eritrea began to recruit and organize the first indigenous units, which soon became known as *ascari*, from the Arabic word for soldiers, just as they were in German East Africa.[40] Eritreans and Somalis were joined by Yemenis and a few volunteers from the Arabian peninsula, and by 1914 even some Ethiopians. From just four battalions, colonial troops grew dramatically in number, soon taking on chief responsibility for upholding order in the east African colonies. The infantry was joined by both regular and irregular cavalry, all under white Italian command. The men were accompanied on campaign by their families, which increased the appeal of military service and facilitated recruitment, but which made moving the troops costly, slow, and inefficient. Indigenous troops played an important part in the First Abyssinian War in 1895–6 and paid a high price—Eritreans captured by the Ethiopian forces after their victory at Adwa suffered death or mutilation for their 'disloyalty'. By 1914 there were twenty-six battalions of Eritrean *ascari* and a handful of companies in Somalia. Meanwhile, recruitment of indigenous troops began in Libya in May 1912: infantry (*ascari*) and regular (*savari*) and light (*spahis*) cavalry forces were accompanied by a gendarmerie force (*zaptiè*). As in east Africa, Libyan units had indigenous NCOs (initially Eritrean or Yemeni *ascari*) but an exclusively white officer corps, recruited where possible from

---

[37] 'Convention Between the United States and Italy Providing for Reciprocal Military Service', *The American Journal of International Law* 13, no. 2 (1 April 1919): 147–9.
[38] Ufficio Storico, Corpo di stato maggiore, ed., *L'esercito italiano nella Grande Guerra, 1915–1918* [hereafter IOH], *Vol. VII, Operazioni fuori del territorio nazionale*, t.2: *Soldati d'Italia in terra di Francia* (Rome: Provveditorato generale dello stato libreria, 1951), 290–1.
[39] See Italia. Ministero della Guerra, *Militari caduti nella guerra nazionale 1915–1918: albo d' oro*, for many examples; online at http://www.cadutigrandeguerra.it.
[40] For the German *ascari*, see Michelle R. Moyd, *Violent Intermediaries: African Soldiers, Conquest, and Everyday Colonialism in German East Africa* (Athens, OH: Ohio University Press, 2014).

among men with prior experience of commanding African soldiers—of course this falsely presupposed that Eritreans and Tripolitanians were fundamentally the same people with the same needs and priorities.[41] These troops were organized and controlled entirely separately from the metropolitan armed forces. The Regio Corpo Truppe Coloniale—Royal Corps of Colonial Troops—was created in 1891 as a command structure for the permanent colonial forces in Eritrea; new corps followed in Somalia in 1908, and in Tripolitania and Cyrenaica in 1914. Each was a distinct entity, its officers transferred or seconded from the regular Italian army, and answerable to the governor of its respective colony. Since these governors were in turn answerable to the Minister of Colonies—after 1912, when this position was created by Giolitti—this meant that Italy's colonial armies were answerable not to the minister of war (still less the Chief of General Staff) but to the colonial ministry. Moreover, there was no overarching command structure through which to address military issues common to all four Corps—whether questions of training, equipment, personnel, doctrine, or organization.

Unlike France and Britain, Italy would not deploy colonial troops in its European war. However, the possibility was explored in great detail in 1915–16, with the vigorous support of no less a figure than the chief of general staff. There were several obstacles to the use of indigenous troops in Europe: perhaps the most important was the ongoing need to garrison the colonies themselves. In 1915 there were around 100,000 men in Libya, and by May 1916 Tripolitania and Cyrenaica were still garrisoned by about 40,000 men each, including 15,000 *ascari* (though a full metropolitan division, the 48th, of around 10,000 men would be repatriated in June 1916). By October 1917, there were still some 30,000 men in Tripolitania (including 11,000 *ascari*) and 35,000 in Cyrenaica (including 12,000 *ascari*).[42] However, there was one indigenous group who were not considered for service in the two provinces: the Libyan troops themselves, recruited since 1912. It was thought dangerous to send these units into a situation which might require them fight against their fellow tribesmen or even family members. There was considerable fear of betrayal, rooted partly in events of April 1915 where Tripolitanian irregulars turned on Italian troops at Qasr bu Hadi; although regularly constituted troops had not been involved in this 'treachery', their loyalties were nonetheless seen as suspect.[43]

---

[41] On the *ascari* in general, see Alessandro Volterra, *Progetto Ascari* (Rome: Libreria Efesto, 2014). For their role in the Libyan war, see Massimo Zaccaria, *Anch'io per la tua bandiera: il V Battaglione Ascari in missione sul fronte libico (1912)* (Ravenna: G. Pozzi, 2012). On the question of their deployment at the Italian front, see Alessandro Volterra, 'Askaris and the Great War. Colonial Troops Recruited in Libya for the War but Never Sent to the Austrian Front', in *The First World War from Tripoli to Addis Ababa (1911-1924)*, ed. Shiferaw Bekele et al. (Addis Abbeba: Centre français des études éthiopiennes, 2018), DOI: https://doi.org/10.4000/books.cfee.1400.

[42] ACS PCM GE 1915–1918, busta 75 19.3.1, f. 18. The term *ascari* was generically used to refer to all indigenous troops though properly it meant infantrymen.

[43] See Chapter 6—110.

Accordingly, four infantry battalions and four dismounted cavalry squadrons were dispatched to Sicily, where they ended up in a large camp at Floridia in the province of Syracuse. This small town hosted nearly 5,000 Libyans—some 2,500–3,000 soldiers and their families—for almost a year, not without some tensions emerging. At one point the white officer in command even wrote demanding the 'urgent dispatch of plenty of native prostitutes' to Sicily in order to avoid seriously disciplinary problems in the area, presumably involving the unwanted disruption of racial hierarchies via sexual relationships with local white women.[44] It would be ironic indeed to vigilantly police racial and sexual separation in the colonies only to see it overturned within the metropole itself. There was also anxiety over the experience of these colonial subjects in a remote, extremely poor, and underdeveloped region of the Sicilian interior: would the rhetoric of the Italian civilizing mission not be undermined by seeing the deprivation of the Sicilian peasantry?[45] Another ongoing problem was the leadership and command of the indigenous units. Experience proved that it was critically important to find and retain the right commanding officers for these men, ideally having prior experience with African troops. Frequent dismissals of unsuitable junior officers, including for racially motivated brutality, highlighted the difficulty in appointing appropriate leaders for the *ascari*. But during the war little effort was made to ensure continuity of leadership or enable the specialization of officers within the colonial forces. No sooner were experienced officers promoted—even to the rank of captain—they were urgently recalled to the metropole to serve at the front, and replaced by newly commissioned 2nd lieutenants with no colonial experience and no knowledge of Tripolitanian or Cyrenaican society, customs, religious practice, or military and political situation.[46] The needs of the colonies, in this case, were clearly subordinate to the more immediate demands of the minister of war and the army.

In September 1915 Cadorna first proposed using the *ascari* stationed in Sicily on the Italo-Austrian front, with the further possibility of bringing more colonial soldiers over from Libya in the future. He had already made it clear that he saw no objection on racial lines: 'our war cannot exclude use of coloured troops, who are subjects of the state', he wrote in July 1915, also emphasizing that Italy's allies were already deploying indigenous troops without lessening the 'patriotism' of their war effort. He also believed that using these troops at the front would increase their patriotism and boost recruitment in the colony.[47] According to officers, some of the men themselves had also expressed a desire to support the Italian war effort

[44] ACS Fondo Giovanni Ameglio, busta 1, fasc. 4, letter dated 7/10/1915. More imams and NCOs were also requested.
[45] Berhe, 'Il fronte meridionale della Grande guerra', 14.
[46] ACS Fondo Giovanni Ameglio, busta 3, fasc. 14.
[47] AUSSME, L8, busta 5, fasc. 19—letters of August and September 1915.

by fighting at the front.[48] Cadorna further planned to transfer some units from Eritrea to the Mediterranean colony, so that troops stationed there—in his view an excessively large force—could be sent to Italy. As well as stabilizing Libya, Cadorna hoped to recruit sufficient Eritreans to deploy a full colonial brigade against Austria.[49] The governor of Eritrea was not enthusiastic and the government was dubious, though Salandra showed himself initially open to persuasion, and debates proceeded through the following months. At this time the Libyan *ascaris'* own commander, Colonel Nigra, advised Cadorna that deployment to the national front might be premature, especially given the likely effects of the Alpine winter on North African soldiers; reluctantly, the chief of general staff agreed to postpone it to the following spring, but confirmed that he planned to send at the minimum a brigade to the front. Minister of War Vittorio Zupelli was hostile to the plan, noting the practical problems created by the *ascari* practice of taking wives and children to war, and fearing for the political repercussions of such deployment.[50] Early in 1916 Cadorna returned to the issue: he hoped to be able to deploy at least a brigade, of mixed Libyan and Eritrean troops, by late April or early May. Cadorna's determination to use indigenous forces reflects less an enlightened outlook on the abilities of all men than an iron resolve to maximize all possible resources for use on the Italo-Austrian front.

> The possibility of using a share of the troops of colour in the war in Italy only partially resolves the larger problem of the build-up of available forces in the colonies. I have drawn His Excellency the Prime Minister's attention to this problem several times such as to affirm the fundamental principle that not one man, not one gun should be diverted for purposes not <u>directly</u> connected to the great undertaking upon which Italy has embarked (the resolution of which will permit us to easily resolve all other secondary questions). All available forces, every energy of both the metropole and the colonies, must be controlled and directed towards the essential aims of our war.[51]

In March 1916 military plans for the deployment of the Libyans from Sicily began. Colonel Nigra advised that their chief strength was as a mobile force and their preparation for trench warfare was limited; consequently, they would need training and preparation for the war they were likely to encounter. The seriousness of Cadorna's intentions can be seen from the fact that not only was an officer

---

[48]   ACS Fondo Giovanni Ameglio, busta 1, fasc. 1, July 1915.
[49]   Volterra, 'Askaris and the Great War'.   [50]   AUSSME, L8, busta 5, fasc. 19.
[51]   ACS PCM GE 1915–1918, busta 106, Letter from Cadorna to Zupelli, 7/4/16, n. 192, 'Costituzione di un gruppo di colore per la guerra in Italia'. He sent an almost identical letter to the Prime Minister. Correspondence from September 1915 is also in this file: busta 106, s.f. Truppe Coloniali 19.4.13.1 Invio Ascari al fronte. For more on his views, see Cadorna, *La Guerra alla fronte italiana*, 7–8.

dispatched from the front to train up the Libyans in the use of gelignite, wire-cutters, and hand grenades, but subsequently an officer of the general staff, Colonel Andrea Graziani, was sent to report back on the quality and preparation of the troops. After a two-day inspection, he proclaimed himself 'Fully satisfied by the progress of the special instruction ordered by Supreme Command and in admiration of the discipline and military spirit of these wonderful troops.'[52] Nigra added that 'They are mercenaries in form only, instead they feel very Italian and the unit is constituted on strongly moral grounds.' The indigenous troops would be keen to 'fight for Italy's interests' and would 'follow their officers everywhere'. The only problem he foresaw was the need to organize accommodation for the families who would accompany the men; at least 800 Bedouin tents would need to be found, he estimated, and transported to the war zone.[53] Even the governor of Tripoli, Ameglio, was persuaded at last to change his mind and support the troops' deployment in Italy, writing in mid-May that 'their military qualities and their loyalty' would be highlighted on the Italo-Austrian front (while avoiding the difficulty of having them back in Tripolitania, creating possible tensions within the colony). But it was all to no avail.

Throughout April and May the matter was discussed repeatedly by the cabinet until the government decided to block the proposal definitively, apparently to the dissatisfaction of the minister for war Paolo Morrone, whose initial misgivings had been overcome by Cadorna (or who was perhaps fed up with arguing with his difficult colleague). The documents make it clear that this was a political and not a military decision. Above all, the minister for the colonies, Ferdinando Martini, was firmly opposed to the proposal. He accepted that the Libyan troops could not stay in Sicily any longer—the prefect had begun to complain quite vigorously by March 1916—but preferred that they should return home rather than fight against the Austrian enemy. It was politically unacceptable to the colonial authorities and also to Sonnino to countenance the use of indigenous troops against white soldiers: this was what seems to be meant by the government's 'reasons of international and moral order' for refusing the proposal.[54] Martini also held profound reservations over the Libyan troops' reliability; as Muslims, he feared their loyalty continued to lie with Italy's enemy, the Ottoman Sultan, in his spiritual role as Caliph.[55] Cadorna was reluctant to accept his defeat at Martini's hands, making yet another demand for the troops stationed in Floridia on 29 May—but by this date Martini was pleased to be able to reply that the men in

[52] ACS Fondo Giovanni Ameglio, busta 5, fasc. 27, Reparti Libici.
[53] ACS Fondo Giovanni Ameglio, busta 6, fasc. 39, Truppa indigene.
[54] ACS PCM GE 1915–1918, busta 75, 19.3.1, fasc. Colonie, s.f. 1 Truppe in Colonie, Letter n.3093, 15/4/16 Urg. Ris, Minister of Colonies to Salandra.
[55] ACS PCM GE 1915–1918, busta 75 19.3.1, fasc. Colonie, s.f. 1 Truppe in Colonie, Letter from Ferdinando Martini to the Minister of War, 4/3/16.

question had already embarked on ships to return to the colony.[56] This was not quite the end of the matter. In 1917, Libyan governor Giovanni Ameglio raised the possibility once more, requesting that four battalions of local *ascari* who he could not fully trust within the colony should be used for military operations in Europe, but once again the minister of the colonies—by this time Gaspare Colosimo—was opposed to the idea and it came to nothing.[57] In this matter at least the determination of the colonial ministry overruled the wishes of the military hierarchy and Cadorna was (most unusually) thwarted in his ongoing battles with the powers of civilian government over who had ultimate direction of the war. The limited wartime value of Italy's colonial manpower resources was thus partly a result of the metropole's doubts and uncertainties about how best to make use of them. Yet, as shall be seen below, colonial troops did make an essential contribution to the overall war effort of the Italian empire. By taking on much of the responsibility of fighting in Libya, the colonial theatre of war, as well as garrisoning the more secure colonies in East Africa, indigenous troops were a crucial resource for the Italian army and freed up white troops for the European theatre.

4.5 The Year of Crisis: 1917

By 1917 comfortable assumptions about a relatively brief war had long been forgotten. This was in many ways the great year of crisis, in Italy as elsewhere. Yet it also witnessed some of Italy's greatest successes on the battlefield. Campaigning began rather late in spring 1917, as both Austria-Hungary and Italy needed time to reorganize and replenish themselves before launching major operations. Eventually Cadorna launched the Tenth battle of the Isonzo on 12 May 1917, attacking towards the Bainsizza plateau from the bridgehead at Gorizia acquired the previous year and simultaneously southwards on the Carso. It was a disaster, bloody and hopeless even by the standards of the previous year's fighting on the Isonzo: forty-one regiments lost over 50 per cent of their men. Supreme Command complained that officers and men on the ground were completely ignoring all their efforts to refine the army's operational and tactical doctrine.[58] The offensive launched the following month on the Ortigara mountain, on the Alpine front, was another costly failure, despite the heroic determination of the Alpini fighting there. Against all expectations, however, in August 1917 the Eleventh Battle of the Isonzo—fought over much the same ground as the Tenth—was a success. Luigi Capello's Second Army managed to capture

[56] ACS Fondo Giovanni Ameglio, busta 5, fasc. 30, Richiesta truppe di S. M., Letter from Martini 29 May 1916.
[57] AUSSME, Libia, b. 170.   [58] Cappellano, *The Evolution of Tactical Regulations*, 41–3.

the Bainsizza plateau, though suffering appalling losses in the process.[59] By mid-September, operations ground to a halt with both sides facing exhaustion. This, then, was the backdrop to the single most devastating battle on the Italian front: the battle of Caporetto, which began on 24 October and lasted for around a month. A surprise attack by nine Austro-Hungarian and six German divisions, under the joint command of German general Otto von Below, was launched at dawn through heavy rain and mountain fog. An intense artillery bombardment was followed by innovative infiltration tactics by the Germans. Poorly prepared for the assault, inadequately led, and generally fatigued, the Italian troops in the sector were in no condition to fight effectively. Many rapidly ran out of munitions and were forced to surrender; there were no reserves ready in the area to replace them. Terrible decision-making at middle-ranking and senior levels compounded the disaster, and within 48 hours the line had been smashed around Caporetto (now Kobarid in Slovenia). Thousands of prisoners were taken and, as a dramatic retreat began, equal numbers began to flee homewards into the interior. As Second Army disintegrated, Third and Fourth Armies to the south and north were obliged to retreat too, to prevent further gaps opening up in the front. By 30 October the Italians had retreated to the Tagliamento river; within a few days this position too proved untenable and a further retreat to the river Piave was ordered. From around 3 November Italian forces began to stabilize, and discipline returned, though the retreat continued. By 12 November the new positions on the Piave were adopted, and the fighting ended on around 26 November (see Map 2 for the final position of the Austro-German advance). Overall, the battle would cost Italy 11,000 dead, 30,000 wounded, 280,000 prisoners of war, and some 300,000 dispersed men, many of whom were temporary deserters while others were simply lost and unable to find their unit.[60]

Caporetto heralded a major domestic political crisis and created serious alarm within the Entente. The entire Italian cabinet was forced to resign, Boselli's government having been noted for its passivity in the face of Supreme Command's demands over the previous seventeen months. The new prime minister, liberal jurist Vittorio Emanuele Orlando, would seize the reins of government much more firmly. Meanwhile the international implications of the defeat were not lost on anybody. Italy's reputation was tarnished in the eyes of its colonial subjects (Ottoman propagandists in Tripolitania made much of the news) and its allies. A request for allied help was sent out almost immediately and generals Ferdinand Foch and Sir William Robertson arrived in Italy to inspect the Italian positions on 30 October. Deeply unimpressed with Cadorna and his leadership, and inclined to view the situation pessimistically, the two men agreed conditionally to send six divisions across from the Western Front but told the Italians that 'it is up to Italy

[59] Gooch, *The Italian Army*, 222–6.
[60] The literature on Caporetto is vast; a recent synthesis is Nicola Labanca, *Caporetto: storia e memoria di una disfatta* (Bologna: Il Mulino, 2017).

to defend herself'.[61] On 6 November the Entente leaders gathered at the exclusive seaside resort of Rapallo. Here the generals reluctantly accepted Lloyd George's insistence on making a significant gesture of support, eventually sending six French and five British divisions to Italy. Lloyd George and his French counterpart Paul Painlevé also backed the creation of the Supreme War Council, to better coordinate the strategic decision-making process at the heart of the Entente.

Cadorna was dismissed on 8 November. Foch had made his replacement a condition of French support, but in fact, the decision had already been taken in connection with the appointment of Orlando as prime minister. As Boselli's minister of the interior, Orlando's efforts to protect the prerogatives of civilian government had more than once put him into direct conflict with Cadorna and there was no prospect of the two men working together successfully. Politically and military discredited, the former chief of general staff was kicked upstairs to the Supreme War Council at Versailles, where his failings would have a much more limited impact. His replacement, Armando Diaz, was a very different man in almost every way. Diaz was a bourgeois southerner and a freemason who had held active combat command before taking up his staff position. Diaz was to dramatically revolutionize the Italian army's command culture and its policies towards troop welfare and morale management, with important effects for the final twelve months of the war. His appointment was immediately welcomed by much of the army, and within days the military situation began to stabilize. By the time that French and British troops began to actively take over defensive duties in certain sectors of the new lines, the battle was almost over, and the Italian troops had successfully halted the Austro-German advance.

4.6 From Disaster to Victory: 1918

In 1918 the programme of reforms introduced by the Orlando government and Diaz began to improve civilian and military morale. Despite the terrible blow of Caporetto, and the ongoing problems created by the presence of hundreds of thousands of refugees from the newly occupied region in the north-east, concerted propaganda efforts helped the public mood to stabilize. The need to eject the invader and liberate Italian families now living under occupation served to provide a real motivation for the war effort, perhaps for the first time. Rationing and food distribution systems were reformed, to alleviate the most urgent cause of civil protest; likewise the army's systems for leave allocation, pay, and pensions

---

[61] Angelo Gatti, *Caporetto: Diario di Guerra* (Bologna: Il Mulino, 1964), 286–9.

were overhauled to remove key sources of discontent among the troops.[62] It would be wrong to suggest that these changes solved all problems: despite a lull in the early months of 1918, demonstrations and strikes resumed in spring. In the army, despite significant improvements in overall morale indicators, desertion and self-mutilation continued to occur at rates that showed that problems remained—and Supreme Command lacked the confidence or the resources to launch any major offensives for most of the year. Nonetheless, the major Austrian offensive launched in June 1918 on the Piave—the Habsburgs' last-ditch attack on this front—was repelled with vigour and determination. Victory on the Piave was an essential stepping-stone towards final victory in the war. Diaz was still cautious, but eventually in October 1918 Italy would be ready to launch its final battle of the war, at Vittorio Veneto, which would bring Austria-Hungary to the negotiating table.

[62] On the changes after Caporetto, see Gian Luigi Gatti, *Dopo Caporetto. Gli Ufficiali P nella Grande guerra: propaganda, assistenza, vigilanza* (Gorizia: Libreria Editrice Goriziana, 2000).

5

Societies at War

The mobilization of Italian society, industry, and culture for total war, in the face of widespread indifference to the country's war aims, was an enormous challenge for the liberal state. The mechanisms by which Italy's political and economic systems responded to this challenge were deeply transformative, with legacies that lasted into the 1920s and beyond. But it was not only the state and institutions which underwent this hour of trial, but ordinary men, women, and children in Italy and beyond. In this moment of crisis, the resources of the much-vaunted 'Greater Italy' of emigrants and colonies would also be called upon, with mixed success. The responses of Italian citizens and institutions to the war, and their experiences once mobilized, reveal the dual nature of the conflict as both a national and an imperial war.

5.1 Cultural Mobilization

The idea of the First World War as the moment in which a true national culture was formed—both in a political sense and more widely—was embraced both popularly and by scholars for many years. Beyond the triumphalist rhetoric of the fascist regime, a 'popular-democratic' vision of the war predominated among liberals and characterized the first few decades of historiography produced after the fall of fascism.[1] In this vision, the war was not only necessary for the completion of the national territory but completed the nationalization of the people, revealing the true underlying unity of the Italian people for the first time. While this depiction ignores many important aspects of the war experience and sectors of Italian society, it is not wholly false. The Libyan war had already shown that Catholics could be brought into the national fold in the name of colonialism; the interventionist campaign revealed that many republicans and democratic socialists could also be mobilized in the cause of war and national expansion. Now both the state and the institutions of civil society worked to unite Italians behind the war effort using a range of moral and political rhetoric.

Given the open neutralism or anti-war sentiment of many sectors of society, including the peasantry and much of the industrial working class, this was an

---

[1] Mondini, 'L'historiographie italienne face à la Grande Guerre'.

The Italian Empire and the Great War. Vanda Wilcox, Oxford University Press (2021). © Vanda Wilcox.
DOI: 10.1093/oso/9780198822943.003.0005

uphill task. There was no moment of national unity to compare to the much mythologized spirit of August 1914 elsewhere. Unlike in other European nations, the mainstream Italian socialist party did not embrace the logic of the *union sacrée* in 1915—reflecting, among other things, the very different circumstances under which Italy had joined the war compared to the situation in France, Germany, or the UK. Although the Partito Socialista Italiano (PSI) had itself been internally riven over the question of war during the period of neutrality, losing numerous high-profile members ranging from Benito Mussolini to Leonida Bissolati, once the war began the party crystalized around a firm position developed by its ageing secretary and founder Costantino Lazzaro. His formula, which was also adopted by the chief socialist trade union, the Confederazione Generale del Lavoro (CGdL), was: '*né aderire né sabotare*'—neither support nor sabotage. This position had the merit of temporarily bridging the growing internal divides within the movement (the PSI would formally split at its 1921 party conference in Livorno, leading to the creation of the Italian Communist Party). It also marked a concession towards a national consensus in comparison to the Italo-Turkish war, which the PSI had unequivocally condemned. However, it was neither morally nor politically satisfying: it simultaneously left the PSI open to accusations of disloyalty and defeatism while doing nothing to materially prevent or end the war. Nonetheless, the socialists' condemnation had in important effect in limiting state efforts to create a homogenous, unified home front, and certainly helped to underpin the many workers' protests which took place throughout the war.[2]

Beyond the socialist party, however, a political truce was established within the (now-muzzled) parliament, and when Boselli became prime minister in June 1916, he led a 'unity government' including all pro-war parties, including those on the left. Critically, if socialism remained opposed to the war, the Catholic Church soon began to adapt, ultimately playing an important part in the production and mobilization of consensus. Arguably this process, by which Catholics were at last fully integrated into the national polity, was one of the most important changes which the First World War wrought in Italian society.[3] A war which set the Catholic peoples of Europe against one another inevitably created interpretative difficulties for the Church at first, compounded by the death of Pius X in August 1914 which necessitated holding a conclave with the war already under way. The new Pope Benedict XV tried to tread a path of cautious neutrality, delegating responses to the war to each country's episcopate; many in Italy suspected him of austrophile leanings. At the national level, however, while some bishops denounced the war as a punishment from God or a form of apostasy, there was a general consensus within the Church that obedience to

---

[2] Valiani, *Il Partito socialista italiano nel periodo della neutralità*.
[3] Mario Isnenghi, *Convertirsi alla guerra: liquidazioni, mobilitazioni e abiure nell'Italia tra il 1914 e il 1918* (Rome: Donzelli editore, 2015), 10.

legitimate earthly powers was a core teaching and that this required support for the respective authorities of each episcopate. The idea of the war as an affliction caused by secularism and sin prompted calls for spiritual mobilization as early as August 1914, but the Italian clerical response was mixed and uneven: especially in the early period of the war there was a distinct lack of enthusiasm from many clergymen, some of whom were even attacked in the press as inadequately patriotic. Others, however, immediately adopted a nation-centric framework for responding to the war. Few went so far as Pietro Maffi, the notoriously nationalist archbishop of Pisa, who was even denied entry to Vatican territory during the conclave of 1914 on account of his political activism; he became a central figure in religious patriotism, spearheading an approach which married faith and nation, and which became increasingly widespread as the war went on. In the words of Daniele Menozzi, the First World War witnessed 'a true sacralisation of war, often based on a Christianization of the political religion of the nation', in Italy as elsewhere.[4]

This was a two-way process in which both the Italian state and the Catholic Church actively participated. Benedict XV created a military vicariate (or 'field bishop'—*vescovo del campo*) to manage the wartime pastoral care of the armed forces, thus avoiding the tricky issue of directly endorsing an individual belligerent, and appointed Monsignor Angelo Bartolomasi to the role. Under his leadership, a huge network of military chaplains attended to the spiritual needs of the troops (alongside a much smaller team of Jewish chaplains, under the direction of the Chief Rabbi of Rome, Angelo Sacerdoti). Nearly 25,000 ecclesiastics, including 15,000 priests, were mobilized into the army, though the large majority served not as chaplains but within the medical services. These efforts were not only welcomed but actively encouraged by the armed forces. Cadorna, himself very devout, was keen to promote faith as a key element in managing morale and discipline. Chaplains had also supported the war in Libya, sometimes embracing not only colonialist but crusading rhetoric in the process. Several high-profile churchmen such as Agostino Gemelli, Giovanni Semeria, and Giovanni Minozzi took up strongly nationalist, pro-war positions, and worked closely with the military authorities. Perhaps the apotheosis of this close relationship came in January 1917, when the soldiers of the Italian army were consecrated to the Sacred Heart of Jesus (immensely popular across Catholic Europe in this period, the rite already been undertaken in 1914 for France and for the Austrian imperial family, and for the German nation in 1915). In a collective act of devotion sponsored by Gemelli, soldiers at the front—whether in Italy or overseas in Albania, Macedonia, or Libya—took part in a solemn Mass and were given

---

[4] Daniele Menozzi, *La Chiesa italiana nella Grande Guerra* (Brescia: Morcelliana, 2015), 7.

commemorative postcards and pamphlets to mark the occasion.[5] The rite suggests the complexity of Church-state relationships at the time: as the state hoped to use the Church to increase soldiers' patriotic loyalty, so the Church—and men like Gemelli—used the army as a way to grow closer to the people.

His colleague Don Minozzi was one of the prime movers in the creation of leisure facilities for soldiers, the so-called Case del Soldato, which he established with Cadorna's daughter Carla in the rear areas behind the front. While designed as places of recreation, they were also sites of both patriotic and religious indoctrination through the reading matter and entertainment they offered. Local and regional Catholic organizations mobilized in support of the troops, raising funds and distributing devotional materials including printed prayers and holy images on postcards. The resources of the Church were put at the disposal of the medical services, with ecclesiastical buildings made available for use as hospitals or soldiers' accommodation, while support for widows, orphans, prisoners, and refugees placed the Church at the heart of the wider processes of mobilization. Religious mobilization was not a simple matter of unquestioned support for the war— prayers for peace were as much a part of the spiritual landscape as prayers for victory. But, largely thanks to the reactions and leadership of the clergy, the war offered a major opportunity for reconciliation between Catholics and the Italian state, and offered new scope for the practice of the faith to be reconciled with patriotic duty.[6]

For Italy's small and generally assimilated Jewish community, the war occasioned a renewed exploration of the relationship between religious and national loyalties; most Italian Jews responded with a strongly patriotic outlook. A relatively high proportion pursued professional military careers and were over-represented at senior levels in the army and navy; of the Jewish men who served in the war, around 50 per cent were officers.[7] A number of these were ardently committed to the most expansionist, imperialist vision of the war, such as Lieutenant Aldo Finzi, who took part in Gabriele D'Annunzio's famous flight over Vienna and later was elected to parliament with the fascist party. Another key figure was Venetian naval captain, later admiral, Augusto Capon (father-in-law to Enrico Fermi) who, under the pen name Adriacus, wrote tracts on Italy's need to control Dalmatia and Albania right down to Vlorë.[8] More

[5] Sante Lesti, *Riti di guerra. Religione e politica nell'Europa della Grande Guerra* (Bologna: Il Mulino, 2015), especially ch. 3.

[6] For a concise introduction, see Carlo Stiaccini, 'The Catholic Church and the War', in *Italy in the Era of the Great War*, ed. Vanda Wilcox (Leiden: Brill, 2018), 272–86. DOI: https://doi.org/10.1163/9789004363724_015.

[7] Vanda Wilcox, 'Between Faith and Nation: Italian Jewish Soldiers in the Great War', in *The Jewish Experience of the First World War*, ed. Edward Madigan and Gideon Reuveni (London: Palgrave Macmillan, 2019), 183–206, DOI: https://doi.org/10.1057/978-1-137-54896-2_9.

[8] Adriacus, *Da Trieste a Valona: il problema adriatico e i diritti dell'Italia* (Milan: Alfieri & Lacroix, 1918). Both men were murdered during the Holocaust, Capon at Auschwitz and Finzi during the Fosse Ardeatine massacre in Rome.

commonly, Italian rabbis and Jewish intellectuals saw the war in a liberal Risorgimento framework which rendered it fully compatible with Jewish narratives of exile and redemption.

Italian society rapidly adopted at least some of the ideas of total war: the belief that every sector of society was required to contribute, and to make sacrifices, was widely embraced. Despite some initial suspicions, the contribution of women, as well as children, teenagers, and the elderly, was soon accepted by both military and civilian authorities, and by the institutions of civil society. National organizations and societies played an important part in cultural mobilization, including taking the lead in the production of patriotic propaganda. Bodies such as the Dante Alighieri Society or the General Union of Italian Teachers published books and pamphlets, organized events and distributed postcards. However, civil society also undertook many practical tasks, such as tracing soldiers' families and communicating news between home and front. Committees of civilians proliferated across the country, dedicated to civil protection, fund-raising, local healthcare, knitting of socks and blankets, running soup kitchens, patriotic education, agricultural development, support for orphans, assistance to refugees, care for convalescents, and more besides. These associations filled the vacuum left by the almost complete lack of state support for the needy (along with local administrations, even where socialist run, which endeavoured to make up for the central government's failings). Whether in Italy or in overseas communities, families who were left in financial hardship after the mobilization of their chief breadwinner were often dependent on this type of community support, since separation allowances were generally inadequate and did not keep pace with rapidly skyrocketing food prices.

Many patriotic associations were run wholly or chiefly by women, for whom this was an important opportunity to participate actively in public life, especially at the local level. This form of civic mobilization in support of the war was led almost exclusively by the aristocratic and upper-middle class, but women of all social sectors were mobilized in the cause. Associations for or led by women were active throughout the peninsula and islands, as well as in emigrant communities. In Italy the feminist movement was less developed than in some other European combatant nations, and Catholic social teachings certainly underpinned many women's approach to the war, which often centred on supporting—and supportive—roles. Nonetheless, women's war work was varied and significant in Italy as elsewhere, and Italian women were mobilized effectively to make numerous contributions to the war effort. Thousands of women volunteered through the Red Cross to work as nurses or as medical assistants (around forty were killed at the front). As artists, poets, and journalists, Italian women represented the war in its many forms; women found employment in offices, shops, as sex workers in army brothels, or as spies working behind enemy lines. Peasant women took on unprecedented responsibilities for the farm and the household, an experience at once liberating and burdensome; without the manual labour of women and children on farms, Italy's food supply would certainly have suffered even more severely. Albeit in lesser numbers than in some countries, women were also mobilized into industry in wartime (or switched to military production out of other industrial sectors such as textiles). At least 22,000 Italian women worked in munitions factories, out of some 200,000 in war-related industries, while some 60,000 teenagers were also mobilized into factories. In a more unusual form of women's war work, local women from Friuli and Venezia Giulia worked at the front as porters, carrying food, munitions, and other essential supplies through the mountains up to the lines, and even helping construct trenches.[9] Women were essential to the survival of Italian communities overseas, which not only lost those men who went into the armed forces but could no longer rely on a steady flow of new young male immigrants, the traditional source of labour upon which Italian businesses overseas relied. With emigration forbidden to men of military age, and increasingly strict controls on the issue of passports, Italians abroad began to call upon women to emigrate and join them. Wives, sisters, and daughters who had previously remained in Italy were summoned abroad to join family firms (as were older men) and take on new responsibilities within emigrant communities.[10] Children were also mobilized for war, and were a major target of nationalist propaganda, both through the children's illustrated press and via the formal structures of primary education, which was a critically important institution for propagating national sentiment in this period.[11]

More widely, artists, scientists, and intellectuals were mobilized in support of the war effort too. This took the form both of public propagandistic efforts, and of scientific-technical work for the Ministry of War; a dedicated historiographical office, the Ufficio Storiografico della mobilitazione industriale, was created to document, preserve, narrate, and promote the work of industrial mobilization. Prime Minister Paolo Boselli, in his capacity as head of the National Committee for the History of the Risorgimento, urged all local councils and civil organizations to collect materials about mobilization and the war effort (pamphlets, posters, photographs, journals, etc.) to record the country's historic experiences; this

---

[9] For an introduction to the ample literature on women's work in the war, see Elpidio Ellero, *Le donne nella Prima Guerra mondiale: in Friuli e in Veneto* (Udine: Gaspari, 2016); Allison Scardino Belzer, *Women and the Great War: Femininity under Fire in Italy* (New York: Palgrave Macmillan, 2010); Barbara Curli, *Italiane al lavoro, 1914–1920* (Venice: Marsilio, 1998); Mondini, *La guerra italiana*, 86–106.

[10] Caroline Douki, 'Les Italiens de Glasgow: identités et appartenances communautaires à l'épreuve de la Première guerre mondiale', in *Les petites Italies dans le monde*, ed. Marie-Claude Blanc-Chaléard et al. (Rennes: Presses Univ. de Rennes, 2007), 248–9.

[11] Fava, 'War, "National Education" and the Italian Primary School'; see also the essays in Part II of Daniele Menozzi, Giovanna Procacci, and Simonetta Soldani, *Un paese in guerra: la mobilitazione civile in italia (1914–1918)* (Milan: Unicopli, 2010).

collection would eventually form the core of the Biblioteca di Storia Moderna e Contemporanea in Rome.[12]

5.2 Resistance, Repression, and Crisis at Home

Undertaking a total war in the face of mass popular indifference—or even hostility—to the war effort was a task which required the mobilization of a powerful coercive apparatus. During the war the Italian state created and extended a range of repressive techniques designed to control the civil and military population. As Giovanna Procacci has observed, Italian wartime administration was perhaps closer to the models adopted in the Central Powers than in the liberal democracies of the Entente. Italy suspended the normal legislative processes of parliamentary scrutiny and stripped civilian workers of their normal rights by placing them under military law; the wartime disciplinary regime ranged from censorship of press and private communications through to limitations on citizens' free movement including the introduction of internal passports and curfews.[13] Critically, civilians were placed under the jurisdiction of military tribunals. Cadorna's fear of 'internal enemies' was bordering on obsessive, but he was not alone in his preoccupations; the fear of anti-war activism or sabotage was widespread in government circles. The deployment of troops for public order duty, including the systematic use of violence against civilians, was hardly a new phenomenon. In 1898, for example, four days of food riots in Milan had been suppressed by General Fiorenzo Bava-Beccaris with extreme brutality, killing 80 and wounding well over 400; a state of siege had also been declared in the provinces of Florence, Livorno, and Naples. Leaving a legacy of popular mistrust towards the army itself (not helpful in wartime), this spectre of this massacre would be evoked in Turin in 1917.

The position of the Italian Socialist Party, and the open anti-war sentiments of most Italian leftists, had important consequences: perhaps the most important was the forced militarization of labour, which took place very rapidly once the war was under way. The army was handed control of industrial mobilization, and workers in all key war-related industries were placed under military discipline. Essential industrial workers, exempted from the armed forces, performed this work as their 'military service'. They were even obliged to reside in barracks and wear uniform in the factories. More remarkably, the same laws also applied to

---

[12] Luigi Tomassini, 'Gli effetti sociali della mobilitazione industriale. Industriali, lavoratori, stato', in *Un paese in guerra: la mobilitazione civile in Italia, 1914–1918*, ed. Daniele Menozzi, Giovanna Procacci, and Simonetta Soldani (Milan: Unicopli, 2010), 48–51.

[13] Giovanna Procacci, 'La società come una caserma: La svolta repressiva degli anni di guerra', in *La violenza contro la popolazione civile nella Grande guerra: deportati, profughi, internati*, ed. Bruna Bianchi (Milan: Unicopli, 2006), 283.

civilian workers, including women. The authorities felt that they could place no dependence on the reliability or patriotism of the industrial working class.[14] Military law was also extended to the areas behind the front lines and to key garrisons or fortified cities including ports and other coastal towns, placing many other civilians under its rule. These repressive measures were not sufficient to eliminate signs of discontent, however. On the contrary, in the words of social historian Roberto Bianchi, 'the period 1915–1918 was entirely marked by a thick web of anti-war protests'. Demonstrations against mobilization continued through 1915; by 1916 more substantial protests began, involving ever increasing numbers and a growing range of social groups. Some were focused on specific grievances such as soldiers' separation allowances or workers' pay and conditions, but by 1917, as war-weariness grew, so too did generalized anti-war demonstrations. Women were very prominent in civilian protests throughout the war, especially those centred on food and supplies: already by April 1917 there had been more than 450 protests by women, most of which centred on food shortages.[15] This reflected the fact that they were 'safer', since they could not be sent to the front as a punishment as male protestors were. Forms of civilian protest ranged from graffiti-ing or singing anti-war slogans, along with petitioning, leafleting, or organized marches, through to stone-throwing, riots, street fighting, the setting up of barricades and even the use of firearms. Anti-war activism in Italy exceeded that seen in any other Western European country.[16]

5.2.1 1917: Domestic Crisis

By 1917 matters were beginning to come to a head, with anti-war demonstrations an increasing problem. These were not solely an urban phenomenon: peasant discontent too grew throughout the war. Serious violence broke out in some places as 1917 proceeded: in May in Milan and then most dramatically in Turin in August, where around fifty demonstrators were killed by the police and armed forces. In the latter case a women's food protest was joined by workers from militarized factories in what soon escalated into a potentially revolutionary moment rooted in the most working-class neighbourhoods of the city, with barricades built in the streets; the failure of the movement to win over the support

---

[14] Tomassini, 'Gli effetti sociali della mobilitazione industriale', 30–8.

[15] Maria Concetta Dentoni, 'Food and Nutrition (Italy)', *1914–1918-Online International Encyclopedia of the First World War*, 2014, https://encyclopedia.1914-1918-online.net/article/food_and_nutrition_italy. DOI: https://doi.org/10.15463/ie1418.10511.

[16] Roberto Bianchi, 'Social Conflict and Control, Protest and Repression (Italy)', *1914–1918-Online International Encyclopedia of the First World War*, 2014. https://encyclopedia.1914-1918-online.net/article/social_conflict_and_control_protest_and_repression_italy. DOI: https://doi.org/10.15463/IE1418.10367.

of the troops prevented it from becoming a real political force for change.[17] This was the high point of public anger against the both the war itself and the perceived inequalities and injustices which arose from its (mis-)management.

To add fuel to the fire of popular disaffection came important statements from different leaders which seemed to undermine the war effort. Two of the country's largest and most important blocs, socialists and Catholics, had generally offered at best a begrudging and partial support for the war; in summer 1917 it seemed as though both groups were being further turned against the war effort. First came an ambiguous declaration by reformist socialist leader and journalist Claudio Treves, who had once fought an intense sabre duel with Mussolini (in which both men wounded one another). A committed pacifist, in a parliamentary address on 12 July 1917 he urged his listeners to listen to the 'voice which rises from all the trenches...uttering the ultimatum of life to death: next winter no longer in the trenches'.[18] Was this the verbal expression of a collective heartfelt wish, or, as his critics held, an incitement to mutiny and revolution? A few weeks later, on 1 August, it was the turn of Pope Benedict XV to earn the ire of nationalists and the army high command when he issued his Peace Proposals. The text used the critical phrase 'useless slaughter' to describe the war, confirming what some Catholics had long felt about the conflict and making it harder for many of them to fully endorse the war effort. These public statements were analysed by the Commission of Inquiry into the defeat at Caporetto as possible contributing factors to disaffection and low morale among the troops as well as the general public, but the inquiry ended by (rightly) concluding that they made no significant contribution to the defeat.[19] Historians today concur that Caporetto was a military defeat and not, as initially alleged by commentators on both sides of the political spectrum, a military strike, an attempted revolution, or a failure of will and determination on mass scale. Nonetheless, it is clear that by 1917 the war was increasingly unpopular in many sectors of Italian society: latent opposition had come to the fore, empowered by the growing socio-economic crisis in the country, while previously tacit and cooperative individuals and groups began to articulate criticisms of the war for the first time.

Within the armed forces, discontent was rarely openly political. Instead, individual acts of indiscipline and defiance indicated personal refusals to fight or, more commonly, a form of temporary rejection of army authority. Military tribunals operating in civilian areas were joined by many more in the war zone;

---

[17] Paolo Spriano, *Torino operaia nella grande guerra (1914–1918)* (Turin: G. Einaudi, 1960).

[18] Italia. *Atti del Parlamento Italiano*—Sessione 1913–1917 (20/06/1917–16/10/1917), Vol. XIII: I Sessione (Rome: Tip. Camera dei Deputati 1917): 14323–86, https://storia.camera.it/lavori/regno-d-italia/leg-regno-XXIV/1917/12-luglio;14367.

[19] On the work of the inquiry and its political context, see Andrea Ungari, 'The Official Inquiry into the Italian Defeat at the Battle of Caporetto (October 1917)', *Journal of Military History*, 76, no. 3 (2012): 695–725.

all served to enact a remarkably repressive body of wartime regulations aimed at disciplining speech and actions. Italian military discipline was notoriously harsh, with some of the highest rates of execution of all combatant nations.[20] For many socialists, and later communists, the struggle of Italian workers and peasants against this oppression was both parallel to and intimately linked with anti-colonial struggle, including the ongoing resistance to Italian colonialism in Libya.[21] In this sense, a post-colonial reading of the war—and an awareness of the centrality of empire to the Italian war effort—might illuminate the experiences of Italian civilians and soldiers alike. The working class were depicted (especially in military discourse) as inherently disloyal, even as inferior by birth, in a eugenicist framework—serving as a domestic 'Other'.[22] The restrictions on representative governance, the functional elimination of the powers of parliament, and the comprehensive apparatus of censorship and repression which the Italian state instituted beginning in March 1915 in several respects replicated a colonial system: Italy turned itself into a kind of auto-colony. It may seem contradictory to state that coercion played such an important part in the Italian experience of the war, and that protests against the war were so significant, when the counter-narrative of mass mobilization and nationalization is also clearly well supported by much evidence. In fact, this highlights the extremely divisive nature of the war experience and the radical fracturing of public opinion—with very long-lasting effects. Here we find another paradox of Italy's war: from the first truly national experience, unprecedented national disunity emerged.

5.3 The Greater Italy at War

Across Italy, citizens responded to the challenges of military and cultural mobilization according to multiple intersecting dynamics of age, class, gender, faith, and political ideals. But they were not the only Italians facing a high complex set of demands on their loyalty and service: their fellow nationals overseas also faced difficult choices about how to respond to the war. Emilio Franzina, the leading scholar of Italian emigrants during the war, has noted that the whole topic is still dominated, even in the historiography, 'by the interpretative model set into circulation by the fascist propaganda machine between the wars'.[23] This analysis saw the Italian communities overseas as unequivocally patriotic and enthusiastic.

---

[20] See Marco Pluviano and Irene Guerrini, *Le fucilazioni sommarie nella prima guerra mondiale* (Udine: Gaspari, 2004) and Vanda Wilcox, *Morale and the Italian Army during the First World War* (Cambridge: Cambridge University Press, 2016), chs 4, 8.

[21] Srivastava, *Italian Colonialism and Resistances to Empire*, 34–6.

[22] See, for instance, Nicola Maria Campolieti, 'La disciplina militare e la disciplina del lavoro sociale', *Nuova Rivista di Fanteria*, VII, no. 5 (1914): 440–53; Ezio Bottini, 'La preparazione alla guerra e l'educazione militare della gioventù in Italia', *RMI*, LIX, no. 2 (1914): 278–304.

[23] Franzina, 'La guerra lontana', 57–8.

Unprecedented numbers left Italy in 1910–13, meaning that in 1915 many emigrants had left but recently, presumably keeping ties to their homeland fresh in their hearts and minds. But even these first-generation Italian emigrants varied considerably in their sense of *italianità*, while the second and third generations almost inevitably had a weaker connection to the nation. Scholars have not always distinguished between loyalty to the nation or to an ideal of *italianità* and support for the war effort; in fact, the former did not necessarily entail the latter. Italians overseas might contribute in many ways to the war: military service, fund-raising activities and subscription to loans, upholding community life, or (in some cases) participation in host countries' own war efforts.

In Argentina, for instance, the Italian *colonie* underwent similar debates as the motherland in 1914–15, and the same range of political positions on the war were adopted; Italian socialists and anarchists in the US demonstrated against the war just as they did back in Italy. Many communities had for decades been strongly divided along regional lines, with divergent groups retaining strong ties to their original hometowns or regions rather than a collective Italian identity—which would therefore have to be constructed in wartime (though arguably the Libyan war had already facilitated this process). Once the war began, Italian-language newspapers around the world such as *Il Patria degli Italiani* (Buenos Aires), *Fanfulla* (São Paolo), *Il Progresso Italo-Americano* (New York), and *L'Italia* (Chicago) dedicated considerable space to the conflict, sometimes publishing syndicated content from the *Corriere della Sera* or other Italian newspapers. They also focused heavily on community-building patriotic endeavours, fund-raising, and mutual support, and on issues particular to emigrants in times of war, such as economic instability, the new difficulties of travel to the motherland, or issues around military service. Even non-Italian periodicals could strongly promote loyalty to Italy: much of the US media was pro-Entente and published many articles praising returning reservists and celebrating the Italian war effort as part of the Garibaldian legacy, while in both the USA and Brazil entry to the war would lead to an emphasis on the positive contributions of diaspora communities. The war saw a huge growth in all form of associationism, with a huge range of Italian community organizations springing up in colonies across the world; most of these not only promoted a sense of *italianità* but also supported the war effort. Local Italian Catholic churches also tended to endorse the war as a patriotic duty (though more research on the role of Italian churches in this era needs to be done).[24]

The war might promote the cohesiveness (and patriotism) of the emigrant community, but it could also undermine it. Once the USA entered the war, Woodrow Wilson's commitment to Americanization of minorities encouraged

---

[24] Fiorello B. Ventresco, 'Loyalty and Dissent: Italian Reservists in America During World War I', *Italian Americana* 4, no. 1 (1 October 1978): 99.

many to use the war as a demonstration of American loyalty. The drive for '100% Americanism' was a powerful coercive force, imposing demonstrations of public loyalty ranging from Fourth of July events to subscribing to war bonds. But even before this date, many Italians in the US and elsewhere were keen to prove that their allegiance lay with the land of their residence, not their origins.[25] A perceptive contemporary observer, the German sociologist Roberto Michels, noted that the higher the social class—original or acquired—of the migrant, the greater their chances of assimilation. Only the 'wretched and illiterate masses of the Mezzogiorno' were able to long resist 'this process of denationalisation', whereas those families which achieved wealth and prominence in the Americas soon became psychologically as well as legally naturalized.[26] Meanwhile, many of the peasants who emigrated had low rates of literacy and an attachment to primarily local rather than national cultural traditions, meaning that although their identity was less rapidly assimilated it was also less truly 'Italian'. This phenomenon had important implications for the reactions of emigrant communities to the war: precisely those middle- and upper-class men and women who within Italy were most likely to lead the processes of civic mobilization were those who in the emigrant colonies were least likely to have maintained close and lasting ties to the *patria*.

5.4 Fundraising Overseas

Since the 1890s an important consequence of Italian emigration had been the steady flow of remittances into the country. The informal empire of emigrants, especially in the USA, made a vital contribution to the growth of the Italian economy in the pre-war period, and was at least partially supported by the Banco di Napoli, which operated as a quasi-colonial bank designed to protect emigrants' savings and funnel them safely back to Italy. On the eve of the war, remittances worth close to one billion Lira a year were sent back to Italy, making up more than 20 per cent of the international balance of payments.[27] Unsurprisingly therefore, Italian communities overseas also made an important contribution to the war economy, through both direct remittance payments and fund-raising.

[25] Christopher Sterba, *Good Americans: Italian and Jewish Immigrants during the First World War* (Oxford: Oxford University Press, 2003); Nancy Gentile Ford, *Americans All!: Foreign-Born Soldiers in World War I* (College Station: Texas A&M University Press, 2001), ch. 1.
[26] R. Michels, *L'imperialismo italiano*, 1914, cited in Bechelloni, 'De petites Italies au service d'une plus grande Italie?', 349–50.
[27] See Dino Cinel, *The National Integration of Italian Return Migration: 1870–1929* (Cambridge: Cambridge University Press, 2002), ch. 6.

Fund-raising efforts in Italian communities took place all over the world. In the USA, money was raised by committees in New York, Connecticut, Chicago, Philadelphia, Reno, Mechanieville, Columbus, and New Orleans. Community donations were sent from Rauch, Rafaela, Felicia, and Plata in Argentina, from the 'Colonia Italiana di Bangkok', from Hankow (China), Sydney, Montevideo, and Asuncion. Contributions arrived from a women's organization in Demetrio, Rio de Janeiro; a group of businessmen in São Paolo sent 300,000L in July 1915. Five wealthy families in Buenos Aires offered the government the use of their villas in northern Italy for the duration of the war, as hospitals or convalescent homes. A 'Pro-Italia' committee of nine Italian traders and professionals even raised money for the war effort in Elisabethville-Katanga in the Belgian Congo. Fundraising efforts were often timed to mark special patriotic occasions. In 1917 the Società Italiana Vittorio Emanuele II° in Rafaela (Santa Fé, Argentina) raised over 5000L on the weekend of 20 September (the anniversary of the capture of Rome in 1870). Over this three days they held buffets and tea concerts, sales of medals, handicrafts and flowers, raffles, fairground games such as target shooting, a theatrical performance, and culminated with a grand masked ball; it is impossible to say how far patriotism genuinely entered into the merrymaking. Cheques were sometimes made out directly to ministers themselves: in June 1915 the Salerno-born owner of a (newly electrified!) hotel in Rio de Janeiro sent 500L directly to Salandra personally, with the request that it be used for soldiers and sailors from his hometown. Others sent cheques to the queen, to spend as she thought best.[28]

Individual donations might be as substantial as 100,000L (sent from a senator's widow for a new hospital) but many were extremely modest. In July 1915, an elderly and impoverished veteran of the 1860–1 wars of the Risorgimento, living in Le Havre, offered to donate a year of his military pension to the 'Propaganda List of the National Party', an entity which did not exist; he was persuaded to devolve this money to the Italian Red Cross, though the bureaucratic procedures which this entailed, including the act of sending money back and forth between France and Italy, consumed much of the value of his modest donation (200L). In the process his pension book, which he had sent in via the consulate, was mislaid and had still not been returned to him by May 1916; it is hard not to wonder whether he regretted his patriotic impulse. Donations were not always so spontaneous: in San Salvador, the Consul organized a formal meeting of the local community to announce the news of the war and then requested those present 'to make an effort and give the largest sums possible to the subscription which was immediately to be opened', which he then passed on through diplomatic channels to the foreign minister.

---

[28] ACS PCM GE 1915–1918, busta 72/19.1.72.

The question of how monies were to be spent could be vexed, revealing conflicts within the Italian 'colonies' and differing visions of the role of patriotic activism. Huge sums were raised in Buenos Aires in the early months of the war but by late 1915 serious tensions had developed between the Italian Red Cross and the local Comitato Italiano di Guerra. This body had been working to facilitate the repatriation of Italian soldiers from across Argentina, but its founder and president refused to cooperate with the Red Cross which he saw as a rival. He wanted local donations made to the Red Cross to be kept in Argentina and used to support the families of serving soldiers, supplementing the inadequate separation allowances. In his view, men would not answer the call if they could not be assured their families wouldn't suffer; consequently, the most helpful way the Committee could serve the war effort was to use the money within the colony itself to facilitate the maximum departure of troops, rather than sending the money back to Italy (to treat non-Argentine Italians, as the Red Cross intended).[29] The Buenos Aires committee was not alone; patriotic bodies in Lyon, London, Cairo, and New York focused much of their attention on supporting the indigent families of serving soldiers. In Tunisia, much of the Italian community lived in extreme poverty and around one-third of all soldiers' families were dependent on charitable support.[30] Caroline Douki, in her analysis of the Italian community of Glasgow, identifies two parallel forms of support: one a 'micro-solidarity' of Italians based on personal acquaintance, most often rooted in shared geographical origins and local identity, the other on the Italian community as a whole. The former, which embodied the *campanilismo* still present in many emigrant communities, was much more proactive in providing real financial solutions (including employment), while the latter, operating at the level of *italianità*, was more rhetorical than anything else, offering real but much more limited and occasional support than the micro-networks. Thus, while wartime community fund-raising and mutual support did serve to increase patriotic loyalty and a sense of connection to Italy, it did not necessarily replace or diminish older, narrower loyalties.[31]

These demonstrations of transnational patriotic enthusiasm were not always welcomed in Italy. In March 1916 Sicilian duke Giovanni Colonna di Cesarò—a nationalist, pro-irredentist politician who also happened to be the nephew of Sidney Sonnino—raised the question in parliament. He was concerned that fundraising in other countries, 'while it might demonstrate the sympathy which other countries feel for Italy', could also encourage 'false judgements on the condition and equipment of our army, and the energy with which the country meets all the needs of the moment'. Charity, he further noted, led swiftly to

---

[29] All details in ACS PCM GE 1915–1918, busta 72/19.1.72.
[30] Montalbano, 'The Italian Community of Tunisia', sections 24–6. See also Leila El Houssi, 'Gli "italiani" dell'altra sponda. La collettività italiana di Tunisia fino all'avvento del fascismo'. In *Circolazioni Mediterranee*, ed. Valerio Giannattasio (Naples: Guida, 2017).
[31] Douki, 'Les Italiens de Glasgow', 250–2.

contempt; the benefits incurred could not outweigh the damage to Italian status. For Colonna di Cesarò, international prestige was more important than any contribution which this community activity might bring. In replying, the under-secretary for foreign affairs agreed with his analysis but noted that where Italians overseas themselves acted, or when 'notable persons' intervened, motivated by 'racial affinity', they ought not to be prevented.[32] The relationship between the Italians overseas and the homeland was therefore complex, and it is perhaps no coincidence that it was precisely in this period that the Liberal model of emigrant colonialism began to decline.

5.5 Mobilizing the Italian Colonies for War

How far did the formal colonies support the war effort? One of the main reasons for acquiring a colonial empire was to strengthen the metropole, better preparing it to face war. The French and British colonial empires made considerable contributions to mobilization, providing vital manpower for the army and for labour, and supplying raw materials and economic resources.[33] When it comes to the Italian empire, however, it can be hard to avoid the conclusion that it was nothing but a drain on national resources; far from an asset in the face of total war, the colonies were a source of weakness and vulnerability, which had to be defended and fed. As John Gooch memorably writes, 'Before 1911 Italy had been militarily weak on one continent; after 1912 she was weak in two.'[34]

5.5.1 Civilian Manpower

As we have seen, colonial subjects were recruited into the Italian army where, even if they never fought on the national front against Austria, they were essential to meeting the overall requirements of the war effort. But the use of colonial manpower was not limited to the military realm: nearly 5,000 Libyan workers, of whom at least 800 were Jewish, were employed in Italy in war-related industries. The idea originated with a proposal from metalworking firm Ansaldo, which wrote to the government in May 1917 suggesting that Eritreans might be usefully

---

[32] Italia. *Atti del Parlamento Italiano*—Sessione 1913–1916, Vol. IX, I Sessione, https://storia. camera.it/lavori/regno-d-italia/leg-regno-XXIV/1916/16-marzo; 9315.

[33] The literature on the contribution of the British and French empires in the First World War is now vast. For a few recent examples, see Ashley Jackson, ed., *The British Empire and the First World War* (London: Routledge, 2016); Gerwarth and Manela, *Empires at War*; Andurain and Zytnicki, *Les empires dans la Grande Guerre*. On colonial soldiers, see the essays in Eric Storm and Ali Al Tuma, eds, *Colonial Soldiers in Europe, 1914–1945: 'Aliens in Uniform' in Wartime Societies* (London: Routledge, 2015).

[34] John Gooch, *Army, State and Society in Italy 1870–1915* (London: Macmillan, 1989).

brought to Sampierdarena, near Genoa, to work in their factories.[35] While this proposal was rejected, since it was impractical to ship men to Italy from East Africa, the proximity of Libya made it an ideal source of labour. Recruitment began swiftly. Posters advertising excellent working conditions proliferated: in return for a 7-hour day, men would receive 3–3.5L, of which 1L would be paid directly to their family at home. Paid over-time, accident insurance, accommodation 'appropriate for natives', and medical benefits would also be provided, the posters claimed, along with free travel from Libya.[36] Men were assured that each would work at his own established trade, a point apparently emphasized by Ameglio in his farewell speech to the newly hired men as they boarded their steamship to Italy. More than 80 per cent of the Libyan workers ended up in the industrial north-west, at industrial giants like Ansaldo and FIAT or at smaller firms working to state contracts. A smaller number ended up at establishments around Naples or Palermo. However, despite the promises made before departure, nearly all were assigned to work for which they had no prior experience or skills (the vast majority were farmers or village artisans), which soon caused problems for workers and employers alike. Within a few months of the 'experiment' beginning, many employers considered that the Arab workers were perhaps more trouble than they were worth, being unskilled and unfamiliar with the local environment; most ended up working as porters or operating forges. Only in Sicily, where they were set to collecting and cutting wood, was there a good match between the workers' skills and their employment. Within a few months the Central Committee for Industrial Mobilization decided that the experiment was a failure, and by the end of the year had ceased to ship over new cohorts of labour; however, those who had already been recruited and despatched were retained in Italy until the war's end, most not returning home until the beginning of 1919.[37]

The Central Committee for Industrial Mobilization had hoped that this scheme would not only support the war but build colonial spirit and a rapprochement between the colonized—who would witness the might and allure of Italian civilization—and the metropolitan population—who would perceive the loyalty and utility of their new Arab subjects.[38] It failed on both counts. The workers were not well-treated: housed in hastily erected wooden barracks, where many fell sick, they were placed under an even harsher military discipline than their fellow

---

[35] ACS Fondo Giovanni Ameglio, busta 22, fasc. 207.

[36] See BSMC, *La Guerra Italiana*, 6 ser n. 13, 27 January 1918, 207–8.

[37] Francesca Di Pasquale, 'Libici per la patria Italia. Esperienze di lavoro e di vita nelle lettere degli operai coloniali durante la prima guerra mondiale', *Zapruder. Storie in Movimento* 18 (2009): 50–6; http://storieinmovimento.org/wp-content/uploads/2017/07/Zap18_5-zoom4.pdf.

[38] See 'Primo esperimento d'impiego della manodopera libica in Italia', *Bollettino del Comitato centrale di mobilitazione industriale*, n. 8–9, febbraio–marzo 1918. Libyan governor Giovanni Ameglio was particularly optimistic on these counts: See ACS Fondo Giovanni Ameglio busta 19, fasc. 171, 175, 275; busta 20, fasc. 179–80; busta 21, fasc. 190–91; and others.

'militarized workers' in the same factories. Although it was not official policy, evidence suggests extensive and brutal use of corporal punishment; Jewish workers recounted that they had been whipped for refusing to work on the first day of Sukkot, a holy day, and claimed violence had been threatened against their rabbi.[39] Even the Prefect of Milan concurred that the Libyans had been unfairly treated, deploring the 'excessively severe disciplinary measures often consisting of corporal punishment'.[40] Unsurprisingly, a number of protests, strikes, and riots took place among the Arab workers through late 1917 and throughout 1918; by the time the men went home they were extremely keen to leave—and the local populations were generally not sorry either, this brief (token) effort at integration having little lasting legacy.[41] On the other hand, in light of the small population of the Italian colonies and the extent of the anti-colonial uprising during the war, it is remarkable that nearly 5,000 men voluntarily took up this work, and there is some evidence that it was not solely for economic or practical reasons.

In a sign of the globalization of the national war, another external source of manpower was also briefly considered: Chinese workers from London. These crew members of sunken ships were seeking employment within continental Europe since the trades unions in the UK made it hard for them to find jobs there. The Chinese embassy in London proposed sending 7,000–8,000 labourers to Italy, and the Sikelia sulphur mining company in Catania expressed an interest in hiring them. The ministry for arms and munitions was willing to consider the issue, but Sonnino was unenthusiastic; he suggested that the Sicilian mines ought to hire colonial labourers instead, and the proposal came to nothing.[42] Unlike the UK, Italy had no interest in using Chinese auxiliary workers in the war zone either, instead relying on women and adolescents (suggesting that in expanding the pool of manpower, it was easier to bend the rigid delineations of gender and age than of race and nationality). The only significant source of labour to be imported from outside the metropole would be the small group of Libyans brought across in 1917.

These men were not, however, the only colonial subjects to be found in Italy during the war. As Francesca Di Pasquale and Simone Bernini have revealed, a significant number of Libyans were interned within metropolitan Italy throughout this period in an effort to remove the 'rebellious' elements of the population, allowing for the pacification of the colony in their absence. Some were simply suspected of disloyalty or political activism; others had even been acquitted of any crime by colonial courts but were still seen with suspicion by military

---

[39] Di Pasquale, 'Libici', 56–61.   [40] Cited in Di Pasquale, 'Libici', 58.
[41] Federico Cresti, 'La prima emigrazione di lavoratori maghrebini in Italia', in *Conflitti, migrazioni e diritti dell'uomo: il Mezzogiorno laboratorio di un'identità mediterranea*, ed. Maurice Aymard and Fabrizio Barca (Soveria Mannelli: Rubbettino, 2002), 47–59.
[42] ACS PCM Guerra Europea 1915–1918, busta 75, 19.3.1, fasc. 29 Manodopera cinese.

authorities.[43] During the initial conquest of Tripolitania and Cyrenaica and during the era of the First World the Italian authorities deported not only individual leaders but large groups of hundreds of people at a time, making it hard to establish accurate figures. Around 4,000 people were most likely deported between 1911 and 1918, both to punish and to further intimidate the resident population. Men, women, and children of all ages and social backgrounds were deported, from beggars to wealthy landowners.[44] Debate continued as to where legally convicted prisoners ought to serve their terms: the many prisons in Libya itself were mainly used for short-term purposes, such as housing men condemned to death, or for imprisoning convicted people's family members. Increasing numbers were therefore deported to Italy, along with deserters from indigenous units, despite some discussion of sending them to Eritrea. A shift in terminology gradually occurred, with the Libyans held in Italy being termed 'hostages'—as indeed to some extent they were, being used in prisoner exchanges for Italians captured by the anti-colonial insurgency in North Africa. Around 2,400 deportees ended up in Sicily and Sardinia, as the authorities of metropole and colony fought a running battle over who was to take responsibility for these 'disruptive elements'. Ustica, Lipari, Favignana, Ponza, and other island penal colonies were used to house the deportees, as was the military prison at Gaeta and a few civilian prisons across the southern mainland. Treatment of the prisoners was extremely harsh, diseases proliferated, and corrupt contractors pocketed the provisions budget leading to starvation. Some penal colonies saw death rates of over a third: at Ustica, so many dead bodies were dumped in the sea that locals stopped buying fish. Not only accused individuals but their families were deported, often with tragic consequences; parents died of sickness leaving young children orphaned in prison.[45] Hugely damaging to Italy's chances of winning popular support in Libya, these measures were also unpopular with the local island populations, who regarded the transported Libyans as racial inferiors, carriers of disease, and traitors who, in a bizarre reversal, were now 'colonizing' their idyllic home spaces.[46] For political reasons, there was no effort to use these deportees as labour during the First World War (though apparently in 1911–12 there had been some forced labour on the mainland).[47] On the contrary, there was a concerted effort to distinguish the treatment of the internees from any suggestion of forced labour which might further damage perceptions of Italy back in the colonies.

[43] Simone Bernini, 'Documenti sulla repressione italiana in Libia agli inizi della colonizzazione (1911–1918)', in *Un nodo: immagini e documenti sulla repressione coloniale italiana in Libia*, ed. Nicola Labanca (Manduria: Lacaita, 2002).

[44] Di Pasquale, 'The "Other" at Home', 214–15.

[45] Aesha Mohammad Suliaman, 'The Impact of the Italian Occupation of Cyrenaica with Reference to Benghazi, 1911–1942' (Bangor, Bangor University, 2017), 125–31.

[46] Di Pasquale, 'The "Other" at Home', 222–5.

[47] Mohammed Suliaman, *The Impact of the Italian Occupation of Cyrenaica*, 128.

5.5.2 Colonial Economies

If colonial manpower made only a marginal contribution, there were other ways that colonies might help a war effort: France and Britain successfully drew on theirs for a variety of resources. By contrast the Italian colonies were not even fully self-sustaining. Tripolitania and Cyrenaica were wholly dependent on imports throughout the war. Having closed the internal markets and suspended all regular commerce with the interior, the governor was obliged to buy in cattle and other livestock as well as forage to feed them; significant quantities of wheat, barley, rice, beans, and pasta had to be imported from Tunisia and Egypt. Wood, coal, and (ironically, in view of later discoveries) oil were imported along with military essentials like explosives.[48] The Dodecanese were also dependent on food imports, above all of wheat—the governor estimated in December 1914 that the islands needed 800 tonnes each month. Historically the Dodecanese had relied almost wholly on imports from Anatolia, but after the Ottoman declaration of war this source of food disappeared. The government in Rome initially proposed only sending enough to feed the Italian troops in occupation, which would have led to starvation among the civilian population since neither Greece nor Egypt could meet the islanders' needs. Italy soon realized, therefore, that it had no choice but to take on the responsibility of feeding the people.[49] As Sonnino noted, it would scarcely advance Italy's political goals as a colonial power to leave the population hungry; already by October 1915, he noted, the people were 'starting to suffer'.[50] The war thus accelerated the transformation of the Dodecanese from an occupied area into a genuine colony.

In September 1917 a new committee was created to tackle these ongoing problems: under Treasury guidance, representatives of the ministries of foreign affairs, the colonies, war, finance, arms and munitions, agriculture, industry and commerce, along with the navy and ministry of transport, all worked together to plan the provisioning of the colonies within the framework of the national war effort. This committee set priorities and allocated a monthly budget, supervising overseas supply delegations, and identifying outside sources of food and supplies from allies or neighbours. Eritrea and Somalia were expected to be self-sufficient or supply a surplus, but it was clear that Libya and the Dodecanese would have to be supplied with nearly all their food and much more besides for the duration of the war. This was unarguably a significant drain on national resources which the country could ill-afford during the war.[51]

---

[48] ACS Fondo Giovanni Ameglio, busta 1, 3, 30 and others.
[49] ACS PCM GE 1915–1918, busta 37, fasc. Isole dell'Egeo.
[50] DDI, Quinta Serie, Vol. 4, Doc. 945, Sonnino to Salandra, 20 October 1915.
[51] ACS PCM GE 1915–1918 busta 75 19.3.1, fasc. 13, Approvigionamente delle colonie.

If Italy's colonies were not a great asset during the conflict, this did not mean that no efforts were made to extract resources from them. Eritrea, for example, was a producer of meat, hides, and other raw materials which were of great importance to the Italian war effort (and to the supply of meat in Libya).[52] However these exports created difficulties not only with Britain (which was seeking to restrict and control shipping in the Red Sea and Eastern Mediterranean) but above all within the colony itself, where wartime over-production, along with military loss of manpower, had a devastating effect internally and left the region severely impoverished afterwards. The production of canned meat for the army had been planned before the war, with dedicated modern processing plants and canning factories opening in 1913. But the colony's beef production was not as high as the Italian authorities had hoped, and by 1916 they began requisitioning cattle to meet demand. Cattle were also imported into Eritrea for processing from Yemen and Ethiopia. Ultimately, at a terrible cost to the Eritrean people (and to the government, which paid over the odds), the colony would produce more than 12 million cans of beef which helped to feed the troops at the front.[53] But for the most part, precious few supplies could be extracted from the colonies; like the contribution of Italians overseas, the empire was doomed to disappoint the optimistic expectations of nationalists.

[52] ACS PCM GE 1915–1918 busta 35, fasc. 17.2/Colonie.
[53] Massimo Zaccaria, 'Feeding the War: Canned Meat Production in the Horn of Africa and the Italian Front', in *The First World War from Tripoli to Addis Ababa (1911–1924)*, ed. Shiferaw Bekele et al. (Addis Abbeba: Centre français des études éthiopiennes, 2018); DOI: https://doi.org/10.4000/books.cfee.1619.

6

War in the Italian Colonies

If the main Italian war effort was against Austria, it had a secondary enemy—the Ottoman Empire—and a secondary theatre of its own: Libya. The general tendency of international historiography has been to see the whole Italian theatre as a sideshow, making Libya the sideshow's sideshow; but the conflict there had lasting repercussions for the whole region and, of course, was hugely important to all those who lived and died in it.[1] Counter-insurgency operations had begun there almost as soon as the official Italo-Turkish war had ended in 1912; by 1915 Italy was fighting against an indigenous enemy which boasted Austrian, German, and Turkish support. While the Tripolitanians and Cyrenaicans engaged in this conflict would have rejected the idea, the Ottoman Empire envisaged them as its agents, operating on its behalf in a form of proxy war. This chapter explores the war in North Africa and its influence on Italy's evolving war aims.

6.1 The War Against Turkey

The Italo-Turkish war left some Italian imperialists with a sense of unfinished business. After the Treaty of Ouchy in 1912, the Dodecanese remained officially under Turkish sovereignty while the Italian military occupation was only—in theory—temporary. Italy justified its failure to withdraw its troops from the islands with the excuse that Turkey was still supporting the ongoing resistance to Italian rule in Libya. In reality, Italy hoped to retain the islands and convert its temporary occupation into a permanent one (even as many in Greece hoped to see Italian withdrawal and a transfer of the islands into Greek sovereignty). In 1915 this aspiration was codified by Article 8 of the Treaty of London, which proclaimed that in the event of Entente victory 'Italy shall receive entire sovereignty over the Dodecanese Islands which she is at present occupying.'[2] The Ottoman Empire was equally dissatisfied with the situation and hoped to recover its position in Libya and the Aegean should any opportunity offer itself. In January 1914 Enver Pasha, formerly overall commander of Turkish forces against Italy in 1911–12, was appointed minister of war: he held an ongoing personal interest in

---

[1] For the importance of the African theatres to wider understandings of the war more generally, see Moyd, 'Centring a Sideshow: Local Experiences of the First World War in Africa'.
[2] *Agreement between France, Russia, Great Britain and Italy.*

The Italian Empire and the Great War. Vanda Wilcox, Oxford University Press (2021). © Vanda Wilcox.
DOI: 10.1093/oso/9780198822943.003.0006

the region and supported efforts to continue intervening there.[3] In autumn 1914, so active was the Sublime Porte in promoting pan-Islamic ideas across North Africa that Germany—still trying to keep the peace with Italy—grew seriously irritated with its ally. Vienna and Berlin repeatedly tried to reassure Salandra and Sonnino that Ottoman activity was directed only against the British, and not at Italian control over Tripolitania and Cyrenaica, but reports of Turkish troop build-up near the Suez Canal were particularly alarming to Italy which needed to secure its maritime route to East Africa. As a result, Ottoman sabre-rattling helped to accelerate the deterioration of the relationship between Italy and Germany in September and October 1914.[4]

During the preparatory discussions for the Treaty of London in the early months of 1915 it had been clear that Italy was intended to declare war on Turkey, but in fact this declaration was delayed. The ambassador in Constantinople, Camillo Garroni, wrote on 3 June 1915 that his situation had become 'really exceptional' owing to the state of war between the two alliances and requesting that he be withdrawn immediately, but Sonnino replied coolly on 8 June that he saw no reason to break off diplomatic relations or to declare war at this time.[5] Not until 22 June did he send his ambassador instructions about the imminent declaration of war on the Ottoman Empire, which was couched entirely in terms of Turkish violations of the Treaty of Ouchy, regarding both Turkish troops in Libya and the failure to release Italian prisoners of war after 1912.[6] For some 6 weeks, the ambassador held Sonnino's authority to present this declaration whenever ultimatums over the mistreatment of Italian nationals in the Ottoman Empire failed of their effect; fortified by this document, Garroni pushed for Italians— especially reservists—to be free to depart from Turkish ports and protected from reprisal attacks. Sonnino left the precise date of the declaration in the ambassador's hands, and not until 20 August would it be delivered to the Grand Vizier, with a state of war existing from 21 August 1915.[7] This timeline shows that the Italian government saw war with the Ottoman Empire as inevitable but was in no particular hurry to declare it, waiting until as many Italians had been evacuated as possible and a propitious moment presented itself. Italian diplomats reported closely on events in the Caucasus and at the Dardanelles; it is hard not to conclude that it suited Italy nicely to allow its Allies to do all the fighting against this new enemy.

---

[3] Rachel Simon, *Libya between Ottomanism and Nationalism: The Ottoman Involvement in Libya during the War with Italy (1911–1919)* (Berlin: K. Schwarz, 1987), 106.

[4] Ulrich Trumpener, *Germany and the Ottoman Empire, 1914–1918* (Princeton, NJ: Princeton University Press, 1968), 114–16.

[5] DDI, Quinta Serie, Vol. 4, Doc. 88, Garroni to Sonnino, Doc. 116, Sonnino to Garroni.

[6] DDI, Quinta Serie, Vol. 4, Doc. 241, Sonnino to Garroni.

[7] DDI, Quinta Serie, Vol. 4, Doc. 626, Garroni to Sonnino, 19 August; Doc. 659, Garroni to Sonnino, 25 August.

What form, then, did the Italian war against Turkey actually take? Italian forces had not participated in the Dardanelles and Gallipoli campaigns, nor would they serve in Mesopotamia. After 1917 there were some small contributions to the land war against the Ottomans, as we shall see, but for the most part this war was waged by the other Entente powers. Italy did, however, contribute some naval capacity to the war in the Mediterranean, taking responsibility for patrolling its own coasts and the coastal waters off Libya—but the rest of the Mediterranean was allocated to the British and French navies. Nearly all of the Italian navy spent the entire war locked up safely inside the Adriatic, lest the Austrians attack; the Austrians, meanwhile, were locked up safely inside the Adriatic lest the Italians attack, leading to a prolonged stalemate deeply irritating to the allies of both parties. Beyond this, even in areas where Italy had direct strategic interests, there were no major naval battles. In the eastern Mediterranean, once the Dardanelles campaign ended, the French and British presence was scaled back. Aside from a few very limited British amphibious raids on the southern Anatolian coasts in 1916, there was minimal activity in the area, and both the Aegean and the Levantine were relatively untroubled by major operations; the Entente navies limited themselves to supporting the land campaigns in Macedonia, Egypt, and Mesopotamia.[8] The war in this region—and indeed across the whole Mediterranean—became primarily a submarine war as both sides attacked one another's vital shipping lanes. Much of the Central Powers' naval war was carried out by Germany, which had far more submarines; until war was officially declared between Germany and Italy in August 1916 these sailed under an Austrian flag. On the Allied side, the French were initially in command of Mediterranean operations, but the British took on an ever more important role and in 1917 assumed overall control of the anti-submarine war.[9] Relations between the allies were often tense, since Italy was dependent on continuously shipping considerable quantities of material across the Mediterranean (to the mainland from its allies, to Libya from the mainland, to and from Eritrea via the Suez Canal), yet the bulk of the burden of defending this sea fell to the British and French. Italy protected its own shipping routes but was reluctant to contribute fully to the shared convoy routes into the western Mediterranean and out to the Atlantic. The naval war with Turkey was thus conducted at arms' length—Turkey relying on Germany, and Italy on its allies.

The major impact of the declaration of August 1915 was actually within the territories which Italy had seized from the Ottomans in 1911–12, rather than on Turkish soil. Italian forces in the Dodecanese began to openly lay the foundations for a colonial administration rather than a temporary occupation. The war itself offered opportunities for this colonizing endeavour, in which military governance

---

[8] Paul G. Halpern, *A Naval History of World War I* (Annapolis, MD: Naval Institute Press, 1994), 132–4.

[9] Halpern, *A Naval History of World War I*, 381–5.

would gradually be flanked by civil rule; although the Treaty of London was secret, it was very clear to many observers—including in Greece—that this was Italy's intention.[10] During the war, Italy extended its influence in education and language policy, as well as seeking to wrest control over the islands' Catholic institutions from France (which still held some rights to protect Catholicism in the Middle East), all in the name of prestige and security.[11] The islands would also be used as a strategic bridgehead for naval operations in the Eastern Mediterranean more broadly, though this role was most important from 1919 onwards. But if in the Dodecanese the war facilitated the consolidation of colonial rule, it was quite otherwise in Tripolitania and Cyrenaica.

6.2 The Libyan Theatre of War

Within the Libyan lands, war did not begin in 1915; arguably it had barely finished in 1912. Gabriele Bassi writes that the period 1912–14, 'cannot be defined as a time of peace, owing to the continual armed skirmishes between Libyans and the Italian army, [but it] certainly represented a period of greater military inactivity'.[12] An artilleryman who was deployed there in 1913—when no war was officially under way—wrote that 'it has been ten months of war, of long marches... of seeing nothing but weapons, the dead, the wounded, of hearing no words but combat, fire, hanging'.[13] Certainly by 1914 a serious and often brutal conflict was ongoing between Italy and a determined if loose coalition of anti-colonial forces.[14] Dierk Walter's typology of imperial violence observes that non-state or sub-state indigenous societies frequently engaged in long-term, mobile, limited warfare, with contained and pragmatic goals, against Western imperial forces—a description which accurately reflects the period 1912–15 in Libya. Ongoing insecurity 'made violence on the periphery an intrinsic social condition there'.[15] Italian governance was flawed from the start, based on a inadequate (though not uncommon) approach known as the *politica dei capi*. This 'policy of notables' meant governing indirectly through an existing ruling class which proclaimed loyalty to the Italian state in return for the protection of its position. Since the early years of the century, Italian diplomatic emissaries in Cyrenaica had therefore been cultivating links with the Sanusiyya—a Sufi religious order with a variety of political and

---

[10] DDI, Quinta Serie, Vol. 4, Doc. 643, De Bosdari to Sonnino, 23 August 1915.
[11] DDI, Quinta Serie, Vol. 8, Doc. 382. On the French religious protectorate in the Middle East, see Roberto Mazza, 'Churches at War: The Impact of the First World War on the Christian Institutions of Jerusalem, 1914–20', *Middle Eastern Studies*, 45, no. 2 (2009): 207–27, DOI: 10.1080/00263200802383248.
[12] Bassi, Labanca, and Sturani, *Libia*, 31.   [13] Cited in Labanca, *Posti al sole*, 297–8.
[14] Berhe, 'Neutralità in Italia e guerra in colonia'.
[15] Dierk Walter, *Colonial Violence: European Empires and the Use of Force*, trans. Peter Lewis (London: Hurst & Company, 2017), 46–51, 76.

economic roles.[16] In Tripolitania, tribal delegates and a coastal merchant elite seemed to offer viable intermediaries for Italian governance. They would make a formal 'act of submission' involving both written declarations and a ritual, sometimes incorporating the surrender of weapons; in return for ongoing loyalty to the regime they would then receive regular stipends from the colonial state. The problem was that the notables in question were only a subset of the indigenous ruling class, many of whom held radically opposed views, and were in any case often unrepresentative of the general attitudes of the population. The extent to which this pro-assimilation ruling class commanded the loyalties and confidence of the wider population was more limited than the Italians had initially realized. It was extremely difficult for the occupying authorities to identify 'suitable' tribal or village chiefs, given their limited knowledge and understanding of Tripolitanian society.[17] Intrinsically anti-representative, it is not surprising that this approach, combined with a poor understanding of the realities of indigenous society, had little success in winning loyalty or cooperation from the majority of Libyans.[18] Italy underestimated the intellectual, cultural, and political sophistication of its enemies as well as the extent of their existing loyalties, which could not easily be accommodated within the framework of national patriotism. Consequently, Italian hopes to exploit tensions between differing religious, ethnic, or tribal groups regularly foundered upon inadequate understandings of the society which they sought to control. Moreover, as one Tripoli notable observed, it was hard to find Italian protestations of its civilizing mission convincing when it in fact instituted a more repressive regime than its Ottoman predecessor.

At least treat us as the Turks did: then we were citizens of the Turkish Empire, we had our deputies in Constantinople, we had a kind of provincial council in Tripoli which met every year [...], we had elected municipal councils; ... we had freedom to meet, freedom of association; [...] we had a good number of newspapers which freely criticised the central government.[19]

If the Italian regime was seen as a step backwards from the Ottoman system, it was not clear how it ought to go about winning the loyalty of its new subjects. It is perhaps not surprising that under these circumstances, fluctuating levels of violent resistance continued; this met with brutal and violent efforts to suppress it (witness the mention of death, 'fire, hanging' in 1913, above), continued. This should not, however be taken as a sign of uniquely Italian incompetence as an

[16] Though dated, the famous ethnography by E. E. Evans-Pritchard, completed during the Second World War, is still worth reading: *The Sanusi of Cyrenaica* (Oxford: Oxford University Press, 1949).
[17] Ryan, *Religion as Resistance*, 36–56, 79–85.
[18] Simona Berhe, *Notabili libici e funzionari italiani: l'amministrazione coloniale in Tripolitania (1912–1919)* (Soveria Mannelli: Rubbettino, 2015).
[19] Cited in Del Boca, *Tripoli bel suol d'amore*, vol. 1, p. 89.

imperial power: Walter notes that in general, 'peace and war on the periphery were legally and practically barely distinguishable from each other', suggesting that the Italian empire was not as abnormal as sometimes suggested.[20]

Further undermining the Italian position was the fact that under the terms of the 1912 treaty, the Sultan retained his role as Caliph, or spiritual authority, over all Libyan Muslims. His 14 November 1914 declaration of jihad against Britain and France greatly alarmed the Italian authorities, who correctly feared that it would inspire resistance among the Muslim population of Libya as much as it did in neighbouring North African states. The Sublime Porte, meanwhile, repeatedly tried in this period to send Nuri Bey (1889–1949), younger brother of minister of war Enver Pasha, to Cyrenaica. Ostensibly his mission was to ensure the peaceful cooperation of the Sanusiyya with Italy, though why he would have wanted to do so was never made clear; Sonnino was—rightly—deeply sceptical about this explanation and refused to allow him passage across Italian territory.[21] It soon emerged that the Ottomans were determined to send Nuri with or without Italian approval; he would eventually spend most of the war in one part of the colony or another, advising the leaders of the anti-Italian insurrection. In 1915–16 he spent considerable time with the Sanusiyya, encouraging their belligerence against both Italian and British enemies; once this conflict had been settled he moved into Tripolitania, and eventually was appointed to lead the Ottoman 'Africa Groups Command', with overall responsibility for the entire theatre.

6.2.1 Anti-colonial Resistance

If the war in Libya is to be understood as part of the First World War, who then were its main protagonists? The forces which faced Italy in Libya were diverse in motivation and background, with Libyan notables of many ethnic and religious origins involved in a shifting and unstable set of allegiances. Within Cyrenaica, although some tribes and villages did formally submit to Italy, the leading regional force was undoubtedly the Sanusiyya: from their base in Jaghbub, they proved a continual thorn in the side of the fledgling colonial administration in eastern Libya. From 1912, their leader Ahmad al-Sharif had become the de facto leader of anti-Italian resistance; in 1916 he was replaced by his younger cousin, and grandson of the order's founder, Idris al-Sanusi, who would steer the brotherhood through the tricky shoals of war and diplomacy with Britain and Italy alike. He would eventually be crowned king of all Libya in 1951, with British support. The Sanusiyya's wartime resistance to Italy was also part of the brotherhood's much broader anti-colonial struggle across French-ruled North and West Africa: in

---

[20] Walter, *Colonial Violence*, 80.
[21] ACS PCM GE 1915–1918, busta 37, fasc. 17.2 Turchia, November–December 1914.

Algeria and northern Niger, Sanusi adherents (and others) fought against France in 1916–17, inspired by a blend of religious and political motivations.[22] In Tripolitania and Fezzan, the situation was more complex, with a number of emergent political leaders, from various tribes, seeking both to end Italian rule and establish dominance over local rivals. These men operated within a range of political contexts from their own village, family, or tribal power bases through to regional and international networks.

Anti-Italian resistance was not narrowly confined to the borders of Libya. Outside the Ottoman provinces, the Italian invasion of 1911 had provoked a considerable movement of solidarity among Algerian and Tunisian Muslims. For instance, Tuareg leader Kaocen ben Mohammed, who would lead a major rebellion against France in 1916–17 in northern Niger, joined the resistance against Italy in 1911–12 even though his home lay outside Libyan borders.[23] The continuing presence of the Ottoman Empire in North Africa was considered by many as an important bulwark against French power as well as a vital connection between French-ruled Maghrib and the rest of the Muslim world. The Arab media rallied behind the Ottomans, boycotts against Italian businesses were organized and fundraising campaigns were launched to support the wounded. In essence, the invasion brought into being a form of pan-Maghribism which accepted the necessity of Ottoman leadership within the anti-colonial movement, at least in the short term.[24] This had important implications for the First World War in North Africa: although the anti-Italian insurgency was a diverse and complex set of movements, a pre-existing narrative which located Maghribi resistance within a pan-Ottoman framework allowed native leaders to accept or even welcome Turkish leadership, funding, and supplies. On the eve of the First World War many indigenous North African activists were actively engaged in building ties with the Ottoman Empire, which they perceived as a key ally in the anti-colonial struggles against France and Italy.

The war against Italy in Libya also incorporated cross-border Maghribi elements which did not necessarily fit with an Ottomanist framework. Many Tunisian volunteers crossed into Tripolitania in 1911–12, while some Tripolitanians who had fled Italian repression during or after the war joined the 1915 uprising against France in southern Tunisia.[25] Anti-colonial groups in Algeria also provided funding and volunteers to the fight against Italy. The rise of pan-Arabism and pan-Islamism offered alternative conceptual models which intersected with tribal and local loyalties such that even before the end of Ottoman rule, Libyan notables had begun to develop and articulate their own models for local self-governance.[26]

[22] Jonathan Krause, 'Islam and Anti-Colonial Rebellions in North and West Africa, 1914–1918', *The Historical Journal* (2020): 1–22, DOI: https://doi.org/10.1017/S0018246X20000357.
[23] Krause, 'Islam and Anti-Colonial Rebellions', 11.   [24] Ghazal, 'Counter-Currents', 82.
[25] Ghazal, 'Counter-Currents', 83.   [26] Berhe, *Notabili libici e funzionari italiani*.

One such aspiring state builder, and one of the most important anti-colonial leaders in Tripolitania, was Sulayman al-Baruni, formerly a member of the Ottoman parliament and enthusiastic supporter of the Committee of Union and Progress (though he had also had several major clashes with the Turkish authorities). Forced to leave Tripolitania after the Italo-Turkish War—a conflict in which he had earned many local enmities for apparently favouring Berber interests over Arabs—in 1914 the Ottoman Empire sent him back into Tripolitania, with a mandate to agitate for insurrection. A highly learned and complex man, al-Baruni had close contacts not only with Constantinople but also in Tunisia, and continued to receive support from Tunis throughout his operations. As an Ibadi—a member of minority sect largely composed of Berbers—he had important links to the Mzab region in Algeria, which was becoming a centre of anti-colonial activism in the early twentieth century.[27] Contrary to the popular image in Italy at the time of isolated, primitive tribespeople, anti-colonial activists like al-Baruni were embedded into multiple transnational networks along ethnic, political, and religious lines; they were also highly mobile. In 1912 al-Baruni proclaimed himself head of his own autonomous province in Jabal Nafusa, close to the Tunisian border, though he was still willing to cooperate with the Ottomans when it suited him (and indeed in 1916 he was delegated the Caliph's authority in Western Tripolitania).[28] During the war of 1911–12 al-Baruni earned the implacable hatred of Mohamed Fekini, leader of the Rojeban tribe and one-time Italian prefect, who later became one of Italy's most persistent opponents right through until 1930. Al-Baruni's ability to profoundly alienate such potential allies was perhaps one of the major obstacles to his ambitions.[29]

During the First World War al-Baruni's major rival in western Libya was Ramadan al-Suwayhili, from an influential Misrata family, who had fought in the 1911–12 war and then led the successful insurrection at Qasr Bu-Hadi in 1915. Consistently described as a brigand and a traitor in Italian sources, his power base in the Misrata region in fact made him a credible political force in Tripolitania. Like al-Baruni he had his own ambitions which did not always chime with the Sublime Porte's plans, but he was happy to work closely with Nuri Bey for the duration of the war and accepted the title of 'Governor of Misrata' from him. Both men extended tax collecting and administrative powers throughout their respective regions of Tripolitania, though they were regularly contested by other local notables.[30] And again like his rival al-Baruni, Ramadan al-Suwayhili had wider transnational links beyond Ottoman power networks, as he received advice and support from the young Egyptian pan-Arabist activist Abdul Rahman Hassan

---

[27] Ghazal, 'Counter-Currents', 84–5.   [28] ACS PCM GE 1915–1918, busta 19.3.1.
[29] Fekini's biographer appears to have absorbed his subject's prejudices, describing al-Baruni as 'shameless' and 'unscrupulous'. Del Boca, *Mohamed Fekini and the Fight to Free Libya*, 34–8.
[30] Anderson, 'The Tripoli Republic', 47–8.

Azzam, who had earlier collaborated with Nuri Bey advising the Sanusiyya in Cyrenaica.[31] Azzam, who later was an important politician and diplomat in his own country as well as the inaugural Secretary-General of the Arab League, spent several years supporting al-Suwayhili and encouraging unity between the Tripolitanian tribes.

Another contender for power in Tripolitania, particularly the Zuwara region, was Muhammed Suf (or Sof) al-Mahmudi, despatched from Constantinople in 1914 to act as governor general on behalf of the Sultan. Suf too had connections across the border into French-ruled territories and was generally on good terms with al-Baruni. Nonetheless, he retained his own freedom of action and fought ambitiously as much for his own position as for any discernably Ottoman cause. All three of these men, along with the Rojeban resistance fighter Fekini, were declared enemies of the Italian state and considerable bounties placed upon their heads (10,000 or 20,000L each).[32] Italian intelligence also endeavoured to track the Bedouin Sef en Nasser family and local leaders like sultan Ben Sciaben who was active around Zuwara. Tribal leaders took advantage of the power vacuum created by the end of Ottoman rule to jostle for advantage, to fight one another, and to settle old scores—but were equally able to unite when it suited them, to connect into transnational networks for financial and military support, and to use outsiders as much as they were themselves being used. The Ottomans hoped that these indigenous leaders were serving as their agents. But from May 1915 onwards, all across Tripolitania, this successful group of mainly young, anti-colonial indigenous leaders began to establish—and contest among one another—forms of local self-government, functionally free of either Italian or Ottoman control.

6.2.2 The Central Powers in Libya

As the war went on it became increasingly clear that the Ottoman Empire stood no chance of recovering the provinces lost in 1912, since even a resounding Italian defeat would only have led to some form of Libyan autonomous state(s). However, at the start of the war, the Ottoman Empire—or at least some of its ruling class—did not by any means accept that the loss of Libya was definitive. And while it was the Arab and Berber population on the ground who would do most of the actual fighting against Italy, there was no shortage of external intervention in Libyan affairs. From autumn 1914, representatives of the Central Powers were highly active within the colony. Otto Mann, the German consul in Tripoli, met so regularly with the Sultan's spiritual representatives there—under Mehmed V's

---

[31] Dirk Vandewalle, *A History of Modern Libya* (Cambridge: Cambridge University Press, 2006).
[32] Del Boca, *Mohamed Fekini and the Fight to Free Libya*, 55–7.

continued authority as Caliph—that di Sangiuliano ordered him to leave. He moved to Italy, where he established a clandestine arms-smuggling network to support the insurgency. Meanwhile in Cyrenaica rumours circulated about the presence of several German officers including Baron von Bentheim, who had served as adjutant to Enver Pasha from 1911 to 1914. German staff had of course supported Ottoman forces during the Italo-Turkish war itself; well before the formal breaking of the Triple Alliance it appeared that Germany was actively supporting its Turkish ally's efforts to undermine Italian control of Libya.[33] The wealthy orientalist Max von Oppenheim, who hoped to incite Islamic rebellions against the Entente powers, had spent many years in Cairo and had connections to the Sanusiyya as well as to the Khedive. German activity in the Italian colony was likely more a source of alarm than of real damage to the Italian cause, but the attention which successive colonial governors paid to the issue shows the nature of their fears.

In August 1915 Italy had denounced the Ottomans' supposed violations of the Treaty of Ouchy; once the war began, the Sultan formally declared that the Treaty was null and void and hence Turkey intended to resume its authority in Tripolitania and Cyrenaica. It did so by sending senior officers—like Nuri Bey— and their staffs to provide leadership to the insurgency, and above all by sending funding and supplies. In this cause, Turkey required significant assistance from its allies. The chief task of the German submarine fleet in the Mediterranean was making war on Allied shipping routes there, but this was 'continually threatened' by the requirement to transport materials to the Sanusiyya and other anti-Italian forces in North Africa, a project which consumed considerable resources.[34] Turkey continued to press for transport to be made available to send men, materiel, food, and money into Libya. Early in 1916 no fewer than three German submarines were entirely deployed for several weeks purely in supplying the Sanusiyya, while others were dispatched to Tripolitania. In 1916 and 1917 a submarine landed at Misrata fortnightly, stocked with cash, rifles, and even small artillery pieces. Throughout the conflict, pressure on the naval high command was sustained by the German Foreign Office and army, which both considered that dedicating time and resources to undermining Italian control of Libya in this way was an effective means to pursue the war.[35]

Even in the later stages of the war, the Ottoman Empire sought to uphold its commitment to the Tripolitanian insurrection. In April 1918, a German submarine sailed from Turkey carrying Prince Osman Fuad to join the insurrection. This young grandson of Sultan Murad V had seen active service as a teenage volunteer

[33] ACS Archivio Salandra, busta 2, fasc. 14.
[34] Erwin Sieche, 'La guerra sottomarina tedesca nel Mediterraneo 1915–1918', in *La guerra navale 1914–1918: un contributo internazionale alle operazioni in Mediterraneo*, ed. Achille Rastelli, Alessandro Massignani, and Andrea Curami (Novale, Vicenza: G. Rossato, 2002), 63.
[35] Halpern, *A Naval History of World War I*, 388–9.

in Italo-Turkish War and then studied at the German military academy in Potsdam. He fought at Gallipoli before being appointed to the suite of Nuri Bey. It was hoped that his rank and dynastic status would inspire the enthusiasm of the local tribes. In July 1918, the Ottomans recalled Nuri to take command of the Army of Islam in the Caucasus, and Osman Fuad assumed command of the Turkish forces in Libya, from Ramadan al-Suwayhili's base in Misrata. His military inexperience and youth were to be offset by the competence of his chief of staff, a confidant of Enver Pasha; his main role was to be a figurehead.[36] But by this stage in the war, the enthusiasm of Tripolitanian notables for Ottoman leadership had waned almost entirely and certainly young Osman Fuad was in no position to revive it. Tripolitania had been fighting effectively against Italy for more than three full years by now and pan-Ottomanism was on the decline.

6.2.3 The Anti-Italian Revolt in Tripolitania

The revolt had begun at the end of November 1914, just a fortnight after Sultan Mehmed V's declaration of jihad, in the interior Fezzan region. An isolated desert nicknamed by Italians 'the Siberia of the sun', home to nomadic and semi-nomadic peoples such as the Tuareg and Toubou, the Fezzan was only barely under Italian control. Its inhabitants were deeply resentful of the imposition of conscription within the region by Colonel Antonio Miani (in direct violation of Italian promises and indeed of practice in other parts of the colonies).[37] Miani's failure to respect the policies decided centrally in Rome was emblematic of the problems of Italian colonial governance: the state struggled to effectively impose its authority in the periphery, where colonial administrators, whether military or civilian, were prone to taking matters into their own hands, sometimes with disastrous results. The Fezzanese, already bitterly hostile to Italian authority, were also encouraged by the Sanusiyya and the declaration of jihad to target their anger against the Italian colonial regime, with stunning effect. Where Fezzan led, Tripolitania soon followed. As Angelo Del Boca writes, 'The outbreak of World War One inflicted the final and decisive blow upon the fragile structures of the Italian presence in Tripolitania.'[38] In the view of Giulio Cesare Tassoni, the governor of Tripolitania, 'spirits generally averse to us for reasons of natural religious and racial hostility are inflamed by the historic moment which Islam is undergoing', while rumours about the war in Europe stoked anti-Italianism more

---

[36] Mustafa Serdar Palabıyık, 'Contextualising the Ottoman Dynasty: Sultan Mehmed V Reşad and the Ottoman Princes in the Great War', in *Monarchies and the Great War*, ed. Matthew Glencross and Judith Rowbotham (Basingstoke: Palgrave Macmillan, 2018). After the Second World War, he became head of Ottoman imperial family in exile, and died in poverty in France in 1973.
[37] Angelo Del Boca, *La disfatta di Gasr bu Hàdi* (Milan: Mondadori, 2014), 74–5.
[38] Del Boca, *Mohamed Fekini and the Fight to Free Libya*, 46.

generally.[39] Soon Italian forces were withdrawing from all their remote fortresses. As the uprising spread into the Jabal region in the west of Tripolitania, home to many Berbers, Italian troops began to fall back towards the coast, abandoning the Fezzan completely and retreating towards Misrata in the gulf of Sirte (see Map 4). As they withdrew, they were harassed by steadily increasing numbers of armed tribesmen.

On 29 April 1915—just days after the signing of the Treaty of London—the minister for the colonies Ferdinando Martini, along with Tassoni, ordered Miani to clear the region of Qasr Bu-Hadi, near Sirte, where numerous camps of anti-Italian 'rebels' had gathered. Setting out with a mixture of metropolitan and colonial troops along with irregular 'bands' of local forces under the command of local notable Ramadan al-Suwayhili, Miani suffered an unexpected and devastating defeat when many of these forcibly conscripted irregulars turned on him and his men. Miani's propensity for violating the established system of colonial recruitment proved deadly: several hundred Italians were killed along with similar numbers of loyal Eritrean *ascari* soldiers. Al-Suwayhili became one of the most committed enemies of the occupation from this moment forwards. Much of the blame must rest with the senior commanders who planned and ordered this operation, which was hampered from the start by inadequate equipment and woefully poor intelligence. Indigenous forces also seized Miani's baggage train, comprising thousands of rifles and millions of rounds of ammunition. Not only was the defeat a terrible humiliation and a devastating blow to Italian morale, but it left Italy's enemies materially much better equipped to continue their fight.[40]

The consequences of this defeat—which raised uncomfortable echoes of the supposed 'betrayal' at Sciara Sciatt in October 1911—were very serious. The surviving Italian forces took a terrible and brutal revenge on the local population and any whom they suspected of complicity in the attack. This did not, however, prevent the occupation from losing its grip on much of Tripolitania. First the region's second city—the port of Misrata—had to be hastily abandoned, the small Italian population fleeing in a disorderly fashion towards Tripoli (and in many cases leaving the colony altogether). Misrata would become a stronghold of the insurgency, Ramadan al-Suwayhili's headquarters, and the landing point for Turkish and German supplies for the remainder of the war. Misrata was also home to a powerful radio, which comfortably sent and received communications from Constantinople. Radio was brought to Libya as an Italian-invented technology, symbol of the superiority of imperial conquerors; its new purpose as a tool of anti-colonial resistance infuriated the Italian occupiers. This was not all: from May 1915 it was no longer possible to guarantee the security of garrisons in the interior. Tarhuna was soon besieged; Beni Walid, a significant oasis town

---

[39] ACS Archivio Salandra, busta 2, f. 14, Tassoni to Martini, 18 February 1915.
[40] Del Boca, *La disfatta di Gasr bu Hàdi*.

equidistant from Tripoli and Misrata, would endure two months' siege before it, too, fell to anti-colonial forces.

On 8 May 1915 Cadorna proposed abandoning the entire Tripolitanian interior. On the eve of war, he wrote, the 'national army' must be devoted to the national war effort, 'sacrificing all secondary theatres', such that 'all that could be done in Tripolitania was to withdraw the armed occupation to the coast and return the excess forces to Italy'.[41] But bolstered by Tassoni's declared conviction that he could hold onto the region, the government initially rejected this proposal. In the event, Cadorna was to be entirely vindicated. By mid-June, it was decided in Tripoli and Rome to withdraw all the garrisons of the Jebel region, before in July the Gefara plain and the important oasis of Zanzur were also abandoned. A number of Italian soldiers surrendered to the resistance and were taken prisoner, creating a complex legal and political problem (since Italy had no desire to accord *ius in bello* to its 'internal' enemy, but was thus unable to insist upon its protection for its own men).[42] Tassoni's governorship was doomed.

From the Italian perspective, so devastating was the situation in the western portion of the colony that the government decided to withdraw its remote outposts in Cyrenaica as well, lest the insurgency spread there. This was probably a sensible choice which saved lives and resources. Cyrenaican governor General Giovanni Ameglio withdrew his men progressively from the interior in an orderly fashion, avoiding the humiliating defeats suffered by his Tripolitanian counterpart, and disarming the tribes in areas he controlled to prevent them from joining the uprising. His reward was to be made governor of both regions, a position he would hold until August 1918. Knowing that no further aid could be summoned from the metropole, one of his first actions in charge of Tripolitania, starting on 16 July, was to withdraw the remaining garrisons at Misrata Marina and Zuwara.[43] His telegrams back to Rome report the steadily growing numbers of enemy forces he faced through the summer months. By August, the occupation only controlled a narrow coastal strip of land around Tripoli and Khoms—ironically, the location of Italy's very first landings in October 1911. In Cyrenaica, tiny islands of Italian control remained around Benghazi, Derna, and Torbruk. Communications between the two halves of the colony were by radio, telegram, and ship only.

Italian attempts to push back into the interior were at best half-hearted for much of the war. A policy of stoking rivalries between Arabs and Berbers, and between different tribal groups, cost many indigenous lives but bore relatively little fruit politically. Inadequate intelligence made it hard for Ameglio's forces to even identify their enemies adequately: while large-scale monitoring programmes

---

[41] ACS Archivio Salandra, busta 2, f. 15.
[42] This was a typical problem when distinguishing between 'external' and 'internal' forms of colonial war. Walter, *Colonial Violence*, 119.
[43] ACS Fondo Giovanni Ameglio, busta 28, fasc. 236.

were instituted, requiring indigenous people to show travel passes issued by Italian authorities whenever challenged, it proved almost impossible to police the loyalty of subjects who were so little understood. One idea briefly raised by General Giuseppe Moccagatta in Benghazi was to simply declare anyone found on the wrong side of a demarcation line as a rebel; this was not only totally impractical but showed how far crisis management risked fundamentally undermining long-term efforts to establish consensual governance.[44] So the interior was left in the hands of the native peoples and, even on the coast, Italian territory was strictly limited. A rare exception to the policy of inaction came in May 1916, when the Tripolitanian port of Zuwara was reoccupied. The importance of this was chiefly as a sign that Italy was still committed to retaining the region; in strategic terms it helped Italy to disperse a few local bands of resisters but did little to change the overall situation in the colony to reopen land communications along the coast to Tripoli were made in January under General Giulio Latini and again in April by General Giuseppe Cassinis but in both cases the Italians met stiff resistance and were forced to retreat. Very little further progress in the region was made.[45]

To the irritation of successive governments in Rome, Ameglio argued that he had insufficient manpower to do any more. From the 100,000 men present in Tripolitania and Cyrenaica at the outbreak of the war numbers fell to 80,000 a year later, and by the time of Caporetto were closer to 60,000.[46] A significant share of the wartime garrisoning of Tripolitania and Cyrenaica was undertaken by East African *ascari* troops. If the Italian government was unwilling to send indigenous African soldiers to fight in Europe—as explored in Chapter 4—it was certainly keen to make use of them on African soil. Soon, however, this proved to be a source of intra-colonial tensions. In Asmara and Mogadishu, the governors of Eritrea and Somalia were far more concerned about the possibility that neighbouring Ethiopia might take advantage of Italian distraction to launch an attack than they were about far-off Libya. Communications between the colonial governors reveal a striking lack of intra-colonial solidarity, and the Minister for the Colonies frequently had to intervene to overrule their decisions in the name of the wider national and imperial interest. In the event, while there were some German and Turkish efforts to incite trouble in Ethiopia, nothing came of it, and the two East African colonies continued to be ordered to send the majority of their forces to Libya. By contrast the number of white troops deployed there fell steadily—though it is noteworthy that after Caporetto some men suspected of defeatism or desertion were sent there. This decision combined a punitive element with the desire to remove potentially untrustworthy troops from the national front.[47]

---

[44] ACS Fondo Giovanni Ameglio, busta. 30, fasc. 289.
[45] Del Boca, *Mohamed Fekini and the Fight to Free Libya*, 61–4.
[46] ACS PCM GE 1915–1918, busta 75 19.3.1, fasc. 18.
[47] Berhe, 'Il fronte meridionale della Grande guerra', 808.

Short of troops, Ameglio turned to other methods to conduct the war in Tripolitania. In summer 1917, he employed the air force to destroy crops and oases in the interior, in the hope of starving the resistance into submission.[48] Much of his time and attention in late 1917 was devoted to the problem of the radio in Misrata, which was staffed by Ottoman operators and provided the vital lifeline between the insurgents and Constantinople, coordinating the arrival of German and Turkish submarines. Italian prisoners captured by Ramadan al-Suwayhili in 1915 were housed very close to the radiotelegraph station, and Ameglio repeatedly refused to make any effort to bomb it least they be inadvertently killed.[49] The topic was just one of many disagreements between the governor and the minister of colonies in Rome; Colosimo felt it was essential that by the time the war ended, Italy should be able to present itself at the peace conference with this important port in its hands. In the event, it was not until September 1918, on the direct orders of the prime minister, that a concerted bombardment of Misrata and the radio station were undertaken by both Italian aircraft and British seaplanes operating out of Malta; only at this late stage in the war was the resistance's submarine lifeline finally cut off.

6.2.4 War in Cyrenaica

The relative quiescence of Cyrenaica in 1914–15—from the Italian perspective—was due not to any greater acceptance of Italian rule than in Tripolitania, but rather to the priorities of the Sanusiyya under the leadership of Ahmad al-Sharif, who was generally cautious. However at least one section of the brotherhood hoped to exploit British preoccupation with the war against Turkey to expand into Egyptian territory. Jaghbub, the long-term headquarters of the Sanusi network, lay in the disputed borderlands between Libya and Egypt. In Jason Pack's words, 'In [...] this un-demarcated zone many actors were competing to build institutional and commercial frameworks to exercise sovereign functions over the local population of nomadic herdsmen and oasis date farmers.'[50] The Sanusiyya were one of the various competing groups in the area. Before the Italo-Turkish War, the inexactitude of this desert boundary had been relatively unimportant, as the Ottoman Empire officially held suzerainty on either side of the border. However, in November 1911, in response to Mark Sykes' question in the House of Commons, Sir Edward Grey announced that Britain considered Jaghbub to be Egyptian.[51] This was followed by the seizure of the coastal settlement of Sollum

[48] Del Boca, *Mohamed Fekini and the Fight to Free Libya*, 65.
[49] ACS PCM GE 1915–1918 busta 75 19.3.1, fasc. Colonie, s.f. 4, Atti riservati riguardanti la Libia, 1918.
[50] Pack, 'The Antecedents and Implications of the So-Called Anglo-Sanussi War', 46.
[51] *The Times*, 7 November 1911.

and a charm offensive to win over the Sanusiyya. Friendly contacts were established between the Sanusi leadership and the Anglo-Egyptian authorities, who even hosted the order's heir, Idris, on his return from Mecca in March 1915.[52] Notably, the British authorities in Cairo prioritized positive relations with the Sanusiyya over the instructions they received from London to support Italy, even allowing weapons and supplies to cross the border into 'rebel' Cyrenaica for use against the Italians; after Italy's entry to the Entente the differing positions of London and Cairo became increasingly fraught.[53]

These friendly Anglo-Sanusi relations did not at all suit the Sublime Porte, which was hoping to reclaim Egypt with the assistance of indigenous allies from both Egypt itself and Cyrenaica (and through coordinating attacks from Sinai and Sudan). The Ottoman government initially sent Sulayman al-Baruni to sound out the Sanusiyya for a possible attack on British interests in Egypt, but as a Berber and Ibadi he shared neither ethnic nor confessional common ground with the brotherhood, who viewed him with considerable suspicion. This was the context for Nuri Bey's mission, accompanied by experienced staff officer, Ja'far al-'Askari, from 1915. Thereafter, Sanusi relationships with Italy and Britain degenerated rapidly, in both cases leading to war. Arguably this was a sign that Ahmad al-Sharif was losing his grip on the brotherhood and that more volatile, pro-Turkish elements within the order were able to manipulate the Sanusiyya into hostilities through financial means.

The Sanusiyya launched their struggle against the British in November 1915, following the torpedoing of the HMS *Tara* by a German U-boat on 5 November. The *Tara*, newly arrived from the UK, lost twelve men; ninety-two survivors were captured and sailed to Bardia, from where they were taken into the interior as Sanusi prisoners. This was to mark the beginning of some eighteen months of war in Egypt's Western Desert. T. E. Lawrence wrote home from Cairo the following month: 'Perfect peace here, except in the West, where there is a little war going on.'[54] Sanusi forces next attacked Sollum (see Map 4), then held by Anglo-Egyptian and Sudanese units, on 20 November and quickly seized the town; a massive British counter-attack soon dislodged them. A Western Frontier Force was created under the command of the Egyptian Expeditionary Force (EEF), bringing British, Indian, New Zealand, and South African troops together to defend the western borders of Egypt. The Anglo-Sanusi war which followed was a limited war, with neither side seeking a decisive battle; Anglo-Egyptian forces progressively cleared the Sanusiyya from Egyptian territory but had no desire to eliminate the

[52] Russell H. McGuirk, *The Sanusi's Little War: The Amazing Story of a Forgotten Conflict in the Western Desert, 1915–1917* (London: Arabian Publ., 2007), 86.
[53] Pack, 'The Antecedents and Implications of the So-Called Anglo-Sanussi War', 49–50.
[54] McGuirk, *The Sanusi's Little War*, v.

brotherhood, simply to steer it away from its pro-Turkish (and pro-German) position—and confine its activities, where possible, to Italian-claimed lands.

Was it Turkish and German pressure which led the Sanusiyya to abandon their friendly relationship with Britain? Certainly, contemporary British analyses concluded as much; the economic pressure of the Anglo-Italian blockade, which caused terrible food shortages and even famine in the Cyrenaican interior, may also have contributed. By contrast John Slight has argued that Sanusi decision-making should be interpreted in context of the brotherhood's position within the wider Muslim world. They were 'a reformist Sufi order that had been involved in a decades-long militant reaction to European imperialism, couched in traditional religious terms of jihad' and they saw themselves as part of a wider revivalist spiritual movement, linked to Arabia despite their African focus.[55] The Sanusi wars against France and Italy were also understood as specifically religious conflicts: jihad and anti-colonialism were inextricably linked. In 1916–17 the brotherhood launched a decisive anti-French crusade in the southern Sahara around the Aïr mountain range and the city of Agades (now in Niger), which was a traditional Tuareg–Berber stronghold and quite a long way from the historic area of Sanusi control. By contrast, Pack contends that the Sanusi war on British-held Egypt was very much a part of the wider Anglo-Ottoman war. He writes that the 'sanctity and administrative structures of the Sanusiyya were temporarily hijacked by Ottoman agents', placing the conflict within the framework of the First World War.[56] For Jean-Louis Triaud, the First World War transformed the Sanusiyya, prompting their evolution from a largely apolitical religious and commercial network into an anti-imperialist, jihadi group implacably opposed to the French and Italians and with pro-German links. Ironically, this was precisely the image which had previously quite falsely circulated in Francophone circles.[57] But as Eileen Ryan shows, the wartime policies and transformation of the order, including the change in leadership from Ahmad al-Sharif to Idris al-Sanusi, reflected an ongoing response to internal debates as well as outside pressures.[58]

In February 1916 the minister of the colonies urged Sonnino and Salandra to push France and Britain to comprehensively implement the Second Chantilly Conference agreements on inter-Allied cooperation (made in December 1915) to the colonial theatre. Relations with Britain along the border with Cyrenaica were particularly thorny: the view in Benghazi was that Britain was actively

[55] John Slight, 'British Understandings of the Sanussiyya Sufi Order's Jihad against Egypt, 1915–17', *The Round Table* 103, no. 2 (2014): 238.
[56] Pack, 'The Antecedents and Implications of the So-Called Anglo-Sanussi War', 43.
[57] Marco Lenci, review of *Review of La légende noire de la Sanusiyya. Une confrèrie musulmane saharienne sous le regard francais (1840–1930), 2 tomi*, by Jean-Louis Triaud, *Africa: Rivista trimestrale di studi e documentazione dell'istituto italiano per l'Africa e l'Oriente* 51, no. 4 (1996): 607–9.
[58] Ryan, *Religion as Resistance*, 90–103.

undermining Italian interests in the region. In particular, Martini wrote, 'the Sanusi movement cannot be considered a local or distinct episode which only affects us, but one which is connected to the general war effort owing to the part which our enemies have and continue to play in it.'[59] The implications of this analysis were two-fold: firstly, if the Sanusi problem was general and not specific to Italy, no blame could attach to Italian colonial administrators for their failure to deal with it effectively. Secondly, if the conflict in Cyrenaica and Egypt's Western Desert were firmly a part of the greater war, then British policy ought to be constrained by wartime agreements rather than self-interest. However, it was not Sonnino and Salandra who needed to be convinced of this approach, or even the British government in London, but rather policymakers in Cairo—who had little interest in or sympathy for the Italian position. Given the fragility of Italian control in Cyrenaica, both Henry McMahon and his successor Reginald Wingate prioritized positive relationships with local indigenous leaders.

By March 1916, the Western Frontier Force had recaptured Sollum and successfully liberated the surviving crew of the HMS *Tara* from imprisonment. This was soon followed by the Italian re-occupation of the adjacent port of Bardia, in a rare example of (limited) cooperation between the allies.[60] Minor operations continued in the interior, with the Sanusiyya establishing temporary strongholds at a succession of oases in the western Egyptian desert. Already by mid-1916 Ahmad al-Sharif's leadership had become fatally associated with the war on Britain, and his young cousin Idris al-Sanusi was able to assume the position which he had long considered rightfully his. Since 1914 colonial officials had become progressively more interested in replacing al-Sharif with a more compliant interlocutor, while within the order al-Sanusi had become 'known for his vocal opposition to Ahmad al-Sharif's support of Ottoman war efforts'.[61] Al-Sanusi's great skill as leader of the Sanusiyya was to create a lasting relationship with Britain—making the order Britain's preferred interlocutor in the region not only throughout this period but throughout the Second World War as well. Fortified by this backing, which also served to legitimize the Sanusiyya as the organized representatives of all the Cyrenaican Bedouin peoples, Idris embarked on negotiations with Italy in July 1916.[62] The Anglo-Sanusi conflict culminated in the order's defeat at Siwa early in 1917; by the end of February, the Sanusiyya had withdrawn from Egyptian territory to their headquarters at Jaghbub.

On 17 April 1917 the Akrama Agreement was finally signed, settling the conflicts between the Sanusi and both European powers. It formally recognized the de facto Italian abandonment of the Cyrenaican interior, which was now effectively in Sanusi hands; only the coastal strip remained under Italian control.

[59] ACS Archivio Salandra, busta 2, fasc. 14, 14 February 1916, n. 302.
[60] ACS Fondo Giovanni Ameglio, busta 5, fasc. 28, Porto Bardia.
[61] Ryan, *Religion as Resistance*, 93–4.   [62] Vandewalle, *A History of Modern Libya*, 27.

This concession helped secure Idris al-Sanusi's position within the Sanusiyya against supporters of his ousted predecessor, and to ensure his lasting control over the brotherhood Italy agreed that the Sanusiyya could keep their arms. In return Idris worked to stamp out Ottoman influence within the order. The agreement brought a form of conditional peace to the eastern portion of the colony, allowing some respite to Ameglio's beleaguered forces there. It was, nonetheless, in many ways a bizarre turn of events. In Pack's words, 'rather than the British wishing the Italians to crush those Bedouin ruffians who had just invaded Egypt, British policy was predicated on strengthening their former enemies as a buffer against their supposed allies, the Italians'.[63] From this moment onwards Idris was expected to serve as Italy's agent in Cyrenaica in a modified form of the old *politica dei capi*—a system which had already decisively failed in Tripolitania by 1915. But if in Cyrenaica the brotherhood's position was now unassailable, their 1915 efforts to extend their region of control and tax-raising into Tripolitania were not successful; Ramadan al-Suwayhili was implacably opposed to what he perceived as an attack on his power, and indeed the two groups came to battle at Bani Walid early in 1916 (highlighting the profound divisions between Cyrenaica and Tripolitania and thus the extent to which it is misleading to speak of a 'Libyan resistance' in this period).

6.3 Ethiopia and the Stability of East Africa

If Libya could not be Italy's priority in wartime, far-off Eritrea and Somalia seemed even less important. Nonetheless, the war's long shadow even briefly threatened to fall across the Horn of Africa. Italy's defeat at Adwa in 1896 had not only created a lasting sense of imperial anxiety but a concrete focus for opportunist revanchism. Eritrea's borders with Ethiopia had been demarcated in 1902 and through the pre-war period Italy's East African policy focused on developing the colonies it had already acquired rather than expanding them further, but the sense lingered that Ethiopia was unfinished business. As events turned out, however, rather than the war offering Italy a chance to destabilize the Ethiopian Empire, it was to be Ethiopia which jeopardized Italian control in Eritrea.

After several years of failing health, the aged victor of Adwa, Menelik II, died in 1913 leading to a short spell of turmoil under his grandson Lij Iyasu. Iyasu, just 18 years old when he became the designated Emperor, was (and remains) a controversial figure: was he a modernizer and nationalist determined to overcome intra-religious conflict, or an apostate—selfish, frivolous, and capricious—dedicated

---

[63] Pack, 'The Antecedents and Implications of the So-Called Anglo-Sanussi War', 59.

to undermining traditional Orthodox Christianity? If his legacy is obscure owing to its suppression by his rival and successor, Haile Selassie, what is undeniable is that Iyasu's increasing proximity to Islam and to the Ottoman Empire became a pressing concern for the European powers once the First World War broke out.[64] Iyasu and his father, Ras Mikael, made contact with the Somali Dervish leader Mohammed Abdullah Hassan, who had been engaged in anti-colonial war for over a decade. Dealings with the Ottomans and Germany suggested that Hassan and Iyasu might have had big plans; the Italian authorities were very anxious about the activity of Germans and Turks in Eritrea in 1915, fearing that they might fund an Ethiopian uprising to match that underway in Libya.[65] By early 1916 the Italian authorities were thoroughly alarmed; the Eritrean governor even wrote to the minister of colonies in March to demand that artillery pieces be diverted from the Italo-Austrian front to protect the colony against its neighbours (receiving predictably short shrift from Cadorna), while Martini described the situation in Ethiopia as 'uncertain'.[66] Britain and Italy alike were concerned at the prospect that an Islamic rebellion might spread from Somalia into Ethiopia and through the Horn of Africa, pinning down troops and resources—especially dangerous in light of the ongoing war in German East Africa. But Iyasu's vision was never really more than a pipe-dream, more remote even than Italian fantasies in the region. Coptic Orthodox Ethiopia was deeply hostile to his scheming and in September 1916, with the encouragement of French and Italian agents, a coup deposed the young emperor before he had ever been crowned. The prospect of a major anti-colonial insurrection in this part of East Africa was both remote and short lived. Mohammed Abdallah Hassan's Dervishes continued their resistance in Somalia, where they caused more trouble to the British than to the Italians; Ethiopia soon settled down under its new rulers. Nonetheless, Italian anxieties around the Ethiopian borders with Eritrea and Somalia obliged the colonial ministry to keep more indigenous troops there than they would have liked, thus damaging the counter-insurgency operations in Libya.[67]

6.4 From the Akrama Agreement to the End of the War

While Cyrenaica was reasonable tranquil after April 1917, in Tripolitania the resistance continued. Despite the frequent conflicts and disagreements between various tribal leaders—and particularly between Ramadan al-Suwayhili and Sulayman al-Baruni—Italy was unable to win over any of the warring factions.

---

[64] Bosworth and Finaldi, 'The Italian Empire', 44–6.
[65] ASMAE Rappresentanza Diplomatica in Egitto 1915, b. 150, fasc. 1: Eritrea, Eritrea e Sudan, Somalia, Benadir.
[66] ACS PCM GE 1915–1918, b. 75, 19.3.1, f. Colonie, sf.1 and 2.
[67] ACS Fondo Giovanni Ameglio b. 6, fasc. 35.

The assistance supplied by the Central Powers was enough to keep the Tripolitanians fighting throughout 1918. In November 1917, during the crisis after Caporetto, Cadorna announced that the national peril was such that all remaining troops in Tripolitania should be withdrawn. At no time committed to the Libyan cause—it is worth remembering that he had not taken any active part in the war of 1911–12—the chief of general staff saw the colonies as an expensive millstone, which in a time of disaster ought to be jettisoned. But in this he received no support: unsurprisingly the colonial lobby, as represented in the cabinet by Colosimo and Sonnino, were vigorously opposed to the proposal. So too was the new prime minister Orlando, who had little time for any of Cadorna's ideas; once Diaz had taken charge the plan was abandoned.[68] But the idea of abandoning the colony altogether was seriously contemplated on several occasions. This reveals the extent of internal divisions over imperialism in Italy: for some, including influential members of the cabinet, empire was absolutely central to the war, while for others it was at best an irrelevance and at worst actively distracting from the true national cause. Certainly, it is unarguable that Libya was a drain on Italian resources, diverting considerable quantities of soldiers, ships, money, livestock, food, cloth, and fuel which were badly needed elsewhere. In this respect, attempts to retain the colony actively undermined the wider Italian war effort; the refusal to abandon Libya altogether and prioritize the war against Austria shows the importance of the ideal of imperialism even when its reality was damaging.

The First World War was devastating to Libya, inflicting a terrible loss of life on the indigenous peoples. Contemporary estimates suggest that by 1918, the population of Tripolitania was little more than one-third what it had been before the Italian invasion in 1911. Hunger and starvation—not least caused by Ameglio's deliberate destruction of crops and closure of internal markets—played a major role in this dreadful suffering. Government efforts to seize wheat harvests led many indigenous farmers to hoard food, further increasing shortages in towns.[69] War, famine, and contagious diseases—including the 'Spanish' flu epidemic—killed at least 100,000 civilians and perhaps many more in Tripolitania alone.[70] The wider world war made Italy at once unwilling to abandon the struggle and unable to commit full resources to it. Without the First World War, the anti-Italian resistance would have lacked the support of the Central Powers which enabled it to fight so effectively, while Italy would have been better positioned to mobilize fully and perhaps thus bring operations to end more rapidly. The political fate of the country might have been the same, simply with fewer casualties.

[68] Bassi, Labanca, and Sturani, *Libia*, 37.
[69] Mohammad Suliaman, 'The Impact of the Italian Occupation of Cyrenaica', 165.
[70] Anderson, 'The Tripoli Republic', 50.

In April 1919 Colosimo wrote a report which summed up the war's impact on Libya; his verdict was damning. He was sharply critical of Ameglio, who had refused his repeated instructions to attempt the reoccupation of Misrata or to end the Central Powers' flow of supplies to the colony. Indeed, he candidly admitted that 'given the international situation and our Great War, we must consider it a success that we managed to hold on to the Colony. We owe this in no small part to our agreement with England in 1916 and with the Sanusiyya Brotherhood in April 1917.'[71] Perhaps characteristically, he identified the failure of the Italian navy to prevent Austro-Hungarian or German submarine warfare as the most significant element in Italy's difficulties. By attributing Italy's problems primarily to its European enemies, and refusing to acknowledge the extent to which it was the actions and determination of the indigenous resistance which had undermined Italian control, he at once reinforced the colonial racial and cultural hierarchy and promised a more successful future in which, now the European war was over, there would be no effective opposition to Italian rule. Colosimo's optimism would prove misplaced: only the extreme brutality of fascist violence would succeed in crushing the resistance to Italian rule in Libya in the late 1920s and early 1930s.

[71]   ACS PCM GE 1915–1918, busta 221, fasc. 201, sf.12; 6 April 1919.

7

The War Beyond Italy

Expeditionary Forces and Expansionist Ambitions

In October 1915 a small group of Italian military men walking peaceably together were ambushed by Austro-Hungarian sailors and an exchange of fire took place, leaving several men wounded; the episode was remarkable only for its location— the streets of Beijing. As the Italian consul there observed, such incidents were not uncommon given the build-up of military forces of the various combatant nations in a small area.[1] Such incidents serve to remind that the war was indeed a global one, as recent historiography has sought increasingly to emphasize; as yet, however, the Italian aspects of the global war have yet to be fully incorporated into the wider story.[2] Like its Entente Allies, Italy was involved in fighting beyond its own principal fronts, participating in various 'sideshows' (even while some in Britain and France viewed the entire Italian theatre as a side-show). Italy contributed expeditionary forces to the war in the Balkans, sending troops both to Albania and to the Macedonian front, and later deployed forces to the Sinai and Palestine campaigns, Murmansk, and Siberia. In addition, a significant number of troops and labourers would be sent to the Western Front in 1918. These missions served to support the Allies, emphasizing Italian commitment to the Entente, but also promoted the idea that Italy had legitimate interests in the Balkans, the Eastern Mediterranean, and further afield. Firmly committed to the principle of post-war territorial compensation, Italy saw wartime participation in other theatres as an essential precursor to asserting post-war claims. At the same time, the resources committed were always limited, and thus so was their impact.

---

[1] ACS PCM GE 1915–1918, Busta 75-bis, fasc. 19.3.5 Cina; Italian Chargé d'Affaires to Sonnino, October 1915.

[2] For a few examples, see Michael S. Neiberg, *Fighting the Great War: A Global History* (Cambridge, MA: Harvard University Press, 2005); Hew Strachan, 'The First World War as a Global War', *First World War Studies* 1, no. 1 (2010): 3–14, DOI: https://doi.org/10.1080/19475021003621036; F. R. Dickinson, 'Toward a Global Perspective of the Great War: Japan and the Foundations of a Twentieth-Century World', *The American Historical Review* 119, no. 4 (2014): 1154–83, DOI: https://doi.org/10.1093/ahr/119.4.1154; Robert Gerwarth and Erez Manela, 'The Great War as a Global War: Imperial Conflict and the Reconfiguration of World Order, 1911–1923', *Diplomatic History* 38, no. 4 (30 July 2014): 786–800, DOI: https://doi.org/10.1093/dh/dhu027; Heather Streets-Salter, *World War One in Southeast Asia: Colonialism and Anticolonialism in an Era of Global Conflict* (Cambridge: Cambridge University Press, 2017).

The Italian Empire and the Great War. Vanda Wilcox, Oxford University Press (2021). © Vanda Wilcox.
DOI: 10.1093/oso/9780198822943.003.0007

7.1 The Balkans

The Balkans were an important focus of Italian ambition before the First World War, featuring heavily within the imperialist calculations in favour of intervention in 1914–15, and one of relatively few areas in which Italy directly fought in pursuit of its expansionist goals. On average some 100,000 men and extensive logistical services were deployed at any one time in Balkan theatres from 1916 to 1918; given troop rotation, the overall number of men who served there is much higher.[3] In fact military action to secure Italian interests began as early as 30 October 1914 when a small naval unit occupied Sazan island, strategically positioned at the mouth of the bay of Vlorë, just north of the Otranto straits (it would remain in Italian hands until 1947). By the end of December more than 2,000 Italian troops had disembarked in the city, ostensibly in response to the request of local inhabitants for protection in the face of the rapidly degenerating security situation within Albania.[4] Cadorna was strongly opposed both to the occupation, which he thought a poorly timed distraction, and to the manner in which it was carried out. If such an endeavour had to be undertaken at all, he proposed that a full army corps should be sent rather than this reinforced regiment. He pointed out that in Libya, an initially simple landing undertaken by limited forces degenerated very quickly into a fiasco requiring urgent reinforcements; far better, he thought, to send an adequate force from the start. This would limit the future risks of insurgence and enable a solid occupation to be established—an interesting transference of colonial lessons to the European theatres of war. However, his concerns and insights were overruled by the government—Sonnino was set on a quick, low-key occupation.[5]

Once the war broke out, the Vlorë occupation became awkward to justify: Italy could no longer present itself as a neutral peacekeeper, and not unnaturally the other states directly concerned in the region—Greece, Montenegro, and Serbia—became increasingly hostile to Italy's presence there. Montenegro, while welcoming Italian intervention, retained an interest in Shkodër (Scutari); Serbia was interested in central Albania, while Greece maintained its long-standing claim to the northern Epirus, one of its own *terre irredente*. Although Serbia's priority in 1914–15 was trying to protect its territories from Austro-Hungarian invasion, it too had long-term interests in Dalmatia, another area of rivalry with Italy.

[3] Vagnini, *L'Italia e i Balcani nella Grande Guerra*, 11.
[4] Vagnini, *L'Italia e i Balcani nella Grande Guerra*, 40–1.
[5] IOH, Vol. VII, t.3: *Albania—Macedonia—Medio Oriente* (Rome: Provveditorato generale dello stato libreria, 1983), 28–9.

7.2 Albania

By autumn 1915 the Entente situation in the Balkans had become critical. Encouraged by Allied failures at Gallipoli and in Poland, Bulgaria joined the Central Powers on 6 September, making Serbia's position extremely vulnerable. Although Greece offered the use of Salonika to permit France and Britain to send reinforcements, Serbia could now be attacked on two sides (the north and east) and it was clear that it was in deep crisis. By November Serb forces were retreating steadily to the south-west into Albania, where they ended up along the Adriatic coast. Paris and London urged Rome to assist them in supporting Serbia—and indeed an Austro-Hungarian victory in the Balkans would clearly not have suited Italy. A debate arose over to how best to contribute: Cadorna advocated participation in the collective efforts at Salonika, while Sonnino suggested sending more units to Albania, an option which offered more direct political benefits in establishing a long-term Italian foothold there. Cadorna's analysis was purely military, noting the impossibility of fighting and resupplying effectively in Albania's terrain, and the desirability of cooperating with the Allies in a theatre which might offer a real breakthrough; instead, Sonnino's political vision won out. He feared that Greece might exploit the chaos in the Western Balkans at Italy's expense. Zupelli, the minister of war, agreed with his cabinet colleague, chiefly since a Salonika expedition might be inordinately expensive. An expeditionary contingent, the Corpo speciale in Albania, was therefore approved in mid-November 1915 (and a brigade recalled from Tripolitania to offset this loss to the main front, showing the interconnection of imperialist projects).[6] The Albanian Corps consolidated the defences of Vlorë, and in December—after a long, unpleasant march—occupied the northern port of Durrës (known in Italy as Durazzo), then serving as the capital of independent Muslim Albania (insofar as it existed).

By this date a huge concentration of Serbs had reached the coastal region under horrific winter conditions and suffering desperate shortages of food and medical supplies; Entente efforts to support them from Salonika had been decisively blocked by Bulgaria. Some 140,000 soldiers were accompanied by at least 10,000 untrained recruits (17 or 18 years old) and tens of thousands of civilian refugees. Simple geography made this into an Italian problem: if the survivors of the retreat were to be fed and supplied, and then evacuated to safety to hopefully fight another day, they would need Italian assistance. At the same time, Cadorna was unwilling to risk undermining Italian prestige by undertaking operations in this challenging area, for instance by advancing into the interior towards Berat, as some proposed. Instead the medical and administrative resources of the Albanian

---

[6] IOH Vol. VII, t. 3, 32–4. See also DDI, Quinta Serie, Vol. 4, Docs 916, 922. Some historians have accepted Zupelli's reasoning at face value, discounting the political aspects: Mario Montanari, *Le truppe italiane in Albania: (anni 1914–20 e 1939)* (Rome: Stato Maggiore Esercito, Ufficio Storico, 1978), 110.

Corps were mobilized, while throughout December 1915 and January 1916 the Italian navy worked to resupply the massing numbers of troops and refugees along the coast. Soon an enormous programme of evacuation began, lasting until early March, in which more than 260,000 people were transported: the army and government to Corfu while refugees and the sick or wounded were sent to French or Italian islands. The bulk of the craft involved were Italian, but British and French steamers also took part, covered by cruisers of all three nations. Naval historian Paul Halpern describes the successful evacuation as 'one of the more notable achievements of sea power in the First World War'.[7] The rescued Serbian army, once recovered from its ordeal, would join the Allied forces at Salonika.

The Serbs had also captured in the region of 100,000 Austro-Hungarians between August 1914 and November 1915. As it retreated towards the coast, it had endeavoured to bring along some 40,000 (the Italian official history suggests as many as 70,000) of these prisoners. Only 24,000 ever reached Albania, having been used as forced labour on the march; the survivors, suffering from extreme hunger and exposure, were taken by Italy to the prison island of Asinara, off the coast of Sardinia, where they experienced atrocious living conditions in a hastily built tent city, at least 7,000 dying in transit or on arrival.[8] The original plan had been to send these men to France, but Sonnino was keen to keep them as a possible source of labour—the spoils of war.

The evacuation completed, Cadorna reasserted his views on the irrelevance of the Albanian expedition and his determination to wrest the final decision-making power away from civilian authorities whenever possible. To his fury, the government had sought to circumvent his authority by making the Albanian Corps answerable directly to the minister of war rather than the chief of general staff—a clear sign of the political leadership's intentions to go far beyond his begrudging acceptance of a token presence in Albania. The gulf between Cadorna's vision of the war, in which the defeat of Austria-Hungary on Italy's principal front was paramount, and Sonnino's wider, more imperialist view, was once again abundantly clear.[9] The northern Albanian city of Durrës was extremely vulnerable and only precariously held; vigorous civil–military debates about the advisability of holding onto it in the face of any determined assault ensued. In the face of advancing Habsburg forces, the Italians withdrew at the end of February 1916, an act which certainly undermined their prestige in Albanian eyes (and indeed it might have been better, from this perspective, never to have occupied the city at all). Like the rest of northern Albania, Durrës would remain in Austrian hands until the closing weeks of the war in 1918.

---

[7] Halpern, *A Naval History of World War I*, 158.

[8] On this grim episode, see Luca Gorgolini, *I dannati dell'Asinara: l'odissea dei prigionieri Austro-Ungarici nella Prima Guerra Mondiale* (Turin: UTET, 2011).

[9] AUSSME Fondo E2, b. 55, correspondence between Cadorna and Salandra, March 1916.

In the aftermath of this embarrassment, Supreme Command managed to wrest direction of the Albanian force away from the government; from April to June several units were withdrawn, despite Salandra's opposition. The government remained committed to further action in the area, and after the Greek parliament voted to annex northern Epirus on 18 March 1916 Sonnino began to contemplate a pre-emptive southern expansion of the Italian occupation, to forestall any Greek action. He justified this manoeuvre as 'the defense of Valona [Vlorë]', showing a colonial logic of expansion wherein new territories were continually needed to protect previous acquisitions. In response, the Greek government attempted to call his bluff, offering to protect Vlorë themselves with a guarantee that they would permit no Central Powers forces to pass through any part of Epirus.[10] Meanwhile in the Italian parliament, ardent nationalists like Federzoni were calling for the formal annexation of the Dodecanese as a response to the Greek declaration.[11] Ultimately, the Greek position grew weaker through spring and summer of 1916 and by autumn Italy was ready to expand southwards despite Greek protests. This decision was taken unilaterally, without the approval of the other Entente powers. The Albanian Corps—now renamed XVI Corps—advanced from Vlorë along the coast to take Porto Palermo without resistance from the Greek gendarmerie in possession, while further troops disembarked directly at Saranda, opposite the northernmost point of Corfu. Subsequently parts of the interior, such as Gjirokastër (Argirocastro), an ancient hill-town just inland from Saranda, were also seized; by mid-October 1916 a substantial portion of southern Albania was occupied—though Sonnino emphasized to his allies that it was simply a military measure to guarantee Allied security in the face of enemy espionage and subversion, and that no permanent occupation was intended.[12] This advance—against minimal opposition—was simultaneous with Romanian entry into the war and the offensive launched from the Macedonian theatre by Entente forces. French and Italian troops eventually met up with one another after the Allied capture of Bitola (then known as Monastir) in November, effectively joining the two fronts together (see Map 3). To Italian alarm, the French also established their own small protectorate in December 1916, run by local stakeholders, under the name of the Autonomous Albanian Republic of Korçë. This encouraged Sonnino to begin considering how best to consolidate Italy's gains in Albania.

By this time Vlorë had been occupied for almost two full years, and the Italian administration in Albania was beginning to settle down. An army-run Secretariat for Civilian Affairs was created in March 1916 to administer the areas under Italian control and manage relationships with the local population. Given the

---

[10] DDI, Quinta Serie, Vol. 5, Docs 683, 793, 794.
[11] Italia. *Atti del Parlamento Italiano*—Sessione 1913–1916, Vol. IX, I Sessione, 9745–9814; 9808; https://storia.camera.it/lavori/regno-d-italia/leg-regno-XXIV/1916/22-marzo.
[12] Vagnini, *L'Italia e i Balcani nella Grande Guerra*, 60–2.

multi-ethnic, multi-faith character of the population, and the country's recent history of political turmoil, this was no sinecure. Maintenance of public order was a key priority for the occupiers, who stationed some 1,400 *carabinieri* (military police) in Vlorë and across southern Albania. They were tasked with suppressing brigandage and supervising the local gendarmerie. Beyond this, the office for Civilian Affairs headed complex efforts to rationalize and 'modernize' all aspects of civil life: Italian attachés and commissioners worked with local authorities to improve the administration of justice at national and local levels, reform public finance and municipal administration, and provide education in both Italian and Albanian. Public works campaigns included substantial road, railway, bridge, and port building programmes, construction of sewers, installation of street lighting, the institution of a first ever public bus network, and improvements in postal and telegraph services. Interventions were also made into agriculture, animal husbandry, and forestry, where Italian experts were deployed with the aim of improving standards through imparting technical and scientific knowledge.[13] In reality, inadequate knowledge and understanding of the local language, customs, or society, combined with poor planning and the lack of a clear Italian purpose in the region, meant that the impact of this work was strictly limited.

Perhaps the single most important responsibility, and greatest achievement, of the Italian wartime regime in Albania was its public health programme, which focused above all on the fight against malaria. Since Italian units were generally stationed in or around significant population centres, troops and civilians lived in close contact with one another, making infectious disease among the local population a military as well as humanitarian concern. Malaria had been endemic in the region for some time, afflicting troops and civilians throughout the war; the Italian administration endeavoured to fight it both through building new hospitals, clinics, and healthcare infrastructure, and through prophylactic measures to halt the spread of the disease among civilians.[14] Other medical measures included the licensing of surgery, general practice, and midwifery as well as promoting preventive medicine. Early on this work had been undertaken by the navy before the army stepped in, supporting refugees suffering from malaria or diseases such as typhus and tuberculosis.

As this summary makes clear, in occupying Albania, the Italians implemented an essentially colonial regime. The occupying authorities themselves were keen to deny any such thing: use of the word 'colony' was carefully avoided and any suggestion that Albanians were treated in the same way as African subjects was

[13] Segretario per gli affari civili d'Albania, *Relazione sulla gestione dei servizi civili* (Vlorë: R. Officina Tip. Italiana, 1920).

[14] Vagnini, *L'Italia e i Balcani nella Grande Guerra*, 99–101.

hastily suppressed.[15] However, the links between this wartime administration and the colonial management of both Libya and the Dodecanese were explicit, especially when it came to governance of a religiously diverse population. Orthodox Albanians were seen with suspicion, as likely to be Hellenophile; the Muslim population was seen as more likely to be amenable to Italian control. Considerable attention was paid to careful administration of local *waqfs* (inalienable mortmain land, held by Islamic religious bodies, usually to support schools or religious education). To improve and support *waqf* management, the Albanian occupation drew directly on the experience of colonial personnel from the Dodecanese and North Africa who could explain the intersection of Islamic law with Italian administrative procedures.[16] Given the close ties between religion and the administration of justice, one intelligence report proposed importing loyal Italophile *qadi* (sharia judges) and *ulema* from the existing Muslim-inhabited colonies to help build loyalty among the Albanian people. This would also integrate Albania into the existing Italian colonial framework, the author believed. He proposed that in return Albanian gendarmes could be sent to serve in Libya, since as fellow Muslims they would be more welcome than Italian Christians to the local populace; their loyalty would be guaranteed by the fact that their families were left behind in Albania.[17] These suggestions for intra-colonial personnel exchanges were never implemented, but they are revealing of military perceptions of wartime Albania and Italian colonial administration more generally (showing how religion was conceived as a potential tool for behavioural management).

The government also made plans during the war for future economic exploitation of the region. The occupying forces were accompanied by an army-run 'chemical-mineral' mission of chemists, geologists, and mining engineers, who surveyed Albania with an eye to its future development (though the war ended before much of the proposed analysis could be completed). The project's 1919 report noted that Albania 'would never be a Peru or a California' but that considerable mineral resources might be extracted; the author expressed his hope that Albania would become at least an Italian protectorate, and equally that 'every colony will soon boast an institution like this' to survey and plan extractive industries, a sign of the extent to which scientists were co-opted into the

---

[15] Renaud Dorlhiac and Fabrice Jesné, 'Une alliance de circonstance: l'Italie et les musulmans d'Albanie (1912–1920)', *Revue des mondes musulmans et de la Méditerranée*, no. 141 (15 June 2017): 51–67, DOI: https://doi.org/10.4000/remmm.9812, sections 6–9.

[16] ACS PCM GE 1915–1918, busta 75 19.3.1., Fasc. 5, Operazione della legge e giustizia Islamica; compare also the administrative and judicial procedures outlined in ACS Fondo Giovanni Ameglio, busta 30, fasc. 290.

[17] ACS PCM GE 1915–1918, busta 75, fasc. Colonie, Relazione sulla situazione in Albania, Nov–Dec 1916.

military–imperial project.[18] Wartime railway-building in order to provide a basis for a post-war Italian-controlled Trans-Balkan line was also discussed.[19]

From economic and administrative rule to political control was but a short step. On 3 June 1917 a declaration was issued by occupying general Giacinto Ferrero that all of Albania would be unified and independent under Italian protection. 'By this act, Albanians, you will have free institutions, militias, tribunals and schools run by Albanian citizens, you can administer your own property and the fruit of your labour for the ever greater good of your Country,' he announced. He then went on to invoke Albanians' 'centuries-old traditions which date back to the Roman and Venetian civilisations', somehow taking credit for all that was good in the land while also asserting the continuity of an Italian presence.[20] The so-called Proclamation of Argirocastro [Gjirokastër] marked a significant step in formalizing Italian control, though the Albanian flag would henceforth fly alongside the tricolour to indicate that Italy was a partner and protector, not simply a master. However, this declaration was a clear violation of the Treaty of London's (secret) provisions for the country, as Paul Cambon soon pointed out to the Italian ambassador in Paris.[21] Italian officials reported that this announcement was well received among the local population, but the Allies, who had not been consulted, were less pleased—as was Nikola Pašić, the Serbian prime minister, who had his own plans for Albania, and who protested formally to the Italian minister to the Serb government in Corfu.[22] The Italians claimed, however, that the Proclamation was a response to French ambitions in the area, as evinced by their protectorate in Korçë. By allowing Ferrero to make the declaration, Sonnino was in effect testing the waters: if it proved necessary to change course, the general could be blamed for acting precipitately and without full authorization.

Around the same time, new military occupations were undertaken in the regions of Chameria and the Pindus mountains, reaching well down into Greek territory—though some of these positions were quickly abandoned once Greece entered the war at the end of the month.[23] This advance also led to further tensions with French forces, particularly the Senegalese units in the region.[24] Cadorna's disinclination to support any further action in Albania, combined with political anxieties about relationships with France, Greece, and Serbia, meant that Italy ceased any further expansion after mid-June and even withdrew

---

[18] Federico Plate, *Ricerche chimico-minerarie eseguite in Albania: relazione* (Vlorë: R. Officina Tip. Italiana, 1919). For the remarkably similar work of German scientists in the Ottoman Empire, see Oliver Stein, 'Scientists in Uniform: The German Military and the Investigation of the Ottoman Landscape', in *Landscapes of the First World War*, ed. Selena Daly, Martina Salvante, and Vanda Wilcox (London: Palgrave Macmillan, 2018), 139–56.

[19] ACS PCM GE 1915–1918, busta 75 19.3.1, 3/2.A, Letter to Gen. Ferrero, Comm. XVI corps, Valona.

[20] IOH, Vol. VII, t.3. 94–5.   [21] DDI, Quinta Serie, Vol. 8, Doc. 305.

[22] DDI, Quinta Serie, Vol. 8, Doc. 300.   [23] DDI, Quinta Serie, Vol. 8, Docs 289, 292, 293, 296.

[24] DDI, Quinta Serie, Vol. 8, Docs 327, 373.

from a few outposts. Endemic malaria in the region was forcing the repatriation of around 2,400 troops each month through the summer, further limiting Italian scope for action.[25] The theatre stabilised over the next few months, until events in Italy threatened to upset the equilibrium in the region: encouraged by the Italian defeat at Caporetto, Austria-Hungary repeatedly attacked the perimeters of Italian-held areas in November 1917, in the interior around Ciflik, though without success. In Rome, the idea of withdrawing troops from Albania altogether to shore up the main front was very briefly mooted, but the navy soon quashed this proposal, emphasizing the centrality of Vlorë for the control of the Otranto Straits and the maintenance of the barrage there.[26] After a relatively static winter, the Italian commander in Vlorë began to develop more ambitious plans early in 1918. With the reluctant agreement of new chief of general staff Armando Diaz, the joint allied offensive of Fieri-Berat was eventually launched in July 1918, and Italian forces soon occupied the town of Berat. Overextending themselves in support of neighbouring French units, however, in direct contravention of Diaz's instructions, they were forced to abandon the town just a month later.[27]

Finally, taking advantage of the main allied offensive on the Macedonian front which had begun in September 1918, an Italian assault on Austrian-held northern Albania was launched on 2 October (just as Bulgaria signed its Armistice). By 14 October Italian forces had reached Durrës, and the following day they occupied Tirana; Shëngjin (also known as San Giovanni di Medua) was taken on 28 October and by the end of the month the first units had entered Shkodër (Scutari). Here they found a Serb regiment in occupation which they promptly dislodged. By the time the Austrians had surrendered, on 4 November, Italian forces occupied almost all of Albania—a far greater area than promised in the Treaty of London—with only a narrow strip of land to the east held by French, Serbian, and Greek forces.[28]

7.3 The Macedonian Front

The opening of the Macedonian, or Salonika, front, had its origins in the Serb crisis of autumn 1915 and the Bulgarian entry to the war. Initially invited to use the port of Salonika by Greek prime minister Eleftherios Venizelos, French troops arriving from the disaster of Gallipoli were formed into a new unit, eventually named the Armée de l'Orient (or more correctly, with the addition of British and

---

[25] Borgogni, *Tra continuità e incertezza*, 40.
[26] On the importance of the barrage, see Paul G. Halpern, *The Battle of the Otranto Straits: Controlling the Gateway to the Adriatic in World War I* (Bloomington: Indiana University Press, 2004).
[27] Vagnini, *L'Italia e i Balcani nella Grande Guerra*, 90–5.
[28] Borgogni, *Tra continuità e incertezza*, 42–3.

imperial forces, the Armées Alliées d'Orient). The Entente hoped to encourage Greece to join the war at this time, but the ongoing conflict between the pro-Allied Venizelos and the pro-German King Constantine made it impossible. The initial aims of this new theatre of war—to shore up Serbia and keep a bulwark between the Central Powers and the Ottoman Empire—were rapidly thwarted, despite some bitter fighting, and for a time the Macedonian front lacked a clear strategic purpose. But at the Chantilly Conference of December 1915 the Allies agreed to keep the front open: though Britain might have preferred to deploy its troops to Mesopotamia and Egypt, France was determined to keep fighting in the Balkans— perhaps on political rather than military grounds. From the Italian perspective, the continued Allied presence at Salonika was an essential pre-requisite for the survival of Italy's occupation in Albania.[29] Salonika soon became a defensive encampment, effectively under Allied occupation (a clear violation of Greek neutrality which produced considerable tensions between the two parties) in the hope of one day being able to relaunch offensive operations. French and British forces were soon joined by the survivors of the Serbian retreat through Albania— some 150,000 additional men by June 1916. Despite the growing allocation of men and resources, however, the front remained extremely static until 1918.

Italian participation in the theatre had been requested by France in October and November 1915, but neither Salandra nor Sonnino were convinced it would be useful to Italy. Perhaps surprisingly, Cadorna was somewhat more positive, even drawing up a preliminary study for Italian deployment there in December 1915 based on the withdrawal of troops from Libya. Instead, at this stage troops were only sent to Albania; only later in 1916 did the government come to believe that failure to participate in the Macedonian theatre would compromise the entire Italian war effort in the Balkans, making it appear that Italy was not pulling its weight within the alliance. Eventually it was agreed that the 35th Division, commanded by General Carlo Petitti di Roreto, would be sent to Salonika. Disembarkation began on 11 August 1916, and by 8 September troops were at the front, under General Maurice Sarrail, who held the newly unified command of the Armées Allies d'Orient.[30] The front was extremely challenging in logistical terms: the terrain and climate were harsh, infectious diseases rife, and troops' equipment often inadequate. Italian troops finally found themselves engaged in offensive operations starting on 14 November 1916, with a joint attack alongside French, Serbian, and Russian units against Bulgarian positions in the Bitola sector (part of the Monastir Offensive). The Cagliari Brigade distinguished themselves in several attacks and the allies succeeded in capturing the town of Bitola itself.[31]

In 1917 events on the Macedonia front did not much improve. General Ernesto Mombelli, who had served before the war as military attaché in Constantinople,

---

[29] AUSSME Fondo E2, b. 55, Carlo Porro to Cadorna, March 1916.
[30] Vagnini, *L'Italia e i Balcani nella Grande Guerra*, 77–9.   [31] IOH, Vol. VII, t.3, 225–9.

was appointed to the command of the division in May.[32] Under Mombelli, the 35th Division fought in the unsuccessful joint offensive known as the battle of the Crna Bend in May 1917 alongside French colonial forces, suffering losses of 120 officers and 3,034 other ranks in the process.[33] Cadorna, alarmed at the lack of progress and concerned that the other Entente powers might be planning a withdrawal, began to wonder whether the Division should be returned to Italy.[34] Politically, meanwhile, relations with Greece grew ever trickier in spring 1917, as Allied forces violated Greek neutrality both in northern Epirus and in the Salonika sector and Venezelist forces in Salonika began to adopt military means. Sonnino found himself in an awkward position: while not wanting to push Constantine I into abandoning neutrality and allying with the Central Powers, he certainly did not want to see the pro-Entente Venizelos return to power either, rightly identifying him and his politics as key threats to Italian imperial goals. In late June, Venizelos finally won his long power struggle with the king, and took over in a form of dictatorship, immediately declaring war on the Central Powers.[35] While this was perhaps good news for the Macedonian front, where several hundred thousand more men would eventually be ready to reinforce the Allied armies, to Sonnino it was a terrible blow. There was no way to avoid the conflict between Greek and Italian aspirations in northern Epirus, but perhaps even more importantly in the Dodecanese and Asia Minor.

On 14 September 1918, the Armée d'Orient launched a major offensive, under the leadership of the French general Louis Franchet d'Espèrey, who was keen to adopt a more aggressive approach in the theatre. This massive assault on Bulgarian forces at Dobro Pole soon began to pay off, with French and Serbian forces advancing steadily. The Italian 35th Division, in the western sector of the front, provided supporting actions designed to prevent the enemy from transferring reinforcements into the main sector. By 22 September the division was on the advance through a mountainous sector, fighting hard and providing valuable flanking support to the main offensive.[36] At the same time, Sonnino considered it useful to embark on a connected assault in Albania, to maintain the Franco-Italian balance of power in the region. On 25 September, the Bulgarian government decided to seek an armistice, signing an agreement just four days later; the Entente meanwhile pushed on to liberate Serbia from Austro-Hungarian

[32] Mombelli was a successful infantry commander in the Italo-Turkish War and went on to serve as the Italian representative in occupied Turkey in 1922; from 1924 to 1926 he was Governor of Cyrenaica. He serves as a good example of a varied but consistently pro-imperial military career spanning the Liberal and Fascist eras.

[33] IOH, Vol. VII, t.3, 261–7.   [34] DDI, Quinta Serie, Vol. VIII, Doc. 211–12.

[35] Loukianos Hassiotis, 'Greece', in *1914–1918-Online International Encyclopedia of the First World War*, ed. Ute Daniel et al. (Berlin: Freie Universität Berlin, 2014), http://encyclopedia.1914-1918-online.net/article/greece/2014-10-08.

[36] IOH, Vol. VII, t.3, 304–11.

occupation by the end of October. To the lasting chagrin of Mombelli and his men, the Italian contribution to allied success on this front was not considered particularly significant; in this sense it did not achieve its main political goal of displaying Italy's value to the Entente.

7.4 Imperial War Aims and Expanding Ambitions, 1916–17

Italian intervention in Albania and Macedonia was just one part of the wider, extra-national war effort, putting boots on the ground to support the expansionist goals outlined in the Treaty of London. Soon Italy would begin to enlarge its horizons even further. The debates carried out during the period of neutrality over Italy's imperial ambitions highlight the diversity of opinion within the ruling class over the role which colonial expansion—of whatever kind—ought to play in determining war aims. With the victory of the interventionists in 1915, nationalist and imperialist voices became increasingly prominent politically. Once the war began, and neutralism was denigrated as defeatist or unpatriotic, it also became politically harder to make a case against imperialism (except, of course, for the socialist party which maintained its principled position of not supporting the war). To cast doubts on the capacity of the army was unthinkable in wartime; to suggest, as many had in the years before the war, that national unification ought to be completed *before* colonial expansion was undertaken implied some doubt over the outcome of the war which was supposed to be achieving that very task. Why not pursue both goals, imperialists began to argue, since victory was inevitable and imminent? On a more practical level, as it became clear that the other Entente powers would not hesitate to think about their war effort in a global and colonial framework, Italian imperialists were struck with an acute fear of missing out.

By 1916 the scope of Italian war aims discussions was widening. A parliamentary address by deputy Piero Foscari—scion of one of Venice's greatest patrician families—gives a flavour. Foscari was a close associate of Giuseppe Volpi, with ties to the Banca Commerciale Italiana and financial interests in the Balkans and the Eastern Mediterranean; he was an active member of the Associazione Nazionalista Italiana and had served during the wars against Ethiopia and Turkey. On 15 April 1916 he addressed his fear that France and Britain were benefiting from the war to expand their colonies while Italy lagged behind. He called for Italian possession of the port of Kismayo in Somalia, the Farasan islands and Yemen, Djibouti, Sollum and Jaghbub on the Libyan–Egyptian border, and adjustments to the Tunisian border as well as greater protection for the Italian community in British-held Egypt. He then proceeded to discuss northern Epirus and the 'tragic situation of Italian Dalmatia' where 'the name Trieste means Istria and Fiume; Trieste cannot be understood without Fiume' since 'the Adriatic is none other than the continuation

THE WAR BEYOND ITALY   133

of the valley of the Po'. This was a significant claim with major implications for post-war events, since Fiume had not featured in discussions around the Treaty of London. Foscari also wanted Split, 'which gave a great Emperor to Rome' (Diocletian, 244–311) and therefore could never, he claimed, be a Slavic city. 'The principle of nationality cannot be applied with superstitious meanness,' he declared, explaining his highly flexible interpretation of that ideal (and apparently unaware that such an approach might just as well be applied by rival nationalities at Italy's expense). Invoking the blood sacrifice already made—an increasingly common rhetorical justification for expanding war aims—he demanded 'the total realisation of our future of independence and greatness' and, critically, requested that more funds be allocated for the foreign office.[37] Foscari would go on to serve as under-secretary in the colonial ministry. When Paolo Boselli took office, his inaugural speech to parliament on 28 June 1916 described the national war effort in Risorgimento terms, invoking king and country in pursuit of national unity; his position largely reflected that of April 1915. Just two days later, however, Luigi Federzoni reproached the new prime minister for his failure to address 'the grave and urgent international questions' of Italian domination of the Adriatic and the need for 'political and economic expansion in the Eastern Mediterranean as well as the right to be consulted about matters in the Arabian peninsula'.[38] Such open advocations of imperial expansion in the Italian parliament grew more frequent and more pressing as 1916 wore on.

Salandra's resignation and the creation of Boselli's unity cabinet might have suggested that the new government would embrace less openly expansionist positions, particularly thanks to the inclusion of Leonida Bissolati and Ivanoe Bonomi, the reformist socialists. In fact, they tended not only to support the war but also to look with an indulgent eye upon (limited) colonial expansion. Moreover, Boselli took an extremely hands-off approach to leadership, allowing Sonnino free reign to continue his chosen policies. Unsurprisingly then, the Italian government's evolving war aims followed Sonnino's own inclinations and assessments.

7.4.1 Colonial Pressure Groups and the War Aims Debate

If Sonnino was the chief architect of expansionist claims, his views did not evolve in a vacuum. By 1917 public interest in colonial affairs appeared to be growing,

[37] Italia. *Atti del Parlamento Italiano*—Sessione 1913–1916, Vol. IX, I Sessione, 10448–54; https://storia.camera.it/lavori/regno-d-italia/leg-regno-XXIV/1916/15-aprile.
[38] Italia. *Atti del Parlamento Italiano*—Sessione 1913–1916 (06/06/1916–11/12/1916), Vol. X, I Sessione (Rome: Tip. Camera dei Deputati, 1916): 10847–76, https://storia.camera.it/lavori/regno-d-italia/leg-regno-XXIV/1916/28-giugno; pp. 10848–50; 10943–96, https://storia.camera.it/lavori/regno-d-italia/leg-regno-XXIV/1916/30-giugno; pp. 10988–9.

perhaps spurred in part by news of Japanese and Anglo-French conquests of German colonies in Asia and Africa, which highlighted the potential gains at play in the wider war.[39] Pro-colonial publications proliferated, and formal pressure groups and campaign organizations were joined by private initiatives in embracing an ever more imperialist vision of the conflict.[40] In March 1917 a group of seven bankers, lawyers, and investors from Bologna wrote to Sonnino asking for government support. They had a detailed proposal for what they called agricultural colonization in Turkey: they planned to rent or lease certain very large estates in the Pamphylia region—modern-day Antalya province—which they believed they could profitably farm using a mixture of local labour and emigrant Italian farmers, with imported Italian equipment, machinery, and livestock.[41] Given that this endeavour, they believed, would be both highly profitable and a great patriotic service to Italy, they asked the foreign minister what kind of tax breaks or other financial incentives the government proposed to offer them.[42] As Sonnino observed rather drily in his note of response, this request was not a little premature. At this date the Italian army was making no direct contribution whatsoever to the Allied war against the Ottoman Empire, although they had been at war since August 1915 (and were fighting against Ottoman agents in Libya). Nor, at this stage, had there been any clarification over the location and extent of possible Italian gains in Asia Minor with the other Entente nations, beyond the original Treaty of London; but of course the Bologna entrepreneurs were hardly alone in their territorial aspirations.

At the end of March 1917 the prominent nationalist senator, philanthropist, and economist Baron Leopoldo Franchetti wrote to Boselli in a letter co-signed by a further 335 public figures including prominent names like Federzoni, D'Annunzio, and Ernesto Artom, President of the Italian Colonial Institute.[43] Signatories included senators and MPs, mayors, journalists, lawyers, university professors and rectors, doctors, engineers, archaeologists, librarians, local officials, chamber of commerce representatives, and even a few prelates. The letter drew on themes raised in parliament by Foscari, Federzoni, and others during the

---

[39]   Luciano Monzali, 'La politica estera di Sidney Sonnino e i fini di guerra dell'Italia (1915–1917)', in *La guerra di Cadorna 1915–1917*, ed. Pietro Neglie and Andrea Ungari (Rome: Ufficio Storico, Stato Maggiore dell'Esercito, 2018), 320; See also Luciano Monzali, *Il colonialismo nella politica estera italiana 1878–1949: momenti e protagonisti* (Rome: Società Editrice Dante Alighieri, 2017).

[40]   Typical examples include Savino Acquaviva, *L'avvenire coloniale d'Italia e la guerra* (Rome: Atheneum, 1917); Giuseppe Piazza, *La nostra pace coloniale: l'Italia e l'alleanza in Oriente e in Africa* (Rome: Ausonia, 1917).

[41]   The idea of organized, mass transplantation of peasant farmers to form agricultural colonies was not new; it had been much discussed, though little implemented, between 1900 and 1915, with proposed destinations varying from Florida to the Congo basin. Soresina, 'Italian emigration policy', 733–5.

[42]   ACS PCM GE 1915–1918, busta 138, fasc. 19.11.14/12, Colonizzazione Agricola in Turchia.

[43]   Franchetti, a convinced imperialist from a wealthy Tuscan Jewish family and one of the first employers of Maria Montessori, died by suicide on 4 November 1917 in despair over the Italian defeat at Caporetto.

preceding twelve months, arguing that the only guarantee of a lasting peace would be through fair and equitable territorial compensation to Italy after the war, and that consequently, in addition to the *terre irredente* and Dalmatia, major colonial adjustments were required. The signatories wanted the borders of Libya to be 'corrected' where they encountered Tunisia and Egypt, the creation of an Italian sphere of influence in Ethiopia, and the cession of Djibouti (a French colony since 1894) which, they asserted, was of no conceivable use to the French but would nicely round out Italian East African possessions. Across the Red Sea from Italian Eritrea, the group demanded the Farasan Islands—where oil had been discovered in 1912—and some kind of interest in Yemen (a series of demands largely identical to Foscari's April 1916 programme). However, by far the longest part of the document focused on Italian aspirations in Asia Minor, where they wanted 'continental and maritime Asia Minor with all its coasts and ports on the Aegean and on the Mediterranean, and with all its nearby islands'. The Black Sea ports and coast were to be handed over to Russia (apparently the authors anticipated that Turkey would entirely cease to exist as a sovereign entity). So modest was this proposal in comparison to British and French aspirations, the letter suggested, that it would also be appropriate to freely grant all public works across Anatolia to Italian businesses. These aspirations were not, the writers asserted, motivated by greed but by sound geopolitical reasoning:

> Italy, in occupying Asia Minor, will not only satisfy a legitimate aspiration but will render a valuable service to the cause of European harmony. No other Entente power could occupy all or most of this area without thereby acquiring an overwhelming strength in Asia and the Mediterranean, which would be unacceptable to the other allies. Italy, however, will merely restore the disturbed equilibrium of the Mediterranean as well as open indispensable outlets to her emigration. The other Entente powers, in which this emigratory phenomenon does not occur, must acknowledge Italy's rights which arise from this grave necessity.[44]

As in the Bologna investors' proposal, finding suitable land for poor emigrants and investment opportunities for wealthy industrialists were presented as paired objectives that Anatolia was almost uniquely suited to provide. The twin strands of emigrant colonialism and formal annexation, so long presented as alternatives, were here woven into a single argument.

On 26–27 April 1917 a major colonial conference was held in Naples, hosted by the Società africana d'Italia (SAI), to discuss Italy's war aims and to explore the idea that the war's unforeseen scale and importance should be reflected in greater

---

[44] ACS PCM GE 1915–1918, busta 138, 19.11.14, letter dated 24 March 1917.

and more imposing ambitions. The SAI, founded by colonial army officers and administrators, had always promoted a conquest-led model of colonialism, centred in Africa, rather than the Liberal emigration-focused model of 'colonies' across the Atlantic. In Naples the now familiar list of objectives in North and East Africa and Asia Minor was augmented by discussions of access to lake Chad or other sub-Saharan water sources (such plans were linked with schemes to irrigate the Fezzan and make Libya more fertile).[45] This detailing of specific objectives in West Africa and beyond created tensions with France, to Sonnino's irritation; relationships were already difficult, without private initiatives of this kind further imperilling them.[46] The SAI's role organizing this national event—rather than the ICI, sometime supporter of the liberal emigrant model—reflects the way in which wider national debate was shifting precisely at this moment, away from the 'emigrant nation' towards a more conventional formal empire of direct-rule (settler) colonies. Federzoni and other MPs had already noted that the war marked a decisive shift in this regard, arguing that in wartime, emigration and emigrant colonies offered little direct benefit to the country.[47]

Encouraged by these and other similar initiatives, the Italian government was by this time working on very specific and detailed proposals for an Eastern Mediterranean Empire. The choice of Asia Minor for this scheme was in reality no choice at all: little territory was available in Africa for the projected expansion and even the most grateful of allies were unlikely to give away vast tracts of their own land. It was also clear that Italian gains were unlikely to come at the direct expense of Germany, whose colonies did not—unluckily for Italy—border onto any Italian lands. A satirical postcard from the popular 'Casa del Ridere' series depicted Britain (shown as a kilt-wearing Scot) and Japan carving up the German colonial empire, which is shown as a kind of strange pink blancmange. The Kaiser is powerless to intervene, one hand trapped in each of the Eastern and Western fronts, captioned 'the end of a dream'; meanwhile a small child labelled Portugal— with an orange for a head, in reference to a southern Italian dialectal nickname— seeks to grab a slice of the empire. The impossibility of Italy claiming any of this bounty made it safe to satirize other southern European empires seeking to enrich themselves in this way.[48] Instead, it was the dissection of the Ottoman Empire which would offer the greatest possible benefits to the Italian empire.

[45] Giuseppe D'Andrea, ed., *Atti del convegno nazionale coloniale (Napoli 26–28 aprile 1917)*, Società africana d'Italia (Naples: A. Trani, 1917).
[46] ACS PCM GE 1915–1918, busta 75, 19.3.1, fasc. 28.
[47] Italia. *Atti del Parlamento Italiano*—Sessione 1913–1916, Vol. IX, I Sessione, 9503; https://storia. camera.it/lavori/regno-d-italia/leg-regno-XXIV/1916/16-marzo.
[48] Biblioteca Estense Universitaria, Raccolta Formiggini, Casa del Ridere: 'La Fine di un sogno', http://www.14-18.it/cartolina/BEU_cart_0906_v4/001?search=37a6259cc0c1dae299a7866489dff0bd& searchPos=5.

7.4.2 St Jean de Maurienne

The first step in pursuit of this vision was the formalization of the April 1917 agreement of St Jean de Maurienne. This was the culmination of months of laborious and often highly fractious negotiations with Britain and France. Italy's relationship with its Entente allies had been strained from the start, owing in part to Italy's refusal to immediately declare war on Germany in May 1915, which was seen as an unacceptable violation of the spirit of the Entente (even if technically within the terms of the Pact of London). Although Italy had declared war on the Ottoman Empire on 21 August 1915, it was excluded from the secret Anglo-French-Russian discussions on the future partitioning of the Middle East in 1915 and 1916, including the May 1916 Sykes–Picot Agreement. It appeared (and with reason) that Italy was pursuing its own war, not an allied endeavour, so it could not be a surprise that the Allies tended to exclude it.[49] But given that French and British war aims continued to evolve, and their plans for post-war settlements likewise, this side-lining was inevitably to Italy's disadvantage.

Once Italy finally declared war on Germany in August 1916, it requested full information on the proposed colonial settlement. After considerable delaying tactics, incomprehensible and highly irritating to the Italian foreign office, the text of the Sykes–Picot agreement was at last shared with the ambassador in London, Imperiali, in October of that year. Sonnino was absolutely furious: it seemed to him a direct violation of the Treaty of London, as the supposedly equitable partition of Turkey referred to therein was nowhere to be found. With his tendency to regard the April 1915 treaty as his own personal achievement, Sonnino was most jealous in guarding its every detail and saw the Sykes–Picot deal almost as a personal insult. Even Lloyd George conceded that Sonnino could not be blamed for his displeasure at the 'discourteous' treatment he had received.[50] Italy's counterclaim was for an enormous swathe of southern Anatolia, including not just Antalya but also Aydin, Konya, Mersin, and most controversially Smyrna. Sonnino laid out his wish-list in exhaustive, not to say tedious, detail in a memorandum dated 4 November 1916.[51] Arguably, the successive signing of the Italo-Russian accord of 2 December suggested that Russia implicitly accepted these demands (which did not, in any case, impinge on Tsarist claims to the Straits or any Black Sea provinces). For Britain, however, these demands were not easy to accept. Quite in keeping with their practice of secretly bestowing other

---

[49] Mario Toscano, *Gli accordi di San Giovanni di Moriana; storia diplomatica dell'intervento italiano (1916–1917)* (Milan: Dott. A. Giuffrè, 1936), 74–94.

[50] Cited in Nir Arielli, 'Hopes and Jealousies: Rome's Ambitions in the Middle East and the Italian Contingent in Palestine, 1915–1920', in *Palestine and World War I: Grand Strategy, Military Tactics and Culture in War*, ed. Yigal Sheffy, Haim Goren, and Eran Dolev (London: I. B. Tauris, 2014), 43–56.

[51] Toscano, *Gli accordi di San Giovanni di Moriana*, 42.

peoples' lands upon multiple, conflicting beneficiaries, the British had already offered Smyrna to Greece—albeit very informally—in January 1915.[52] This idea circulated once more as Greek entry to the war was discussed early in 1917. In London, meanwhile, foreign office officials like Charles Hardinge were anxious to prioritize British interests there, making for some complex horse-trading.[53] From the Italian perspective Smyrna was not only a town with a considerable Italian population but also an important trade partner of Trieste, through which much of Austria-Hungary's effort to penetrate Ottoman commerce had been directed. To acquire not only Trieste but its crucial trading partners was thus an especially appealing possibility, offering the mirage of cross-Mediterranean trade monopolies.

In January 1917 Boselli wrote to the French prime minister Aristide Briand to follow up on an earlier face-to-face conversation, not only stating that the allocation of Smyrna to Italy was essential to assure a viable economic future for the whole Antalya region but also asserting that the presence of an existing Italian community there—including schools, religious institutions, commercial interests—made it a logical step. But Boselli's interests also reached eastwards across Cilicia, following an incremental logic. If Italy were to be assigned the Vilayet of Konya then it would also require Konya's traditional maritime outlet, the Vilayet of Adana, which would in turn also require the allocation of the Adana–Mersina railway (currently in German hands). This really was a stretch: a similar logic could eventually have extended the Italian claim all the way to Iran! It also brought the Italian claim uncomfortably close to the French zone in Syria and Lebanon. Despite Boselli's assurance that 'France and Italy are destined to pursue a noble civilising mission in the Orient, hand in hand, on the basis of their common traditions and for the preservation of their interests as Mediterranean Powers', the French were not having it.[54]

Gradually, however, in a series of inter-Allied conferences in spring 1917, culminating at St Jean de Maurienne on 19 April, an agreement was slowly hashed out. Much of what Sonnino had asked for was indeed allocated to Italy under this agreement; according to Hardinge, the British cabinet felt the agreement represented 'enormous concessions by Lloyd George to Sonnino'.[55] In return, Italy would accept Allied support for Greek entry to the war and for the return of Eleftherios Venizelos to power, two policies it had vigorously opposed up to this point.[56] Venizelos was a personal friend of Lloyd George, who had become

---

[52] Michael M. Finefrock, 'Ataturk, Lloyd George and the Megali Idea: Cause and Consequence of the Greek Plan to Seize Constantinople from the Allies, June-August 1922', *The Journal of Modern History* 52, no. 1 (1980), 1050; https://www.jstor.org/stable/1881129.
[53] BOD Rennell Rodd Correspondence 18–1917: e.g. Hardinge to Rodd, 7 March.
[54] ACS PCM GE 1915–1918, busta 75, fasc. Colonie.
[55] BOD Rennell Rodd Correspondence 18–1917: Hardinge to Rodd, 30 April 1917.
[56] Marcuzzi, 'A Machiavellian Ally?', 110–13.

increasingly convinced of the need to involve Greece in the Balkan theatre of operations. Italy, by contrast, had no desire to share influence in Albania or the southern Adriatic with Greece and saw this development as a considerable threat; in Sonnino's view this was a major concession in return for what was, after all, the rightful assignation of territorial compensation. Italy also made a commitment to increase its military contribution to the war effort in the Middle East (hitherto non-existent). The April meeting did not entirely resolve the matter: diplomatic discussions with France continued through May and June over the precise borders to be established between the French and Italian portions of Anatolia. The two powers could not decide whether to rely on the pre-existing divisions between the Ottoman sanjaks or to create new boundaries around natural features and commercial interests.[57] At last, the agreement was confirmed in an exchange of notes with London and Paris in mid-August 1917, and a new map of the Middle East created which added Italy's 'C' zone to the French and British 'A' and 'B' areas (see Map 5 for details). Though often forgotten—certainly compared to the Sykes–Picot Agreement which remains notorious—this represents the fullest extent of European wartime colonial aspirations in the Middle East.

7.4.3 The Italian Expeditionary Corps in Sinai and Palestine

Sonnino and the minister for Colonies Gaspare Colosimo were both strong supporters of the plan to deploy Italian forces in the Middle East, as agreed at St Jean de Maurienne, and the very first contingent disembarked in Port Said on 19 May 1917. This was a tiny group, initially consisting of just 300 *bersaglieri* and 100 *carabinieri* (military police) with their few officers and auxiliary services in support, but Sonnino hoped that more would soon be sent, thus making a meaningful contribution to the Sinai and Palestine campaign. This would justify Italy's subsequent territorial claims and reap the propagandistic benefits of 'liberating the Holy Places' for Catholicism; it was also a response to the French military presence in the Middle East.[58] Troops might be redeployed from Cyrenaica, where the war against the Sanusiyya was now ending, and others could perhaps be found from other expeditionary forces such as that based in Albania or perhaps from new units raised in Italy. Muslim *ascari* from Somalia were earmarked for potential future action in the Hijaz; the (extremely remote) prospect of an Italian sphere of influence in Yemen was again invoked. The force sent in May 1917 also included some Italians resident in Egypt and it was hoped by the

---

[57] DDI, Quinta Serie, Vol. 8, Docs 326, 344.
[58] Antonello Battaglia, *Da Suez ad Aleppo: La campagna alleata e il distaccamento italiano in Siria e Palestina (1917–1921)* (Rome: Edizioni Nuova cultura, 2015). See DDI, Quinta Serie, Vol. 7, Docs 412, 420 on concerns about the French presence in the Middle East.

government that perhaps more could be identified. Even before the signing of the St Jean de Maurienne Agreement, the minister of war and Sonnino had discussed sending as many as 6,000–7,000 men to the theatre.[59]

In the event, this was not to be. Firstly, the foreign office's plans were energetically opposed by the chief of the general staff, Cadorna, who saw every man deployed away from the Italo-Austrian front as a waste, and who campaigned continually to abandon even existing commitments such as the occupation of Libya (still absorbing some 40,000 men at this time).[60] Colosimo also refused to contemplate the redeployment of troops from Cyrenaica, while so far as Italians in Egypt were concerned, most of those men of military age who were willing to serve were already under arms. Secondly, despite the Italian government's repeated requests to send more units to the theatre, the British were entirely opposed to the idea; they wanted a purely representative presence with minimal military or political significance. The Italian expeditionary corps would be primarily a public order unit, which the British requested should be composed of white troops (thus denying one possibly useful assignment for the largely unused Libyan *ascari*).[61] In fact, although the Agreement called for an Italian detachment in Palestine, Britain had already formally abandoned this requirement by June 1917, just two months after signing the deal.[62] Thereafter, they would determinedly block every effort to deploy further Italian forces—it was, in Allenby's view, already bad enough to have to accommodate the French.[63] The tiny Italian force took part in Edmund Allenby's Gaza campaign and the subsequent occupation of Jerusalem, making almost no appreciable contribution to the Allied victory but infuriating the British with their demand for equitable treatment with the French at all times. In fact the Italians spent more time and energy bickering with the French over questions of status than engaged in military activities.[64] The dispatch of a second, larger detachment was eventually agreed with the Allies, and assembled in Naples in October 1918; this group consisted mainly of indigenous Libyan *ascari* and five regular battalions, under the command of General Mario Riveri, and was preparing to embark for Palestine when the Armistice at Mudros forestalled their departure.[65] The units were sent to Rhodes instead, still with the intention of proceeding to Syria or Palestine, but finally in March 1919 this plan was

[59] AUSSME, E3, b. 151, fasc. 14. See also Arielli, 'Hopes and Jealousies: Rome's Ambitions in the Middle East'.
[60] DDI, Quinta Serie, Vol. 8, Doc. 371; ACS PCM GE 1915–1918, busta 241-bis, Militari Vari: Cadorna to Sonnino, 27 June 1917, n. 2984 di Prot. G.M.: Colloquio col Generale Foch. See also Luigi Cadorna, *La guerra alla fronte italiana (24 maggio 1915–9 novembre 1917)* (Milan: Fratelli Treves, 1921), 7–8.
[61] Battaglia, *Da Suez Ad Aleppo*, 117–19.
[62] Paul C. Helmreich, 'Italy and the Anglo-French Repudiation of the 1917 St. Jean de Maurienne Agreement', *The Journal of Modern History* 48, no. 2 (1976): 130, https://www.jstor.org/stable/1877819.
[63] Aimée Fox, *Learning to Fight* (Cambridge: Cambridge University Press, 2018), 140.
[64] Arielli, 'Hopes and Jealousies: Rome's Ambitions in the Middle East', 47–8.
[65] ACS PCM GE 1915–1918, busta 241-bis.

cancelled.[66] The paucity of the Italian contribution in the Middle East was largely due to British refusal to countenance any greater deployment there; the Italians were pardonably annoyed when in 1919 Lloyd George complained about their lack of military contribution given that his own military hierarchy had actively and repeatedly blocked all efforts to participate.

The British were not the only political force with whom Italy had to contend in Palestine. Rather begrudgingly, in 1918, the Italian government tried to respond to the emergence of Zionism. The foreign office sent a young Jewish naval officer, Commandant Angelo Levi-Bianchini, to Palestine to collect intelligence. Sonnino was persuaded in May 1918 to issue a formal endorsement of the Balfour declaration and Levi-Bianchini was thereafter admitted to Chaim Weizmann's Zionist Commission. Both an observant Jew and an enthusiastic patriot, his position was awkward: was he there to represent his government—after all, he owed his job to Sonnino—or to represent Italian Jewish interests? The ministry hoped he would promote Italian economic interests in the new Palestine and collect valuable intelligence on both Zionism and the British, although Sonnino, typically, did not formally request this until Levi-Bianchini was already in the field. The Italian Union of Jewish Communities (UCEI), however, saw him as Italy's delegate to the Zionist movement. From a wealthy Venetian family (his brother was a colonel), Levi-Bianchini was tactful, personable, and a talented linguist who got on equally well with Weizmann and the British authorities. He worked to mediate between various positions within the Commission, to promote the totality of Jewish interests in Palestine and to protect local Jews. Sonnino appears to have had no real interest in Zionism, other than an opportunistic desire to see whether it might in some way be used to promote Italian interests in the Middle East; he hoped that Levi-Bianchini might serve as a tool of informal empire-building. In reality, Levi-Bianchini's success in moderating local tensions appears to have strongly—if inadvertently—promoted the British position.[67]

7.5 Italy and the Global War

As the war went on and new belligerents joined, its world-wide dimensions grew ever more apparent. In 1918 Italy began to contribute more significantly to the wider global war effort, owing to both external and internal developments. Within the Entente, the impact of the Supreme Allied War Council—created at the

---

[66] IOH Vol. VII, t.3, 357–8.
[67] Sergio Minerbi, 'Angelo Levi-Bianchini in Levante (1918–1920)', *Rivista di studi politici internazionali* 34, no. 1 (1967): 45–108.

Rapallo Conference in November 1917—was doubtless making itself felt.[68] The improved allied coordination in the final year of the war meant that there was not only more effective pressure on Italy but also greater incentives for Italian cooperation within this body. Domestic attitudes had also changed. The new willingness to engage beyond the pursuit of narrowly national interests was largely the result of Allied intervention in Italy after Caporetto in 1917, which encouraged a general perception that the country was fighting as part of a collective war effort and also suggested, if not a debt to repay, at least the desirability of a reciprocal gesture. Greater intervention outside the Italo-Austrian front was also intended to convey the clear message to Allies and enemies alike that the defeat of Caporetto had been overcome and had left no lasting mark on the battle-worthiness of the Italian army or on Italy's capacity to continue to resist. Almost certainly, the removal of the eternally pig-headed Cadorna also played a part: where he had fought tooth and nail against sending troops outside Italy, Diaz was much more politically accommodating.

The political dimensions of this new approach were of paramount importance, even to military commentators. Its most important consequence was the decision to send troops to France. In February 1918 Diaz himself prioritized 'the high morale value of the material presence of all the Allied powers on all of the chessboards of the war' and undertook to dispatch troops to support Entente powers as rapidly as possible, even if this meant reducing the forces on Italy's own front.[69] Orlando, speaking in the parliament, invoked lofty rhetoric of liberty and solidarity; it was a source of 'pride and pleasure' to think that 'the Italian tricolour would fly above the fields of Flanders and Picardy alongside the allied flags'. Perhaps the persistent international denigration of the Italian front as secondary to the Western Front helps explain this outlook. Even the official history, written after the Second World War, caught this mood, suggesting that the troops were sent to show they could 'proudly fight and Italian-ly win or perish on any battlefield, against any enemy'.[70] Lesser expeditionary forces in support of Allied missions in Russia and the Far East would also follow later in 1918.

7.5.1 Italians in France

In February and March 1918 extensive discussions over the distribution of Italian, British, and French forces ensued. At length Italy committed to send several divisions to the Western Front, partly to forestall the full Franco-British

---

[68] On the Council's relationship with Italy, see Meighen McCrae, *Coalition Strategy and the End of the First World War: The Supreme War Council and War Planning, 1917–1918* (Cambridge and New York: Cambridge University Press, 2019), ch. 4.
[69] IOH. Vol. VII, t.2, 5.   [70] IOH. Vol. VII, t.2, 8.

withdrawal of their forces from Italy, seen by Diaz as both politically and militarily undesirable. Originally, two infantry divisions were due to be sent by Italy to form part of the joint strategic reserve, as agreed in February 1918.[71] When this plan was abandoned, the units were instead allocated instead to an active sector of the front.

At the end of April, II° Army Corps was duly dispatched to the Western Front. While it was not the first time Italians had fought in France, the contribution of the volunteer Garibaldian Legions in the Argonne in 1914 had been of minimal operational importance. By contrast, II° Army Corps was a complete and sub-stantial unit, composed of two infantry divisions with their own artillery, cavalry, *Arditi* shock troops, and all the necessary auxiliary services from logistics to medical staff, making it operationally independent and ready to deploy. With around 52,000 men, this was the largest single unit deployed outside Italy during the war (more men were sent to the Balkans but dispersed between multiple units). Considerable care went into the selection of the units to be sent to France. The corps had a good reputation, having served well on the Isonzo and being free of the negative associations attached to the former units of Second Army after Caporetto. Its commander, Alberico Albricci, was also well regarded—he was a former military attaché in Vienna with experience both on the general staff and in combat roles (he would later serve as minister of war under Francesco Saverio Nitti's government in 1919–20). One of the four infantry brigades selected was the 'Alpi' Brigade, historically a prestigious unit with a record stretching back to the wars of the Risorgimento, under the command of one of Garibaldi's surviving grandsons (Peppino). Many of the former 'legionaries' of 1914 had ended up in this unit, including the writer Curzio Malaparte, so the brigade had ties to service in France as well as evoking Garibaldi's leadership in the Army of the Vosges in 1870–1 in defence of the Third Republic.[72]

Upon arrival, II° Army Corps spent some time training and acclimatizing to the new front and its fighting expectations in the training camp at Mailly-le-Camp, followed by a period in a quiet sector in the Argonne. But French and Italian authorities were united in their desire to see the Italian troops actively engaged. The corps was soon transferred into the Reims sector where it fought with the French 5th Army along the river Ardre and was deployed at Bligny during the Second Battle of the Marne. In these battles, more than 9,000 men were lost (of whom nearly 4,000 were captured by German forces).[73] Italy's most famous war poet, Giuseppe Ungaretti, served with the corps and wrote several of his best-known works in this period, some in Italian and others in French. In September

[71] McCrae, *Coalition Strategy and the End of the First World War*, 100–3.
[72] Alberto Caselli Lapeschi and Giancarlo Militello, eds, *1918: Gli italiani sul fronte occidentale: nel diario del ten. Giacomo Tortora e in altri documenti inediti* (Buccinasco (MI): Società storica per la Guerra Bianca, 2007), 13–17.
[73] IOH. Vol. VII, t.2, 37–58.

and October the corps fought on the Aisnes and the Chemin des Dames, taking part in the final Allied offensives and reaching the Meuse on 11 November 1918, shortly before 11 a.m. It would spend most of the next few months in Belgium, awaiting repatriation. By the end of its deployment, it counted at least 4,375 dead and 6,359 wounded, and some 3,500 missing.[74]

Significant numbers of auxiliary troops were also deployed—the Truppe Ausiliarie Italiane in Francia (TAIF)—from January 1918. This followed almost two years of formal requests from France for manpower which had been mostly ignored or rejected while Cadorna was in charge (though in reality there were tens of thousands of emigrant Italians working in France in a variety of unofficial capacities before 1918 too).[75] The TAIF was made up of some 60,000 unarmed men, no longer fit for combat duty (including on grounds of age or of service-related disability), serving as labour battalions. The decision to send these men to France was much criticized within Italy, not least because there was a fear that these aged or wounded men risked giving a poor impression of Italian strength, but also on the grounds of humanity (why should men honourably wounded in the service of Italy be sent to build roads for the French?).[76] The widespread practice on the Western Front of employing racially othered and implicitly 'inferior' manpower for these non-combat roles—such as the Chinese Labour corps or the various colonial labour units—explicitly underpinned some of these Italian anxieties about the TAIF and how it might influence perceptions of Italy and of Italians. The head of Italian military intelligence in Paris, General Nicola Brancaccio, made this very clear: writing to the minister of war, he argued that it was wrong to send Italians 'to perform services which up until now have been carried out by colonial natives'.[77] Like the men of II° Army Corps, the TAIF remained in France until after the Armistice, despite repeated efforts by Diaz to reclaim them in summer 1918 which were politely rejected by Foch, on the grounds that their services were essential. They were demobilized in January and February 1919.[78]

7.5.2 From Murmansk to Manchuria

Italy's new outlook towards participation in the greater war also led to the deployment of troops much further afield than France. In August 1918 a new

---

[74] IOH. Vol. VII, t.2, 218.   [75] IOH. Vol. VII, t.2, 289–94.

[76] IOH. Vol. VII, t.2, 345–6.

[77] Mario Caracciolo, *Le truppe italiane in Francia. Il II Corpo d'armata e le T.A.I.F.* (Milan: Mondadori, 1929), 26–7, 235–7.

[78] For more on their experiences, see Hubert Heyriès, *Les travailleurs militaires italiens en France pendant la Grande Guerre: héros de la pelle et de la truelle au service de la victoire* (Montpellier: Presses universitaires de la Méditerranée, 2014).

overseas detachment was organized, in accordance with agreements made at Versailles by the Supreme War Council to send a force to Murmansk.[79] After the signing of the Treaty of Brest–Litovsk between Germany and the new Bolshevik government in Russia, the Allies intervened on the Eastern Front to try to prevent Germany from seizing Allied supplies and further strengthening their position with additional Russian resources. A multinational force was accordingly deployed into northern Russia, and Italy was keen to participate. Consequently, the IV battalion of the 67th infantry regiment, with a machine-gun company, some *carabinieri* and engineers, and a field hospital with its staff—a total of some 1,300 men in all—was dispatched to join the Allied Expeditionary Force against the German presence in Finland and the Archangel region.[80] They were accompanied by their own translator (an aristocratic Russian-born cavalry officer named Nicolò degli Albizzi) and two fully equipped meteorological experts. The Italian units travelled via Le Havre to Southampton, where they welcomed not only by Sir Henry Wilson but by an Italian emigrant in her nineties named Signora Operti greeted who the troops with a tricolour flag she had kept since the 1860s—'our *first* Risorgimento', the commanding officer of the unit remarked pointedly.[81] This contingent, finally disembarking at Murmansk on 2 September 1918, was yet another sign of Italian determination to maintain its position and prestige within the Entente.[82] Serving under British command as the Savoia Column they were joined by French, Serbs, Americans, Poles, and Karelians, with French and British naval support. The Savoia Column was initially engaged in defending the Kola–St Petersburg railway line from the Red Army, and later was engaged in the Lake Onega region where it saw action in May and June 1919. It returned to Italy in August 1919, after suffering a total of twenty-two fatalities.

In August 1918 Italy was also firming up plans to contribute to the Allied forces in the Far East (these had been developing since at least January 1918 when the French first sent troops to Irkutsk). In May and June the revolt of the Czechoslovak Legion—consisting mainly of former Habsburg prisoners of war—against the Bolsheviks encouraged the Allies to intervene, and in July 1918 Woodrow Wilson proposed a joint US–Japanese expeditionary force should land in Vladivostock.[83] The Italian government, 'motivated by reasons of politics,

[79] See AUSSME Fondo F3, b. 272, f. 22.

[80] For a military history of this force, see Giuseppe Cacciaguerra, *Corpo di spedizione italiano in Murmania 1918–1919* (Rome: Stato maggiore dell'Esercito, Ufficio storico, 2014).

[81] ACS PCM GE 1915–1918, busta 75-bis, fasc. 19.3. x Russia.

[82] For an interesting analysis of Murmansk as a colonial theatre of war, this time from a British perspective, see Steven Balbirnie, 'Small War on a Violent Frontier: Colonial Warfare and British Intervention in Northern Russia, 1918–1919', in *Small Nations and Colonial Peripheries in World War I*, ed. Gearóid Barry, Enrico Dal Lago, and Róisín Healy (Leiden: Brill, 2016), 193–210.

[83] Paul Dunscomb, 'Siberian Intervention 1918–1922', in *1914–1918 Online. International Encyclopedia of the First World War*, ed. Ute Daniel et al. (Berlin: Freie Universität Berlin, 2018), https://encyclopedia.1914-1918-online.net/article/siberian_intervention_1918-1922.

morale and prestige', accepted the Allied invitation to participate.[84] Officially the intervention was designed to protect the Czechs, but in reality the intervention had a variety of overlapping or even conflicting objectives. Ever since the Bolshevik revolution, there had been discussions over sending some Allied units to Vladivostok—to protect Allied supplies, to support the anti-communist forces in the Civil War, to ensure that Russia did not in any way further support Germany, or to boost the Japanese position, depending on who was asked. Italian interests were not directly touched but as in northern Russia the principle of 'acting as a great power come what may' governed the decision-making process. The Italian legation in Beijing had been keen to see Italian troops join the Allied forces there since the French were very active in deploying to the region and the Legate was seriously concerned about Italy's prestige within China if no Italians were present.[85] Several officers had already been sent out, with equipment and machine guns, with instructions to disembark in China and then meet up with the main Allied forces; a military attaché was appointed to join the Japanese command in Vladivostok. The Expeditionary Corps for the Far East (Estremo Oriente) was finally formally constituted on 19 September 1918 after many months of discussion. Zupelli was already planning which units to deploy in April—he envisaged that it would be necessary to staff the mission with units from Eritrea.[86] The Expeditionary Corps which set off from Naples on 19 July 1918 was little more than a command, some carabinieri and a solitary mountain artillery unit; they travelled via Malta and Port Said to Massaua where they collected the remaining forces—an infantry company and two-machine gun sections—before proceeding via Singapore to Tianjin, where they arrived on 2 September. In total there were some 25 officers and 700 other ranks, mostly Sicilians and Sards.[87]

This unit would be joined in Tianjin by the volunteers of the Legione Redenta—the 'redeemed Legion', also known in Italy as Siberian Legion. Like the more famous Czechoslovak Legion, the unit was made up of volunteers formerly serving in the Austro-Hungarian armies. Even before Russia's exit from the war, Italian irredentist prisoners in Russian hands had been seen as an important group, embodying as they did the national cause of liberation. The Italian Military Mission in Russia spent several years trying to recruit them, successfully extracting

[84] IOH, Vol. VII, t.1: *Il Corpo di Spedizione Italiano in Estremo Oriente* (Rome: Provveditorato generale dello stato libreria, 1934), 51.
[85] ACS PCM GE 1915–1918, busta 75-bis, fasc. 19.3.5 Cina. Franco-Italian rivalry was a major driver of Italian policy in China in this period, even down to debates over the appointment of a new Papal Nunzio.
[86] Ministero della Guerra Segretariato Generale, 3 April 1918. Reproduced in Antonio Mautone, *Trentini e Italiani contro l'Armata Rossa: la storia del Corpo di Spedizione in Estremo Oriente e dei Battaglioni Neri, 1918–1920* (Trento: Temi, 2003), 313–14.
[87] IOH, Vol. VII, t.1, 51–6.

99 officers and 3,949 other ranks in 1916 and 1917 from prisoner of war camps and repatriating them via Britain. Most of the officers and several hundred men immediately joined the Italian army upon their return.[88] After the Bolshevik Revolution this work became almost impossible and the Military Mission left the country. Instead, the remaining Italian irredentist prisoners ended up travelling east to Vladivostock and Tianjin, where those who wished to fight for Italy were formed into the Legione Redenta.

The Expeditionary Corps' stay in Tianjin was brief; officials reported they were greeted with enthusiasm 'by our Colony here' but the Italian concession in the city was so tiny that the Corps command had to be housed in the French concession and the troops in a British barracks. The Official History unconsciously contrasts this awkward situation with the impressive military facilities in which the British had easily hosted the Corps in Singapore, highlighting the weakness of a supposed colony which could not even accommodate its own forces. The Corps then transferred its base to Vladivostock, and set off into Siberia, some 40 officers and 1,350 men, chiefly to help defend the Trans-Siberian railway. In May and early June 1919 they saw action against Red Army units, achieving some success at a tactical level, but the overall fate of the Allied expedition was clear and already by the end of June 1919 the Italian government was planning to withdraw the unit. They withdrew from Siberia, reaching Tianjin once more in late August, and arrived back in Italy in late autumn or early in 1920 (many disembarking in Trieste, to the delight of the members of the Legione Redenta).[89]

Between the two expeditionary forces and the Legione Redenta, at least 4,000 Italians served in Russia during and after the war—some born and raised in the kingdom, others from the 'redeemed lands'—and others yet in American uniforms. This last group raised some surprising fears within the Italian government, as revealed by a letter of 27 March 1919 from minister of the colonies, Colosimo, to the prime minister. Officers in both Murmansk and Manchuria, he wrote, feared that their men might have been infected with Bolshevism during their time in Russia. But this was not, as might be expected, thanks to interactions with local populations; on the contrary, it was caused by 'frequent contacts with American troops, largely made up of soldiers of Italian nationality who are already infected with Marxism'. The troops who returned from Murmansk would be carefully inspected in France to check their ideological position before they were permitted to return to Italy in 1919.[90]

---

[88] IOH, Vol. VII, t.1, 16–20.   [89] IOH, Vol. VII, t.1, 84–143.
[90] DDI Sesta Serie, 1919–1922, 4 vols: Vol. 3, Doc. 43.

7.6 Planning for Peace

The greater Italian participation in the wider war which began in 1918 and continued into the immediate post-war period was purely politically motivated. Demonstrating great power status, whether in Murmansk, Upper Silesia, or Palestine, was critically important. The Italian government was looking to the future and planning how best to position itself in relation to its allies with an eye to the eventual peace conference. Contributing to the global war was essential for claiming a share of the global spoils.

By 1918 planning for the post-war development of the colonies was already under way. By mid-summer, the Italian Colonial Institute was already planning a major national conference (eventually held in January 1919) to discuss colonial compensation and popularize its agenda. Colosimo wrote to Orlando on 7 June to outline his most pressing concerns: since both Libya and the East African colonies bordered onto French and British possessions, territorial adjustments could only come through bargaining at the eventual peace conference. Since the 1885 Berlin Agreement had been largely overtaken by events, a new African order was needed—which he hoped would be more favourable to Italy, reflecting its much greater status than in 1885. 'We cannot and must not ignore the colonial question as a cause and an epilogue of this war,' he wrote, and so 'colonial resolutions must be an integral part of our war policy and our peace negotiations'. In a similar report to the Foreign Ministry he argued that colonial questions should be 'one of the chief topics upon which the peace conference must focus'. Reviewing the international press, Colosimo observed that neither in Germany—which still hoped to retain its colonies after the war—nor within in the Entente were Italian interests in Africa anywhere being considered. Ironically, the principles which he outlines as underpinning German colonialism—reflecting a European balance of power, providing an outlet for industrial and population growth—more nearly reflect that Italian position that the French or British approach. He urged his colleagues to begin preparing at once for the peace negotiations, based on the guiding principle that compensation must be commensurate with Italy's sacrifices for the common cause, as well as maintaining the alliance effectively after the war.[91]

What did this mean in practice? Italian colonialists nurtured a range of ambitions, some deeply implausible, others only moderately so. By October 1918 General Marco Nicolis di Robilant was reporting back from the Supreme Allied War Council in Paris—on Sonnino's orders—about rumours and indiscretions about Entente plans for Africa, as part of a concerted effort to position Italy well for the conference ahead. Though France and Britain viewed the German

---

[91] ACS PCM GE 1915–1918, busta 75, fasc. Colonie. Colosimo to Sonnino, 3 June 1918, n. 3412; Colosimo to Orlando, 7 June 1918.

colonies as spoils to share between them, Italy had not yet given up hope of achieving significant compensation in return.

Djibouti recurred frequently in Italian discussions. This tiny French foothold in East Africa was a matter of irritation to Britain and Italy alike; both believed that the French were using it to traffic arms into Ethiopia to expand their influence there. Both Britain and Italy agreed, at least according to reports from April and May 1918, that the best solution would be to kick the French out of East Africa altogether. There the consensus ended, for both parties unsurprisingly considered that they would be the most appropriate beneficiaries. By June 1918 the Italian position was clear:

1) The 'Ethiopian question' cannot be resolved while Djibouti remains French;
2) It would not be resolved for Italy if it became British either;
3) If the alliance is to continue after the war, and is to apply in Africa also, then it is imperative that Djibouti passes into Italian hands;
4) If, as seems most likely, the French won't cede it to Italy directly, then it would still be better for it to pass to Britain and for Italy to do a deal with the British;
5) A lasting resolution of the situation requires elimination of France from the region and exclusive rights for Italy, with exception of British interest in the source of the Nile, but with Djibouti firmly in Italian hands;
6) In the unfortunate event that Djibouti remains French, Britain and Italy should jointly push for a revision of the treaty governing the sale of arms and munitions into Ethiopia.[92]

It was not likely, however, that France would willingly surrender this vital refuelling port on the Red Sea, an essential link to its colonies in Madagascar and Indochina, and indeed the French were quite unwilling to put Djibouti on the table as part of their negotiations at any stage. Italy's hopes relied heavily on driving a wedge between France and Britain in East Africa, but this proved totally unsuccessful.[93] Equally of interest to Italy was Lake Chad, or at least its northern shore, which was an important outlet for trans-Saharan trade on routes through the Libyan interior. But like Djibouti this was a highly unrealistic goal, not least since it could only be of any possible benefit to Italy once the entirety of Libya, including Fezzan, was under its control—which remained a remote prospect in 1918.

Such possibilities lay well beyond the scope of St Jean de Maurienne. But by 1918 these extravagant positions were circulating not only in hard-line colonial circles but even in the heart of government. At the same time, after Caporetto a clear shift in policy making had begun. Where Salandra had generally supported

---

[92] ACS PCM GE 1915–1918, busta 75, fasc. Colonie, 1/6/1918, Colosimo to Sonnino n. 3245.
[93] Robert L. Hess, 'Italy and Africa: Colonial Ambitions in the First World War', *Journal of African History* 4, no. 1 (1963): 105–26; 119–20.

Sonnino, and Boselli left him to his own devices, Vittorio Emanuele Orlando was a much more interventionist prime minister who increasingly sought to shape and direct foreign policy himself. The conflict between Orlando and Sonnino which emerged in this period would go on to become a significant element in the Italian performance at the Paris Peace Conference.

7.6.1   Albania

In late 1918 Italian policy towards Albania was also evolving. The Treaty of London and Italy's wartime Proclamation of Argirocastro were in considerable tension with one another, and Italy once again found itself engaged in a bitter rivalry with France. Bulgarian defeat and Austrian withdrawal should have offered the Italians a much freer hand in Albania, but Italy and France could not agree over Serbia's future role in the region. Serbia hoped to reoccupy Kosovo and assure its access to the sea; with tacit French agreement, Serb troops were also able to occupy the northern city of Shkodër and its surroundings, to Italy's great annoyance.[94] Though by 11 November 1918 Italy occupied the largest share of the country, Serbia in the north and Greece to the south both posed obstacles to its full aspirations there.

In October 1918 Sonnino invited leading Albanian politicians to Rome, where he urged them to form a new 'independent' national council, uniting all religious and provincial groups, under Italian protection. Ostensibly this was in line with the 1917 Proclamation of Argirocastro, though this had actually referred to a national government, which was not quite what Sonnino now proposed. In December 1918 an Albanian congress met in the then-capital Durrës, but rather than forming this half-representative body, which he hoped would agree to be represented at the Paris Conference by Italy, the congress declared a new Provisional Government, and protested against Sonnino's decision to separate Italian-held Vlorë from the rest of the country.[95] This was certainly not what Sonnino had wanted; General Settimio Piacentini, commanding the occupying forces, tried to prevent the government forming but to no avail. Sonnino reluctantly agreed to recognize the Durrës government 'as an expression of Albanian national sentiment' but warned its leaders that only the Peace Conference could definitively settle any territorial questions.[96] In fact many Albanians stigmatized this new government as merely a submissive Italian puppet, and it would not last beyond 1920.[97]

---

[94]   DDI, Sesta Serie, Vol. 1, Docs 76, 77.
[95]   See Sonnino's telegram of 20 November 1918: DDI, Sesta Serie, Vol. 1, Doc. 243.
[96]   DDI, Sesta Serie, Vol. 1, Docs 660, 661, 671, 694–7.
[97]   Fabio Bego, 'The Vlora Conflict from a Trans-Adriatic Perspective', in *Myths and Mythical Spaces: Conditions and Challenges for History Textbooks in Albania and South-Eastern Europe*, ed. Claudia Lichnofsky, Enriketa Pandelejmoni, and Darko Stojanov (Göttingen: V&R unipress GmbH, 2017), 110–11.

8

Race, Nationality, and Citizenship

The Meanings of *Italianità* in Wartime

Early twentieth-century Italians—and especially imperialists and nationalists—conceived of empire as a broad category where formal colonies were accompanied by the projection of global power through emigrant communities. But just what was the nature of the tie between Italians abroad and the Kingdom of Italy? Was it simply a legally framed relationship based on reciprocal rights and obligations, namely citizenship? What did *italianità* actually mean? Italian nationality was conceived of in highly racialized terms, meaning that the 'greater Italy' was bonded not only through language, culture, and citizenship but through birth. This global Italy was an empire based not on territorial sovereignty but on the italianità of emigrants: an empire of blood, not of soil. From unification onwards, racial discourses emerged around the nature of Italian identity and were profoundly shaped by ideas about empire and colonialism, including the internal colonization of the South. These ideas, in turn, underpinned wartime political and military culture. What did it mean, in 1915, to be Italian? And to what extent did that change in the years that followed? The expansionist nature of Italy's war, and the Liberal state's ongoing commitment to imperialism, meant that discourses of nationality, race, and citizenship were intimately entangled in the conflict. In Italy as elsewhere, the war provoked reassessments of how these ideas (and gender) intersected.[1] This chapter traces some of the contemporary debates to show how the imperial and colonial dimensions of the war promoted new understandings of these critical concepts within Italy.

8.1 *Italianità*

If Italy's colonies abroad contributed vital manpower and money to the war effort, they also necessarily complicated the wartime concept of nationality and citizenship. The category of 'Italian' had been constructed in multiple ways since the origins of the Italian nationalist movement with little clear consensus. Language, faith, and culture were all important but not sufficient in themselves to establish

---

[1] See the Introduction to Sara Lorenzini and Simone Attilio Bellezza, eds, *Sudditi o cittadini? L'evoluzione delle appartenenze imperiali nella Prima Guerra Mondiale* (Rome: Viella, 2018).

The Italian Empire and the Great War. Vanda Wilcox, Oxford University Press (2021). © Vanda Wilcox.
DOI: 10.1093/oso/9780198822943.003.0008

italianità. Territory, of course, was not a sufficient basis for identity: no country which embraces strong irredentist beliefs could limit the definition of its nationality to those born or resident within its existing borders. A fundamental strand in Italian nationalist thought was therefore the existence of many Italians outside the kingdom's borders; they might be born far afield, never visit Italy, speak other languages—as well as Italian, of course—and develop roots in those areas, without this lessening their Italian-ness. They might vote or even hold office within other state systems and yet still be Italian—as with Cesare Battisti and Alcide De Gasperi, two very celebrated political figures for Italy, who were both once elected deputies in the Vienna parliament. Indeed, they might live their entire lives across the Atlantic Ocean—as so-called '*oriundi*'—and yet be Italian. Critically, the formation of Italian national identity in advance of the nation-state meant that an essentialist definition of *italianità* emerged from the beginning.

Italian was something one might become or be made into: the internal colonization of the 'degenerate' South was in part a project of making Italians. But—given the inherent fragility of the concept—it was also something which could (and should) be handed down, wherever a family found itself in the world. A core component in *italianità*, therefore, was heritability. As Silvana Patriarca and Valeria Deplano noted, by the early twentieth century 'race (and other semantically related words such as stirpe, "stock") and nation became interchangeable terms'.[2] This superimposition of national and racial identity was manifest in many arenas: citizenship was to be based on *ius sanguinis* rather than *ius soli*, while the Italian literary culture of romantic nationalism celebrated a mythic link between blood, tradition, and landscape.[3] Throughout the late nineteenth and early twentieth century, we find 'Italian' explicitly defined as a race both by Italians and others; at times, it is an ethnocultural subset of the 'Latin races'. The role of racial thinking in defining *italianità* was enhanced by encounters with various external Others, whether through emigration or colonialism, which allowed Italians to define themselves in contrast to a variety of racial and ethnic groups.

The question of who was Italian, and what made them Italian, was of fundamental importance in the First World War. To 'liberate' an oppressed people in a neighbouring land, or to win the greatness which 'the people deserve' one must first be able to clearly identify the people in question. Equally, an expansionist war will—if it succeeds—bring new lands and populations into the control of the state. The status and treatment of these new inhabitants requires a clear articulation of national identity and citizenship policy. During the period 1911–24 Italy grappled with many new peoples within its expanding borders: Arabs and Berbers, Greeks

    [2] Silvana Patriarca and Valeria Deplano, 'Nation, "Race", and Racisms in Twentieth-Century Italy', *Modern Italy* 23, no. 4 (2018): 349–53, DOI: https://doi.org/10.1017/mit.2018.38; 350.
    [3] See Alberto Mario Banti, *La nazione del Risorgimento. Parentela, santità e onore alle origini dell'Italia unita* (Turin: Einaudi, 2011).

and Turks, Ladino-speaking Jews, Tyrolese Germans, Slovenes, Croats, and Albanians all came under Italian rule. As this multitude of linguistically, religiously, and ethnically diverse inhabitants encountered the Italian state, the state and the ruling class were forced to grapple with important questions involving both nationality and citizenship.

8.2 Race in Italy Before the First World War

While the Fascists' interest in biopower and racial categorization is well known, it is sometimes assumed that this marked the origins of racial thinking in Italy. Not so: in the last twenty years scholars have shown that Italian racial 'science', and the construction of Italian whiteness, began with the Risorgimento.[4] As Rhiannon Welch illustrates, 'race underpinned the discursive constitution of Italians as modern political subjects—a process often referred to as "making Italians"', and indeed it was a core foundation for the whole process of nation formation.[5] Enrico Corradini, like many other nationalists, was in no doubt that race was an essential component of the Italian national identity, connecting the Italians of his time to their ancestors and to their descendants.[6] Despite the lack of a colonial empire, often assumed to be an essential prompt for the development of racial thinking, in the 1860s and 1870s sociologists, criminologists, and anthropologists began to formulate extensive 'scientific' theories which relied upon two key ideas: firstly white supremacy and secondly the inalienable whiteness of Italians.[7] In this way, 'coloniality' predated functional colonialism. In fact, the acquisition of a colonial empire was imagined as a proof and validation of Italian claims to whiteness. The notorious eugenicist Cesare Lombroso was at the forefront of this movement, and his colleagues and students were numerous. Racial thinking was pervasive not only in academic circles but also within the military, where one of Lombroso's followers, psychologist Placido Consiglio, was highly influential in the years before

---

[4] Italy has proven an especially fertile field for scholars and theoreticians of biopower in recent years, see Welch, *Vital Subjects*; Aaron Gillette, *Racial Theories in Fascist Italy* (Abingdon: Routledge, 2003); Alberto Burgio and Luciano Casali, eds, *Studi sul razzismo italiano* (Bologna: CLUEB, 1996); Alberto Burgio, ed., *Nel nome della razza: il razzismo nella storia d'Italia 1870–1945* (Bologna: Il Mulino, 1999); Giuliani, *Race, Nation and Gender in Modern Italy*;Aliza Wong, *Race and the Nation in Liberal Italy, 1861–1911: Meridionalism, Empire, and Diaspora* (New York: Palgrave Macmillan, 2006).

[5] Welch, *Vital Subjects*, 5–6. See also anthropologist Miguel Mellino, 'De-Provincializing Italy', in *Postcolonial Italy: Challenging National Homogeneity*, ed. Cristina Lombardi-Diop and Caterina Romeo (New York: Palgrave Macmillan, 2012), 83–102.

[6] Cited in Gillette, *Racial Theories in Fascist Italy*, 38.

[7] Giuseppe Finaldi and Daniela Baratieri, '"Without Flinching": Facing up to Race in Liberal Italy', *Australian Journal of Politics & History* 65, no. 1 (2019): 1–16. On the construction of Italian whiteness, see Gaia Giuliani and Cristina Lombardi-Diop, *Bianco e nero: storia dell'identità razziale degli italiani*, (Florence: Le Monnier, 2013).

and during the war.[8] The insistence on the scientific superiority of whiteness, and Italian whiteness specifically, was a response both to the 'superstition' of Catholicism and its hold on Italian society, and to the international tendency to present Italy as backwards and under-developed. Indeed, Italians were regularly held up as a cautionary example of 'degeneracy' in comparison to their own glorious past in the writings of nineteenth-century northern European race scholars. Racial prejudice against Italian emigrants in the United States was another driver of Italian rebuttals and assertions of whiteness.[9] Racism in the early Liberal period was therefore, in the words of Finaldi and Baratieri, 'a crusade espoused by progressive cosmopolitan scientists and intellectuals seeking to provide novel solutions to the urgent questions besetting the new state and nation'.[10] Italy's most pressing concerns in its first fifty to sixty years—the 'southern question', irredentism, emigration, and the acquisition of colonies—were all wholly or partially rooted in racial understandings, which these scientists sought to articulate more explicitly.[11] But racial thinking was equally important outside scientific (or social scientific) circles: the fields of literature and journalism were also pervaded by ideas about race, while the visual media of photography and the cinema also made a major contribution to Italian racial discourse.[12]

Racial thinking and anxieties about degeneracy were very much prompted by the encounter with Italy's internal colony, the South: Lombroso himself accompanied the army as it brutally crushed the 'brigandage' of the 1860s where he witnessed first-hand what he considered the 'atavism' of the southern peasantry. The views of Leopoldo Franchetti—'meridionalist' and dedicated colonialist— are also illuminating here.[13] But the colonial comparison has its limits. Class *always* mattered: even the most prejudiced Piedmontese aristocrat did not really believe that his Sicilian counterpart was innately uncivilized, and within a few decades of unification, southern politicians held some of the highest offices in the land. Interestingly, many of these southerners—Francesco Crispi, Antonino di Sangiuliano, Antonio Salandra—were also committed colonialists. Perhaps relative marginalization within the homeland increased the southern ruling class's support for empire. Meanwhile all Italians—including southerners—were understood as a racial stock ripe for improvement and growth, through collective management. Italian whiteness, in other words, was actively constituted in this

[8] Andrea Scartabellati, 'Un *Wanderer* dell'anormalità? Un invito allo studio di Placido Consiglio (1877–1959)', *Rivista Sperimentale di Freniatria* 134, no. 3 (November 2010): 89–112, DOI: https://doi.org/10.3280/RSF2010-003008.

[9] Wong, *Race and the Nation*, 120–36.   [10] Finaldi and Baratieri, '"Without Flinching"', 9.

[11] On Meridionalism and the implications of racial thinking about the Italian South, see Wong, *Race and the Nation*.

[12] Lucia Re, 'Italians and the Invention of Race: The Poetics and Politics of Difference in the Struggle over Libya, 1890–1913', *California Italian Studies* 1, no. 1 (2010), 17–18, https://escholarship.org/uc/item/96k3w5kn.

[13] Welch, *Vital Subjects*, Ch.1. On southern stereotypes, see John Dickie, *Darkest Italy: The Nation and Stereotypes of the Mezzogiorno, 1860–1900* (Basingstoke: Macmillan, 1999).

period through racial discourse and conceived as an asset for the national community. The supposed military qualities of the 'superior races' were one aspect which Italian thinkers were particularly keen to promote, as we shall see.

8.3 Race and the Libyan War

If much pre-war racial discourse was centred on revitalizing and strengthening Italian whiteness, the processes of Othering and imposing hierarchy were not lacking. In the earliest phase of African expansion there had been considerable ambiguity over racial status, and non-white Italian colonial subjects were able to occupy a range of positions, but in the 1870s and 1880s this soon receded in favour of a more regimented form of official and popular racial hierarchy.[14] The need to recruit, command, and deploy colonial soldiers was one contributing factor to this process of increasingly rigid racial definition (constructive ambiguity not being a great feature of military organization).[15] It was really the Italo-Turkish war which brought a focus on racial Others—and in particular on Africans—to the fore in Liberal culture, as Lucia Re has argued, marking a new level of integration for previously Othered groups like southerners, Italian Jews, and even devout Catholics.[16] As Italian whiteness expanded to include southerners, Latinity and Meridionalism were reimagined as potential sources of (imperial) strength: unmartial weakness was recast as gentleness, generosity of spirit and kindness which would make the new Italian empire a vision of harmony and benevolence. Unlike the harsh and exclusive Anglo-Saxon system, some theorists proposed, the Latin races were best suited for creating a tolerant, progressive, benign empire.[17] Here the *italiani brava gente* narrative was explicitly recast in essentialist racial terms.

Once the invasion of Libya began, encounters with Italy's enemies—soon to be subjects—were couched in racialized and strongly dehumanizing terms. Soldiers and civilians alike were referred to by Italian troops as animals or as beasts, snakes to be killed or flies to be crushed.[18] Journalistic accounts were little better, referring to the Arabs as 'bipeds' who could only be recognized with great difficulty as fully human.[19] After 1911 there was much interest in, but little knowledge of, Italy's new colonial subjects, who were racially baffling to the

---

[14] Finaldi and Baratieri, '"Without Flinching"', 14–17.
[15] For an example of contemporary thinking about the racial hierarchies 'required' in commanding Black troops, see Errardo Di Aichelburg, 'Gli ascari d'Italia', *RMI* 59, no. 4 (1914): 743–68.
[16] Re, 'Italians and the Invention of Race', 5–6.   [17] Wong, *Race and the Nation*, 86–9.
[18] For a fuller discussion of Italian soldiers' racist views of Libyans during the war, see Vanda Wilcox, 'The Italian Soldiers' Experience in Libya, 1911–1912', in *The Wars before the Great War*, ed. William Mulligan, Andreas Rose, and Dominik Geppert (Cambridge: Cambridge University Press, 2015), 41–57.
[19] Luigi Lucatelli, *Il volto della guerra* (Rome: M. Carra, 1913), 42.

military and civilian men who set out to rule them. In December 1911 Adolfo Orsini carefully explained in the pages of the Italian Military Review that not all Africans were the same. In fact, he informed his readers, they spoke many different languages and had different cultures despite the apparent similarity which—to his eyes—their colour suggested: 'Beneath that uniform black colour with which the tropical sun has varnished their skin, beat hearts which are foreign to one another. All they share are servitude, exhaustion, sadness.'[20] Italy's encounter with Africans had begun at least half a century before but its knowledge of the people it aspired to govern was superficial at best. A 1914 article in the same publication had to refute the rumour that Black soldiers felt no pain (a widespread and enduring nineteenth-century racist trope in the US and elsewhere).[21] The racial Others provided by Arabs and East Africans were often used to promote reflections on Italian racial characteristics: could the white soldier be made as 'bold and brilliant' as the Eritrean *ascari*?, pondered one military reformer. The innate qualities ascribed by this writer to Black soldiers—infantile cheerfulness, vivacity, boldness, strength, fearlessness—were most apparent because he is 'not civilised like us, he has greater powers of resistance, he makes war by instinct'. White Italians, however 'are civilised, and so they are less able to endure in battle, they are motivated by duty and not instinct'; the army should seek to unite the fighting qualities of Black men with the civilized, rational qualities of its white majority, the author concluded.[22] The practice of appointing exclusively white officers to command the indigenous troops exemplified the assumptions which prevailed within the army (as in wider society) about relative racial capacities. Fascinatingly there was at least one exception to this binary vision: the Eritrean-Italian Domenico Mondelli, most likely born as Wolde Selassie in Asmara in 1886, was adopted by an Italian colonel, Attilio Mondelli, and raised in Parma. He was commissioned into the *bersaglieri* from the Modena Military Academy and later qualified as a pilot, serving with both the infantry and aeronautical forces during the First World War before joining the elite *Arditi* with the rank of lieutenant-colonel in 1918. Despite being decorated with five medals for valour, he was forced out of his career in 1925. Resuming his military career after the fall of fascism, he achieved the distinction of becoming Italy's first Black general (having also been one of the world's first Black pilots).[23] Mondelli's education and the socio-economic standing bestowed upon him by his father were apparently sufficient to overcome his racial status; nonetheless, his experience was exceptional and did not challenge the wider racial hierarchy in the army.

---

[20] Orsini, 'Tripoli e Pentapoli', 2593.   [21] Di Aichelburg, 'Gli ascari d'Italia', 748–9.
[22] Pietro Giacone, 'Educazione o istruzione militare?', *RMI* 59, no. 4 (1914): 792–801; 793–4.
[23] Mauro Valeri, *Generale nero. Domenico Mondelli: bersagliere, aviatore e ardito* (Rome: Odradek, 2016).

8.4 Militarism and Race

When the First World War began, it was as commonplace to speak of 'the Italian race' as of 'the Italian people', but the topic was often addressed with as much anxiety as pride. It was specifically within the realms of war and military affairs that racial fears about Italians were most clearly articulated and where the racial stakes were highest.[24] The defeat at Adwa raised fears about the country's blood stock—and some northern Europeans too interpreted the defeat as a sign of Italian racial inferiority.[25] The troubles Italy experienced in handling its new North African colony did little to assuage these fears. The highly influential anthropologist Giuseppe Sergi advocated the existence of a uniquely brilliant 'Mediterranean' race, of which Italians were one example; while Sergi defined Mediterraneans as innately embodying creativity, innovation, individuality, and intelligence, they lacked the industrious, organized, disciplined, and obedient character of Aryans.[26] It was hard to ignore the fact that precisely these qualities were sought after in good soldiers (and effective colonial administrators). During the First World War even Italy's British allies made negative assumptions about the country's military capacity precisely on this racial basis, believing Italians to be emotional and intrinsically more susceptible to propaganda.[27] Throughout the conflict Italian anthropologists continued their race studies, in particular through the study of the Libyan deportees confined on Italian territory and the *ascari* in Sicily, but also of mentally ill people (including colonial psychiatric patients and sexual 'deviants') who were analysed in racial terms to further an understanding of 'degeneracy' and racial weakness. This work aimed to highlight Italy's superior racial stock relative to its colonies but was also indicative of considerable anxiety.[28] Just in geopolitical terms there were fears about Italy's great power status in comparison to its supposed peers, in biopolitical terms there were anxieties about the Italian army's strength and potential relative to its neighbours and enemies. In both realms, active measures to repair and bolster Italy's position were required.[29]

Placido Consiglio—psychologist, psychiatrist, and eugenicist—was a leading prophet of these anxieties, publishing prolifically across medical, military, and

[24] On racial insecurities and 'self-Othering' more generally, see Suzanne Stewart-Steinberg, *The Pinocchio Effect: On Making Italians 1860–1920* (Chicago: University of Chicago Press, 2007).
[25] Gillette, *Racial Theories in Fascist Italy*, 22–3.
[26] Gillette, *Racial Theories in Fascist Italy*, 25–7.
[27] McCrae, *Coalition Strategy and the End of the First World War*, 102–3.
[28] Di Pasquale, 'The "Other" at Home', 226–8.
[29] A comparable rhetorical process underpinned the fascist project to reshape Italians' geographical imaginations in the 1930s: first a supposed deficiency in the Italian people was identified, which was limiting the country's true greatness, and then a plan was evolved to reform it, allowing Italy to reach its highest destiny. See David Atkinson, 'Geographical Imaginations, Public Education and the Everyday Worlds of Fascist Italy', *JMIS* 18, no. 5 (2013): 561–79, DOI: https://doi.org/10.1080/1354571X.2013.839487.

generalist publications.[30] His essays grappled with fears about degeneracy of various kinds and the innate qualities of white (Italian) soldiers in comparison to their European counterparts as well as colonial opponents. Consiglio considered moral infirmity—including alcoholism and pre-marital sex—as much a threat to the army as physical inadequacy; all armies had to find ways to maximize the potential of their raw material which would reflect not only the 'spirit of their race' but also their 'phase of national civilization'. He also wrote that one had to understand the 'cerebral vaso-paralytic action of the sun's rays' and the overall hot climate when trying to analyse the racial qualities of Italian southerners. Neuroses, psychiatric disorders, and idiotism were simply 'an exaggeration and deformation of the southern character' which was 'primitive [...] individualistic and passionate'; this made southerners a potential source of trouble in the armed forces and risked creating manpower problems for Italy.[31]

If the military was the sphere where racial degeneracy posed the greatest dangers, it also offered a prime arena for racial regeneration, Consiglio argued. In a 1916 essay entitled *La rigenerazione fisica e morale della razza mediante l'esercito* (The physical and moral regeneration of the race through the army) he discussed the problems of turning inadequate racial stock into good soldiers. The army was 'the true school of the nation', but, he wrote, 'the psychologically abnormal [...] and degenerates' struggled to adapt to army life, as did the peasantry, who were more 'primitive and superstitious'. Consiglio proposed an extensive eugenic programme, based on forcible detention in penitential institutions for the mentally and physically weak, including sending the psychiatrically abnormal to Africa to deploy 'in the struggle against savage and primitive peoples'. His premise was that the army's social management 'must be essentially biological in origins and method' and that it should practise 'social medicine [which] is a form of collective hygiene'.[32] In espousing these ideas, he found itself surprisingly close to Filippo Marinetti, the father of futurism, whose 1909 manifesto had declared war 'the only cure [or hygiene] for the world', and who envisaged a process of racial purification and purging through military action. War was supposed to restore not only racial vigour but Italian virility: a perceived crisis of Italian manliness, linked to modernity and degeneration, was under discussion in this period, and military service was also the cure for this problem, restoring both discipline and dynamism to Italian men.[33] Colonial and imperial war

---

[30] There is no full biography of him, unfortunately. See Scartabellati, 'Un *Wanderer* dell'anormalità?'

[31] Placido Consiglio, 'Medicina Sociale nell'esercito. Saggi di psicopatologia e di scienza criminale nei militari', *RMI* 59, no. 10 (1914).

[32] Placido Consiglio, 'La rigenerazione fisica e morale della razza mediante l'esercito', *RMI* 61, no. 1 (1916): 23–51.

[33] On the gendered politics of Italian colonialism, see Giulietta Stefani, *Colonia per Maschi: Italiani in Africa Orientale, Una Storia Di Genere* (Verona: Ombre corte, 2007).

specifically would further clarify and enforce a gendered racial hierarchy (white–masculine/black–feminine).

More generally, however, Rhiannon Noel Welch argues that Liberal-era racial thinking offered a 'positive' or optimistic discourse of Italians themselves as racialized subjects who had to be made more (re)productive both economically and biologically.[34] The mechanisms by which this was to be achieved were both preventive—to suppress internal weakness and degeneracy—and incentivizing—to elevate Italian racial stock above all through conquest and colonialism, particularly agricultural colonialism. The 'mutilated body' of the Italian nation-state was to be restored by the labouring arms of Italian emigrant colonies overseas and by the acquisition of new territories (whether these were to be remade into parts of the metropole or remain in an explicitly colonial status). If the Italian race was to be regenerated, strengthened, and revitalized through colonialism and expansionism, it is clear that the First World War—as an imperial endeavour—was among many other things conceived as an essential project for the future of the Italian race.

8.5 A Racial War?

Unsurprisingly, given this background, the war was frequently conceived in racialized terms—even against Austrians and Germans. Contemporary biological and anthropological theory was much focused on the conflict between Aryan and non-Aryan—especially Mediterranean—races; the war offered an opportunity to demonstrate definitively the superiority of the Mediterranean race against its Germanic competitor. This racialized analysis was particularly prevalent in war-time representations and discourses of the Italian communities overseas, which in both the USA and Argentina co-existed with well-organized German communities. Media portrayals on both sides descended into essentialist caricatures, such that mafiosi, lechers, and brigands faced off against ferocious Hunnish barbarians.[35] Ignoring the awkward presence within the Entente of the British (were they Aryan?) and the Slavic Russians and Serbs, race theorists focused solely on France as a fellow Latin or Mediterranean people, engaged in a primordial racial struggle against the Germanic peoples and their barbaric *Kultur*.[36] The idea of a shared racial 'Latinity' as a way to reconcile Franco-Italian differences had already been deployed with some success to lessen colonial rivalries in north Africa in the late nineteenth century.[37] This vision was embraced by an organization named Latina

---

[34] Welch, *Vital Subjects*, introduction and epilogue.
[35] Franzina, 'La guerra lontana'; Emilio Franzina, 'Italiani del Brasile ed italobrasiliani durante il primo conflitto mondiale (1914–1918)', *História. Debates e Tendências* 5, no. 1 (2004): 225–67.
[36] Gillette, *Racial Theories in Fascist Italy*, 35–7.
[37] Montalbano, 'The Italian Community of Tunisia', section 7.

Gens: established before the war, this global network of 'Latin peoples' had Rome as its spiritual and organizational centre, and branches in France, Brazil, Portugal, and Romania. It promoted a Mediterranean-based pan-Latinism centred on the 'Latin sisters' France and Italy—the heart of the Entente—who should lead the charge against both pan-Germanism and pan-Slavism. Blood and culture were inextricably intermingled in a 'Latin' heritage which ran from the Parthenon via Trajan and Christopher Columbus through the French Revolution to the Entente; the war was a global struggle of races and values in which all the far-flung colonies of Latinity had a part to play. Patriotic speeches, fund-raising events, and public celebrations of the supposed birthdate of Rome on 21 April 1916 were organized. Perhaps unsurprisingly, the group achieved little else; when they appealed to the government for funding, Sonnino replied succinctly that he was 'quite unable to identify the least concrete utility or urgency within their proposals'.[38] But for all the marginality of this network, the ideas which they embraced found echoes in many nationalist publications, not least Mussolini's *Il Popolo d'Italia*, which frequently discussed the war in racial terms, including a focus on the 'Latin race' in 1918.[39]

Wartime service brought Italians into contact with multiple Others, whom they were generally quick to assess in racial terms. Some were allies or subordinates— Serbs and Montenegrins, or anti-Habsburg Slavs in the Czech Legion. Others were civilians under Italian occupation, such as the Albanians, whom one Italian intelligence officer described as 'perfectly Oriental or Byzantine', as 'even more complicated than the Libyans and much more impenetrable'.[40] Crucial encounters also came with enemies—Turks and Arabs in Libya, Slavs, Germans, Bosnians, and more from the vast diversity of the Habsburg Empire. Italian soldiers and civilians also encountered the colonial troops and labourers of their Allies (for instance, the British West Indian Regiment was briefly stationed at Taranto in 1918, where it mutinied over poor treatment), and African Americans in the US Army. One young lieutenant in France in April 1918 recorded in his otherwise sparse diary 'going [into the town] to see the huge number of soldiers – French, Americans, Portuguese and Blacks'—leaving the nationality of the Black soldiers unidentified, seeing their racial Otherness almost a nationality of its own.[41] From the Macedonian front, another junior officer wrote in April 1917:

> The Macedonian population here barely exists: they live in earth and mud huts, it's disgustingly dirty. There's a great variety of soldiers, however, of all races: French, English, Russians, Serbs, Indians, Blacks, Annamites [South Vietnamese]

[38] ACS PCM GE 1915–1918, busta 138.   [39] Mussolini, *Opera omnia*, Vol. 5, 81.
[40] ACS PCM GE 1915–1918, Busta 75, Fasc. Colonie, Relazione sulla situazione in Albania, Nov–Dec 1916.
[41] Diary of 2nd Lt Giacomo Tortora, reproduced in Caselli Lapeschi and Militello, *1918: gli italiani sul fronte occidentale*, 104.

and other races too; Bulgarian and German prisoners too, [though] I've not seen any Austrians or Turks yet.[42]

Despite his contempt for the local civilians, his phrasing ('however') suggests that the 'great variety' of 'races' he encountered was a matter of interest and curiosity, as it was for his counterpart in France cited above. Beyond this type of casual day-to-day encounter, the reactions of Italian officers and men serving overseas or engaged in occupations to racial difference reveal much of how the process of oppositional definition could play out in practice. Italian coloniality—and racial categorization—underpinned military practice in crucial ways, as we shall see. When the war ended and final territorial settlements were achieved, over half a million new minorities would find themselves under Italian rule; these so-called *allogeni*—in other words, people of a different genus or 'stock'—would be subject to an ongoing process of Italianization throughout the fascist era.[43] In fact, their experience as ethnic and linguistic Others would begin during and immediately after the First World War.

8.5.1 Encounters with South Slavs

When it came to their near neighbours, the Slavic peoples of the Balkans, Italian official policy was generally motivated by suspicion and a spirit of rivalry. Indeed, a racial and cultural anti-Slavism can be found within border regions as far back as the Risorgimento.[44] In 1915, when the total dissolution of Austria-Hungary did not yet seem likely, it was at that Empire's expense that Italian ambitions were formulated, so Slavs were not yet the chief enemy. As the war went on and Yugoslav nationalism emerged, anti-Slavic rhetoric became increasingly vigorous, though it would find its most virulent form later under fascism.[45] However, the encounter between Slavs and Italians was not a post-war phenomenon. Over 150,000 Slovenes were living in the County of Gorizia and Gradisca immediately before the war; many had already been mobilized into the Habsburg armed forces,

---

[42] Lt Raffaele Merendi of the 35th Division, letter to his father in Terni. 'Tenente Raffaele Merendi', Fronte Macedone 1916–18, accessed 11 November 2019, http://www.frontemacedone.com/tenente-raffaele-merendi.html.

[43] Pergher, *Fascist Borderlands*, 11–12, 56.

[44] Enzo Collotti, 'Sul razzismo antislavo', in *Nel nome della razza: il razzismo nella storia d'Italia 1870-1945*, ed. Alberto Burgio (Bologna: Il Mulino, 1999), 33–61; Tullia Catalan, 'Linguaggi e stereotipi dell'antislavismo irredentista dalla fine dell'Ottocento alla Grande Guerra', in *Fratelli al massacro: linguaggi e narrazioni della Prima Guerra mondiale*, ed. Tullia Catalan (Rome: Viella, 2015), 57–9, 68. On the long-term history of the Italo-Slavic border region, see Marina Cattaruzza, *L'Italia e il confine orientale: 1866-2006* (Bologna: Il Mulino, 2007).

[45] On fascist anti-Slavism, see Stefano Bartolini, *Fascismo antislavo: il tentativo di bonifica etnica al confine nord orientale* (Pistoia: Istituto storico della Resistenza e della società contemporanea nella provincia di Pistoia, 2008).

and others fled at the outbreak of the war, but at least 25,000 Slovene civilians remained.[46]

Within days of the war's beginning, Italy occupied Slovene territory: the towns of Caporetto and Cormons, for instance, fell into Italian hands by 30 May 1915. Despite Cadorna's optimistic plans for advancing deep into Habsburg territory towards Ljubljana, no concrete planning for occupation policies had taken place before the outbreak of the war. On 29 May 1915 the general staff created a Segretariato Generale per gli Affari civili, based in Abano (Padova), responsible for the administration of any occupied territories and the governance of civilians therein.[47] This military unit, answerable to the chief of general staff, was headed up by one Agostino D'Adamo, an experienced bureaucrat from the ministry of the interior. He was required to liaise between the government, the existing local authorities on the ground (such as local mayors, councils, and parish priests), and the Italian military hierarchy for whom operational concerns generally overrode political considerations. Martial law was imposed throughout the war zone and implemented by military police and tribunals, with draconian punishments for a vast range of offenses including sabotage, espionage, resistance, refusal to obey military orders, trafficking with the enemy, and many more. Meanwhile D'Adamo, assisted by a staff of keen irredentists from the border regions, oversaw the administration of justice, public health and education policy, and the management of the local economy.[48] Pre-war Austro-Hungarian legislation was left in place for the duration of the conflict, and Habsburg systems were to be functionally maintained (local markets, the fire service, schooling, the water supply, etc.) though efforts to impart patriotic Italian values were made whenever possible. It was clear to the military authorities that Italian law could not be imposed on these Austrian lands during the war, even though they were classified as 'Italian provinces previously subject to Austrian rule' and would become wholly Italian in the fullness of time. Less clear was the status of local civilians, some of whom— especially the clergy—were seen as intrinsically anti-Italian and untrustworthy for political reasons. Many were also ethnically Othered, whether as Slavs or 'Germans', with practical consequences at local levels. A gulf emerged between policy and practice; moderation and tolerance were often lost in translation between authorities and local actors. Indeed, the army was supposed to be a liberating force, rather than an occupying one—but this rhetoric fell afoul of the reality on the ground where local populations were not predominantly Italian after all. The very existence of a Slovene majority in these 'unredeemed' lands was

[46] Petra Svoljšak, 'La popolazione civile nella Slovenia occupata', in *La violenza contro la popolazione civile nella Grande guerra: deportati, profughi, internati*, ed. Bruna Bianchi (Milan: Unicopli, 2006), 147–63.

[47] ACS PCM GE 1915–1918, busta 72 bis—Terre occupate.

[48] Andrea Fava, 'D'Adamo, Agostino in "Dizionario Biografico"', in *Dizionario biografico degli italiani* (Rome: Treccani, 1985).

embarrassing, compromising the core of the war's ostensible purpose; the Slovenes were soon identified as 'enemies of irredentism'.[49]

The administration of these communities was a tricky and delicate task not facilitated by the general attitudes to Slovenes and other Slavs on both racial and cultural grounds. The 'assumed superiority of Italian culture' underpinned both language policy and general attitudes among the occupying forces.[50] In fact, both sides nurtured ethnic stereotypes about one another: for Slovenes, Italians were untrustworthy, incompetent, boastful, and overly emotional whereas Italians considered Slovenes overly reserved, secretive, and sullen.[51] Unsurprisingly, these ethnic stereotypes led to a heightened anxieties within the Italian army of espionage and betrayal by local civilians, along with fears of attacks from *francs tireurs* and subversion.[52] Rumours circulated of sleeping soldiers killed by Slovene civilians. General Pietro Frugoni of 2nd Army was (perhaps not unnaturally) concerned that some armed and trained members of the territorial militia might be found in the area, and ordered that all locals should be disarmed immediately.[53] By contrast, the Slovene stereotype of Italian volatility encouraged the local clergy to preach calm and cooperation even while they upheld the duty of loyalty to Austria.[54] Even methods which the occupying authorities themselves considered mild and benevolent, such as plans to only gradually replace the Slovene language, place-names, and culture with Italian, were unsurprisingly much resented by their targets.

Underpinning apparently assimilationist measures was a reality of often brutal coercive oppression: by some estimates up to 70,000 people were forcibly displaced, including local notables and community leaders, and at least 5,000—but likely more—were interned in camps in remote parts of Italy, such as Sardinia. Freedom of movement was strictly limited, and the population were subjected to mandatory public health measures.[55] Most dramatic was the use of violence against unarmed civilians: at least twenty-six were summarily executed in the occupied zones, and very possibly more. All but one of the documented instances of summary executions of Slovenes took place between late May and mid-August 1915, after which the area was apparently 'pacified'. The victims, seen as partisans

[49] Piero Melograni, *Storia politica della Grande Guerra* (Milan: Mondadori, 1965), 31.

[50] Petra Svoljšak, 'The Language Policy of the Italian Army in the Occupied Slovenian Territories, 1915–17', in *Languages and the Military: Alliances, Occupation and Peace Building*, ed. Hilary Footitt and Michael Kelly (London: Palgrave Macmillan, 2012), 70.

[51] Petra Svoljšak and Bojan Godeša, 'Italian interwar administration of Slovenian ethnic territory: Italian ethnic policy', in *Frontwechsel: Österreich-Ungarns 'Grosser Krieg' im Vergleich*, ed. Wolfram Dornik et al. (Vienna: Böhlau Verlag, 2014).

[52] It is worth comparing these fears and their effects with the dynamic at play during the initial occupation of Belgium and Northern France. John Horne and Alan Kramer, *German Atrocities, 1914: A History of Denial* (New Haven, CT: Yale University Press, 2001).

[53] AUSSME Fondo E1, b.114, letter dated 29 May 1915.

[54] Pluviano and Guerrini, *Le fucilazioni sommarie*, 197.

[55] Svoljšak, 'La popolazione civile nella Slovenia occupata', 153–4.

or *francs tireurs* by the Italians, were mainly men in their 50s and 60s—farmers, local councillors, a sacristan, a pub landlord—or in some cases deserters from the Habsburg army. Memoir and diary testimonies, whether they accurately represent verifiable facts or not, illuminate Italian military mentalities; suspected or presumed signalling to Austrian troops was often mentioned as a reason for summary executions. One young artilleryman, in a letter to his old professor, described 'an old man of around sixty' who 'we shot where he stood, that dog', while another 'spy was shot with his lantern still in his hand, without [us] thinking too much about it'.[56] Other Italians recorded killing civilian prisoners, or forcing men to dig their own graves before shooting them. Local Slovenian testimonies record casual plunder of monies and food, the gratuitous shooting of livestock, and a young deaf herdsman who was beaten so savagely by Italian soldiers that he died eight days later.[57] On at least one occasion, orders were issued—though later retracted—to raze an entire village, inhabited almost entirely by Slovene women and children, to the ground without prior warning. This was, by any reckoning, a colonial approach.[58] Mussolini, staying in Caporetto in February 1916, wrote revealingly in his diary: 'These Slovenes still do not love us. They suffer our presence with resignation and poorly concealed hostility. They think we are just passing though, that we won't stay.'[59] Instead, he confidently believed, a long-term occupation was being established. Mussolini also described the 'enigmatic faces' of the locals, a classic racial Othering, and noted in passing that the Italian occupation had 'rejuvenated' the town. Most telling of all is the later testimony of a local peasant eyewitness to the mass execution in Villese, near Gorizia, who commented, 'The Italian command didn't know the conditions, the people round here. They had come with an African experience and they took it out on the population.'[60] Indeed the major responsible for the shooting of six men, witnessed by this observer, had served in Libya during the war of 1911–12 and even allegedly been involved in the reprisals against Tripolitanian civilians after Sciara Sciatt.[61] As Bruna Bianchi has written, 'The justifications of violence against civilians during the invasions [of the First World War] did not in fact differ from those advanced during colonial wars.'[62] The process of racial Othering against Slavs clearly facilitated this outlook. It is very hard to fit the wartime policies and practices of the Italian army in the borderlands into the framework of a Risorgimento war for liberation.

---

[56] G. B. Jannuzzi, cited in Pluviano and Guerrini, *Le fucilazioni sommarie*, 198.

[57] Pluviano and Guerrini, 199–214.

[58] For a comparable analysis of the Italian army's colonialist approach to South Slavs in the Second World War, see Teodoro Sala, 'Guerra e amministrazione in Jugoslavia, 1941–1943: un'ipotesi coloniale', *Annali della Fondazione Micheletti* 5 (1991): 83–94.

[59] Mussolini, *Il mio diario di guerra*, 97.

[60] Teodoro Sala, '"Redenzione" e "conquista": la guerra del '15–'18 al confine orientale. I fucilati del 29 maggio 1915 a Villesse', *Bollettino dell'Istituto regionale per la storia del Movimento di liberazione nel Friuli-Venezia Giulia* no. 1–2 (1975): 16.

[61] Pluviano and Guerrini, *Le fucilazioni sommarie*, 204.

[62] Cited in Svoljšak, 'La popolazione civile nella Slovenia occupata', 18–19.

After twenty-nine months, the occupation of Slovene areas around the Isonzo was brought to an abrupt end with the battle of Caporetto before awkwardly resuming at the war's end; by the time the new borders were established, an estimated 450,000 Slovenes and Croats would be living within Italian borders. The general overseeing the post-war occupation was Carlo Petitti di Roreto, who imposed stringent limitations on the local population—belying the rhetoric of liberation. Free movement, speech, and assembly were limited and a military court established; opponents were arrested and interned.[63] Not until 1 August 1919 did the governance of these 'redeemed' areas of Italy pass into civilian administration, and the rights of these new Italian citizens were frequently not respected.

Meanwhile, outside the newly established borders of the victorious state, the encounter between Italians and Slavs came in the contested territories of Fiume, Istria, and Dalmatia. The conflict was chiefly one of national policy and interests, but it was frequently framed in racial terms, even by outsiders. In March 1919 Arthur Balfour wrote to Rennell Rodd that 'fundamental differences of temperament will always prevent anything like intimate cordiality between Jugo-Slavs and Italians', but he blamed Italians for 'deliberate[ly] ... embitter[ing] the relations between the two races'.[64] Prejudices and hostility were felt on both sides: during the war, South Slav soldiers had fought with the greatest determination on the Italian front and indeed showed more animosity to the Italians than any other group of Habsburg soldiers.[65] According to a pro-Yugoslav polemicist in Paris, Italian public discourse regularly referred to Slavs as venomous snakes, barbarians, executioners, lazy, ignorant, and more besides.[66] Serving soldiers also deployed vicious rhetoric against the Slavs: a 1918 postcard from a serving unit of Alpini to the minister of war referred to the Slovenes among whom they found themselves stationed as 'Bedouins', a telling form of racial and colonial transference. They wrote the slogan 'Down with and Death to Serbs Croats and Slovenes' along the side of the postcard.[67] Tensions between Italians and Slavs also marred the cooperation of the Italian Expeditionary Force in the Far East with the Czechoslovak Legion; supposed to be fighting alongside one another, the two units in fact devoted much energy to mutual mistrust on ethnic grounds.[68] By 1919 racial hostility was further deepened by the degeneration of political relations between Italy and the new Yugoslavia.

[63] Svoljšak, 'The Language Policy of the Italian Army', 82–3.
[64] BOD Rennell Rodd correspondence, 20–1919: Balfour in Paris to Rodd, 14 March 1919.
[65] John Paul Newman, 'Post-Imperial and Post-War Violence in the South Slav Lands, 1917–1923', *Contemporary European History* 19, no. 3 (2010): 249–65, DOI: https://doi.org/10.1017/S0960777310000159.
[66] Zdenko Moravec, *L'Italie et les Yougoslaves. Avec un exposé des relations Italo-Yougoslaves pendant la guerre et des documents à l'appui* (Paris: Imprimerie Lang, Blanchong et Cie, 1919).
[67] ACS PCM GE 1915–1918, busta 170 Armistizio, Sf.3 Proposte, voti, consigli.
[68] IOH, Vol. VII, t.1, 71–2; 256.

8.5.2 Germanophobia

Along with Habsburg Slavs, the war also brought about complex encounters with the German-speaking peoples of another area claimed by Italy, the Austrian South Tyrol (which comprised the two provinces later known by Italy as Alto Adige and Trentino). Of the 650,000 inhabitants of the South Tyrol recorded in the 1910 Austro-Hungarian census, around 238,000 (some 36 per cent) were identified as German.[69] The conflation between language and ethnicity in the region was substantial. Once the war began, the Trentino area was rapidly occupied and militarized by the armies on either side of the border which divided it in two. Some 56,000 Trentini south of the border found themselves under Italian military authority, while to the north the Austro-Hungarian army established a zone of military control incorporating most of the region. In each case, the civilian population found itself the subject of mistrust and frequently of mistreatment. The Italians could not be sure that the German-speaking Trentini living close to the border did not harbour Austrian leanings; the Austrians, for their part, were deeply suspicious of all Italian-speaking Trentini and embarked on a programme of mass deportations and internment.[70] On both sides of the border, the authorities viewed the people of the Trentino as potentially disloyal for purely ethnic reasons even in the absence of evidence or actions which indicated support for the enemy. At the same time, for the Italians, this was a people in the process of 'redemption' who had to be treated cautiously. Not until the Austrian offensive of May 1916, the so-called *Strafexpedition*, were some 29,000 civilians forcibly evacuated from the Italian-controlled border zone. Some, despite their Italian cultural and linguistic identity, were loyal citizens of the Habsburg Empire and experienced their forced displacement into Italy as deeply traumatic.[71]

During and after the war, anti-Germanic sentiment was often couched in ethnic and essentialist terms. In March 1919 a father who had lost two sons in the war wrote to the prime minister's office complaining about 'the [German] brutes', who had committed 'barbarities of every kind' such that the entire 'German population should be put to the sword'.[72] This did not augur well for the incorporation of German-speaking Austrian subjects from the Tyrol into the Italian community. In fact, even the newly liberated Italian Trentini would find themselves subject to much distrust—after all, at least 55,000 served in the Habsburg army during the

---

[69] Andrea Di Michele, 'L'Italia in Austria: da Vienna a Trento', in *La vittoria senza pace: le occupazioni militari italiane alla fine della Grande Guerra*, ed. Raoul Pupo (Rome: GLF editori Laterza, 2014), 29–31.

[70] For an excellent recent transnational study, see Francesco Frizzera, *Cittadini dimezzati: i profughi trentini in Austria-Ungheria e in Italia (1914–1919)* (Bologna: Il Mulino, 2018).

[71] Frizzera, *Cittadini dimezzati*, 69–75.

[72] ACS PCM GE 1915–1918, busta 221, fasc. 204, sf. 4/3.

war. As a result, a highly centralized administration was imposed after the war which destroyed the traditional local rights and autonomies enjoyed by towns and provinces under Austrian rule. This new system quickly earned the hostility of even patriotic irredentist Italians. General Guglielmo Pecori Giraldi, formerly commander of I Army, was appointed as military governor of the region in November 1918; he initially advocated a cautious policy to avoid alienating new German subjects. He wanted to use Italian Trentini as administrators not only across the southern portion of the new lands but also within the German-speaking northern sector, the South Tyrol. His idea was that by deploying bilingual staff, who were not outsiders to the region, it would be easier for the German population to accept the new regime. However, he faced an ongoing struggle with hardline anti-Germans such as the local nationalist and irredentist Ettore Tolomei. Tolomei was implacably hostile towards German culture, language, and people, who he saw as racially incompatible with Italian values. His career blossomed under fascism and he went on to become a senator under Mussolini, but his vitriolic anti-Germanism was so notorious that after Italy's surrender in 1943 he was arrested by the SS and deported to Dachau. Tolomei saw the post-First World War occupation as his long-awaited chance to fully Italianize the entire region, including immediately and forcibly changing all place names into Italian variants (thus turning the Südtirol into Alto Adige). Even so loyal an Italian patriot as Alcide De Gasperi critiqued the post-war Italian regime in the region as a 'colonial one' in 1919.[73] In fact, in the late 1930s Tolomei directly compared the annexation and Italianization of the Alto Adige to the processes underway in Libya, showing that this was intentional goal and not inadvertent.[74] In mid-1919 the military occupation of Pecori Giraldi ended and was replaced by a civilian administration under the liberal Luigi Credaro, but the active presence of militantly anti-German officials continued. Meanwhile the Italian military occupation of Innsbruck, in the northern Tyrol, lasted until 1920, and was guided by an essentialist understanding of the local population who were considered 'innately disciplined' but also inherently simple and rustic, and who by nature needed a strong authoritarian system set over them.

8.5.3 Colonial 'Others' at War

Racial encounters within the existing colonies were also fraught with prejudice, misconceptions, and ignorance. Experienced administrators and officers frequently acted in ways which exacerbated divides and demonstrated the deep-seated racialization of their thinking. For example, colonial officials transferred to

---

[73] Di Michele, 'L'Italia in Austria', 35–40.   [74] Pergher, *Fascist Borderlands*, 10–11.

Libya from East Africa grossly offended the local Arab elites by comparing them to the Black population of Ethiopia and Eritrea—who many Libyans, no less than the Italians, saw as racially inferior. The Libyan Muslim elite complained that to treat them in the same way as Italy's East African subjects was 'an offence against their race, their dignity, their history as an Arab people'.[75] At times, the colonial administration spoke of its 'Muslim policy' and categorized the indigenous population of Tripolitania and Cyrenaica in chiefly religious terms; at other times, it described them in a uniquely racial framework. The pressures of the ongoing war of (re-)conquest in the colony made it almost impossible to prioritize the development of a more coherent approach to these problems. Instead, racial stereotypes were circulated through myths, rumours, and apocryphal tales, especially within the armed forces. The Eritrean novelist Gebreyesus Hailu's important 1927 work *The Conscript*—one of the earliest African novels—follows the experiences of a young *ascari* soldier in Libya, at some unspecified point in the period 1911–22.[76] He describes the ways white officers used racism to try to motivate their East African troops who were deployed against the anti-colonial insurgency: 'According to the stereotype which was passed along by the Italians, to say that an Arab would respect a deal would be to lie.' The protagonist Tuquabo describes the native Libyans as 'untrustworthy, treacherous', and 'merciless' but immediately qualifies these utterances by emphasizing that these are the Italians' views; he recounts several anecdotes passed on by Italians, or even 'copied from a book [...] written in Italian' to illustrate the Arabs' 'so-called indolence'.[77] Here racial stereotypes of the enemy were apparently used to motivate troops in battle. A similar process was certainly employed among white troops during the original invasion of Libya in 1911–12.

The rhetoric of the civilizing mission in Libya concealed a reality in which racial contempt could easily shape military actions. Operations in June and July 1915, as the Italian forces withdrew to coastal positions in Tripolitania, clearly illustrate this. Reports collected by the minister of the colonies in November 1915 highlight the occurrence of racially motivated atrocities against the civilian population by Italian patrols; the racist motivations of these acts were clearly acknowledged in official investigations. On 19 June, thirteen Arab civilians were killed inside the border fence at Al-'Aziziyah (a town in north-western Libya which would later be proclaimed the capital of the short-lived Tripolitanian Republic in 1918). On 7 July, around seventy-five Arab farmers were massacred along the road to Al-'Aziziyah from Zanzur on the coast. Racist atrocities were not committed both by ordinary soldiers and by officers: in September 1915 one Captain Pietro

---

[75] ACS Archivio Giovanni Ameglio, b. 30 f. 284, report dated 9 October 1915.
[76] Despite the translator's choice of title and the repeated description in the English text of the *ascari* as conscripts, they were in fact volunteer professionals—as plenty of internal evidence in the novel itself makes clear.
[77] Gebreyesus Hailu, *The Conscript: A Novel of Libya's Anticolonial War*, trans. Ghirmai Negash (Athens, OH: Ohio University Press, 2012), 32–3.

De Angelis, of the 7th indigenous battalion, summarily executed an old man, his young grandchild, and a female relative, without any judicial process or higher authority. He ordered several further executions and corporal punishments of local civilians. Meanwhile in a separate incident, an elderly woman and a child, along with three adult men, were thrown into a cistern to drown near Tripoli by a second lieutenant. The minister's report laconically observed that the atrocities reported here were simply a small selection of the numerous 'deplorable facts which have occurred in Libya' and that there were others not included in the report (it is unclear why).[78] Brutal Italian war crimes in Libya are often primarily associated with the fascist era, but clearly they were also a feature of the Liberal regime, albeit less systematically. Official reports into these atrocities emphasized racial hatred, vindictiveness, and 'psychological flaws' as their underlying causes, but also noted that these sentiments were a sign of weakness. Both officers and men, it was reported, had declared that 'we must destroy the Arabs'—least they threaten Italian security at this delicate time. The fears provoked by the world war were seen as legitimizing atrocities: Adwa syndrome in action. Yet as the colonial minister Colosimo noted, events of this kind seriously undermined Italian claims of moral superiority, and ultimately national prestige and power within Libya. There were wider political implications too: he feared that the Sublime Porte planned to publicize Italian war crimes and capitalize on them to support their ongoing war effort in the region.

Despite atrocities of this type, the rhetorical ideal of racial harmony was regularly proclaimed by Italian officials. Upon his replacement as governor of Tripolitania in 1918, General Ameglio issued a final proclamation addressed to 'the Italians, Arabs and Israelites of Libya' in which he rather surprisingly asserted that he had been 'Rigid with the powerful, [since] I felt spiritually closer to the humble sort, to whom I never denied my assistance without distinction of caste, race, religion or party.'[79] Yet quite unintentionally, Ameglio had earlier put his finger on the heart of Italy's racial problem. In a 1915 memorandum to Italian forces in Tripolitania he had written:

Instead of hating or despising the native it is necessary to study him, understand him and equip oneself with the same ancient forces which motivate him in order to guide him towards our ends, all the while demonstrating that we are ahead of him in this work and in showing in all our activities that calm and certain energetic dignity which is innate to those races which have a certain knowledge of their own high destiny.[80]

[78] ACS PCM GE 1915–1918, busta 75 19.3.1, fasc. Colonie, sf. 4, Atti riservati riguardanti la Libia: Atrocità. The drowning took place at 'Cussabet'—perhaps Cusseba near Janzur.
[79] ACS PCM GE 1915–1918, busta 75 19.3.1, fasc. 20.
[80] ACS Archivio Giovanni Ameglio, b. 28 Governo della Tripolitania—Ufficio Politico Militare, 25 September 1915.

A position of racial assurance and self-confidence on the part of the governing class was intrinsically linked in his view not only with effective rule over the indigenous population but with a moderate, liberal approach rooted in understanding of its culture; the unspoken corollary was that racial insecurity, such as Italy was suffering acutely in this era, was linked to episodes of hatred and contempt for those supposedly lesser races against which Italy sought to assert its superiority. The greater the fears about Italian status in its colonies and in the world, the more likely it was that atrocities would occur. And yet as Colosimo had noted, racist atrocities, rooted in a fear that Italy looked weak, actually further weakened the Italy's position.

In Venezia Giulia, Istria, South Tyrol, and Libya, Italy would continue to face political difficulties for many years after the war; these borderlands posed direct challenges to Italian sovereignty throughout the fascist period, since the majority of their indigenous populations did not wish to be Italian.[81] In all three cases, racial Othering furthered the divide between Italian rulers and reluctant subjects even before the increasingly rigid racial distinctions introduced by the Fascist regime.

8.6 Race, Biopower, and the State

In a war in which manpower was of critical importance it is no surprise that the logic of biopower politics was applied. Cultivating, strengthening, and husbanding the vital strength of the nation was indispensable for victory. The army's attitudes to internal colonialism and the fight against domestic degeneracy were therefore intimately linked to the concern about emigration. Emigrants were typically men of working—and hence military—age; very commonly it was the strongest, fittest, most enterprising, and energetic individuals who chose to emigrate—but these were precisely those that the army most needed. While economists lamented the loss of these men's working capacity, for the military the loss was even more critical. Italian nationals overseas were still citizens—and still subject to conscription. And the quality of conscripts was a matter of very serious concern: in the 1911 draft, no fewer than 22 per cent of men were rejected as being unfit for service.[82] Under these circumstances, the loss of fit, healthy young male emigrants was a serious blow to the body politic. The difficulties created by mass emigration for military service was one of the issues debated in detail by the 1911 Congress of Italians Overseas, held in Rome under the auspices of the ICI, under the heading

---

[81] Pergher, *Fascist Borderlands*, 15–17, concisely summarizes the similarities between these regions.
[82] 'Statistica sulla leva della classe del 1891', *RMI* 59, no. 7–8 (1914): 2291.

'The Problem of citizenship specially in regard to Italians overseas'.[83] With the application of *ius soli* in the Americas, dual citizenship was increasingly common; what happened if dual citizens were to be drafted by two different states? How was military service as a mandatory element in citizenship to be managed when so many young men were resident overseas? This was one important reason why many army officers supported the creation of settler colonies close to home: while it was functionally impossible to coerce the thousands of fit young reservists in the Americas to return in time of war, and might also prove practically impossible given the likely wartime pressures on transatlantic shipping, no such obstacles would impede men's return from Mediterranean colonies. Settler colonialism meant control over the vital strength and hence military power of the nation—the young staff officer Achille Vaccarisi wrote in 1911, 'it is the duty and interest of every state to connect, as far as possible, its emigration to its political supremacy and economic development'.[84] But to secure this strength and deploy it for the purposes of the nation, it had to be channelled by means of citizenship. As many scholars have noted, this concept contains within itself two quite separate ideas—first the legal status of an individual and their rights and responsibilities within the state, and secondly an active participation within the life of the community, generally with commitment to its interests.[85] It was not enough, from the perspective of the army, that emigrants to the Americas remain legal citizens if they lacked a commitment to active participatory citizenship within the Italian community. Equally, throughout the war, colonial soldiers from Eritrea or Libya were active, voluntary contributors to the interests of the national community—but were not actually citizens, with all the rights or duties which that entailed.

8.6.1 Citizenship and Nationality

The First World War was an important watershed moment for the interlinked concepts of citizenship, subjecthood, and nationality for many participants, especially those living within empires, whether of land or sea. For the white serviceman from the British Dominions, the Senegalese tirailleur, the Pole in the Imperial German army, or the Serb in the Habsburg forces, the war brought the relationship between national identity and citizenship or subjecthood into new light—and

---

[83] Nissim Samama, *Il problema della cittadinanza specialmente nei rapporti degli italiani all'estero: Tema primo (Istituto coloniale italiano. Secondo Congresso degli italiani all'estero (Roma, giugno 1911), sezione I, legislazione)* (Florence: Tip. E. Ariani, 1911); Nissim Samama, *Contributo allo studio della doppia cittadinanza nei riguardi del movimento migratorio* (Florence: Tip. E. Ariani, 1910).

[84] Vaccarisi, 'Importanza dell'odierna espansione coloniale', 1686.

[85] Eric Lohr points out that in Russian these are two distinct concepts each with its own term, highlighting the different cultural development of these ideas. Eric Lohr, *Russian Citizenship: From Empire to Soviet Union* (Cambridge, MA: Harvard University Press, 2012), 1–11. Understandings of citizenship are thus nationally distinct.

this was no less true in the Italian case. Refugees and displaced persons—in Italy and in the former Habsburg lands—highlighted the importance and the difficulties in establishing citizenship status in a moment of fluctuating borders and states. Many Italian Austrians were forcibly removed from the war zones around Trento and Trieste—some 140,000 were deported—in despite of their rights as citizens (so too were 70,000 Slovenes and 12,000 Croats).[86] Others faced difficult choices, as the high-profile examples of Cesare Battisti and Alcide De Gasperi highlight. Both were born in Trento, of Italian nationality, both were Austrian citizens, and—as elected members of the Reichsrat—both were the sworn subjects of the Habsburg emperor. De Gasperi kept his position in parliament and worked for his fellow nationals within the empire, seeking to defend the interests of Habsburg Italians in the face of deportation and mistrust; Battisti abandoned the country and took up arms as a volunteer in the Italian army—violating his oath of personal loyalty to the Emperor in the process. In 1916 he was captured and executed as a traitor by the Austrians: whatever his nationality, his citizenship was unquestionably Austrian. At the end of the war, when Trento became Italian, De Gasperi became an Italian citizen and pursued his future parliamentary career within the kingdom (culminating as prime minister of the republic after the Second World War). Their fates show that only once Italy's formal claim to Trento had been secured could the nationality and citizenship of Italian Trentini be made to correspond.

Such questions were further complicated by the slipperiness and elision of the three concepts subjecthood, citizenship, and nationality in this era.[87] Contemporaries sometimes used them interchangeably, and at other times made subtle distinctions, as can be seen most clearly in the colonial realm. Before the 1930s, the Italian state officially classified its peoples primarily by citizenship status rather than by race.[88] In fact, Italian citizenship is still largely constituted in racial terms today, with the political debate about the status of children born to immigrants—generally Black or Asian in the white popular imaginary—rumbling on for much of the early twenty-first century. Italy continues to follow the *ius sanguinis* rather than the *ius soli* and thus claims to citizenship and nationality are still today staked on a variety of competing (and gendered) bases.[89] During and

---

[86] Francesco Frizzera, 'Dai pieni diritti all'esclusione dalla cittadinanza. I profughi di guerra nell'impero Asburgico e negli stati successori', in *Sudditi o cittadini? L'evoluzione delle appartenenze imperiali nella Prima Guerra Mondiale*, ed. Sara Lorenzini and Simone Attilio Bellezza (Rome: Viella, 2018), 51.

[87] For an overview, see Sabina Donati, *A Political History of National Citizenship and Identity in Italy, 1861–1950* (Palo Alto, CA: Stanford University Press, 2013).

[88] Ester Capuzzo, 'Sudditanza e cittadinanza nell'esperienza coloniale italiana dell'età liberale', *Clio* XXXI, no. 1 (1995): 65–6.

[89] For a recent analysis of contemporary issues, see Camilla Hawthorne, 'Making Italy: Afro-Italian Entrepreneurs and the Racial Boundaries of Citizenship', *Social & Cultural Geography* (28 March 2019): 1–21, DOI: https://doi.org/10.1080/14649365.2019.1597151.

after the First World War these issues presented themselves in a variety of ways: Italians born in the unredeemed lands, emigrants, and their descendants were nationals who might nor might not be citizens, according to circumstance; non-Italian nationals—whether white Europeans or Black and Arab colonial subjects—might in some cases hold, or aspire to, citizenship. The categories of citizen, national, and subject became newly significant even as the complexity of wartime opened liminal spaces in which these ideas could be contested. An excellent example of how race, citizenship, and nationality were brought into new relations by the war can be seen within the Italian community in Egypt.

8.6.2 Egypt

At the start of the war, there was a sizeable group of Italians resident in Egypt, many of whom were liable to the draft.[90] Some believed that being born overseas should exempt them from this obligation and considered that they were not exactly like the 'kingdom-born' Italians; others actively sought out military duty and identified passionately with a far-off fatherland which they had never themselves seen. Several 17-year-olds tried to volunteer in May and June 1915, one of whom asserted his 'rights as a colonial' to sign up from his home in Cairo, seeking full acknowledgement of his patriotism as an overseas Italian.[91] This phrase suggests the internalization of the Italian emigrant colonialism model. Also present in lesser but still significant numbers were *irredenti*: citizens of the Habsburg Empire, born in the unredeemed lands around Trento and Trieste (or their descendants) now living in Egypt. Many claimed Italian nationality, especially once the British authorities increased their programme of expulsion or internment of enemy aliens. Some wrote impassioned letters of patriotic devotion to the national cause, while others were—allegedly—'good Austrians at home but Italians in the street', as they sought to evade repressive measures. A local *pro-irredenti* committee worked to support them, and in general the Italian consular authorities were happy to claim anyone who applied as an Italian national, though they did not necessarily want to vouch for them with the military authorities. Born in Egypt after his Italian-speaking father had moved from Istria in the 1880s, one Alexandrian man refused to answer his Austrian call-up papers in 1914. Instead, as soon as Italy declared war, he applied for his Italian citizenship, amid declarations of irredentist enthusiasm. As 'an Italian from outside the kingdom', he asserted his claim to citizenship by right of blood, further noting that 'in our

---

[90] More generally on this topic, see Marta Petricioli, *Oltre il mito: l'Egitto degli italiani, 1917–1947* (Milan: Mondadori, 2007).

[91] Archivio Storico del Ministero degli Affari Esteri [ASMAE], Rappresentanza Diplomatica in Egitto, 1915, busta 152, fasc.1.

family we speak only Italian and I know no other languages except English and Arabic'.[92] The majority of Egypt's 'unredeemed' Italian nationals, however, did not apply for citizenship during the war and were happy enough to secure notes which demonstrated their 'Italian sympathies' and entitled them to better treatment during the war, while they awaited its outcome to resolve their legal circumstances.

Italy was also concerned with the status of indigenous Libyans, who were neither Italian nationals nor citizens, but who as colonial subjects were still entitled to the protection of consular authorities and to benefit from the judicial provisions of the capitulations. This raised extremely complex questions of identity and statehood. In what sense could Libyans permanently resident in Egypt be considered Italian? As with the Austrian citizens of Italian nationality, the consular authorities were keen to strongly assert their claims in this regard: a Tripolitanian-born person resident in Cairo since 1880 was still, the consulate claimed, an Italian subject. The Consul was also concerned to ensure that Italian colonial subjects were treated exactly as French or Spanish Algerians or Moroccans were, as an illustration of colonial parity. Such conflicts about legal status reveal less about the private interests of the individuals in question than about British respect for the standing of the Italian empire.[93]

Egypt's large Jewish community also retained strong Italian links. Many Jews living in there—and generally considered to be of Egyptian nationality—claimed descent from families in Livorno or Pisa, although most had arrived in Alexandria via one or two generations in Aleppo or Beirut. Many still held Italian citizenship, in some cases with documents tracing their heritage back to pre-unification Tuscany. These citizens retained only the loosest of cultural connections with their homeland: Italian Jews in Alexandria were not generally active within the Italian community there and rarely spoke Italian at home, but nonetheless they answered their call-up papers and served alongside their fellow citizens, some with a considerable degree of patriotic enthusiasm. The same was also true of Italian Jews living in Palestine or Syria.[94] Their stories illustrate the difficulty of determining what an Italian really was: religion was not a deciding factor; language use was important but perhaps not decisive among those who used Arabic or Hebrew more often in their daily lives. Place of residence was clearly unimportant, after two generations in Syria or Egypt. Could they then be defined as racially Italian? Or was it simply that willingness to answer the draft proved their Italianness?

[92] ASMAE, Rappresentanza Diplomatica in Egitto, 1915, busta 152, fasc. 4.
[93] ASMAE, Rappresentanza Diplomatica in Egitto, 1914; 1915, busta 148.
[94] ASMAE, Consolato Generale di Gerusalemme, Pos. 30, fasc. 58—nazionalità.

8.6.3 Citizens of Empire

All those who were under the authority of the Italian state and its head, the king, were Italian subjects, while citizenship was reserved to native-born nationals from the metropole, or to their descendants overseas. Although the terms subject and citizen were often used interchangeably within the metropole, in the colonies they described two very different and distinct conditions. For the inhabitants of Libya, the Treaty of Ouchy had meant among other things the loss of citizenship status (within the Ottoman Empire), being downgraded to merely subjects of Italy. The metropolitan citizen retained his privileges even if he moved to the colony; the colonized subject shared none of his political rights; women's citizenship status was lesser in both cases, as well as contingent upon marital status. Instead, colonized subjects were granted certain rights which derived from previous legal and administrative structures—specifically, the Ottoman system in operation prior to 1911—and to religious custom, most importantly the right to polygamy (for Muslim men) and to religious rules on family composition, inheritance, and property. However, while colonial subjects were denied many rights, they were also exempt from some of the obligations of citizenship—chief among them military service.

As part of the evolving debate on war aims and on the post-war settlement, the question of how colonial subjects were to be treated acquired increasing signifi- cance over time. In March 1917 so-called 'Indigenous Advisory Committees' were created in Tripolitania and Cyrenaica, following the suggestion of governor Giovanni Ameglio, in a first step towards a (very limited) form of participatory representative government.[95] In January 1918 Lloyd George's 'war aims' speech discussed the future of German colonies, suggesting that (some form of) self- determination ought to operate there, and that in any case colonies ought not merely to be exploited by European powers but 'the natives' [. . .] chiefs and councils' should 'consult and speak for their tribes'.[96] The Minister for the Colonies, Gaspare Colosimo, copied an Italian translation of this speech into his diary and annotated it carefully; Wilson's Fourteen points, and their implications for Italy's imperial possessions were also subject to his scrutiny.[97] Clearly Colosimo was aware that not only internal matters but international policy positions emerging from the war were likely to influence the development of the colonial administration and governance; through 1918 he repeatedly emphasized

---

[95] Federico Cresti, 'Quale futuro per la Libia italiana? Dal dibattito sulla politica coloniale del dopoguerra alla promulgazione degli Statuti (1918⊠1920)', in *Sudditi o cittadini? L'evoluzione delle appartenenze imperiali nella Prima Guerra Mondiale*, ed. Sara Lorenzini and Simone Attilio Bellezza (Rome: Viella, 2018), 167–8.
[96] British War Aims. Statement by the Right Honourable David Lloyd George [—]. Authorized Version as published by the British Government (New York: George H. Doran, 1918), 6.
[97] Cresti, 'Quale futuro per la Libia italiana?', 153–5.

to both parliament and his ministerial colleagues the potential dangers which the coming 'Wilsonian moment' might present to Italian plans in Libya.[98] In response to both the internal situation and the evolving international climate, the legal status of Italy's north African subjects clearly required some kind of resolution.

In June 1919, in both Tripolitania and Cyrenaica, a new Statute (or constitution) was introduced, which created 'colonial citizenship', loosely based on the French provisions for Algeria.[99] This hybrid citizenship was a clear improvement on the previous status of 'colonial subject' (which continued to be all that was available to the peoples of Eritrea and Somalia): the new category of '*cittadinanza italiana in Tripolitania e Cirenaica*' (Italian citizenship in Tripolitania and Cyrenaica) offered significantly increased personal liberties including freedom of conscience, freedom of the press and association, equality before the law, and the inviolability of private property. It was nonetheless different from (and in key ways lesser than) full Italian metropolitan citizenship. Participation in national politics and in the regular metropolitan army were still excluded, while the possibility of following Islamic or Jewish law on family matters and inheritance was preserved. This status kept the colonial population at arm's length while still offering the appearance of integration and assimilation. It was also possible for indigenous Libyans to apply for full metropolitan citizenship through a series of lengthy bureaucratic procedures, an option which only a few individuals sought to take up (though we lack substantial archival evidence to explore this question more fully). Those who did were assessed on multiple criteria: only prosperous, literate, loyal, Italian-speaking, morally upstanding young men, single or monogamous, and permanently resident in the colony, might receive favourable responses to their applications. As Sabina Donati makes clear, these examples allow us a glimpse of an active participation by a (small) colonial elite, participating in Italian administration, and seeking personal and professional advancement through citizenship.[100]

The Italian recognition of Tripolitanian rights was presented as an enlightened step: a kind of Wilsonian colonialism, perhaps, almost an informal Mandate. In truth it was more a sign of Italian uncertainty than a sincere desire to grant civil liberties to imperial subjects; how could it be other, when the express purpose of the colonization of Libya was to create a settler colony?

---

[98] e.g. his report to parliament, 23 February 1918: Italia. *Atti del Parlamento Italiano*—Sessione 1913–1918 (12/02/1918–26/04/ 1918), Vol. XV, I Sessione (Rome: Tip. Camera dei Deputati 1918): 16047–114; 16076–102, https://storia.camera.it/lavori/regno-d-italia/leg-regno-XXIV/1918/23-febbraio.

[99] On French Algeria, see Dónal Hassett, 'Reinventing Empire in the Wake of the Great War: Imperial Citizenship and the "Wilsonian Moment" in Colonial Algeria', *Comparativ. Zeitschrift Für Globalgeschichte und Vergleichende Gesellschaftsforschung* 26, no. 6 (2016): 37–55.

[100] Sabina Donati, ' "Cittadinanza", "sudditanza" e "nazionalità" in contesto imperiale: Riflessione sul caso italiano tra guerra e dopoguerra, 1914–1925', *Italian Culture* (forthcoming); see also Donati, *A Political History of National Citizenship*, 130–3.

8.6.4 Citizens and Subjects Beyond North Africa

In the Dodecanese, citizenship was used explicitly as a tool of Italianization. The inhabitants of Italy's only 'white colony' were treated quite differently from those of the African colonies. Greek ambitions in the area also shaped Italian policy. More than 80 per cent of the population was Greek-speaking and Orthodox, with the remainder made up of Muslims and Jews; the Greek majority preferred Italy to the previous occupier, Ottoman Turkey, but irredentism was nonetheless a growing force. Greeks and Turks alike hoped the Italian occupation would be short lived—each hoping to see its own nation prevail. Greek irredentists saw the war as an excellent opportunity to force the issue, leaving Italy scrambling to 'pacify' local restlessness and undermine Venizelos' appeal to nationalism by transforming the military occupation into a civil administration.

War gave Italy a chance to offer the islands' inhabitants a concrete benefit: Italian diplomatic protection. Potentially subject to either Greek or Ottoman conscription, men of military age could instead turn to the Italian authorities and receive a passport which exempted them from such service. This did not, however, make them into Italian citizens (liable to Italian conscription). Armed with this passport, men of the Dodecanese and their families could emigrate and evade the war altogether—some even travelled to the USA. Italian passports were also granted to those born in the Dodecanese but living elsewhere, such as in Egypt. Granting diplomatic protection was a low-cost measure with the great benefit of undermining the Greek nationalist cause and strengthening the Italian colonial hold on the islands. Somewhat bizarrely, the Italian foreign office decreed that although these men were 'of the Hellenic race' they could, if needed, be recognized as Italian subjects—even though Italian sovereignty over the islands was still unrecognized internationally.[101] Dodecanese residents were treated as colonial subjects who by virtue of their whiteness might receive a form of privileged 'national' status (still well short of citizenship). Here we can see both the impact of Italian racial thinking at work, and the willingness and ability of the state's colonial structures to respond creatively in wartime to these thorny questions of identity and legal status, when it proved politically expedient.

Citizenship was also used as a tool of wartime politics in the far-off Italian territory of Tianjin, where the Legione Redenta was assembled. While in Russian captivity, many Austro-Hungarian prisoners had sought to claim Italian citizenship; since this status would guarantee a completely different treatment from their captors than that reserved to German or Hungarian prisoners, this cannot be taken as firm evidence they were Italian nationals (and it is not impossible that

---

[101] Valerie McGuire, 'An Imperial Education for Times of Transition', 145–63.

some German or Hungarian soldiers falsely asserted Italian status).[102] Of course since Italians in the Habsburg army were nearly all by definition from the *terre irredente*, this was a chance for a personal 'redemption', which could come in the form of military service or other support for the Italian war effort. Those who volunteered for the Legion guaranteed their individual acquisition of Italian citizenship, which they received in a ceremony in August 1918.[103] Individual Italians were thus 'redeemed' into the nation even before the lands of their birth, which remained firmly in Austrian hands at this date. Italian wartime expansionism was multi-stranded: not only the national territory but its most vital resource, manpower, were to be enlarged. And as Donati observes, by swearing their new allegiance to Italy on Italian colonial soil, in far-off China, these new citizens explicitly exchanged one imperial allegiance for another.[104] In essence, these few hundred souls enacted a dual demonstration of the war's expansionist character, joining not just an extended national community but the ruling element of a colonial empire. However, though they acquired their citizenship within a colony, they were offered not colonial but metropolitan citizenship. The determining criteria was not the location in which they found themselves but their nationality, as conceived in ethno-cultural terms. And the process of acquiring full metropolitan citizenship was also radically differentiated on racial grounds: a white Austrian citizen could earn it through military service, whereas an Arab Italian subject could not.

In 1921 the National Fascist Party included the equivalence of race and nation within its founding manifesto. But this was neither new nor particularly surprising, given both the nineteenth-century traditions of Italian racial thinking and the widespread emphasis on race and nation during the First World War. The need to classify and to manage differing groups during and after the war led to a re-articulation of both nationality and citizenship centred on the new borderlands and the colonial empire. Race was 'less a contingent component of national identity than one of its constitutive elements' and that in turn underpinned Italian thinking about the treatment of minorities within the state.[105] This approach, informed by and constitutive of a colonial mindset, deeply shaped wartime practices both towards Italians and towards the Others they fought or governed.

[102]   See Marina Rossi, *I prigionieri dello zar: soldati italiani dell'esercito austro-ungarico nei lager della Russia, 1914–1918* (Milan: Mursia, 1997).

[103]   Sabina Donati, 'Citizenship and Identity Issues in the Italian Concession of Tientsin (1902–1922)', in *Ideas and Identities. A Festschrift for Andre Liebich*, ed. Jaci Eisenberg and Davide Rodogno (Bern: Peter Lang, 2014); Donati, '"Cittadinanza", "sudditanza" e "nazionalità" in contesto imperiale'.

[104]   Donati, '"Cittadinanza", "sudditanza" e "nazionalità" in contesto imperiale'.

[105]   Patriarca and Deplano, 'Nation, "Race", and Racisms in Twentieth-Century Italy', 350.

9

The Paris Peace Conference and Beyond

On 24 October 1918, precisely one year after the battle of Caporetto had begun, Italy launched its final offensive at the battle of Vittorio Veneto. The 4th, 8th, 10th, and 2nd Armies attacked along the Piave and despite some solid Austro-Hungarian resistance and the difficulties of the terrain, flooded by the autumn rains, the 10th Army was able to make a significant breakthrough at Grave di Papodopoli. This joint Italian–British unit, under the Earl of Cavan, created a bridgehead which could then be exploited starting on 27 October. The Austrian retreat began the following day, as Hungarian, Czech, Slovenian, and Croatian troops refused to obey orders. On 29 October the Habsburg high command made contact with their Italian counterparts to request an Armistice, and the following day Italian forces reached the town of Vittorio Veneto. Not everyone was convinced that it was advisable to sign an Armistice straight away: given the unsatisfactory military legacies of the Risorgimento, there was a current of thought— supported by Giocchino Volpe, Gaetano Salvemini, and others—which held that Italy should fight on until all the *terre irredente* had been redeemed by force of arms, and even perhaps push on to seize any additional desired territories.[1] This might have put Italy in a stronger position when it came to later negotiations. Certainly, if Fiume had been conquered by force of arms, rather than claimed retrospectively, it must have affected the negotiations that followed; but there was no general appetite to delay the end of hostilities. The Armistice was signed on 3 November at Villa Giusti, a handsome villa outside Padova, just as Italian troops were raising the tricolour flag over Trento and Trieste (after a hasty rush to seize both cities before the document was signed).[2] Hostilities ended at 3 p.m. on 4 November 1918: Italy was the first of the great powers to secure its victory. The human cost was immense: around 600,000 servicemen were dead, including around 100,000 who died as prisoners of war, and another 100,000 would die of wounds or war-related ill-health in the next few years. Around 1 million men were wounded, of whom around half suffered permanent disability, and another 2.5 million experienced

---

[1] Carlo Ghisalberti, 'Il mito della vittoria mutilata', in *La Conferenza di pace di Parigi fra ieri e domani (1919–1920). Atti del Convegno Internazionale di Studi Portogruaro-Bibione. 31 maggio-4 giugno 2000*, ed. Antonio Scottà (Soveria Mannelli: Rubbettino, 2003), 132–3.
[2] See Angelo Visintin, *L'Italia a Trieste: l'operato del governo militare italiano nella Venezia Giulia, 1918–1919* (Gorizia: LEG, 2000).

The Italian Empire and the Great War. Vanda Wilcox, Oxford University Press (2021). © Vanda Wilcox.
DOI: 10.1093/oso/9780198822943.003.0009

significant sickness, of whom more than 200,000 were permanently disabled. From a population of 37 million in 1915, some 5.5 million men served in the armed forces; roughly 11–12 per cent were killed, 18 per cent were wounded, 11 per cent were captured, 45 per cent fell sick, and 12 per cent were permanently disabled.[3]

The heightened psychological and symbolic significance for Italy of defeating Austria-Hungary has often been ignored. Whereas the emotional weight of Franco-German hostilities is commonly acknowledged, it is easy to overlook the fact that Italy had fought Austria in 1848, unsuccessfully; in 1859, when victory was largely French; and in 1866, when victory was entirely Prussian. Italy's victory in 1918 thus assumed truly epic proportions, the end point of seventy years of conflict and rivalry; it was in many ways experienced as a coming of age. We need not accept the liberal-national interpretative framework of the 'Fourth War of the Risorgimento' to acknowledge the emotional impact of this victory, or to understand the scale of the expectations which it aroused.[4]

9.1 Demobilization and Domestic Politics

When the Armistice was signed, some 3.9 million officers and men were under arms. Their hopes of a rapid return home now that the war was ended would be dashed, as many would not be demobilized until December 1920.[5] In fact the geographical dislocation of Italian forces was still spreading after the Armistice, as Italian troops were sent to occupy Bulgaria and later Upper Silesia, as well as continuing in the various expeditionary corps.[6] Arguably, the war did not so much end as spread out eastwards along the margins of Europe.[7] Demobilization, therefore, was slow. The first to receive their release papers were the sick and the oldest classes of conscripts, along with those whose families were in great difficulty—around 1 million men in the first few months after the war. However, most of these were territorial militia or even militarized workers, rather than serving soldiers in the field army. In June 1919 Orlando, Sonnino, and Diaz agreed to start bringing most of those still stationed overseas back to Italy—a decision which would happily combine cutting costs with general popularity. They ordered

[3] Pierluigi Scolè, 'War Losses (Italy)', in *1914–1918-Online. International Encyclopedia of the First World War*, ed. Ute Daniel et al. (Berlin: Freie Universität Berlin, 2015), https://encyclopedia.1914-1918-online.net/article/war_losses_italy.

[4] Raoul Pupo, ed., *La vittoria senza pace: le occupazioni militari italiane alla fine della Grande Guerra* (Rome: GLF editori Laterza, 2014), v.

[5] Giulia Albanese, 'Demobilisation and Political Violence in Italy, 1918–1922', in *Italy in the Era of the Great War*, ed. Vanda Wilcox (Leiden: Brill, 2018), 234–35, DOI: https://doi.org/10.1163/9789004363724_013.

[6] On the Italian presence in Upper Silesia and in north-eastern Europe more generally, see Irene Guerrini and Marco Pluviano, 'L'area baltica tra il 1919 e il 1922 nelle fonti archivistiche diplomatiche e militari italiani', in *Da Versailles a Monaco. Vent'anni di guerre dimenticate*, ed. Davide Artico and Bruno Mantelli (Turin: UTET, 2010), 91–121.

[7] Gooch, *The Italian Army*, 311.

a significant reduction of the forces serving in Tripolitania and Cyrenaica (down to a maximum of 50,000 men) along with the withdrawal of Italian forces in Murmansk and Siberia, as well as the return home of at least 20,000 men from Albania.[8] The units serving in the Eastern Mediterranean were also to be scaled back as much as possible. Through 1919 prisoners of war were also slowly returning home from camps in Austria and Germany—or even further afield: a number of prisoners of war captured at Caporetto by the Germans had ended up working as road-builders in the Ottoman Empire.[9] By summer 1920 some 200,000 men were still overseas. At home, the government was loath to add dramatically to the already high unemployment figures by too rapid a demobilization, while the growing number of strikes and protests encouraged the authorities to keep men in arms ready for use in public order duties. How were veterans to be supported? The promises of better treatment made in the aftermath of Caporetto would require a great deal in the way of funding and administration; the government's failure to act effectively in this area led to the springing up of multiple new veterans' associations, which would soon become major political forces in their own right.

Italy's domestic political situation was complex. Wartime political unity, always stronger in rhetoric than in reality, quickly broke down. In November 1918 discussions began around a major new political force which embraced Catholic values: the Partito Popolare Italiano (PPI), founded the following January by charismatic Sicilian priest Don Luigi Sturzo to serve as a mass party which could attract the working class away from socialism. Socialist critiques of the war had earned the party further support (in the November 1919 elections, the PSI would earn nearly one third of the vote). The weeks and months after the Armistice were politically chaotic, and the PPI was intended to act as a stabilizing force.[10] Democracy was already under severe strain, with the very real possibility of a military coup d'état in the final months of the war and the first period of the peace.[11] As Marco Mondini highlights, many regular officers regarded the return of peace with unease if not open hostility: none wished to return to the pre-war liberal state of affairs, in which the army's position had always been somewhat constrained, after enjoying several years of unprecedented social and political power. The weakness of civilian government during the war had raised questions about the entire constitutional structure, and many officers regarded the entire political class with mistrust and contempt.[12] The war had ended but the climate of militarization continued, especially in public spaces; in social and psychological

---

[8]   ACS PCM GE 1915–1918 busta 221, f. 201, sf.3 Smobilitazione.
[9]   ACS GE b. 214, sf. Anno 1921.
[10]   On the PPI, see John Neylon Molony, *The Emergence of Political Catholicism in Italy: Partito Popolare 1919–1926* (London: C. Helm, 1977).
[11]   See Giulia Albanese, *La marcia su Roma* (Rome: Laterza, 2006), 4–8; Roberto Vivarelli, *Storia delle origini del fascismo* (Bologna: Il Mulino, 1991), 497–505.
[12]   Mondini, *La guerra italiana*, 358–9.

terms, demobilization happened slowly if at all. By the winter of 1919–20, public order had degenerated drastically across the country, with low-level street violence increasingly common. As in many other countries, the formalization of political violence into paramilitarism often involved the remobilization of veterans who felt that the war was not yet complete. In the Italian case, internal enemies on the left had replaced the Austrians.[13]

9.2 The Peace Conference Begins

On 18 January 1919, precisely forty-eight years since the proclamation of the German Empire in the Hall of Mirrors at Versailles, the Paris Peace Conference opened with a ceremony at the Quai d'Orsay. Just as in 1871, it was the fate of Germany and its place within Europe which were the heart of the matter—but the key actors were the heads of government and foreign ministers of the main victorious powers. Italy was internationally perceived as the least of the principal players and was frequently marginalized at the conference (tellingly, John Maynard Keynes' classic account of the conference makes almost no mention at all of Orlando) compared to the US, France, and Britain.

Yet the impact of the Peace Conference, its treatment of Italy, and the failures of Italian diplomacy there were to have enormous significance. Spencer Di Scala suggests that 'many historians ignore or view with scepticism the idea that the Paris Peace Conference following the Great War contributed to the destruction of Italian democracy',[14] but this is an argument worth serious consideration. Vittorio Orlando's comment that the outcome of the conference 'would cause violent conflicts in Italy in the more or less near future'[15] was prescient indeed. Given the extent of scholarly attention to the question of links between the Versailles Treaty and the rise of Nazism, it is odd that the relationship between the conference and fascism has been generally downplayed.[16]

Underpinning all Italy's problems in Paris was a huge divergence in under-standing of Italy's contributions to the Allied victory. To the French and the British, the pre-eminence of the Western Front was self-evident while Italy's military contribution to Allied victory was generally downplayed. As Supreme

---

[13] Compare case studies in Robert Gerwarth and John Horne, eds, *War in Peace: Paramilitary Violence in Europe after the Great War* (Oxford: Oxford University Press, 2012). On squadrismo, see Mimmo Franzinelli, *Squadristi: Protagonisti e tecniche della violenza fascista* (Milan: Mondadori, 2004).

[14] Spencer Di Scala, 'Liberalism, Civil Rights, and Reform: Vittorio Emanuele Orlando and the Great War', in *Italy in the Era of the Great War*, ed. Vanda Wilcox (Leiden: Brill, 2018), 187, DOI: https://doi.org/10.1163/9789004363724_011.

[15] Spencer Di Scala, *Vittorio Emanuele Orlando: Italy* (London: Haus Pub., 2010), 52.

[16] Gaetano Salvemini argued that the widespread disparagement of the Italian war effort was an important issue in the collapse of the Liberal State: *The Origins of Fascism in Italy* (New York: Harper & Row, 1973), 13–18.

Allied Commander, Foch had repeatedly made known his irritation with the Italians: he considered them to have been unjustifiably passive in the closing period of the war, as well as excessively demanding of Allied resources, and therefore saw their political claims as unfounded.[17] Many Italians were (and remain) convinced that this was a misreading of the war, and that the Italian contribution to victory was central. In D'Annunzio's words, '[the Allies] won just on a single front fighting a single nation of 77 million men' which they faced with 'all the forces of France, the British Empire, the United States, thousands of Italian, Portuguese and Polish auxiliaries and colonial troops of every kind'. Meanwhile Italy fought 'alone, always alone' (despite the arrival of French and British troops, which he does concede) while also sending troops to France, Macedonia, Syria, and even Murmansk. The bizarre assertion that the Allies fought only on the Western Front while Italy fought a global war led him to ask: 'which nation is more purely and fully victorious than Italy?'[18] This was a characteristically extreme version of the position, to be sure, but a sense that Italy's contribution had been crucial to allied victory whereas the Western Front's importance had been overplayed was widespread across many sectors of society—a view which clearly influenced the Italian position at the Peace Conference.

The Italian delegation to Paris suffered from considerable internal tensions. Orlando and Sonnino personally disliked one another and had different political visions, especially over the fraught problem of the upper Adriatic. But the real problems lay in Italy's relations with its former allies. Even before the conference began, the Italian government found itself increasingly isolated. Robert Cecil wrote to the British ambassador James Rennell Rodd in Rome on 3 January 1919:

> The fact is that the greediness of Italian foreign policy in all directions is leading Italy into serious difficulties. I do not deny that the French are not always tactful in their dealings with the Italians, and that they also have an exaggerated appetite, nor am I prepared to maintain that the Yugoslavs have never claimed more than their due, but Sonnnino's stubbornness and the extravagant nature of Italy's claims have had as a result that it is now literally true that Italy has not a friend in Europe except ourselves, and she is now doing her best to make her isolation complete.[19]

That isolation was literal as well as metaphorical. Notably, the Italian delegation in Paris tended to keep to their own hotel; they did not dine or take tea with their Allied counterparts, as many of the other delegations did, nor did they throw

---

[17] By November 1918 both military and political authorities in France were weary of what they saw as Italian prevarication and selfishness. McCrae, *Coalition Strategy and the End of the First World War*, 124–32.

[18] Gabriele D'Annunzio, *Contro uno e contro tutti* (Rome: Presso la Fionda, 1919), 130–1.

[19] BOD Rennell Rodd correspondence 20–1919, Cecil to Rennell Rodd.

themselves into the hurly-burly of Parisian social and cultural life, which was reviving rapidly after the war. Their absences from balls and concerts was doubtless insignificant, but their failure to participate in the regular informal meetings with their colleagues did not help their position.[20] The delegation failed to appreciate the importance of interpersonal relations: when Orlando and Sonnino travelled from London to Paris in December 1918, they took the same train as Georges Clemenceau but without once making the effort to speak to him on the journey, or even to take leave of him at its end—a failure of common courtesy as much as international diplomacy which left Clemenceau 'astonished and offended'.[21] Orlando was also frequently under-prepared and ill-informed about any matters not directly relating to Italian interests; as a result, he sometimes gave the impression that Italy only cared about itself and not about resolving the wider problems of Europe.[22]

The opening months of the conference saw a great quantity of work but little real progress on matters of substance. Broad outlines of the eventual settlement were agreed by the end of January but the devil was all in the details. Not until March 1919, when Woodrow Wilson and David Lloyd George returned from their respective homelands, did a much smaller working group emerge capable of really determining the knottiest questions: the Council of Four. By restricting the meetings to the 'Big Four', it became possible to focus solely on critical issues; by excluding all but the heads of government, troublesome presences such as Sonnino were removed (no bad thing, said some at the time).[23]

By mid-April, the Council of Four was ready to invite—or perhaps summon— the German delegation to Paris. Originally the Conference had been intended to serve as a preliminary conference at which the Allied position could be drawn up, in advance of the 'real' negotiations with the defeated enemy. Somehow, tacitly, this preliminary conference turned into the real thing. Rather than negotiate a treaty with the Central Powers, the Allies would simply present it to them. But at this critical moment, the Italian delegation provoked—or from an Italian perspective, found itself thrust into—a crisis which temporarily blocked the work of the conference altogether.

9.2.1 Italian Hopes in Paris

To fully understand the international crisis which broke out in April 1919, we must examine the fraught domestic scene which underpinned it. In parliament in November and December 1918, Orlando had carefully—and perhaps typically— avoided presenting any overly specific programme, instead sticking to platitudes

---

[20] Macmillan, *Paris 1919*, 143–9.   [21] Macmillan, *Paris 1919*, 289.
[22] Caccamo, 'Italy, the Adriatic and the Balkans', 127–9.   [23] Macmillan, *Paris 1919*, 273.

about the completion of the national territory and Italian reasonableness. At meetings in December 1918, members of the government had acknowledged that compromise would be essential to achieve a successful outcome in Paris.[24] But this spirit would soon be lost, in part due to the changing circumstances of domestic politics but also owing to the actions of the other Allies and Greece.

The wartime coalition, which under the pressures of the conflict had managed to put to one side its inherent differences, could not hold up well under the new requirements of peace negotiations. The leader of the democratic interventionist left, Leonida Bissolati, whose views were almost diametrically opposed to Sonnino's, resigned after a cabinet meeting on 27 December. He then made his views known both in the press and in a public address in Milan on 11 January, where a large and organized crowd of nationalists, including Mussolini, shouted him down so effectively that he could not be heard—a sign of things to come. Bissolati was a full supporter of Wilsonian idealism: peace without annexations, no territorial compensation, international arbitration by the League of Nations. He was also an inheritor in many ways of the Mazzinian tradition. Yet this important strand of public opinion was increasingly marginalized in this period: the Mazzinian press, and the liberal *Corriere della Sera*, offered little clear policy lead in the strange post-war lull between the Armistice and the conference; Albrecht-Carrié called it 'supine'.[25] Strong socialist support for a Wilsonian peace allowed nationalists to smear democratic interventionists as unpatriotic (even, potentially, Bolshevik) and play into a widespread middle-class fear of the left.

Public debates soon focused on the Adriatic and on Dalmatia, and quickly came down to the question: how much should Italy demand? In naval circles, the idea of making the Adriatic into an Italian pond was quite appealing, and proposals for claiming the entire eastern shore down as far as the bay of Kotor (Cattaro) ensued, entailing a long narrow strip of land along the coast. Wiser minds in the army greeted this prospect with horror—how on earth was such a land border to be defended?[26] Nostalgia for the glory of the Venetian Republic in the heyday of the Serenissima encouraged some to argue that since Dubrovnik (Ragusa) had once been Venetian, Venice's claims to the entirety of the Dalmatian coast had a strong historical basis. But in general, debates over Dalmatia were more modest, though still greedy in Yugoslav eyes. By February Fiume had rather unexpectedly emerged as the key issue in public opinion. Throughout the war, Fiume had barely been mentioned: the press, politicians, propaganda all focused exclusively on Trento and Trieste. Why, then, did Fiume become such a sticking point? Although the

[24] Francesco Caccamo, *L'Italia e la «Nuova Europa». Il confronto sull'Europa orientale alla conferenza di pace di Parigi (1919–1920)* (Milan: Luni Editrice, 2000), 41.
[25] Albrecht-Carrié, *Italy at the Paris Peace Conference*, 69.
[26] Giorgio Rochat, *L'esercito italiano da Vittorio Veneto a Mussolini (1919–1925)* (Bari: Laterza, 1967), 33.

town itself did have a majority Italian population (though only just), its suburbs and hinterland were entirely Slav; the Treaty of London had explicitly excluded it from Italian claims.

It was Orlando, desperate to preserve his own position, who came up with the Italian claim for 'The Treaty of London plus Fiume'; Sonnino by contrast was not interested in Fiume at all, but simply wanted to fully impose the original Treaty, perhaps adding some less important parts of Dalmatia. Bissolati, to whom no-one was inclined to listen, was happy to abandon the Treaty of London and hand the Dodecanese over to Greece—which would in turn have allowed a much stronger claim to Fiume.[27] Possibly Orlando, sensing that under these changed circumstances Italy was unlikely to receive Dalmatia, thought Fiume could be a suitable replacement he could present to the public as fruit of successful negotiations. He himself admitted to Wilson's aide Colonel House that had the territorial questions been resolved in November 1918 Fiume might never have been mentioned at all.[28] But in the event, the Italian Memorandum of Claims, drafted by Trieste-born lawyer Salvatore Barzilai and presented on 7 February, made Fiume almost its central focus.[29] Critically this document made no mention of colonial matters: of course, to have included them here would have laid bare the fiction that Italian claims to Dalmatia were in any way compatible with the ideal of self-determination. By suggesting that claims in the Western Balkans could have been swapped for some African or Middle Eastern territory would have been to decisively destroy the very basis for those claims; nonetheless, this could have been one way out of the impasse. Instead, the need to appear 'Wilsonian' stifled the colonial party—including Sonnino—from presenting its demands more clearly at an early stage of proceedings in Paris.

Although to outsiders, this focus on Fiume and Dalmatia appeared without foundation, within Italy itself wartime discourse had shifted the boundaries of the debate. The *Giornale d'Italia*, which was very close to Sonnino and the foreign office, was promoting a strongly anti-Yugoslav position, while the *oltranzisti* (hard-liners), whether appealing to the heritage of ancient Rome or of the Venetian Republic, made such exaggerated claims—including Split, Kotor, and Dubrovnik—that by contrast Orlando's chosen formula of 'the Pact of London + Fiume' seemed quite moderate.[30]

Colonial questions made a sudden and short-lived appearance in the Italian press in mid-December. What, precisely, did Italy want in Africa at the end of the war? The diversity of opinion within government circles and even among supporters of a colonial policy made it hard to agree a single set of demands. The

[27] Albrecht-Carrié, *Italy at the Paris Peace Conference*, 72.
[28] Albrecht-Carrié, *Italy at the Paris Peace Conference*, 102–3.
[29] Reproduced in Albrecht-Carrié, *Italy at the Paris Peace Conference*, Doc. 17, 370–87.
[30] Ghisalberti, 'Il mito della vittoria mutilata', 128–30; Vivarelli, *Storia delle origini del fascismo*, vol. 1, 322–3.

high-profile conference organized by the Italian Colonial Institute at the Campidoglio in Rome, planned since June 1918, finally opened on 15 January 1919 and was still in session when talks began at Versailles. Designed to plan the future of the colonies, the event was open to the public and was semi-official: Colosimo and former colonial administrators were joined by scholars and ambitious activists. Some delegates made life rather difficult for the government, with extravagant calls for Italy to receive a share of Cameroon or descriptions of self-determination as unjust and superficial.[31] The conference attracted a great deal of attention, succeeding in increasing public interest in colonial questions, but it resolved little. The very nature of Italian colonialism as born from wishful thinking mitigated against the development of a coherent programme.

Most revealing of Italy's official position is the detailed memorandum and accompanying map which Colosimo prepared for House (and Wilson) as the war ended, which laid out Italy's colonial case very clearly.[32] Unlike Sonnino, who was increasingly interested in the Asia Minor project, Colosimo's focus was almost wholly on Africa and the Red Sea. The memorandum first outlined Italy's 'rights pre-dating the war', essentially a potted history of Italian imperialism, and then its 'rights born during the war', which were inevitably somewhat more speculative. Finally, the memorandum turned to the post-war world. Colosimo attempted to present acquisitive colonialism in the language of Wilsonian self-determination, a herculean rhetorical task which was inevitably a failure. Nonetheless, it is worth examining this document in some detail, as it represents perhaps the fullest summary of the official Italian programme in Africa.

Colosimo began with the principle that 'states should be given benefits proportionate to the contribution each one has made to the common victory *relative to their own strength* [my emphasis]. That said, there can be no doubt about the rights which Italy has earned during the Great War.' Italy's contribution should thus be assessed not relative to British, French, or American strength but to its own position. He then enumerated a long list of Italian naval, military, and economic achievements, in which he even tried to claim that credit should be given for Italy's initial neutrality, on somewhat spurious grounds. In North Africa,

Italy's continued occupation of Libya, with its enormous sacrifice of blood and gold, maintained in the face of the rebellion in Tripolitania which the Turks and Germans fomented, prevented the enemy from securely occupying that Mediterranean coast which would have been gravely damaging not only to Italy but to France and Britain.

---

[31] Istituto Coloniale Italiano, *Atti del Convegno nazionale coloniale per il dopo guerra delle colonie: Roma, 15–21 gennaio 1919* (Rome: Unione editrice, 1920).
[32] A copy was also presented to Balfour in December 1918.

In reality, it seems likely that even a hostile Ottoman Libya would have proved only a minor annoyance to Allied naval routes or to French Tunisia and British Egypt. Colosimo continued by asserting that Italy had faced 'the entire weight of the Austrian Empire along its borders', breezily ignoring the existence of Russia, Romania, and Serbia in his effort to display the scale and significance of Italy's war effort. As a result of this superlative endeavour, a 'just, equal and lasting peace in line with the ethical ends of President Wilson' required a long-term alliance based on a complete and satisfactory colonial settlement, in which colonies should be organized into homogenous, organic, independent entities. Just as French control reached from Morocco to Tunisia, or British rule from Egypt to the Cape, so too a coherent, homogenous entity should be created for Italy. Only thus could Italy 'develop the latent energies of its youthful people and its future' and 'meet our needs for development, life, and a lasting peace'. Peace required a degree of distributive justice between the three allies, Colosimo concluded, before proceeding to outline the details of his proposed African settlement—a maximalist vision.[33]

A report by *Comando Supremo* in November 1918 addressed more directly the question of how to present Italian claims in the most positive light. The anonymous author outlined the predominant French, British and American views on colonialism and speculated how best this new system might be gamed—perhaps, he suggested, a case might be made for Italian rule as a source of economic growth and development which would benefit the indigenous peoples? Alternatively, if arguments for territorial equity were no longer viable, then why not argue for economic equity—consider the vast wealth gained by Britain and France in oil; should Italy not be compensated for these new monopolies? The report proposed that rather than full sovereignty over large areas of worthless land, Italy should fight for special privileges in coal and wheat-producing areas, to which Italian surplus population could also be directed, even if sovereignty remained in other hands.[34] Both these documents show Italian policymakers struggling to fit decidedly non-Wilsonian world views into an unwelcome new framework in preparation for the Paris Conference.

Perhaps unsurprisingly, therefore, little was done to formalize colonial proposals in this preparatory period. When the Italian official memorandum was presented on 7 February 1919, it focused on Europe and the Mediterranean rather than prioritizing Africa; by February, the press and parliament in Italy were already beginning to develop that almost exclusive focus on Fiume which was to prove so disastrous.

---

[33] ACS GE 1915–1918: busta 75, fasc. Colonie, 30 October 1918: Colosimo's Memorandum for Colonel House, and Carta Segreta. On the minimum and maximum programmes already drawn up during the war, see Hess, 'Italy and Africa', 109–11.
[34] ACS GE 1915–1918: busta 75, fasc. Colonie, 28 November 1918: Contributo alla preparazione per le trattive coloniali, by Comando Supremo.

9.2.2 Territorial Compensation in the Era of Self-determination

The 1915 Treaty of London had offered relatively specific territorial compensation in the core national objectives, the 'unredeemed' lands of Trento and Trieste, as well as extensive claims in Dalmatia and Albania. Italy's frustration at the Peace Conference would come about in part due to changing priorities from its erstwhile allies, and in part owing to its own increased ambitions, which had evolved significantly during the war. Even the terms of the London Treaty were by now seen as an annoyance by the French and British; there would be no sympathy for larger claims. Clemenceau repeatedly tried to persuade Orlando that the Treaty of London should be abandoned as no longer fit for purpose—superseded by the unexpected event of the dissolution of Austria-Hungary. More generally, the extent to which the new Europe would be exclusively formed through territorial agreements between the powers—of whatever date—was now debatable. While Italy assumed that decisions would simply be made in Paris and then implemented, in reality the Peacemakers would face considerable problems in imposing their vision.[35] That Italian leaders ignored the gulf between the conference's discursive power—vast—and its material power—strictly limited—was of course entirely typical, in that Italy frequently mistook its own discourse for reality.

The largest obstacle to Italian success in Paris, however, was undoubtedly the new vision of post-war politics championed by US President Wilson. Wilson's pronouncement on Italy's post-war fate was to be found at point IX of his famous Fourteen Points speech in January 1918: 'A readjustment of the frontiers of Italy should be made along clearly recognisable lines of nationality.' Unfortunately, this apparently simple utterance concealed within it enormous ambiguity: what constituted recognizable lines? and who was to do the recognizing? As Wilson himself was to acknowledge at the end of 1919, the question of national self-determination was rather more complex than he had initially understood. Rather surprisingly, the Fourteen Points also neglected to mention the question of Italian areas occupied by the enemy (whereas Wilson's first remarks on Russia, France, Belgium, and the allied Balkan powers all acknowledged that some part of their territory was under occupation and must be evacuated). Was this mere oversight? The occupation of the Friuli-Venezia Giulia region had taken place two months before Wilson's speech in January 1918, and he could hardly have failed to be aware of it. Perhaps he simply saw Italy as a party which was neither wronged nor particularly vulnerable and did not envisage any great complexity

---

[35] On the challenges of implementing the Peace Treaties, see Leonard V. Smith, *Sovereignty at the Paris Peace Conference of 1919*, The Greater War (Oxford and New York: Oxford University Press, 2018); Marcus M. Payk and Roberta Pergher, eds, *Beyond Versailles: Sovereignty, Legitimacy, and the Formation of New Polities after the Great War* (Bloomington: Indiana University Press, 2019).

arising around an Italian post-war settlement. His visit to Italy in early January 1919—he toured Rome, Milan, and Genoa, and even met with the Pope—was marked by cheering, ecstatic crowds.[36] The Italian 'myth of America' was still in full flow at this stage, leading Wilson to optimistically imagine that his policies would be equally popular. Meanwhile Orlando would later claim that the Italian ambassador in Washington, Baron Vincenzo Macchi di Cellere, had totally misled the Italian government about Wilson's true feelings and intentions through his own incompetence.[37] These fundamental misunderstandings on both sides would prove disastrous.

In the event, Wilson was directly responsible for many of the difficulties Orlando would experience in Paris. The two men were unable to communicate directly, having no common language—as Keynes observed 'it is of historical importance that Orlando and the President had no direct means of communication'.[38] As well as a common language, the two men lacked a common vision of the post-war world, despite the liberal-democratic rhetoric in which Orlando strove to cloak his position. Wilson was resolutely opposed to the territorial compensation set out in the Treaty of London, and even claimed in Paris that he had never seen the details of the treaty—in fact, however, British Foreign Secretary Arthur Balfour had shown it to him in 1917.[39] As for the idea of proceeding beyond the already unacceptable 1915 claims to add Fiume, the only possible way this could have been made acceptable to Wilson would have been on the basis of indisputable Italian nationality. Wilson however considered—rightly—that the surrounding area was clearly Slavic in character and thus the city could not be meaningfully said to fit within the 'recognisable lines of [Italian] nationality'. Instead, it should be part of the new state of Yugoslavia—not least to provide that country with a reasonably large Adriatic port. As he informed the Conference in April, he was prepared to see Italy have the western portion of Istria but not the eastern, and Trieste and Gorizia but not Dalmatia—or Fiume. As Margaret Macmillan puts it, 'The quarrel was over territory, but it was also over principle, since the Italians wanted what they had been promised under the old diplomacy while the Americans stood firm on the new.'[40] Confusingly though, Wilson was prepared to compromise at times; he was willing to accept Italian possession of the Tyrol (Alto Adige), despite its overwhelmingly German character; even the Italian nationalist martyr Cesare Battisti, born in Trento, had been unconvinced that Italy ought to have the Tyrol as well as the Trentino. This

[36] Erez Manela, *The Wilsonian Moment: Self-Determination and the International Origins of Anticolonial Nationalism* (Oxford; New York: Oxford University Press, 2007), 56.

[37] Cedric J. Lowe and Frank Marzari, *Italian Foreign Policy, 1870–1940* (London; New York: Taylor & Francis, 2002), 166.

[38] John Maynard Keynes, *The Economic Consequences of the Peace* (New York: Harcourt, Brace and Howe, 1920), Ch. 3, fn 6.

[39] Macmillan, *Paris 1919*, 10.   [40] Macmillan, *Paris 1919*, 279.

showed that even ardent advocates of self-determination were forced to acknow-ledge that the rhetoric of homogenous nationhood did not reflect reality. But Wilson's apparent openness to compromise was perhaps more simply willingness to sacrifice German interests, since when it came to the Slavs he was intransigent. Moreover, he expected the Italians to be more amenable to compromise else-where, having already received a major concession in regard to the Tyrol; instead it had the opposite effect of suggesting that ethnic boundaries were not, in fact, to be decisive in settling borders—and that Wilson was perhaps a hypocrite.

Contemporaries were unimpressed with the diplomatic skills of the Italian leadership in Paris, and historians have tended to agree. Michael Neiberg writes that Orlando was hampered by 'severe personal and political limitations', while Macmillan describes the delegation's tactics as 'irritating, transparent and fre-quently inept'.[41] The basis on which Italian claims were made shifted radically from case to case: the Tyrol was claimed on the grounds of security, Fiume on the basis of nationality, Dalmatia on the basis of the Treaty of London and of historical links, while African gains were justified in terms of territorial compen-sation. Inevitably, this flexibility looked like rank opportunism and only served to undermine the entirety of the Italian position. By the time that the question of borders between Italy and Yugoslavia came up, in April, Italian public opinion had become fixated on Fiume to an unprecedented (and perhaps inexplicable) degree. Throughout early April a series of unsuccessful meetings were held, with each party growing steadily angrier and more resentful. French patience with Italy, already slim, was quite exhausted. Moreover, stories circulating of Italian mis-treatment of Slavic populations in the areas they occupied were hardening Allied hearts to the Italian claim of Wilsonian benevolence.

Sonnino explicitly cited Italy's blood sacrifice, appropriately enough in Passion Week, and even announced his regret that Italy had ever signed a treaty before entering the war in 1915—making it clear that to 'merely' grant the territories agreed in the Treaty of London was now considered wholly insufficient. But of course, since the Treaty explicitly granted Fiume to Croatia, it was impossible to insist on the complete application of the Treaty when Italy itself was proposing—in one critical area—to violate it. Matters came to a head with a fraught meeting on Easter Sunday, 20 April, when Orlando was apparently reduced to tears in Wilson's office, during a Council of Four meeting.[42] All the leaders were by now feeling the strain, and personal relationships—and politeness—were breaking down. Lloyd George and Clemenceau offered a compromise: the islands, but not the coast, with Fiume as a free city. But Orlando had backed himself into a corner

[41] Michael S. Neiberg, *The Treaty of Versailles: A Concise History* (Oxford: Oxford University Press, 2017), 28; Macmillan, *Paris 1919*, 292.
[42] Macmillan, *Paris 1919*, 279.

and no compromise of any kind could now be acceptable to the nationalists at home.

Wilson then made a major misstep. Given the enthusiasm of Italians upon his visit three months earlier, he sought to win round public opinion with a direct appeal to them, urging them to embrace his vision and reject the Treaty of London. Wilson was apparently convinced that he spoke for the masses and was in some way better suited than Italy's own elected representatives to gauge national feeling there. But his public letter, printed first in the French and then in the Italian press, provoked scenes of public outrage and fury across the peninsula.[43] This was the final straw for Orlando, who had no real options left; he left the Conference altogether and returned to Rome. Some feared that the entire conference might break down and questioned whether it would be possible to enforce the German treaty under these circumstances.

Did Orlando think that the Allies would be forced to back down under the pressure of his departure? If so, he was much mistaken: on the contrary, France and Britain took the opportunity to divide up the German colonies in Italy's absence, formally recognized the Kingdom of Serbs, Croats, and Slovenes, and even contemplated putting aside the Treaty of London altogether. As Sonnino had feared, Orlando's move only weakened the Italian delegation still further.[44] The gambit seems curiously childish and hard to understand; it perhaps reflects Orlando's desperation over domestic affairs as much as any considered diplomatic strategy. Where Wilson saw a shameless lack of principle, Orlando saw his only hope for political survival. Not for the first or last time, Italy had over-estimated its importance in the wider balance of power. On 6 May Orlando and Sonnino returned, crestfallen but with their position largely unchanged. The so-called 'Tardieu compromise' for a small independent Fiume under Italian influence was discussed in May but to no avail. Matters would not be resolved to any party's satisfaction, and in fact Orlando's government had fallen before the Treaty of Versailles was signed. No resolution to the Italo-Yugoslav border would be achieved in Paris.

9.3 Imperial and Colonial Settlements

By the end of the war the international climate had shifted decisively towards a new understanding of sovereignty, with profound implications for colonialism. The cause of self-determination was embraced by international socialists and pacifists—albeit in a different form—such that 'the "Wilsonian Moment" was

---

[43] Lowe and Marzari, *Italian Foreign Policy*, 167–8.
[44] Caccamo, 'Italy, the Adriatic and the Balkans', 121.

also—perhaps even more so—the "Bolshevik Moment"'.[45] Transnational and transcolonial movements began to articulate new forms of politics and imagine a radically transformed new world order, even as Italy was in some ways still trying to force its way into the old order. Even the world's most dominant and established empires, France and Britain, began to modify their approaches to colonial rule; they adopted the rhetoric of trusteeship and began to grant new forms of citizenship (French Algeria) or participatory government (British India), though violent repression continued to underpin their control.[46] In January 1919, as the Supreme Council in Paris began to discuss the future of German colonies, Wilson introduced the concept of League of Nations mandates. Greeted with ambivalence by Britain and with outright hostility by its Dominions and by France, the idea nonetheless took hold rapidly and was approved on 30 January.[47] George Beer, the colonial expert appointed to Wilson's preparatory Inquiry, was a strong advocate of the mandate system and also hoped that the US would itself become a mandatory—perhaps in Africa; his secretary Louis Herbert Gray observed that in effect the US already held a 'self-appointed Mandate for Cuba' and it would thus be perfectly appropriate to formally take on others.[48] Both the rhetoric and the reality of the mandate system showed a transformation in understandings of colonial rule away from the model still envisaged in Italy.[49]

It was clear, even before the Peace Conference opened, that France and Britain both considered the colonial sphere as exclusively their own concern. Neither Wilson nor the minor powers were to intrude upon it. France and Britain had agreed during the war to divide up Germany's African colonies. Vigorous protests from Belgium and Portugal followed, as each pressed for territorial compensation for their part in the warfare which had taken place in Africa; in the event both would be granted some minor concessions, the most important of which was the allocation of the Rwandan mandate to Belgium.[50] Where, then, was Italy in all this? It soon emerged that boots on the ground were the key element in the assignation of post-war control; most of the mandates directly followed upon wartime conquest. Having taken no part in the war against German colonies, Italy would receive no part of them; and the same principle was soon to be asserted in

[45] Eric D. Weitz, 'Self-Determination: How a German Enlightenment Idea Became the Slogan of National Liberation and a Human Right', *The American Historical Review* 120, no. 2 (2015): 462–96, DOI: https://doi.org/10.1093/ahr/120.2.462, 485.
[46] See, for instance, Hassett, 'Reinventing Empire in the Wake of the Great War'; Durba Ghosh, 'Whither India? 1919 and the Aftermath of the First World War', *The Journal of Asian Studies* 78, no. 2 (2019): 389–97, DOI: https://doi.org/10.1017/S0021911819000044.
[47] Macmillan, *Paris 1919*, 98–104.
[48] George Louis Beer, *African Questions at the Paris Peace Conference, with Papers on Egypt, Mesopotamia, and the Colonial Settlement* (New York: Macmillan, 1923), xlii.
[49] On the transformation of empire in the post-war international system, see Susan Pedersen, *The Guardians: The League of Nations and the Crisis of Empire* (Oxford and New York: Oxford University Press, 2015).
[50] Macmillan, *Paris 1919*, 105–6.

the Near East, by Lloyd George among others. The principle of compensation clearly articulated in Article 13 of the Treaty of London had implicitly acknow-ledged this, referring to the 'extension of Italian possessions in Eritrea, Somaliland, Libya and the districts bordering on French and British colonies'. But just as Italian ambitions in the Adriatic had grown since 1915, so too had its aspirations further afield. Little wonder, then, that Italy soon felt the need to assert her claims in Asia Minor more vigorously by deploying an occupation force there.

Interestingly, Beer found Italian claims in Africa mostly reasonable. Their case for a hinterland to Libya he thought 'sound', provided its borders were limited and thus did no harm to French North-West Africa nor to the Anglo-Egyptian Sudan, and he was not unsympathetic to their East African requests either. He rejected as 'undoubtedly exaggerated' the idea of an Italian sphere in Yemen, as advocated by the Oriental Institute of Naples in 1917, or the 'highly indefensible' proposal to cut off all French access to Lake Chad, but he generally accepted the principle that Italy ought to be able to considerably extend its African possessions.[51] Beer's views were influential with Wilson in many areas but not here; Italy's ambitions in Africa found very few friends, and the mandates were actually allocated while Orlando was back in Rome, making it very hard for the Italians to even insert themselves back into the discussion. Clemenceau made it clear that France would not countenance any concession in Djibouti, nor did Britain seem keen to offer compensation in Africa (despite the Treaty of London's explicit, if vague, requirements).

9.3.1 Italy and the Ottoman Empire

So far as Italy's other extra-European objectives were concerned, the 'just share of the Mediterranean region adjacent to the province of Antalya' promised by the Treaty of London (Article 9) had of course been amended substantially by the St Jean de Maurienne Agreement in 1917. But no part of this pact would ever, in fact, be implemented. To the Italians' dismay, the requirement that it be ratified by Russia—which even before the October Revolution had become a clear impossibility—was used by France and Britain in late 1918 to justify the aban-donment of a deal which they had never particularly wanted in the first place. The foreign secretary Sir Arthur Balfour notified the Italian ambassador in London on 14 October 1918 that Britain considered the agreement invalid.[52] By the end of the war, British policy towards the Middle East had changed radically and there was

---

[51] Beer, *African Questions at the Paris Peace Conference*, 391–8.
[52] Riccardi, *Alleati non amici*, 613. Balfour also wrote to the British ambassador in Rome on the same day, see BOD Milner Papers, Box 131, Balfour to Rennell Rodd, 14 October 1918.

little British enthusiasm for any of its wartime agreements.[53] The tense and chaotic situation in Syria and Lebanon, where Britain now found itself caught between French and Arab claims, made Italian interests seem a very minor concern indeed. In a December 1918 meeting, Lloyd George and Clemenceau informally tore up and remade the Sykes–Picot agreement—apparently without at any time reflecting that it had, in theory, already been rewritten once at St Jean de Maurienne.[54]

In any case, self-determination was about to scupper these plans too. With reference to the Middle East, Wilson's Point XII stated that

> The Turkish portion of the present Ottoman Empire should be assured a secure sovereignty, but the other nationalities which are now under Turkish rule should be assured an undoubted security of life and an absolutely unmolested opportunity of autonomous development, and the Dardanelles should be permanently opened as a free passage to the ships and commerce of all nations under international guarantees.

This ruled out any prospect of an Italian zone of control in Anatolia, since it fell clearly into the Turkish portion of the Ottoman Empire. As the French and British had allocated themselves Arab lands, it was possible—with a little rhetorical work—to present their claims as the necessary break-up of Ottoman oppression, and thus compatible with self-determination. But Italy's allotted zone was clearly inhabited by Turks and there was no concealing the fact that it represented an illogical (and unjust) partition of a coherent national territory; the US could thus countenance Franco-British schemes but never the Italian plan, which was a classic example of that 'aggrandizement' which Wilson had directly condemned.[55]

Orlando made clear to his peers that Asia Minor was much less important to him than Fiume or Dalmatia—but once these had been denied, the Eastern Mediterranean project assumed much greater importance. Sonnino of course knew long before the conference began that his approach was not consonant with Wilson's; he briefly floated the idea of arguing that Italian claims in the Eastern Mediterranean would be a counter-weight to Anglo-French imperialism and thereby winning Wilson's support for this version of a 'democratic peace', but the plan never went very far.[56] The most logical ally in this region might, perhaps, have been France, since the French too were seeking to assert ambitious (but generally complementary) claims in Asia Minor. But the overall breakdown

---

[53] Helmreich, 'Italy and the Anglo-French Repudiation of the 1917 St. Jean de Maurienne Agreement', 100–1.

[54] James Barr, *A Line in the Sand: Britain, France and the Struggle That Shaped the Middle East* (London: Simon and Schuster, 2011), 71–2.

[55] Wilson, Woodrow. 'President Wilson's Fourteen Points, delivered to a joint session of Congress, 8 January 1918'. World War I Document Archive. Accessed 17 June 2020. https://wwi.lib.byu.edu/index.php/President_Wilson%27s_Fourteen_Points.

[56] DDI, Quinta Serie, Vol. 9, doc.134, Sonnino to Macchi di Cellere, 27 June 1918.

of Franco-Italian relations, including acute rivalry in Africa, made this almost impossible and it was never seriously attempted. By the time the Peace Conference began, then, the Italian position in the Eastern Mediterranean already looked weak; the delegation's total isolation in Paris rendered it hopeless. In Italy, however, the abandonment of the St Jean de Maurienne agreement was a serious blow. Sonnino was not alone in his fury at its repudiation, as Rennell Rodd reported after meeting with king Vittorio Emanuele III in August 1919:

> His Majesty said that the feeling in Italy against the Allies was very strong. [...] He said that a general impression prevailed that now that the Allies had no longer any use for Italy they could afford to neglect or postpone the consideration of her interests. So long as Italy had been necessary to them, then the Allies were ready to promise her everything, but now that that necessity no longer existed her particular interests were relegated to the indefinite. And here, I am sorry to say, H. M. spoke rather strongly of the rejection of the Agreement of St. Jean de Maurienne.

When the ambassador tried to persuade the king it would have been impossible to implement the agreement, the king grew annoyed: 'in that case the best thing would have been to say so frankly and to reconsider the position'. Rejection on the basis that 'a non-existent Russia had not accepted it' was unacceptable: were that approach to be taken, 'then "one would have to admit that no agreement had any validity." H.M.'s language was strong, even stronger than I have reproduced here,' concluded Rennell Rodd.[57] Feelings ran high outside the Quirinale Palace too: the failure to observe St Jean de Maurienne added insult to the injury of Fiume.

9.3.2 Italy and the Greek Position

Many of Italy's problems in Paris were the result of its poor relations with its Allies. The chief relationship which underpinned its membership with the Entente had always been with Britain and its relationship with France, never strong, had deteriorated steadily.[58] Yet it was the arrival of new partners after 1915 which had most complicated matters: increasingly after 1918 its most tricky interlocutor would lie much closer to home, just across the Adriatic.

Greece, like Italy, had come out of the war with big dreams: the Megali Idea, a vision of a huge Hellenic Empire which spread across the Aegean and into the Eastern Mediterranean had roots back in the nineteenth century, when it had

[57] BOD Rennell Rodd correspondence 20–1919: Conversation with the King, 18 August 1919.
[58] The best account of this relationship is Stefano Marcuzzi, *Britain and Italy in the Era of the First World War. Defending and Forging Empires* (Cambridge: Cambridge University Press, 2020).

included a great focus on Salonika. Like Italian claims in the Adriatic, this 'great idea' deliberately blurred the lines between irredentism and imperialism, by claiming territories with (extremely) old links to the motherland and with relatively small contemporary populations of nationals. Where Italy eyed up swathes of the Western Balkans, Greece pursued Smyrna, Crete, even perhaps Constantinople itself in a neo-Byzantine vision which boasted 'a fluid character as both an irredentist and an imperialist notion'.[59]

The Italians were implacably opposed, of course, to these ambitions at once so similar and so inimical to their own. Early discussions between Venizelos and Sonnino found that while compromise might be possible around Albania, their competing claims in Asia Minor were irreconcilable. Yet while the Italians had steadily exhausted the patience of their Allies, the Greek government had succeeded in retaining the whole-hearted backing of Lloyd George. Indeed, his support for Venizelos and indirectly for the Megali Idea was so strong that it would ultimately help contribute to his political downfall in 1922, when he risked dragging an unwilling Britain towards war in pursuit of Greek glory.[60] At the Paris Peace Conference, this support would manifest itself in ways which directly conflicted with Italian hopes in the Eastern Mediterranean and trampled all over the abandoned agreement of St Jean de Maurienne.

In February 1919 Venizelos first presented the Greek case to the Council. Apparently the polar opposite of Orlando and Sonnino—the one bland, the other charmless—Venizelos' tact, charisma, and diplomatic talent made an excellent impression, even upon Wilson (who might have been expected to be rather suspicious of a cheerleader of the Megali Idea). Even though the basis of the Greek position was really quite similar to that of the Italians, the Greek delegation successfully persuaded people that it was not. Hardinge, much impressed, wrote to Rennell Rodd in Rome, 'The Greeks are much more rational than the Italians, for their claims are really based on substance, while those of the Italians are not. At the same time the Italians are exceedingly voracious and want all they can get. They are suffering from megalomania like the French.'[61]

Venizelos was also perhaps the only Allied leader who already knew exactly what he wanted to happen to the Anatolian portion of the Ottoman Empire, while uncertainty and indecision gripped everybody else. Lloyd George persuaded Clemenceau and Wilson to accept the Greek occupation of Smyrna, in the teeth of Italian opposition.[62] Arguably, Britain adopted this approach specifically in

[59] Anastasia Stouraiti and Alexander Kazamias, 'The Imaginary Topographies of the Megali Idea: National Territory as Utopia', in Spatial Conceptions of the Nation: Modernizing Geographies in Greece and Turkey, ed. Nikiforos Diamandouros, Çağlar Keyder, and Thalia Dragonas (London: I.B. Tauris, 2014), 13.

[60] Finefrock, 'Ataturk, Lloyd George and the Megali Idea', 1048.

[61] BOD Rennell Rodd correspondence 20–1919: Hardinge to Rennell Rodd, 6 February 1919.

[62] A. E. Montgomery, 'VIII. The Making of the Treaty of Sèvres of 10 August 1920', The Historical Journal 15, no. 4 (December 1972): 775–87.

order to thwart the Italians, being 'more concerned with the problem of Italian troop and ship movements towards Smyrna than with preventing a renewal of Greco-Turkish conflict'.[63] Given that Italian relations with France had at all times been tense, and that British support would be essential in any future claims which Italy wished to assert, this marked sign of opposition to the Italian cause was daunting indeed. There was also a clear inconsistency in how Italian claims were treated vis-à-vis other powers' desires. As Albrecht-Carrié notes, 'It was at least awkward to ask the Italians to give up the Dodecanese to Greece, while the British delegation decided that it must retain Cyprus.'[64] Britain and France expected Italy to behave in ways which they themselves would not have thought necessary. Greece too was far happier to demand Italian-held islands than to attempt to pressure Britain, its most important ally, out of (a far more important) island. Once again, Italy's lesser military and economic might was at play.

In mid-April the idea of an Anatolian mandate for Italy was briefly raised by Clemenceau as a solution to the Adriatic impasse, but without success; it was not until Orlando had left Paris that matters would move very suddenly. As the Italian government sought to make good on its claims, sending warships to Smyrna as well as troops to the Antalya region without bothering to even inform their allies, the 'Big Three' swung decisively towards Greece. In a rather undignified turn of events, their outrage at Italian duplicity led them to secretly endorse a Greek expedition to Smyrna (to Venizelos' surprised delight).[65] Clemenceau finally informed Orlando of the authorization for the Greek expedition to Smyrna on 12 May, nearly a week after his return to Paris; the conversation was necessarily a little awkward. At this point new plans for the partition of Anatolia were proposed by the British: they were generally considered unsatisfactory, even by their own architects, since it appeared impossible to 'do something for the Italians' without also violating various core principles of the Conference (self-determination, security, stability).[66] Shortly thereafter, Lloyd George performed one of his typical U-turns and decided that even concessions in Fiume might be worthwhile to 'get the Italians out of Asia Minor altogether'.[67] From there he quickly began to blame Italy for all the problems in the region, despite the enormous differences between the US, Britain, and France.

---

[63] Finefrock, 'Ataturk, Lloyd George and the Megali Idea', 1051.
[64] Albrecht-Carrié, *Italy at the Paris Peace Conference*, 216–17.
[65] Albrecht-Carrié, *Italy at the Paris Peace Conference*, 218–19.
[66] See Balfour's Memorandum, 16 May 1919, reproduced in Albrecht-Carrié, *Italy at the Paris Peace Conference*, 526–9 Doc. 48.
[67] Quoted in Albrecht-Carrié, *Italy at the Paris Peace Conference*, 233.

9.4 Francesco Saverio Nitti and Italy's New Direction

On 23 June 1919 Orlando was replaced as Prime Minister by the economist Francesco Saverio Nitti, an austere man whose main priority was to ensure domestic stability and resolve the country's social and economic crisis. International affairs were less important to him and grandiose, expensive imperial claims were very far indeed down his list of preferred policies. He focused at once on the high cost of living and on unemployment, seeing economic crisis as likely to lead to serious domestic problems. Foreign affairs were placed in the hands of Tommaso Tittoni, a former Triplicist and neutralist, who announced that he would follow the general lines of his predecessor but without going into much detail.

The fall of Orlando and Sonnino was accompanied by some recognition in the press of the impossibility of their tasks in Paris, without any appreciable change in the insistence on those territorial ends which had made their job so impossible. The court of public opinion ruled that Fiume was still to be claimed—somehow. Tittoni's job was immediately made harder by the embarrassing episodes in that city in early July when fighting broke out not only between Italians and Croats but even between Italian regular soldiers and French troops. Luckily for Italy, Clemenceau was not inclined to make too much of the issue (despite the death of nine French soldiers and the wounding of fifty-eight more), but it was symptomatic of feeling on the ground and within the ranks of the Italian army.

Tittoni was active in immediately meeting and negotiating with Venizelos: in July 1919 he made a secret agreement with the Greek prime minister, based on a common enmity towards the Yugoslavs. Italy and Greece would support one another's claims to Albania and to Epirus and Thrace respectively, while Italy would cede most of the Dodecanese to Greece in return for a free port in Smyrna. The Venizelos–Tittoni agreement was greeted with outrage in Albania and would be abandoned the following year, but in any case, Tittoni's attention was soon to be dragged elsewhere, as matters were taken out of his hands by Gabriele D'Annunzio in the most dramatic fashion.

10

Post-war Settlements in the Adriatic and the Balkans

Italian aspirations in the upper Adriatic and the Balkans were to be blocked not only by changing Allied priorities and Woodrow Wilson's principles but also by the active and determined opposition of the new Yugoslavia. Taking the Tyrol from defeated Austria may have been simple enough, but to the east Italy now faced the counterclaim of a friendly nation. To the fury of Italians, their defeated enemy had somehow morphed into a 'friend' which the Allies wished to reward rather than punish. Where for three years Italy had envisaged simply seizing the spoils of war, suddenly a new entity, with a better claim, had jumped to the front of the queue.

But what exactly did the new Yugoslavia want? Was there room for negotiation? Unsurprisingly, the Yugoslav delegation to the Paris Peace Conference was diverse and somewhat divided, like the new country itself. For some—Slovenes and Croats in particular—Italian greed was the main threat, and the paramount priority was the protection of Istria, Dalmatia, and the borderlands (especially when it came to former Austro-Hungarian railways and ports).[1] Not unnaturally, Serbs and others further away from the borderlands were less concerned about these issues and more disposed to compromise with Italian interests, in exchange for advantages elsewhere. These internal differences of opinion slowed the progress of negotiations but were not sufficiently great to allow Italy to meaningfully exploit them. Despite the fact that Italy's queen, Elena, was the daughter of Montenegro's deposed king Nicholas, Italy was disinclined to support him against the claims which Serbia pressed in 1919.[2] Perhaps Orlando hoped that this conciliatory position would win Serbian support for Italy's claims in the Adriatic, but if so it had little apparent effect.

France and Britain were initially willing to delay recognition of the new kingdom, but Wilson recognized it in February and actively welcomed it as a counterweight to Italy—though he still wished to deny the Yugoslavs a navy, on the grounds that they would be a 'turbulent' people who ought not to be trusted

---

[1] Raoul Pupo, 'Attorno all'Adriatico: Venezia Giulia, Fiume e Dalmazia', in *La vittoria senza pace: le occupazioni militari italiane alla fine della Grande Guerra*, ed. Raoul Pupo (Rome: GLF editori Laterza, 2014), 35; Macmillan, *Paris 1919*, 110.
[2] Macmillan, *Paris 1919*, 118–20.

The Italian Empire and the Great War. Vanda Wilcox, Oxford University Press (2021). © Vanda Wilcox.
DOI: 10.1093/oso/9780198822943.003.0010

too far.[3] After the brief Italian leadership crisis in May, however, the pendulum of international opinion would swing decisively in favour of Yugoslavia, and the two Entente powers both recognized the new state at the start of June 1919.

While these political debates wore on in Paris, tensions on the ground were growing. The new minister of war Enrico Caviglia (appointed in January 1919) was keen to proceed as quickly as possible with demobilization for political reasons, but Diaz and his second-in-command Pietro Badoglio were obstructing this process out of a growing fear that troops might actually be needed to engage in operations. Public order duties were already straining the army's capacity to demobilize—seven brigades were sent from the war zone to Rome and to major northern cities to deal with strikes and protests that summer.[4] But it was in the Adriatic that the fear of renewed military action was most focused, despite Nitti's tendency to minimize this threat. Meanwhile, a small group of hard-line 'oltranzisti' generals (the duke of Aosta, commander of Third Army, Gaetano Giardino of Fourth Army, Pecori Giraldi in the Trentino) were either tacitly or openly encouraging extreme nationalism through 1919 among veterans and serving men alike. In April 1919, uniformed officers joined a mob attacking the headquarters of socialist newspaper *Avanti!*—a clear sign that the army was no longer even notionally outside politics.[5] This unrest soon crystallized around a specific interpretation of the war and its outcome: the myth of the mutilated victory.

10.1 The Myth of the Mutilated Victory

In the final weeks of the war, Gabriele D'Annunzio wrote several important poems addressing the nation's circumstances. Achieving a popular impact few poets can hope to emulate, 'La preghiera di Sernaglia' was published in the *Corriere della Sera* during the battle of Vittorio Veneto. It contained the phrase: 'Our victory, you shall not be mutilated!', which quickly resonated with the public. In case anyone had missed the point, in the 'Cantico per l'Ottavo della Vittoria (III–XI novembre MCMXVIII)', published shortly after the Armistice at Villa Giusti, D'Annunzio listed a series of towns and cities along the coast of the Eastern Adriatic which 'await unity with the *madre patria*'.[6] D'Annunzio's famous phrase revealed the fear that this unity might not be achieved—that Italy's wartime sacrifices would not be suitably rewarded with the gains which the country and its gallant soldiers deserved. The timing of these two works is instructive: far from being a retrospective analysis, they show that right from the start the post-war clamour for Fiume was accompanied by anxiety, as if the mutilated victory were in some sense a self-fulfilling prophecy. Fiume was by no means the only target of

---

[3] Macmillan, *Paris 1919*, 110.   [4] Gooch, *The Italian Army*, 312.
[5] Gooch, *The Italian Army*, 315–16.   [6] Ghisalberti, 'Il mito della vittoria mutilata', 125–6.

D'Annunzio's desires; in his May 1919 polemic *Contro Uno e Contro Tutti* he continued to invoke Italian possession of Diocletian's Palace in Split, the Roman roads of Istria, along with Zara, Dubrovnik, and Kotor but also Asia Minor, Africa, and the Eastern Mediterranean. The concept of the mutilated victory was certainly focused on Fiume and on Dalmatia, but it also reflected a wider sense of having been cheated out of territorial (including colonial) gains. By this time, the crisis of Italian diplomacy in Paris meant that the idea that Italy's victory had already been 'mutilated' was gaining currency. As in May 1915, D'Annunzio proved to have a gift for both articulating and shaping public sentiment.

These demands for Fiume underpinned Orlando's walkout from the Peace Conference. However irrational his action may have seemed in Paris, it keyed directly into public sentiment in Rome. As Rennell Rodd wrote to Lloyd George on 6 May 1919:

> It is perhaps not entirely realised in Paris what the situation here is. The nation has now taken charge and the Government is no longer able to control the public feeling, which one cannot acquit them of responsibility for having raised. In my long experience of Italy, covering some twenty years, I have never seen the nation united as it is over this question. [...] It is now only a question of national feeling and not of reasoning. [There is] a condition of feeling here as regards the town of Fiume which I must insist with all earnestness is dangerous. Some months ago had the issue been dealt with then, I think a compromise would have been easy. Now it is almost past praying for.[7]

Orlando and Sonnino were divided as to what to do by this stage—Sonnino was willing to accept Fiume as a free town but Orlando was not. The situation was further complicated by the pot-stirring antics of von Bülow, the former German ambassador, who expressed full support for Italy's claims in the Adriatic and suggested that Italy like Germany was receiving a raw deal in Paris.[8] These claims directly foreshadowed of the two countries' later shared fascist revisionism—or revanchism. As public disillusionment increased, anger among military circles grew particularly rapidly in June and July 1919, leading some fears about the loyalties of the army. D'Annunzio's formula resonated strongly with many veterans, especially officers, and with former irredentists. But it was not only extreme nationalists who embraced his interpretative framework: the jurist, veteran, and university professor Piero Calamandrei, later an important anti-fascist, complained of the 'betrayed war' in 1920.[9]

---

[7] BOD Rennell Rodd Correspondence 20–1919, Rennell Rodd to Lloyd George, 6 May 1919.
[8] BOD Rennell Rodd Correspondence 20–1919, Renell Rodd to Lloyd George, 6 May 1919.
[9] Mondini, *La guerra italiana*, 359.

The state's failure to adequately celebrate the nation's victory compounded the problem. Underestimating the importance of rhetorical gesture and the political theatre of the grandiose victory parades held in Paris and London, there was relatively little clear sign of a nation's gratitude to its soldiers.[10] The war seemed to have ended with a damp squib; in psychological terms, there was little in the way of satisfactory closure. Nor had daily life in any way been noticeably improved by the suffering and sacrifice endured during the war: living standards continued to be poor even with the return of peace. The notion of a mutilated victory was abstract as well as specific, including a generalized dissatisfaction not just with the war's territorial outcomes but also its aftermath at home.

10.2 The Occupation of the Upper Adriatic

The post-war occupation of the new borderlands is historically significant for several reasons. The historiography on Fiume and Italy's claims in the upper Adriatic has generally been focused on the myth of the mutilated victory and the subsequent rise of fascism,[11] and has reflected an almost exclusively national framework (as is common with many studies of fascism). If we re-conceptualize the upper Adriatic as one of those imperial shatterzones which across Europe were undergoing intimately linked, transnational transformations, then this traditional teleological reading must be revised. The new greater Italy was one of imperial Austria's successor states, and thus faced some of the same problems—at least in these areas—as other successor states. By taking this viewpoint, Italy's post-war development (including the rise of paramilitarism and political violence) may appear less of an anomaly. Equally, the upper Adriatic was a post-imperial space; was it also, under Italian rule, a colonial one? What were the priorities of the Italian administration there after the war, and what can this reveal about the imperial and colonialist aspects of Italian national policy?

The Austrian Littoral was entirely occupied by various Allied forces in the aftermath of the war. Venezia Giulia was placed under the governorship of General Carlo Petitti di Roreto, who had earlier commanded the Italian expeditionary forces in Macedonia. In Trieste and much of Istria, the Italian occupation was welcomed joyfully by the local populations, which were majority Italian, but in many border towns—Gorizia, Pola to name but two—locals predominantly supported the new Yugoslavia; in some cases, awkward negotiations took place

---

[10] Mondini, *La guerra italiana*, 360–1.

[11] On D'Annunzio's political activism and its context, see George L. Mosse, 'The Poet and the Exercise of Political Power: Gabriele D'Annunzio', in *Masses and Man: Nationalist and Fascist Perceptions of Reality* (Detroit: Wayne State University Press, 1987); Renzo De Felice, *D'Annunzio Politico 1918–1938* (Rome and Bari: Laterza, 1978); Jared Becker, *Nationalism and Culture: Gabriele D'Annunzio and Italy After the Risorgimento* (P. Lang, 1994).

with the emergent Yugoslav armed forces as to who was to occupy certain locations. On the Dalmatian coast, where for reasons of both necessity and political outlook it was mainly the navy rather than the army which was responsible for establishing the Italian occupations, local populations were generally hostile to the arrival of Italian forces. Alone of the Dalmatian coastal towns, Zadar (Zara) had a genuine Italian majority; they welcomed the arrival of Italian troops on 4 November 1918 (sent by speed-boat in a hasty effort to 'conquer' the town before the Armistice went into effect). The occupation of Dalmatia would prove complex and demanding: not until 20 February 1919 did Italian forces finally reach the entirety of the so-called 'Armistice line' there (see Map 6 for details). Admiral Enrico Millo, former minister for the navy, served as military governor of Dalmatia until the end of 1920. Like many naval men, he was keen to maximize Italian holdings on the eastern shore of the Adriatic and saw the Pact of London as merely a starting point.[12] The navy, in fact, would prove an important factor in the Upper Adriatic, with several senior officers actively working to expand Italian possessions.[13] Millo's efforts to this end on the ground, however, bore no more fruit than those of Italy's political leadership in Paris.

But Italy was not the only military power in the Adriatic: Louis Franchet d'Espèrey had hoped to organize a French occupation of Fiume and Dubrovnik to facilitate the supply lines of his Armée d'Orient, and the emergent Yugoslav army was also active in the region. Fiume was soon placed under joint allied control; Italian troops were supposed to cooperate with French, British, and Serb forces, but any mood of wartime friendship broke down quickly. Open French support for the Yugoslav cause led to growing anti-French sentiment within Italy. Italian cinema audiences loudly jeered newsreel footage of French troops entering Strasbourg in January 1919, while in February a French soldier was killed in a brawl in Livorno.[14] A number of petty incidents had occurred in the Adriatic, such as a row in Italian-occupied Pula over whether the French could also raise their flag there.[15] The situation had been especially fraught in Fiume, where as early as December 1918 incidents of hostility and even violence between French troops and Italian civilians had occurred.[16] Italian officers in the occupying forces became increasingly politicized, and so vexed were Franco-Italian relations in the Adriatic generally that the king made an official complaint to the French prime minister Raymond Poincaré in early February 1919.[17] In May 1919 the government even

---

[12] Pupo, 'Attorno all'Adriatico', 73–82.
[13] Oreste Foppiani, 'The Italian Navy in the Adriatic, 1918–1919. An Unknown Actor between Diplomatic Rivalry and International Competition', *Nuova rivista storica* 101, no. 3 (2017): 969–90.
[14] Alain Marzona, 'Les incidents franco-italiens de Fiume ou l'expression des frustrations italiennes (novembre 1918–juillet 1919)', *Revue historique des armées* no. 254 (15 March 2009): 29–38, 6, http:// journals.openedition.org/rha/6383.
[15] ACS PCM GE1915-1918 busta 170, fasc. Armistizio, sf. Occupazione di Pola.
[16] BOD, Rennell Rodd Correspondence 20–1919; Marzona, 'Les incidents franco-italiens', 3.
[17] BOD, Rennell Rodd Correspondence 20–1919: Rennell Rodd to Curzon, 2 February 1919.

commissioned a sociologist's report on the nature and origins of French anti-Italianism. He reported that the French saw Italians as vainglorious, empty boasters who could almost never actually achieve the things they set out to do, and that this underpinned France's attitude to Italian goals in the Balkans.[18]

In July 1919 matters began to come to a head: while Mussolini's *Popolo d'Italia* was calling for a new Sicilian Vespers (the legendary thirteenth-century rebellion against the French), violence and disorder in Fiume was becoming an almost daily matter. A group of French soldiers were attacked by an Italian mob—allegedly including soldiers—on 6 July, leaving nine Frenchmen dead. The inter-allied commission of enquiry into the episode had no hesitation in attributing their deaths to the nationalist feeling in the town.[19] Fiume had been a point of national and international friction for months: now it was also approaching a state of crisis on the ground. The moderate approach which Petitti di Roreto had embraced was no match for the increasingly lively nationalist organizations in Rome, in Trieste and in Fiume itself.

10.2.1 D'Annunzio at Fiume

In September 1919 Gabriele D'Annunzio took matters into his own hands. He travelled to meet some officers of the Sardinian Grenadiers at a small town close to the Carso named Ronchi di Monfalcone (later renamed Ronchi dei Legionari, in honour of these 'legionaries'). This unit had been stationed in Fiume as part of the occupation and had been removed after stirring up Italian nationalism in the town. On 12 September D'Annunzio, the grenadiers, and an assortment of volunteers set off to 'march' on Fiume in a convoy of cars and trucks; by the afternoon he had entered the city and proclaimed himself in charge. British and French forces, rather than engage in hostilities with an ally, withdrew.

The ambiguity from senior politicians and generals as to whether there was secret official support for the venture led many army officers in Dalmatia to act only tepidly against D'Annunzio and his men. Badoglio, both vice-chief of general staff and regional commander for the Adriatic occupations, was openly sympathetic to D'Annunzio, which hardly helped an energetic repression of the occupation. *Arditi* and *bersaglieri* units sent to end the occupation instead defected and joined it, along with many veterans. By the end of September, the illegal occupation could rely on nearly 5,000 men under the command of several hundred regular army officers. In October they were joined by a newly enthusiastic Mussolini, who had been publishing supportive accounts in his newspaper *Il Popolo d'Italia* from the start. Guglielmo Marconi and Filippo Marinetti also

---

[18] ACS PCM GE 1915–1918 busta 210 Francia e sue colonie, sf. 1918.
[19] Marzona, 'Les incidents franco-italiens', 7–8.

joined him, and the occupation took on an increasingly colourful aspect, with a heady mixture of cultural outpourings, political posturing, and hard drinking. D'Annunzio also visited Admiral Millo in Zara, who—despite his office—embraced him enthusiastically and expressed his support.[20]

Often read deterministically as simply a form of proto-fascism, the occupation was in fact more ambiguous and complex, involving a range of actors with motivations from ultra-nationalism to artistic utopianism through to boredom.[21] However, it is undeniable that many of D'Annunzio's methods were directly reused by fascism. This was a critical moment in the aestheticization of politics: D'Annunzio's politics of spectacle—including the wearing of black shirts, the shouting of slogans, the regular speeches delivered from a public balcony—are immediately recognizable in Mussolini's dictatorship.[22] D'Annunzio's interest in the purely aesthetic functioning of his political practice led him to drew rhetorical links between ancient Roman imperialism, the conquest of Libya, and the seizure of Fiume. At the same time, he evoked anti-colonialism and spoke of the liberation of oppressed peoples (meaning here the Italians as against the world's great powers, or Istrian Italians against their former rulers). This was not merely inconsistency, but a reflection of Italy's ambiguous racial and political status as at once great and wretched. It was blood—and blood sacrifice, as already performed during the war itself—which was to unite Italians to the soil and 'redeem' the land. This redemptive sacrifice drew not so much on traditional Christian rhetoric as on a biopolitical imagery through which blood-letting restored wholeness to the fractured 'body' of the Italian territories and revitalized the moribund Italian race.[23]

10.2.2 Italian Public Opinionand the 'Slavic Question'

Backed by Woodrow Wilson, the new Yugoslavia had proved one of Italy's major obstacles at the Peace Conference, and the Italian attitude towards the South Slavs was almost unrelentingly hostile by 1919. Italian nationalists were happy to back the political claims not only of Romania—a former ally—but also their former enemies Bulgaria and Austria in an effort to prevent the emergence of a dangerous new Balkan power which had prevented Italy from achieving all its goals in the region.[24] In fact, the rise of Yugoslavia was a major factor in the unexpectedly rapid rapprochement between Italy and her old Triple Alliance partners starting immediately after the Paris conference closed. This political hostility towards the

[20] Pupo, 'Attorno all'Adriatico', 103–20.

[21] Marco Mondini, *Fiume 1919. Una guerra civile italiana* (Rome: Salerno, 2019).

[22] Michael Arthur Ledeen, *The First Duce: D'Annunzio at Fiume* (Baltimore: Johns Hopkins University Press, 1977).

[23] Welch, *Vital Subjects*, 132, 165–8.

[24] Caccamo, *L'Italia e la «Nuova Europa». Il confronto sull'Europa orientale.*

Yugoslav project was rooted in territorial questions, stemming from some of the same problems as the 'mutilated victory' myth, but it would also mix with the racial assumptions about Slavic peoples already seen during the war, with important implications for the post-war treatment of Italy's new minorities along the eastern border.

The Italian ruling class largely shared a set of comfortable assumptions about their new Slav citizens. National sentiment was assumed to be confined to urban, bourgeois circles; Balkan cultures were seen as self-evidently inferior to Italian culture, so Italian rule would be unquestionably beneficial. There was slightly more respect for Croatia than Slovenia, leading to marginal differences in the treatment of the two groups. Slovenes, believed to have no more than a superficial sense of nationhood and little national culture, would more easily be absorbed wholesale into Italy. An inherently colonial approach based on a system of ethno-nationalist classification and cultural supremacy was thus adopted, though opinion differed over how best to rule. Some favoured a gradualist system, whereby rising standards of living accompanied by good governance would inevitably Italianize the masses, leaving only isolated pockets of nationalist intellectuals. Others advocated a more interventionist, even aggressive policy, as would of course soon by adopted under fascism.[25]

Upon his arrival in Trieste, Petitti proclaimed that his administration would be benevolent, reassuring Slovenes as to their faith and language rights. Italy, as a land of liberty, would protect their rights far more than Austria ever had, he declared, announcing a gradual transition of legal and administrative practice. Italian law would be implemented in a rather non-systematic fashion, adapting or incorporating existing local practices, and not imposed wholesale in pursuit of national uniformity. However, his approach was directly undermined by other branches of the army—the military police, for instance, or the notoriously aggressive local intelligence forces, known as the ITO (Ufficio Informazioni Truppe Operanti). Education became a battleground, as the right of local Slavs to be taught in their own languages (a right granted to Libyans at this time) was fiercely contested by nationalists and early fascists, for whom school was a key institution in the process of Italianization. The Slavic clergy were also considered—with some reason—to be implacably anti-Italian, and were hence subject to continual harassment.

Unlike in East Prussia or Upper Silesia, no confirmatory plebiscite was held in any of the areas annexed by Italy. The Risorgimento itself had been completed in this way, demonstrating a popular mandate for the national project; some proposed a comparable plebiscite to confirm the outcome of this 'Fourth War' of Unification. But the risk of failure was too great for the government to

---

[25] Pupo, 'Attorno all'Adriatico', 121–4.

countenance, not least since it could have fatally emboldened Wilson to act even more vigorously against Italian claims. Given the ethnic and linguistic diversity of the territories in question, there was every chance that Italy would have failed to win such plebiscites (or at least some of them), revealing that far from an act of 'national liberation' this was in fact an inherently imperialist project. The logic of Italy's new eastern and northern borders was that of military necessity, administrative coherence, and the maintenance of power, not one of liberation and nationality.[26] Their conquered populations had to be controlled through re-education and repression, a distinctly colonial rather than liberationist programme: the new borderlands had to be Italianized because they were so clearly not yet Italian. Some troops on the ground understood the war as an inter-ethnic conflict: a group of young Alpini stationed near Tolmin (Slovenia) wrote in March 1920 declaring that they would not retreat a metre from Italy's natural border on the 'inviolable' Armistice line but, on the contrary, that they were willing to fight all the way to Ljubljana. They framed their position as one of ethnic status-seeking: 'now that we're here we don't want to let the Slavs laugh at us because we Italians are men who should be respected not just by the nations of Austria-Hungary but all the nations of the world'.[27] Ethnic division was compounded by the emergence of Yugoslavia as a powerful alternative focus of loyalty for Slavic minorities in the borderlands.

10.2.3 Post-war Occupation and the Rise of Fascism

The Italian occupation did not succeed in winning over its Slavic subjects. In the Istrian city of Pula, for instance, there were tensions between Italians (both military and civilian) and local Croat families right from the start of the occupation. which led to numerous incidences of violence as well as the burning of houses and destruction of property. Strikes, demonstrations, and socialist protests centred around the shipyards were also numerous, which led to violence including the murder of a local policeman. The Italian military authorities perceived Croat socialist activism to also be inherently anti-Italian and pro-Yugoslav.[28] Pula, like Trieste, also witnessed early fascist violence starting in spring 1920. Attacks against Slav institutions and especially on local socialist newspapers, organizations, and individuals proliferated throughout Istria and Venezia Giulia. This 'fascismo di confine', or border fascism, was among

[26] Ester Capuzzo, 'In vista dell'annessione: i pieni poteri e la legislazione di guerra', in Dall'Austria all'Italia: aspetti istituzionali e problemi normativi nella storia di una frontiera, ed. Ester Capuzzo (Rome: La Fenice, 1996).
[27] ACS PCM GE 1915–1918, busta 170, fasc. Armistizio, sf.3 Proposte, voti, consigli; Pieve del Cadore battalion. Punctuation as in the original.
[28] ACS PCM GE 1915–1918, busta 170, fasc. Armistizio, sf. Occupazione di Pola.

the most virulent local strains. The paramilitary movement here—which aimed to flank the 'regular' occupation of state forces—was closely linked to fascist structures in the rest of Italy as well as recruiting heavily from among D'Annunzio's followers in Fiume.[29]

For fascists in these borderlands, the fight against communism and Slavism went hand in hand; these internal enemies were but two sides of the same coin. Cosmopolitanism and diversity were undesirable and un-Italian—but also signs of enduring 'Austrianness' which the victorious nation needed to stamp out in order to complete and vindicate its triumph. Fascist paramilitarism considered itself a nation-building movement fighting against the 'national indeterminacy' which characterized the region.[30] It is here significant that while the Upper Adriatic was the target for a new kind of imperial thinking from the Italian side, it was also a post-imperial space in its own right, emerging as it did from centuries of Habsburg rule. The failure to develop a strong form of national identity—as demonstrated by pan-Slavism and indeed by Yugoslavism—was read by fascists as another sign of the cultural and racial inferiority of the Slavs. Yugoslavism was denigrated both in the specific—an entity obstructing the full exercise of Italian 'rights'—and in the general—a failure of proper national sentiment.[31]

The experience of post-war occupation in the Adriatic played a crucial part in the development of fascist thought and practice; Trieste, far more than Trento, was a focal point of Italianization and a major location for fascist activism, primarily in the form of anti-Slav violence. This is surely no coincidence, considering that for all the periodic wartime denunciations of Germanic *Kultur*, racist hostility against Slavs was far higher than that against Germans. Trieste had very high numbers of early fascist party adherents and many of Mussolini's important early speeches were given there. Early fascist thinkers also linked this space not just to the Adriatic but to the wider Eastern Mediterranean as a sphere for Italian agency. Conceptually, imperial expansion in this area was not only desirable but also a moral necessity to bring an effective order to the vacuum which Austria had left; later fascist justifications for empire drew directly on structures and systems first devised in the upper Adriatic. Italian post-war governance showed much continuity with wartime practice, unsurprisingly given that the occupation was in the hands of the military throughout 1919 and into 1920.

[29] Marco Bresciani, 'The Post-Imperial Space of the Upper Adriatic and the Post-War Ascent of Fascism', in *Akteure der Neuordnung: Ostmitteleuropa und das Erbe der Imperien, 1917–1924*, ed. Tim Buchen and Frank Grelka, trans. Adam Peszke (Berlin: epubli, 2016), 47–64; [online at https://www. academia.edu/30485986/], 6–9.

[30] On the concept of indeterminacy, see Pamela Ballinger, 'History's "Illegibles": National Indeterminacy in Istria', *Austrian History Yearbook* 43 (April 2012): 116–37.

[31] Bresciani, 'The Post-Imperial Space of the Upper Adriatic', 12–13.

10.3 The Rapallo Treaty

If throughout 1919 the relationship between Italy and Yugoslavia seemed intractable, by mid-1920 the international situation had evolved in ways which opened new possibilities. The new Giolitti government, with Carlo Sforza as foreign minister, was able to develop closer relations with France and Britain—while the approaching end of Wilson's presidency, and the US's declining involvement in European politics, raised the prospect of more flexible negotiations. On 8 September 1920 D'Annunzio proclaimed the 'Charter of Carnaro', a kind of constitution for his regime in Fiume which essentially created a corporatist dictatorship, combining syndicalism with authoritarianism and showing several proto-fascist elements. This so-called 'Regency of Carnaro' was not, however, destined to last.

An agreement between Italy and Yugoslavia was finally reached in November 1920 at Rapallo. A compromise was, it appeared, possible after all. Italy received most of Istria and the town of Zadar (which *did* have an Italian majority) as well as a few Adriatic islands. The majority of Dalmatia, and its chief islands, remained in Yugoslav hands. Fiume was to become a free city, with a narrow stretch of land to link it to the Italian mainland. Now that the fevered atmosphere of the Peace Conference period had passed, it was possible to represent this as a triumph for Italian nationalism since it had kept Fiume out of Slav hands—many disastrous events might perhaps have been averted if this solution had been proposed and adopted from the very start. On the other hand, D'Annunzio's band of adventurers still held out and refused to leave the city; only a frontal assault at the end of December 1920 would finally force D'Annunzio to resign, ending the illegal occupation. As Mondini observes, the last shots fired in Italy's national war were fired not against Austrians in November 1918 but against fellow Italians in Fiume, bombarded by the navy on Christmas Day 1920.[32]

The Fiume episode has long been recognized for its importance in the rise of fascism. It showed the weakness of the Liberal state in the face of decisive action by a small, determined minority and the power of extreme nationalist rhetoric as a mobilizing force, as well as revealing the decline of civilian control over the military. But the occupation of Fiume was also an act of colonialism (albeit not state-directed): the military seizure and administration of territory on ideological rather than national, practical, or economic grounds, following an imperial logic. D'Annunzio himself repeatedly linked the city rhetorically to Libya, Eritrea, and Somalia, with imaginary bonds forged from airpower—another sign of the futurist nexus between modernity, technology, and empire.[33] Rather than simply treating

[32] Mondini, *La guerra italiana*, 7.   [33] Welch, *Vital Subjects*, Ch. 4.

the occupation as a unique harbinger of fascism, it ought also to be given its proper context as an Italian imperial project.

10.4 Albania

At the end of the war, Italy hoped to build on its wartime 'protectorate' to establish a permanent foothold in Albania, particularly in Vlorë and the surrounding area. Some Albanians saw Italy as a bulwark against Greek and Serbian ambitions and were open to cooperation provided Albanian autonomy was assured. However, a series of misjudgements fatally compromised Italy's position; prolonged and ineffective diplomatic wrangling frustrated both sides while errors in Italian local administration exacerbated the problem. Italy spent a great deal of money in Albania on public works—significantly more than in other occupied areas such as Dalmatia or Asia Minor—but without winning over hearts and minds.[34] The Italian wartime rhetoric of self-determination based on historic ties between the Adriatic peoples, exemplified by the Proclamation of Argirocastro, rapidly vanished in favour of comments on Albanian barbarism and savagery. Celebrations in honour of Albanian independence in November 1919 led to a breakdown of Italian control in Vlorë; riots broke out during which some Italian troops dishonoured Albanian flags. From a Risorgimento-style rhetoric of freedom, the hidden script of colonialism became ever clearer: even as late as 1920 there were discussions of establishing agricultural settler colonies in Albanian farmland through transplanting Emilian peasants.[35] Once news finally spread of the secret Venizelos–Tittoni Agreement, effectively partitioning Albania between Greece and Italy with no reference to Albanian wishes or rights, Albanians lost all confidence in Italy and the breakdown in relations spread rapidly.

On the night of 5 June 1920 an anti-Italian revolt in Vlorë broke out; Italy was finally forced to accept that its policy had failed, and the (largely unrecognized) Italian protectorate ended definitively. By this time, the troop presence had been diminished such that Italy could no longer effectively impose its will through force: as Nitti intensified the demobilization process, the number of Italian troops present was scaled back from 33,000 in March to under 15,000 in June.[36] The surprise Albanian attack soon forced the occupiers back into their fortified positions. Meanwhile the ongoing occupation was increasingly unpopular in Italy too: that same month, *bersaglieri* stationed in Ancona, who were due to be deployed to Albania, revolted against these orders. Joining forces with local socialists and communists, they refused to depart, amid calls for Italy to withdraw

---

[34] Rochat, *L'esercito italiano (1919–1925)*, 180.   [35] Bego, 'The Vlora Conflict', 108, 112–13.
[36] Rochat, *L'esercito italiano (1919–1925)*, 170–81.

from this illegitimate and imperialist occupation.[37] On 22 July 1920 new foreign minister Carlo Sforza formally abandoned the Venizelos–Tittoni agreement—which had in reality already lost any meaningful chance of success—and declared that Albanian nationalism had forced Italy to modify its position.

On 2 August the Tirana protocols were signed, recognizing Albanian independence and its pre-war borders; the agreement set down the terms of Italian military withdrawal, which was completed within the weeks that followed. Italy retained only the tiny island of Sazan, first seized in October 1914. Sforza echoed his predecessor Sonnino in agreeing that it was futile to seek to hold onto Vlorë without the consensus of the Albanian population.[38] Italy could simply not militarily control the region—and after five years of fighting in Libya had no appetite for another rebellious colony. Indecision and inflexibility in the face of determined resistance from the Albanians left it empty-handed without even a foothold in a port. Initial military victory (however ambiguous) was followed by political defeat, as so often in Italy's imperialist endeavours. The Corfu incident in 1923—when Italian troops briefly occupied the island –showed that control of the southern Adriatic was a dream which was slow to die after the end of the war. Failure in Albania once more reinforced the myth of the mutilated victory; nationalist and imperialist reactions show the importance of Vlorë (perhaps all the greater considering the failure to claim Dalmatia). Mussolini called the ejection from Vlorë 'another Caporetto, worse than the first', D'Annunzio said it left Italy 'castrated', and leading fascist Dino Grandi, writing many years later, even compared it to the defeat at Adwa, a revealing but astonishingly hyperbolic remark.[39] After nearly six years of military presence in Albania, withdrawal represented a significant failure of Italian policy and leadership; it left a legacy which Mussolini would pick up in the 1930s. Albania—like Ethiopia—was unfinished business as far as the fascists were concerned, and in 1939 it would find itself once again under Italian rule.

---

[37] Marcello Paolini, 'I fatti di Ancona e l'11° bersaglieri (giugno 1920)', *Quaderni di Resistenza Marche* 4 (1982): 95–119.
[38] Vagnini, *L'Italia e i Balcani nella Grande Guerra*, 182–5.
[39] Cited in Bego, 'The Vlora Conflict', 116.

11

Africa and the Eastern Mediterranean
After the War

Italy's wider imperial aspirations, which were at once extensive and loosely defined, had been acknowledged from the start of the war. Although they had been articulated with growing precision as the conflict progressed, by early 1919 Italian goals were still somewhat uncertain (or, more charitably, flexible). This chapter explores the post-war settlement and its effects in Italy's existing colonies in Africa as well as in its hypothetical new empire in the Eastern Mediterranean.

11.1 The Allied Occupation of Constantinople and the Eastern Mediterranean Force

The Armistice signed at Mudros with the Ottoman Empire, on 30 October 1918, included at article 7 the proviso that the Allies might occupy 'any strategic points, in the event of any situation arising which threatens the security of the Allies'.[1] Italian documents on the Armistice negotiations suggests that this important clause was originally proposed by Sonnino at a meeting at the Quai d'Orsay on Sunday 6 October (he also successfully pushed for the inclusion of surrender by Turkish forces in north Africa under the terms of the armistice).[2] Constantinople was duly occupied as early as 13 November 1918 by a small force of French and British troops accompanied by a massive fifty-five warships, which controlled the Bosporus in a highly intimidating fashion. Each of the three occupying powers immediately appointed a High Commissioner, a position which the Italians at least considered to be of great importance for their prestige and the future of their plans in Asia Minor. They appointed the experienced diplomat Carlo Sforza, who had served as chargé d'affaires in Constantinople during the Young Turk revolution of 1908 and had personally overseen the successful confirmation of the Italian concession in Tianjin (Tientsin). Sforza was an interesting choice: ideologically on the Mazzinian wing of the interventionist movement, he was a skilled negotiator

---

[1] 'Mudros Agreement: Armistice with Turkey (October 30, 1918)', *German History in Documents and Images*, Vol. 6, German Historical Institute, Washington, DC, online at: http://germanhistorydocs.ghi-dc.org/pdf/eng/armistice_turk_eng.pdf.
[2] ACS PCM GE 1915–1918, busta 170 Armistizio, sf. Armistizio con Turchia.

The Italian Empire and the Great War. Vanda Wilcox, Oxford University Press (2021). © Vanda Wilcox.
DOI: 10.1093/oso/9780198822943.003.0011

but no great supporter of colonialism. On the contrary, his adherence to the principles of self-determination impressed Nitti, who appointed him undersecretary for foreign affairs in June 1919 (he became Foreign Minister a year later).[3] As High Commissioner in Constantinople, Sforza was essentially the head of local government in the Italian-occupied area; among other things, he claimed on behalf of his country the former seat of the Austro-Hungarian Embassy—the Palazzo Venezia. This grandiose neoclassical building in the Beyoğlu neighbourhood, dating back to 1695, had originally been the embassy of the Venetian Republic, passing briefly through French hands in the Napoleonic period before serving as the Austrian embassy right through until 1918. Sforza ordered the building and its archives to be seized by Italian troops on 1 December 1918, for use as his official seat. Legal and financial wrangling continued for some time, with a payoff eventually being made to Austria since 'the palace is of enormous historic importance to us' and should it fall into foreign hands there would be 'considerable damage to our prestige in the East', in Sforza's words.[4] This story perfectly illustrates Italy's approach in the Near East: opportunistically seizing property to which it had wholly spurious claims (the 1866 treaty between Italy and Austria-Hungary at the end of the Third War of the Risorgimento specifically allocated the building to the Habsburgs) and dressing this up with the fig leaf of historic inheritance from the Republic of Venice. The episode also reveals the amount of time and energy often devoted to issues of little real significance in the wider scheme of things. More obviously important was Sforza's private meeting on 17 December 1918 with Mustafa Kemal (the future Atatürk); the High Commissioner was happy to encourage Turkish nationalists to see Italy as a possible future friend and protector.

On 7 February 1919 an Italian contingent from Franchey d'Espèrey's Armée d'Orient, fresh from the Macedonian front, finally disembarked at Galata in Constantinople; officially named the Expeditionary Force in the Aegean, in practice these troops served as the counterpart of the French and British forces already present. The city was divided into three occupation zones, and the Italians were allocated Scutari (Üsküdar) and Kadıköy in the Asian section, across the Bosporus, while the historically more important neighbourhoods of Pera and Stamboul were held by the British and French respectively; they would administer and police these areas, in close if often ill-tempered co-operation with their allies, until the birth of the Turkish Republic.

---

[3] Sforza went on to be an important anti-fascist leader: one of the only senators to denounce the murder of Giacomo Matteotti in 1924, he fled Italy in 1927, and after years in France made his way to the USA during the Second World War. He returned after the overthrow of the regime and resumed his position as foreign minister from 1947 to 1951; in the twilight of his career, he personally signed the NATO treaty and the Treaty of Paris which created the European Coal and Steel Community.

[4] ACS, PCM GE 1915–1918, busta 214, Min. Aff. Est., Div. IV, to PCM, tel. 45440, 16/11/1920. Today known as the Venedik Sarayi, it serves as the Italian ambassador's official residence in Istanbul.

11.1.1 The Italian Expeditionary Corps in Anatolia

The authorization for occupation encoded in the Armistice at Mudros was so vague as to offer carte blanche for the Allies to dispatch their troops to any part of the Ottoman Empire with great ease. The French began a series of occupations almost immediately—in the Black Sea coalfields, in Thrace, and also in Cilicia, where they occupied Mersin and Adana in November and December 1918. This brought French forces uncomfortably close to the proposed Italian sphere, leading Sonnino to inform Clemenceau that if France occupied Anatolian territories then Italy would follow suit (Clemenceau raised no objection at this time).[5] Given that the Allies had already notified Italy that they did not intend to respect the St Jean de Maurienne agreement, it was becoming clear that only direct action would secure Italy's position in Asia Minor, and Sonnino soon became convinced of the need for a military occupation of 'Italian' lands. Rennell Rodd considered that this was as much about satisfying Italian public opinion as staking a claim with their Allies (the views of the region's Turkish inhabitants were nowhere considered).[6] Though Lloyd George informally suggested that he might be persuaded to support an Italian occupation, he rapidly changed his mind; Sonnino then began to discuss a possible landing on the Anatolian mainland with General Vittorio Elia, the governor of Rhodes, without initially informing Orlando. Sonnino's secret plans were not only unauthorized, but militarily unsound, as the minister of war, Enrico Caviglia, soon pointed out to him. Debates took place between the two ministers in late February and early March as to where the troops for such an expeditionary force were to come from—the Dodecanese? the Balkans? Italy?—as well as how many men ought to be deployed.[7]

To plan effectively for a hypothetical military mission with exceptionally vague and poorly defined objectives, in a rapidly evolving situation characterized by the total breakdown of local political and legal authority, social and economic chaos, and rising inter-ethnic tensions would have been a difficult task even for an army not exhausted by four years of war. Staff officers fretted over the dreadful condition of internal transport and communications networks; intelligence reports were pessimistic about the situation on the ground, where public order appeared fragile. On the other hand, local unrest (brigandage, mass desertion, prison riots, fighting with gendarmes) offered an excellent pretext for an Italian 'peace-keeping' mission. Meanwhile, the Italian institutions in the Antalya region were endeavouring to return to normality through February and March 1919: the Salesian school, the archaeological mission, and the medical centre all reopened,

[5] ACS PCM GE 1915–1918, busta 241-bis, fasc. 5, Asia Minor.
[6] BOD Rennell Rodd correspondence 20–1919, Rennell Rodd to Curzon, 23 Feb 1919.
[7] Cecini, *Il Corpo di spedizione italiano in Anatolia*, 44–6.

and an Italian vice-consul was appointed. Increasingly anxious about the situation in Paris and fearful of missing out in Anatolia (to the Greeks or to the nationalists), Sonnino sent orders on 23 March to Sforza in Constantinople that he should communicate with Elia in Rhodes and prepare for an occupation. On the night of 27 March, a bomb exploded near the Italian girls' mission school in Antalya, and the local naval commander—well primed by Sonnino and Elia—took matters into his own hands the next day, landing several hundred sailors to restore order. By 30 March an agreement was signed in Paris between Diaz and Henry Wilson for the Italian occupation of Konya, and over the next few weeks the numbers of men on the ground was slowly but steadily increased. The troops originally intended for the abortive reinforcement of Palestine, along with some cavalry units and various other troops hastily gathered from here and there, were placed under the authority of General Giuseppe Battistoni, commander of the 33rd Division, for a total of some 15,000 men.[8]

A naval intelligence report from 1 April 1919 suggests that Antalya was not a particularly promising basis for any kind of colony. The town was extremely poor and in dreadful condition with shabby, tumbledown houses, no public lighting, and not a single restaurant or hotel. There were acute shortages of everyday essentials, public order and security were minimal, while rumours held that armed gangs of brigands or Ottoman army deserters were preying on travellers and rural people across the region. The report's author observed almost apologetically that there was great economic potential in the area—for agriculture, forestry, and mining—but that it was all yet to be developed, requiring much investment. The only good news in the whole document was that public views of Italy were now less hostile than they had been during the war for Libya, and reports of Italian good treatment of Muslims in the Aegean islands had found its way to the mainland.[9] Despite these unpromising circumstances, the Italian Expeditionary Force in Anatolia gradually penetrated into the interior, seizing local railway lines and strategic points around Antalya and the Aydin region of southern Anatolia from March 1919, though Aydin itself was occupied by Greek forces in May.[10] Disembarkation of the occupying forces was not completed until June. Battistoni, who remained in charge only until July, complained about the vague, even impossible, instructions which he received from Rome, and the difficulty of complying with foreign office orders as well as his own military chain of command.[11] In Paris, formal protests were made against the occupation, but—somewhat confusingly—the occupation of Konya was approved by the British, and the 1,200 Italians stationed there even received British supplies.

Although this was a military occupation, the Italian expeditionary force neither acted nor was generally perceived as an invading one. In fact, by spring 1919,

[8] IOH Vol. VII, t.3, 357–9.   [9] ACS PCM GE 1915–1918, busta 219.
[10] Cecini, Il Corpo di spedizione italiano in Anatolia, 101–40.   [11] IOH Vol. VII, t.3, 360–1.

Italian aspirations had evolved considerably from the original objectives presented at St Jean de Maurienne in 1917, in recognition of the changed decision-making climate in Paris. Rather than a direct-rule colony, Sonnino was now thinking in terms of a sphere of influence, both economic and administrative—or even, perhaps, a League of Nations Mandate. Italian occupation forces were keen to assure locals that, in Sforza's words, 'the vitality and integrity of the Turkish nation is an essential Italian interest, and in those Turkish regions where we have a special interest this will always take the form of a fraternal and temporary collaboration'. He added that his own priority was to ensure that 'any eventual Mandate operates without the bayonet'.[12]

There were good reasons for Italy to support a viable independent Turkish state: should the whole Ottoman empire be carved up by the British and French, there would be precious few economic opportunities left for Italy to exploit. An independent yet weak Turkey, on the other hand, might conceivably prefer to pick Italy as its preferred great power, rather than one of the more ruthless and successful empires.[13] In this situation, Italy's relative weakness might become its greatest asset. The Italian delegations in Constantinople and Paris were therefore keen to reassure their allies, the Ottoman government, and even Turkish nationalists that they had no desire to dismantle the state. Consequently, right from the start, the Italian military occupation of Anatolia was to be given a distinctly non-military character, emphasizing instead its role in maintaining public order. The expeditionary force was given almost exclusively political objectives, such as building links with the local community, securing public works for Italian investment, protecting Italian enterprises, and reassuring the population as to the benevolence of Italian intentions, all while impressing the other great powers with their seriousness and worthiness.

Unfortunately, these objectives were poorly conceived, and the resources deployed in Anatolia almost wholly unsuited for pursuing them. If by March 1919 the Italian political class were beginning to understand how dramatically the international climate had changed with regard to colonial claims, they were far from understanding the radically changed situation within the Ottoman Empire. The Italians were not alone in their early failure to appreciate the strengths of the new Turkish nationalist movement or its armed forces. France and Britain were soon not only unwilling but also in practical terms quite unable to simply grant lands to Italy at their discretion. The Turkish army might have been defeated but it was far from destroyed, as Greece and the Entente were very soon to learn.

---

[12] ACS PCM GE 1915–1918, busta 214–19.29.17, fasc. Turchia Affari vari, sf. Anno 1921, 9 August 1919, Min. Aff. Est., Div 3, n. 14847.
[13] ACS PCM GE 1915–1918, busta 214–19.29.17, fasc. Turchia Affari vari, sf: Anno 1919: Turchia; Uff. del Capo di Stato Maggiore della Marina, Bollettino Speciale, n. 261, 30 March 1919.

As early as April, Italian military intelligence was reporting on the growing Turkish popular support for the nationalists with some concern, though also showing optimism that humanitarian relief work—especially medical assistance— was winning over local hearts and minds. Turkish local authorities were not above trying to use the Italian occupiers for their own purposes: there was a general consensus in many Turkish circles that the Italians were preferable to the Greeks, and in the void of Ottoman state power which developed in 1919, some local notables approached the Italian occupiers with various proposals for protectorates or enclaves. These approaches, made in July and August 1919, were based on an assessment of Italian strength which was perhaps overly generous; as the reality of Italian weakness became more apparent, local authorities withdrew their enthusiasm for cooperation.[14] By November 1919 reports came in via the military representative in Constantinople, Colonel Vitale, that 'Mustafa Kemal has issued a proclamation urging the population of Adana to resist foreign intervention', although this was as yet having little impact on the ground.[15]

The Italian position on the Greek occupation of Smyrna and the surrounding area was complex: on the one hand, Greece had 'usurped' the position of European occupier there; on the other, British and French support for Venizelos made it hard for Italy to oppose them too directly. Equally, as fellow Christians, there was some sympathy in Italian circles when attacks on Greeks took place. However, reports from the occupying forces reveal determination to distance themselves entirely from the Greeks so that local populations would not tar all Europeans with the same brush—there was a considerable fear that anti-Greek feeling might somehow expand to encompass the Italian presence too. In July 1919 General Alfredo Dall'Olio—a former minister and delegate to the Paris Conference, and generally well regarded by the Allies—was sent to Constantinople, with secret instructions to systematically highlight the flaws and failings of the Greeks and undermine them by all means possible in the eyes of the British and French, while at the same time giving every appearance of impartiality.[16] He made Italian–Greek relations his special area of concern, and quickly grew convinced that any association with Greece would be disastrous to the Italian cause. Anti-Greek sentiment was leading to increasing hostility to all formal military occupations in Turkey, so he pushed for a visibly different

[14] ACS PCM GE 1915–1918, busta 214–19.29.17 fasc. Turchia Affari vari, sf. Anno 1921, 2 June 1919, C.S. n. 636 operazioni report from Battistoni. Battistoni also reported that Assyrian, Armenian, and Greek communities welcomed the Italian occupation on religious grounds and saw it as a guarantee of protection.
[15] ACS PCM GE 1915–1918, busta 214–19.29.17, sf. Turchia—Impero Ottomano—Questioni Politiche, 20 November 1919.
[16] ACS PCM GE 1915–1918, busta 214, sf. Anno 1919: Turchia, Affari Vari; Forze Italiane in Asia Minore.

Italian model.[17] Some agents in Anatolia even argued that Italian troops should adopt a strong anti-Greek approach, to secure local support. This was going too far for the government which, however hostile it was to Greece, could not afford to risk head-to-head conflict with a supposed ally (or, indeed, anybody else).

11.1.2 Reorganization of the Eastern Mediterranean Force

In August 1919 the remaining Italian units serving in Eastern Thrace with the Armée d'Orient were withdrawn. The separate occupying forces in Constantinople and southern Anatolia were then formally united into a single Eastern Mediterranean Expeditionary Force (Corpo di Spedizione italiana nel mediterraneo orientale), then some 17,000 strong, and united with the military command of the Italian occupation of the Dodecanese in Rhodes, under General Vittorio Elia. Sforza— recently promoted to under-secretary for foreign affairs—outlined his new tasks: in the Dodecanese, he should plan the gradually reformation and Italianization of the legal, administrative, and educational systems of the islands, while both reducing costs and avoiding conflict with the Greek Orthodox hierarchy (an almost impossible juggling act). On the Anatolian mainland, while cooperating as much as possible with the British, Elia should at all costs avoid fighting with Turkish forces, redeploying or reducing numbers if necessary, to avoid any direct conflict (an instruction endorsed by the new minister of war, General Alberico Albricci). A new political office was created to emphasize the core business of the Italian presence was to work with the local authorities to create a stable, peaceful, and lasting presence based on 'mutually beneficial' collaboration rather than control.[18] These instructions speak volumes to Italian anxieties but also raise a fundamental question: what is the point of a military occupation which must not engage in military operations?

The restructuring of Italian command in the Eastern Mediterranean was not only a practical measure designed to improve the effectiveness and inter-unit coordination of the various detachments but also a symbolic one: by linking the still-speculative endeavours in Anatolia with the comparatively successful occupation in the Aegean, Italy aimed to demonstrate the logical coherence of its claims in Asia Minor. This drew heavily on the long-standing Italian colonial concept of 'the sea unites, not divides': it was now the Aegean and the Eastern Mediterranean which were to link Italian territories, in line with Italian diplomats' repeated insistence in 1919–20 on the point that Italy was 'the only wholly

---

[17] ACS PCM GE 1915–1918, busta 214, sf: Turchia—Impero Ottomano—Questioni Politiche, October 1919; also Sf: Anno 1919, Turchia: Questioni vari.
[18] ACS PCM GE 1915–1918, busta 214, sf. Anno 1919, Turchia—Affari Vari: Corpo di Spedizione italiana nel mediterraneo orientale.

Mediterranean Great Power'. This assumption would endure into the fascist conception of empire, in which the 'inner sea' was an essential connecting element.[19] But this rhetoric was as unconvincing to the French and British as most other diplomatic approaches deployed by the Italian delegation in Paris, and by the time that the Peace Conference began to seriously address the territorial settlement of the Ottoman Empire in 1920, the evolving international situation did not favour this approach.

What, ultimately, did Italy hope to achieve in Asia Minor in 1919? The variety of perspectives and ideas make it impossible to say: even within government circles there were widely divergent ideas. Arguing against the desire for a geographically defined sphere of influence, Sforza observed in October 1919 that Italy's traditional colonial approach had produced an empire of limited usefulness or prosperity, and questioned whether it was really useful to claim more 'second-rate zones to fill up with bureaucrats, like Eritrea or Libya'; instead, why not respect Turkish sovereignty, winning popularity with the population, and try to position Italy as the leading foreign economic power throughout the entire country?[20] Both ideological differences and differing information about the situation on the ground lay behind the very divergent approaches explored in this period. Meanwhile, in the same month naval intelligence was suggesting that the Italian presence in Adana 'might soon be a thorn in Turkey's heart', and it ought to be withdrawn as soon as possible, to salvage Italian prestige. And yet, still in October 1919, Albricci was arguing that Italy ought to help fund the post-war reconstruction of Lebanon as 'an important measure to assert *italianità* in the East'—at a time when the formerly occupied areas of Italy itself were still in urgent need of funds for reconstruction.[21]

These extravagant dreams were increasingly recognized as unfeasible economically, however desirable they might be. There were doubtless many reasons why Italy could not hope to win over public support across Asia Minor and the Near East through philanthropic endeavour, but chief among them was a simple lack of funds. Indeed, the main impression left by reports on the occupation of Anatolia is one of vastly over-stretched resources. From the beginning of the Allied presence in Constantinople, there was a stark difference apparent in the actions of the three occupying powers. While Britain and France requisitioned barracks, arsenals, factories, warehouses, ships, boats, and docks, while also putting their own men into all key positions for commerce, trade, and industry, Italian officers complained in March 1919 that 'we have done little or nothing, for lack of means and

[19] This contributed to the late 1930s hostility to Britain, whose navy was 'strangling' the empire. Laura Cerasi, 'Empires Ancient and Modern: Strength, Modernity and Power in Imperial Ideology from the Liberal Period to Fascism', *Modern Italy* 19, no. 4 (2014): 421–38, DOI: http://dx.doi.org/10. 1080/13532944.2014.968116;425.
[20] ACS PCM GE 1915–1918, busta 214, sf.: Anno 1920.
[21] ACS PCM GE 1915–1918, busta 214, Sf: Anno 1919: Turchia, Affari vari.

especially for lack of suitable personnel'. The rapporteur, counter-admiral Edoardo Salazar, wrote that it was not entirely too late: shipping companies, insurance, mining, spinning (cotton and silk), electrical materials, and agricultural machinery were all promising sectors in which Italy could still invest—yet time was of the essence. The British and French forces in Turkey had dedicated investment funds ready to use and were accompanied by large numbers of technical experts and industrialists, while Italy had neither the cash nor the experts. Sforza agreed, admitting that the chief obstacle to his vision of large-scale economic dominance was the shortage of capital ready to invest in key industries and infrastructure. Italian business and finance did make efforts to profit from new opportunities in the Ottoman Empire: in March 1919, the Consorzio per il Commercio dell'Oriente (Consortium for Commerce in the East) sent a ship with 25 million lira worth of goods and samples to Turkish ports, while Italy was claiming all warehouses formerly belonging to Austro-Hungarians. The Banco di Roma reopened its Constantinople branch, and other Italian banks were seeking to do the same; yet compared to the French and British efforts, this seemed second-rate. The following year, the Italian Ferrovie dello Stato (State Railways) were forced to stand by as British, French, and US firms snapped up German and Austrian holdings in the Turkish railway system, while Britain sought to exclude Italian shipping interests by upholding a pre-war Armstrong–Vickers monopoly agreement.[22] In the event, of course, the apparent successes of the French and British would not create an enduring sphere of influence either; yet the difference from Italian capability was stark.

Missed investment opportunities were not the only problem. On 23 August 1919 the socialist newspaper *Avanti!* had published a denunciation of the conditions in which Italian troops were living in Konya, and military attaché Vitale's investigation confirmed many of the worst claims: soldiers were significantly underpaid and were sleeping at best on piles of hay but often on the bare earth; medical resources were inadequate to cope with the numerous outbreaks of pappataci fever and malaria. The units were dependent on the local British forces for food supplies. Morale was poor, not least because of the visible difference between Italian forces' conditions and the better-treated French and British troops in the region. The next month, the ministry of war's colonial office found that the units in Constantinople were also seriously under-funded and under-supplied; once again the comparison with the Allies' situation rendered the problem more noticeable.[23] By 1920 the problem was growing ever more obvious: as the Italians steadily scaled back their military presence and replaced soldiers with civilian

---

[22] ACS PCM GE 1915–1918, busta 214—Turchia Affari vari; Sf: Anno 1919: Turchia; Uff. del Capo di Stato Maggiore della Marina, Bollettino Speciale, n. 261, 30 March 1919, and response dated 21 April 1919, Min. per l'Industria, Commercio e Lavoro, Tel. 1115.; Min. dei Lavori Pubblici, 15 July 1920, n. 25104; Rome, 23 June 1920, B.1179., Min. della Marina, to Min. Affari Esteri.

[23] ACS PCM GE 1915–1918, busta 214, Sf. Anno 1919: Turchia, Affari vari.

personnel, they were losing their ability to impress. For instance, while early in the occupation of Constantinople Italian military and civilian aviation had been the best on display, they had now lost ground completely to the French who were building a new airfield—the Italians could simply not compete.[24] Lack of money was also the most common response to the endless flow of petitions which the Italian government received for humanitarian relief from Armenian communities and organizations, and from refugees in Constantinople and across the Ottoman lands.

Not for the first (or last) time, it seemed that Italy was trying to bite off more than it could chew. Without the vast wealth and resources of its allies—ironically, rooted in empire—Italy appeared unable to build an empire of its own. To them that hath empire, it seemed, shall empire be given.

11.2 The San Remo Declaration and the Treaty of Sèvres

Allied discussions over the fate of the Ottoman Empire intensified once the Treaties of Versailles and Saint-Germain had been signed. The delay between the Armistice of Mudros and negotiations for the treaty meant that the situation within the Ottoman Empire—as well as internationally—had evolved considerably, and the Italian position was much weaker. At the Supreme War Council's Conference of London in February 1920, the Italian delegation was still (futilely) upholding the St Jean de Maurienne Agreement as the basis for its claims, but now the designated 'Green and C' territories were to be:

> areas of Italian economic interest, where Italy will have the right of priority over all enterprises of public interest and on mining and forestry concessions, etc. Other Allied Powers' interests in the zone will be respected but may not serve as the means of any political action. [Italy will] work with the Ottoman Government to ensure the best administration and public order in the Green and C areas (nomination of technical advisers and organisation of the gendarmerie). Enemy ownership in all public enterprises in the zone will be transferred to Italy in reparations.[25]

Meanwhile compensation for the 'loss' of Smyrna and its environs to Greece would come via the transfer to Italian ownership of all coal mines in the Zonguldak basin (Eraclea, as the Italians knew it) with the exception of those owned by Allied or neutral powers in August 1914. Italy's lack of coal, a major constraint on its strategic decisions in 1914–15, was a central issue in its planning

---

[24]   ACS PCM GE 1915–1918, busta 214, sf: Anno 1920.
[25]   Archivio Francesco Saverio Nitti, busta 25, fasc. 93, sf.6; Memorandum of 16 February 1920.

for the Anatolian settlement in 1920. In return for this agreement, Italian troops would be immediately withdrawn from Anatolia. The language and style of Italian claims under Nitti was heading inexorably away from a traditional colonial claim based on Italian rights and towards the purely economic sphere. The military occupation, far from paving the way for a long-lasting Italian presence in the region, had now become nothing more than a bargaining chip—like an annoying restaurant violinist who has to be paid to go away.

At last, in April 1920, the Supreme War Council met in San Remo, to finalize arrangements for the Ottoman treaty. Best known for its provisions regarding British and French Mandatory status in Syria, Mesopotamia, and Palestine,[26] the Italians hoped that the San Remo meeting would formalize their '1917 agreement minus Smyrna' model. To the colonial-minded foreign ministry, this already represented a significant act of compromise—accepting both the loss of Smyrna and the changed status of 'Green and C' areas. Nitti's government were not, therefore, minded to make further concessions, especially given the bitter legacies of the Fiume issue.

Instead, the official line was to stick fast to Italy's territorial demands, while offering flexibility as to exactly what kind of rights or administration it would have within the designated territory. The idea of a Mandate appealed since it would indicate equality of rank with France and Britain and acknowledge Italy's Mediterranean status. Some in Italy had hoped the US would accept the proposed Mandate in Armenia, since this would make it easier to argue for an Italian Mandate in Anatolia; but as neither the US nor the other Entente powers showed any enthusiasm for an Italian Mandate—and in any case, the US Congress would shortly reject Wilson's plan for Armenia—this proposal was quietly abandoned. Nonetheless, the Italians withheld their endorsement of the San Remo Declaration on Mandates, noting that 'in view of the great economic interests that Italy, as an exclusively Mediterranean power, possesses in Asia Minor, [the government] withholds its approval of this resolution until Italian interests in Turkey in Asia shall have been settled'.[27] This formal phrase poorly conceals the huge sense of betrayal felt by Italy with regard to its former allies: from the Italian perspective, not only the letter but above all the spirit of wartime cooperation had been utterly abandoned, adding insult to the previous year's injuries in the Balkans.

---

[26] Angelo Levi-Bianchini was part of the Italian delegation there, to advise on Zionist interests and share intelligence about Arab views.

[27] The 'San Remo Convention', based on the April 1920 agreement, was not approved until 24 July 1922, by the Council of the League of Nations. The original text stated that all specific details were to be resolved at a later date. See Britain, 'Minutes of Palestine Meeting of the Supreme Council of the Allied Powers Held in San Remo at the Villa Devachan – April 24, 1920', recorded by Maurice Hankey, online at https://commons.wikimedia.org/wiki/File:Minutes_of_Meetings_of_the_Supreme_Council_of_the_Allied_Powers_in_San_Remo_at_the_Villa_Devachan,_April_24_and_April_25,_1920.djvu [accessed 17/06/2020].

In the run-up to the conference, intense lobbying went on by Greek, Assyrian, and Armenian communities in the Ottoman Empire, Britain, the US, and elsewhere; each produced extensive catalogues of horror and atrocity committed against them in support of their claims. Meanwhile, Turkish groups denounced atrocities committed by Christians against Muslims, publishing long lists of rapes, murders, and thefts along with photographs of ruined mosques and mutilated bodies. These international efforts to influence Italian political leadership and public opinion reframed foreign policy as a matter for ethical concerns and religious solidarity, rather than political and economic gain. In the weeks before the meeting, campaigners and pressure groups within Italy also pushed for a variety of positions. Armenian and Greek sympathizers invoked Christian solidarity, denounced the wartime leadership of the Committee of Union and Progress, called for war-crimes trials, and urged a harsh and punitive settlement which removed sovereignty from the Turkish authorities.[28] At the same time Nitti's government was lobbied by the 'Italo-Turkish Committee', headed by the journalist Italo Sulliotti. He drew up a pamphlet in April 1920 which described terrible wrongs suffered by the Turkish people during the war and the great dangers inherent in an unjust peace such as that which the powers appeared to be contemplating.[29] Sulliotti's position is interesting: he was an ardent nationalist and former war correspondent in Albania and the Balkans who strongly supported Italian expansion and who would later become a keen fascist (and rumoured regime spy). However, he did not see Anatolia as a suitable space for Italian expansion. A would-be coloniser, he thought, should carefully consider the peoples and lands they attempted to claim. Sulliotti saw the San Remo meeting as a chance to move away from the 'accumulated hatreds' which had marred the Versailles Treaty and create a true 'Magna Carta of Europe'. He described the colonial approach as 'vivisection on the body of the Turkish nation', denounced the Greek invasion, and ironized cruelly on the fate of the Armenians, calling them uniquely privileged in Turkish society. Invoking the possibility of a pan-Islamic global uprising against the British and French Empires, he warned: 'let no-one dream of killing Islam and building a mercantile society over its body.... It is so great that even its corpse could poison the world!' Instead, he argued that Italian interests were closely and irrevocably tied to Islam—especially in North Africa—and that fair treatment of Turkey was the only way to achieve a lasting peace. A harsh treaty would only lead to more war and more death, while mistreatment of the Caliph risked a global uprising.[30] Sulliotti's Cassandra-like

---

[28] ACS PCM GE 1915–1918, Busta 214–19.29.17, Turchia: Affari vari, Sf. Pace con la Turchia.

[29] ACS PCM GE 1915–1918, Busta 214–19.29.17, Turchia: Affari vari, b Sf: Turchia—Impero Ottomano—Questioni Politiche.

[30] Comitato Italo-Turco, *La pace con la Turchia al Congresso di San Remo* (Milan: Stab. Yip. Stucchi, Ceretti & C., 1920).

warnings were of course ignored, but his predictions of Turkish resurgence were remarkably prescient.

In Konya, local nationalist notables lobbied Italy in protest over the terms of the San Remo Agreement which suggests that the Italian claim to act as an impartial mediator had won at least some local adherents.[31] Italy was succeeding in its efforts to differentiate itself in the eyes of the Turkish public from the Greeks or the British (and a small but significant number of wealthy Turkish citizens, especially Jews, requested Italian citizenship in 1920). But it was pointless for the Turks—or indeed anybody else—to lobby Italy for change, given that Italy was also an aggrieved party whose ability to shape the San Remo agreement was demonstrably very limited: and what is the use of a protector which cannot protect?

Despite Italian (and Turkish) resentment, the San Remo Agreement would form the basis of the Treaty of Sèvres, signed in August 1920. Section XI (articles 121 and 122) of the treaty confirmed the Italian possession of the Dodecanese Islands, which under the original 1912 Ouchy Treaty were supposed to have been returned to the Ottoman Empire after a temporary Italian administration, and removed the remaining privileges of the Caliph in Libya. Italy also received its dedicated sphere of influence in southern Anatolia, along the Mediterranean shore; more or less the 1917 agreement without the Greek zone around Smyrna. But whereas St Jean de Maurienne had provided for an 'Italian zone' (comparable to the British and French Mandates in Syria and Mesopotamia) and an Italian 'sphere of influence' alongside it, at Sèvres Italy was given purely an economic sphere of influence, without any direct administration at all. It represented a serious blow to nationalist hopes, but by this time it was scarcely a surprise.

If the Treaty of Sèvres seemed to be a defeat for traditional Italian colonialism and its great power pretensions, it was a huge victory for the Greek Megali Idea; the settlement in the south-west relied on the Greek army enforcing Allied will to a large extent. If—as would indeed prove the case—they could not subdue the Kemalists, then the treaty would be entirely unenforceable. This left Italy's claims in Anatolia uncomfortably dependent upon Greek military success, despite the tension between the two.

11.2.1 The Dodecanese Islands

The Greek invasion of Asia Minor made the Italian position in its Eastern Mediterranean colonies even more fraught. After seven years of occupation, the Italian presence was growing no more popular; on the contrary, whereas in 1912

---

[31] ACS PCM GE 1915–1918, busta 214, sf. Anno 1920.

the Greek population saw Italian occupation as preferable to Turkish, the defeat of the Ottoman Empire and the rise of the Megali Idea meant Greek nationalists felt the time was ripe to kick Italy out of the Aegean. As the war ended, the Greek diaspora in the USA sent petitions to the Italian government calling for the complete unity of all Greeks across Northern Epirus, Thrace, Macedonia, Asia Minor, the Sea of Marmora, and the entire Aegean. Greek residents in Egypt joined in this lobbying; from within the Dodecanese islands themselves, extremely harsh wartime censorship had prevented any complaints, but with the coming of peace it would be increasingly difficult to justify the maintenance of such a repressive regime. The Italian position was made awkward by the language of irredentism and natural borders which the Greeks employed when speaking of the Dodecanese, which was extremely close to Italian rhetoric around Trieste and Fiume, and which rendered the hypocrisy of Italy's Aegean claims uncomfortably clear.[32] Nonetheless, Italy was determined not to relinquish the islands. Wartime measures had already extended the occupation from the purely military into the political sphere, and civil policy measures relating to public health, education, and the food supply were increasingly the responsibility of the Italian military governor, laying the stage for a 'regularization' of colonial status.

11.3 The Italian Expeditionary Corps in Palestine

Always chiefly symbolic, by 1919 the Italian presence in Palestine was largely irrelevant to international questions. Beyond appointing a diplomatic agent and pushing for the reopening of the local Banco di Roma in Jerusalem, Jaffa, and Haifa, the Italian government did not waste much effort pursuing economic influence in an area where its options were clearly going to be limited by the British.[33] Instead it focused ever more on questions related to the Holy Places and to Catholic interests. Perhaps the chief priority in Palestine was the ancient Cenacle (or *Cenacolo*), the upper room of King David's tomb on Mount Zion, supposedly the location of the Last Supper. A detailed aide-memoire was sent to Balfour in May 1919, highlighting that the sanctuary had been legally purchased from the Sultan of Egypt in around 1335 by Robert of Anjou and his queen, Sancia of Naples, and was later maintained by Franciscan friars funded by the Kingdom of Naples, which still claimed the crusader kingdom of Jerusalem. According to this document, the Cenacle was the rightful possession of the heirs of the kings of Naples; indeed, until its abolition, the house of Savoy continued to use the title of Kings of Jerusalem (though so too did the Bourbon pretenders to the throne of the Two Sicilies). The Sultan, whose possession it had been since the early years of

[32]   ACS PCM GE 1915–1918, busta 75, sf. 21, Isole d'Egeo.
[33]   Minerbi, 'Angelo Levi-Bianchini in Levante', 47.

the Ottoman Empire, was now willing to cede it to Italy and in April 1919 was persuaded by Carlo Sforza to sign an agreement to this effect. Vittorio Emanuele III was enthusiastic, and the project held inestimable worth as a propaganda move to win over Catholic support, so Nitti considered it worth pursuing.[34] He hoped to make this a quid pro quo for recognition of the British Mandate in Palestine, but Balfour was very discouraging and the issue was eventually dropped (although Italy continued to intermittently press these claims up until 1940).[35] Like the vigorous pursuit of the Austrian embassy building in Constantinople, the Italian desire for the Cenacle reveals the primacy of image and prestige over functional influence overseas; how else to build an empire on the cheap? The episode is suggestive, though, in showing how Catholic interests might connect with foreign policy—or how Catholic voters might be encouraged to support imperialist claims. State efforts to protect and fund Italian missions across Palestine and Syria can also be read in this light.[36] Up until 1921, 150,000L per annum were spent there on 'political' work at the behest of the foreign ministry: two-thirds for religious and educational activities (missions, schools, hospices, clinics) and the remainder on 'scientific' activities (archaeology, geology, history), though from 1922 this budget was cut significantly.[37] The Italians lacked the deep archaeo-logical or cultural tradition in the region which might have supported their ongoing political goals there.

The fate of Catholic interests in the Holy Land appeared particularly pertinent in the aftermath of the Balfour Declaration and of Arab responses to it; intelli-gence sent in by the Zionist delegate Levi-Bianchini reported that Arab Christians preferred the status quo and were apprehensive about the possible implications of Zionism.[38] Levi-Bianchini travelled between Paris, Rome, and Palestine through 1919, trying with growing anxiety to balance the conflicting duties which he owed to his faith, his country, his family, and the navy. He toyed with programmes for uniting the multiple, disparate communities of Italian Jews spread all over the Mediterranean—in Tunisia, Libya, Egypt, Palestine, Lebanon, and southern Anatolia—in such a way as to benefit both the individuals and Italy itself; he was also charged by foreign minister Tittoni, in July 1919, with building pro-Italian sentiment among Turkish Sephardi communities, especially within Italy's proposed sphere of influence along the Mediterranean coast.[39] Levi-Bianchini also worked with Arab leaders, travelling widely into Syria and the Arabian peninsula, hoping to promote peaceful coexistence (and Italian interests); he was sadly

[34] ACS, Archivio Francesco Saverio Nitti, busta 25, f. 93, sf.1.
[35] Arielli, 'Hopes and Jealousies: Rome's Ambitions in the Middle East', 50.
[36] ASMAE, Consolato Generale di Gerusalemme, pos. 68, fasc. 132.
[37] ACS PCM GE 1915–1918, busta 220, fasc. 19.29.38 Siria e Palestina; Min. Aff. Est to Min. del Tesoro, 16/10/1922, n. 58386/366.
[38] ACS PCM GE 1915–1918 busta 214, sf. Anno 1919, Turchia: Affari Vari.
[39] Minerbi, 'Angelo Levi-Bianchini in Levante', 87–94.

assassinated returning from Damascus to Jerusalem on 20 August 1920.[40] With his death, official Italian interest in Zionism as a tool of policy waned.

After the signing of the Treaty of Sèvres and the declaration of the British Mandate in Palestine, it was clear that the various schemes for building influence there were at an end. This also meant that the Italian *carabinieri* unit in Jerusalem had to be withdrawn—a decision already postponed several times on political grounds. The unit would finally embark at Jaffa on 1 March 1921 to sail for home after nearly four years in Palestine.[41]

11.4 Italian Withdrawal From Asia Minor

Like the St Jean de Maurienne Agreement, the Treaty of Sèvres would never be implemented, as the Italian foreign office gradually came to understand. The political authorities decided, and the military hierarchy was happy to agree, that at all costs Italian troops should avoid any direct hostilities with Turkish forces of any stripe. They might cautiously act against armed brigands, but any kind of confrontation with Turkish units—whether loyal to the Sultan or part of the new nationalist army—must be avoided. Nitti's administration hoped that this would indicate Italian desire for a friendly and mutually beneficial sphere of influence. But as the new Kemalist government grew in power and effectiveness, the Italian position became increasingly untenable. The difficulties faced by the French in their Cilicia campaign from 1920 onwards, particularly the horrors of the battle of Marash in February of that year, further convinced Nitti and his successor Giovanni Giolitti of the undesirability of military engagement with the nationalist forces.[42]

The Italian occupation of Antalya, and its dispatch of warships, was militarily insufficient to stake an effective claim or to secure by right of conquest its objectives. Arguably, all it achieved was to further irritate and alienate Italy's allies thus further undermining the chances of success within negotiations at the Peace Conference. Recklessly squandering what remained of Allied goodwill for little concrete return, it is hard to avoid the conclusion that these expeditionary forces achieved nothing but a vast waste of time and money.

Italy's dire economic straits and unprecedented level of national debt led to the ruthless slashing of budgets in all areas in 1919 and 1920. Along with pressure from wartime allies to begin repaying some of their huge war debts, this left the government remarkably little room for manoeuvre. Put simply, Italian resources

---

[40] His posthumous daughter Angela (1921–2018) was a celebrated novelist, translator, and critic.
[41] ACS PCM GE 1915–1918, busta 214, sf. Anno 1922.
[42] The PM received detailed briefings on the French Cilicia campaign, see ACS PCM GE 1915–1918, busta 220: 19.29.38, Siria e Palestina which undoubtedly influenced government thinking on military engagement in Anatolia.

were insufficient to implement the policies which many political leaders and citizens alike ardently embraced. Like the other Allies, Italy seriously underestimated Mustafa Kemal's nationalist forces, and its expeditionary force also found itself continually at a disadvantage compared to the better funded, better equipped, and more experienced French and British contingents.

Italy was an unreliable interlocutor for both the Sultan's government, such as it was, and the Kemalist movement. It agreed in January 1920 to offer the Ottoman government a line of credit in return for coal; at other moments it appeared to be negotiating with the nationalists. Albricci, the minister for war, was anxious that too close collaboration with the Sultan could leave Italian troops open to attack by nationalist forces. By May 1920, Italian intelligence in Anatolia was openly questioning the utility of negotiating with the 'Constantinople government' and speculating as to how best to come to terms with the nationalists (and with the Bolsheviks in the Caucasus).

As a result of both the economic situation and the new political realities in Turkey, Italian units in Anatolia began to be withdrawn from their inland forward positions starting in late 1920 and continuing throughout 1921 and 1922. The occupied zone grew progressively smaller as they fell back towards the coast. This cautious policy also meant that they failed to provide effective security against brigands and raiding forces, which seriously weakened them as a potential administrator of the territory in the eyes of the local population. Elsewhere in the Eastern Mediterranean Italian forces were also gradually withdrawn: the small nucleus of military police remained in Jerusalem only until February 1921, and by 1922 the last forces in Anatolia had been removed to the Dodecanese; finally, in October 1923 the detachment in Constantinople was withdrawn and the experiment was over.[43] Italy's victory over Austria-Hungary had not left it in any position to undertake further military expansion, nor had it earned the diplomatic clout which France and Britain were able to wield in pursuit of their goals. Yet these fruitless endeavours left an important legacy: in the late 1930s and early 1940s, Fascist Italy would seek once more to expand into the Middle East, hoping replace Britain as the hegemonic power there.[44]

11.4.1 The Treaty of Lausanne

On 24 July 1923 the new Republic of Turkey signed the Treaty of Lausanne, which formally resolved the outstanding territorial questions of the Great War in the Middle East. France and Britain had secured their League of Nations Mandates;

[43] Cecini, *Il Corpo di spedizione italiano in Anatolia*, 392–412.
[44] On Fascist policy towards the Middle East, see Nir Arielli, *Fascist Italy and the Middle East, 1933–40* (Basingstoke and New York: Palgrave Macmillan, 2010).

Greece was defeated. Today Italy is rarely even considered as a player in this arena, and yet Asia Minor had been a major focus of Italian political and military activity for the previous six years, and of diplomatic and economic interest for more than a decade. Italian failure in this respect was almost complete, though by this date, the new prime minister Benito Mussolini had abandoned his focus on the area and his citizens had quite other concerns on their minds. The only mentions of Italy within the Treaty were to confirm de facto rights (in the Dodecanese and Libya) rather than to grant any new ones. The history of the occupation of the Ottoman Empire from 1919 to 1923 offers important insights into the functioning of the Entente, with all its many difficulties and misunderstandings, and of Italian foreign policy and its dilemmas. It also illustrates the extent to which Italy shared the Allies' opportunistic attitudes to the war in the Middle East, the complex legacies of which are still with us. Despite the total failure of Italian ambitions in the Eastern Mediterranean, dating back to before the First World War, the colonial expansionist mentality which they embodied lived on into the new regime.

11.5 The African Colonies

Just as critical in the aftermath of the war as Italy's Eastern Mediterranean policy were its efforts to secure, consolidate, and even expand its African possessions. The war had left Libya, the supposed jewel in the Italian colonial crown, in a parlous state.

11.5.1 Tripolitania

The ambitious claims asserted in Rome and presented in Paris could not make up for the fact that the situation in Tripolitania from November 1918 was in fact dire. The Italian coastal strip, centred around Tripoli, was essentially besieged by Arab forces. Italian control survived behind a strongly garrisoned array of trenches, fortresses, and even electric fences.[45] Unsurprisingly, the climate was tense and hostile: the political approach of reconciliation and cooperation which had been officially embraced by many of the colony's administrators was not reflected in the mood of the officers and men actually occupying the front lines, who had become 'frightened, vicious and recriminatory'.[46]

The first step in normalizing the situation was to somehow achieve a cessation of hostilities. The Italian governors of Tripolitania and Cyrenaica had, during the

---

[45] Del Boca, *Tripoli bel suol d'amore*, 1:299.
[46] Bosworth and Finaldi, 'The Italian Empire', 43.

war, attributed great importance to the role of the Central Powers in supporting the resistance; they therefore hoped that the defeat of the Central Powers would significantly weaken the Arab forces. The Armistice of Mudros required the surrender of all Turkish forces fighting Italy in Tripolitania and Cyrenaica. Colosimo had insisted on this point to Orlando in October 1918, specifically mentioning Prince Osman Fuad, commander of the Ottoman forces in Africa, along with Isahag Pasha, Sulayman al-Baruni, Chetua Bey, and several others; he also insisted upon surrender of arms, munitions, and all other war materials including radio equipment in Libya, and the surrender of all Italian prisoners of war and civilian hostages in Turkish or Arab hands.[47] In early December a group surrender was organized at Orfella: Osman Fuad was to be accompanied by one major general, four senior officers, twenty-two junior officers, eleven civilian officials, and forty-six soldiers (all Turkish). He was also accompanied by three German junior officers, with seven men, and three Austrians including Lieutenant Prince Francisco José Braganza.[48] At first the young Ottoman prince hoped to avoid surrender and keep fighting, ignoring this agreement. When it proved impossible without the vital lifeline of German submarines, he preferred to surrender to the French than to the Italians, and accordingly made his way to the Tunisian border. To his disappointment, rather than sending him straight home to Constantinople, the French handed him over to Italy. He and his men would be interned on Ischia for several months.

However, by the end of the war the Ottoman military leaders on the ground had little genuine support from the Tripolitanian resistance, who saw Turkey as a welcome source of cash and weaponry but little more—indeed, many were now fiercely anti-Turkish nationalists. As a result, the loss of external leadership did little to crush the anti-Italian resistance. On the contrary, fortified by the 'global Wilsonian moment' (or perhaps by Leninist anti-imperialism), in November 1918 Ramadan al-Suwayhili, Sulayman al-Baruni, and other tribal leaders of the resistance from Tarhuna and Warfalla, came together to found the Tripolitanian Republic, 'the first formally republican government in the Arab world' (although the choice of a republic was at least in part a reaction to the impossibility of selecting any one man as an Amir).[49] The new leaders were acutely aware of the wider historical moment in which they were operating, denouncing Italian colonial aspirations as anachronistic and incompatible with the emergent world order, and sending a delegation to the Peace Conference in Paris to assert their right to self-determination.[50] Historians' attention has generally focused on the Sanusiyya

---

[47] ACS PCM GE 1915–1918, busta 75, f. Colonie.

[48] ACS PCM GE 1915–1918, busta 170 Armistizio, sf. Armistizio con Turchia. Braganza was an exiled member of the Portuguese royal house, godson of Austrian Emperor Franz Josef, and protagonist of a series of high-profile pre-war scandals involving swindling and gay sex; he died in Italian captivity on Ischia in June 1919.

[49] Anderson, 'The Tripoli Republic', 43.   [50] Pergher, *Fascist Borderlands*, 33.

and on the resistance in Cyrenaica at the expense of Tripolitania, yet this highly significant moment reveals the level of development and organization of the resistance in the western province. The local notables were assisted and encouraged by Abdul Rahman Hassan Azzam, who had worked for several years with al-Suwayhili, and who would now serve as the first secretary to the new republic's ruling council, from its capital in Aziziya (Jafara).[51] Meanwhile the republic also sought to extend its authority southwards, appointing long-term resistance fighter Mohamed Fekini as prefect of Fezzan (he continued his struggle against Italian rule until he went into exile in Algeria, aged 75, in 1930).

By April 1919 the Italian situation in Tripolitania was critical in several respects: troops needed to be demobilized and returned to Italy rapidly—the PSI had threatened a general strike otherwise—but the colony was not yet sufficiently peaceful to safely do so. The hot season was on its way, the money allocated for the year was already running low, and as soon as a peace treaty was wrapped up in Paris there would be nothing left to distract the public or the press from the Libyan mess. Some Turkish officers were still with the resistance, and Colosimo grew increasingly impatient with Ameglio's replacement as governor, Vincenzo Garioni, who he thought was needlessly stalling.[52] The changing international situation had of course created extra complications. The Fourteen Points, Feisal's declarations in Paris, and the establishment of the kingdom of Hejaz were all encouraging both pan-Arab sentiment and the movement for Tripolitanian independence. Meanwhile both French and British actions were creating new problems: the French decision to grant full citizenship to Algerians put pressure on Italy to follow suit, while British actions in Egypt were blamed for further inflaming anti-colonial feeling in Cyrenaica. Against this background, Italy was forced to negotiate with the leaders of the new Tripolitanian Republic—who were now the de facto power across most of Tripoli. This was the background for the proclamation of the new Legge Fondamentale (also known as the *Statuto*) for Tripoli on 1 June 1919. This law created a new colonial citizenship—resolving the highly chaotic and confused situation which had existed since 1911—along with a provincial parliament and local elected councils. Yet while the leaders of the Republic believed they were establishing a fully independent state, the Italian authorities saw this as little more than a dressed-up version of the old *politica dei capi*. Voting rights, exemption from conscription and parliamentary control of taxation were all granted, but it is hard to establish just how sincere the Italian negotiations really were. Was this a new style of colonial regime inspired by the principles of progressive devolution towards self-determination and a spirit of trusteeship, or simply a concession made by a weak and ineffectual metropole? Both in Tripolitania and in Rome many saw the *Statuto* as purely a rhetorical

[51]   Anderson, 'The Tripoli Republic', 51.
[52]   ACS PCM GE 1915–1918, busta 221, fasc. 201, sf. 12.

construct rather than a new form of colonial governance; the events of the war years had abundantly demonstrated that were true self-determination to be granted, perhaps in the form of a plebiscite, Italy would immediately lose sovereignty over the colony. The locally elected parliament would never in fact be created, and elections were never held.[53] The governing council of the republic formed itself into 'An Association of National Reform', tacitly accepting ongoing Italian sovereignty, but in its weakened state achieved very little. Fundamentally, both sides saw the *Statuto* as an unsatisfactory and hopefully temporary compromise, and unsurprisingly it broke down swiftly.

A further compromise was made in this same period over the essential Tripolitanian hinterland. On 12 September 1919 a Franco-Italian Exchange of notes confirmed the new border, which ceded two triangles of French territory to Italy—one between Gadames and Ghat, along the Tunisian border, including the oases of Fehut and El-Baeka; the other between Ghat and Tummo. This was finally signed into law by the French in 1923. The territorial adjustment—while significantly less than Italy had hoped for—at least helped to consolidate Tripolitania into a more coherent and economically secure whole. But the dream of accessing—even controlling—Lake Chad was doomed to failure. For centuries caravan routes from Tripoli via the Fezzan down towards Lake Chad had proved highly profitable, before a decline linked to the arrival of European colonizers in Africa; the dream that this trade could be restored was unrealistic in the face of French power in north and west Africa.[54]

Equally doomed was the Tripolitanian Republic; lacking any international recognition or protection to compare with British sponsorship of the Sanusiyya, it was hard for the nascent republic to overcome internal disputes effectively enough to resist Italian pressure. The arrival of fascism in 1922 certainly doomed this brief experiment, but in fact it had fought a brutal and costly war for survival from its foundation. The economic weaknesses of the tribal leaders enabled Italy to secretly buy some of them off—even the notoriously anti-Italian Ramadan al-Suwayhili was allegedly in their pay by 1919, enabling him to sustain his Robin Hood-like reputation and keep the loyalty of his many followers.[55] Italy also worked to exploit differences between Arabs and the Berbers of the Nafusa mountain area, including between different branches of Islam. Rivalries between al-Suwayhili and other leaders led to renewed fighting through the summer of 1920, and eventually in August he was killed in battle, depriving the nascent republic of an important and charismatic leader.

[53] In fact, the citizenship status(es) of Libyans continued to be shifting and uncertain throughout the fascist era, see Pergher, *Fascist Borderlands*, ch. 4.
[54] Ali Abdullatif Ahmida, *Forgotten Voices: Power and Agency in Colonial and Postcolonial Libya* (New York: Routledge, 2005), ch. 2.
[55] Anderson, 'The Tripoli Republic', 55.

In November 1920 a conference was held at Gharyan to try to resolve some of the internal differences and build an effective resistance to Italian control; by this time the Republic's leaders had abandoned hope that the *Statuto* would ever be worth more than the paper it was written on. The Berber leader Sulayman al-Baruni, so long a key figure in the resistance, refused to attend and left Libya for good in 1921, eventually settling in Oman. A delegation was sent to Rome by the Gharyan conference to present the Republic's position, but despite spending most of 1921 in Italy it was not received by the government—who had other problems on their minds—succeeding only in meeting some socialist opposition MPs. By July 1922, despairing of achieving effective self-governance, the Tripolitanian leaders resolved to offer the Amirate of Tripolitania to the Sanusiyya; Idris reluctantly accepted, becoming Amir of both provinces, and the brief republican experiment was over.[56] In part this decision was hastened by the fact that the new governor of Tripolitania, Giuseppe Volpi, had almost single-handedly decided to embark on a military reconquest upon his appointment in July 1921. Although appointed by the liberal minister Giovanni Amendola, Volpi's methods were energetic to the point of brutality. It was he who brought Rodolfo Graziani, who the Italians would later know as the 'pacifier of Libya', out to Tripoli for the first time in 1921. Graziani's notoriety was yet to come—the atrocities for which he earned the nickname 'the butcher of Fezzan' lay almost a decade away—but he played an important part in the suppression of the Tripolitanian resistance between 1922 and 1924. The process began in 1921 with Volpi's attack on Misrata, long the stronghold of the resistance, but once al-Sanusi had accepted the Amirship the Italian government had all the excuse it needed to formally launch a full 'reconquest' at the end of 1922, with the enthusiastic support of the new fascist regime. By 1923 Azzam had left Libya and returned to Egypt; most of the republic's leaders were dead or in exile across the Arab world. Deprived of its elite, there was little prospect of Tripolitanian resistance enduring for long into the fascist era.

11.5.2 Cyrenaica

As in Tripolitania, the Italian state granted a new *Statuto* in Cyrenaica in 1919, but unlike in Tripolitania, it was actually implemented—perhaps owing to the closer scrutiny applied by the British thanks to their connection with the Sanusiyya. The *Statuto* was a fine example of how moral rhetoric could dress up political necessity: it was designed as much to win the submission of the restive population as to demonstrate Italy's enlightened credentials. Perhaps the most notable

---

[56] Vandewalle, *A History of Modern Libya*, 28–30.

element of the *Statuto* was the creation of the Cyrenaican parliament, to be located in Benghazi; it included representation for the Jewish population and for nomadic Bedouin.[57] But the concentration of political power there, under the watchful eye of the colonial authorities, was by no means popular with the local tribes, not least since it threatened to replace the traditional centres of political, economic, and social power in the region such as Jaghbub, the traditional Sanusi centre, or Ajdabiya, where Idris al-Sanusi had chosen to base himself since signing the Akrama deal. In the end, the parliament met just five times before it was abolished in 1923.[58]

As in wartime, the Sanusiyya continued to hold most of the cards in the eastern province. In the immediate aftermath of the war, the colonial government was keen to placate Idris al-Sanusi and keep his support, which had become essential in their plan to implement the *Statuto*. Indeed, in September 1919 Italy facilitated Idris in his pilgrimage to Mecca, sending him on board the steamship *Massaua*, under the unlikely escort of the Italian Zionist delegate, naval commander Levi-Bianchini. Levi-Bianchini accompanied him to Jeddah, where he was welcomed by the king of Hedjaz, and then on to Jerusalem to visit the Holy Places there before returning him to Benghazi at the end of October.[59] The new negotiations held between Idris al-Sanusi and the Italian government in 1920 were held in this climate of mutual cooperation, against the backdrop of ideas of 'trusteeship' which greatly bolstered Idris's position. The aim was to update the 1917 Akrama agreement, ensuring al-Sanusi's full authority in all Cyrenaican territories and his full acceptance of Italian sovereignty above him. The Accord of al-Rajma, the fruit of these talks, was signed on 25 October 1920: it granted Idris the title of Amir of Cyrenaica (and a monthly stipend) and recognized him as an emissary of the Italian State. By claiming for itself the right to grant this title, Italy asserted its sovereignty the more clearly; this was also the logical conclusion of the 'policy of notables' which it had embraced since the earliest days in Libya. Idris and the Sanusiyya were to govern the areas around Jaghbub, Kufra, and the other Cyrenaican oases in the interior semi-autonomously, while Italy maintained direct rule in the coastal strip where it had been consolidating its control during the war years. Italy immediately reduced troop numbers in the province by around 10,000 men, a notable saving, on the grounds that the al-Rajma accords significantly reduced the likelihood of armed conflict there.[60]

However, the basis of the agreement was that al-Sanusi would implement the terms of the *Statuto* while assisting Italian infrastructure penetration into the interior. The installation of effective transport and communications infrastructure

[57] Mohammad Suliaman, 'The Impact of the Italian Occupation of Cyrenaica', 62.
[58] Berhe, 'Il fronte meridionale della Grande guerra'.
[59] Minerbi, 'Angelo Levi-Bianchini in Levante', 94–6.
[60] Nicola Labanca, *La guerra italiana per la Libia: 1911–1931* (Bologna: Il Mulino, 2012), 136–7.

was fundamental for any future economic development of the colony and so was Italy's top priority; by contrast many of Idris's own followers were deeply suspicious of this idea, rightly seeing it as a tool of future Italian control and unequal distribution of wealth.[61] Critically, new railways and wells were to pave the way for the creation of new cultivatable areas—ready for Italian agricultural colonists to take over. While on the surface the al-Rajma Accord appeared an example of liberal, quasi-Mandatory colonial governance, it was rather a stepping-stone to much greater control and penetration of the region, rooted in the long-term project of creating a settler colony. Soon al-Sanusi was beginning to lose the support of his own power base; the role of colonial collaborator and intermediary was to prove fraught with difficulty. Not all tribes would accept his leadership if it meant he was pocketing all the economic benefits; if he could not successfully command the allegiance of all the Cyrenaican tribes, he lost his value as an interlocutor in the eyes of the colonial regime. Idris's celebratory tour of Italy at the end of 1920 could not conceal the displeasure of his own sheikhs, many of whom rejected the al-Rajma Accord altogether—along with any further expansion of Italian control into the interior.

By the end of 1921 relations between the Sanusi leader and Italy were decaying; by 1922 they were extremely tense. The colonial regime lost faith in its key intermediary and even flirted briefly with the notion of trying to replace him with his cousin, predecessor, and father-in-law Ahmad al-Sharif, who had left Cyrenaica in 1917. Al-Sharif had made his way to the Ottoman Empire where he became a strong supporter of the new Kemalist government in Ankara; his name was even suggested in some circles as a possible replacement for Mehmed VI as Caliph. This would have represented a great snub to British influence and policy in the region, since it was al-Sharif who had launched the Sanusi war against Britain, whereas Idris al-Sanusi, by contrast, was to some extent their client. Less desirable, from the Italian perspective, was the possibility of improved relations between Cyrenaica and Tripolitania, where al-Sharif was much more popular than his successor, and indeed in 1922 the Tripolitanian Republic first proposed offering the title of Amir to al-Sharif rather than to Idris. The Tripolitanian leaders' reluctant turn to the Sanusiyya shows the status which the brotherhood still held as the main resistance to colonial rule, yet by the end of 1922 Idris's position had in fact grown very weak.

In December 1922 Idris fled into a self-imposed exile in Egypt, where he would remain until 1951 when he reluctantly agreed to become the first (and only) king of a united Libya. The Cyrenaican parliament was suspended in 1923, and the experiment of 'enlightened' Italian rule through local Sanusi power was officially at an end. Informally, negotiations of various kinds would continue with the

---

[61] Ryan, *Religion as Resistance*, 116–20.

Sanusiyya for several more years, until Italian policy took a decisive turn towards violence. Idris al-Sanusi's followers, led and inspired by the celebrated 'Lion of the Desert', Omar al-Mukhtar, would continue to fight for their freedom for the next decade, in an increasingly brutal and unequal war against fascist Italy. The so-called pacification of Libya under Rodolfo Graziani lasted until 1932, devastating the countryside and interning huge numbers of civilians in concentration camps. An estimated 25 per cent of the Cyrenaican population were killed in the process, many by execution, others in battle, or through starvation and thirst.[62] Once al-Mukhtar had been captured and hanged in 1931, the resistance was largely at an end, paving the way—in theory—for the mass settlement of poor Italians which had been planned ever since 1911.

11.5.3 East Africa

The war's impact in East Africa had been primarily indirect, and so too were its consequences. Djibouti—the most important and ambitious of all Italy's object-ives in the region—was to remain a pipe-dream.[63] Indeed so far from being willing to give the colony up, France would hang on to Djibouti for longer than almost any of its other possessions, until 1977.

The colonial party's ambitions for Eritrea included the region of Kassala—one of the most fertile regions of Sudan, with an important cotton-growing industry. An Anglo-Italian agreement of 15 April 1891 had permitted a temporary Italian occupation of the Kassala region, which had ended in 1897; now Italy sought to reclaim this territory and incorporate it fully into Eritrea.[64] This was one strand in the plan to create an unchallenged sphere of influence in Ethiopia, by controlling all its trade outlets. This also required control of its waterways and ports, which was the justification behind the Italian claim to the river port of Kismayo and its hinterland, generally known as TransJuba. The Juba river controlled access to Italian Somalia as well as forming the border with British East Africa; Kismayo had been in British hands since the 1891 Anglo-Italian agreement, but now Italy sought to control both sides of the river.[65] George Beer noted that the claims for Libyan borderlands, Kassala, and TransJuba 'command the unanimous sup-port of the colonial party', whereas the more ambitious goals—Djibouti, British Somaliland—were not universally embraced. TransJuba was an area which had been explored by Italians in the late nineteenth century and which some

---

[62] The fullest account from an Italian perspective is Angelo Del Boca, *Dal fascismo a Gheddafi*, vol. 2, in *Gli italiani in Libia*, 2 vols (Bari: Laterza, 1986).

[63] See Francesco Salata, *Il Nodo di Gibuti: storia diplomatica su documenti inediti* (Milan: Istituto per gli Studi di Politica Internazionale, 1939).

[64] Beer, *African Questions at the Paris Peace Conference*, 396.

[65] Beer, *African Questions at the Paris Peace Conference*, 397.

consequently considered a morally and historically legitimate target. It was also an area of relatively little interest to Britain; Alfred Milner, the British secretary of state for the colonies, assured Colosimo in January 1919 that it should be possible to do a deal. However, the initial British offer made in September—a relatively narrow strip of land along the river—was considered 'unacceptable' by Tittoni. In March 1920 the British made a more generous offer; Italy pushed for still more land, but simultaneously were negotiating over the Cyrenaica–Egypt border, and could not afford to risk losing out there. The two negotiations became linked, and when Britain declared the negotiations closed in a note on 31 March 1920 there was not much for Italy to do but to acquiesce.[66]

These agreements, made in 1919–20, would not be fully implemented until 1924–5, as talks dragged on over issues which were tricky but not important enough to either side to prioritize an urgent agreement (possession of certain wells; nomads' travel routes). In Cyrenaica, Italy was confirmed in its possession of both Kufra and the oasis of Jaghbub—birthplace of Idris and the Sanusi heartland (although the gulf of Sollum remained in Egyptian hands). In East Africa, the British were keen to link the Kismayo settlement to changes in the status of the Dodecanese, which the Italians were equally determined to avoid. Consequently, although the basic outline of these agreements was widely known, the formal treaty was only signed in July 1924, and ratified the following year.[67] Popular sentiment in Italy credited Mussolini for unblocking the negotiations, but in reality, it was British desire to get the business over at long last which seems to have done most to finally resolve the impasse.[68] This new 'fascist colony' was in fact the fruit of liberal Italy's earlier policies and negotiations. TransJuba was duly incorporated into Italian Somalia just a year later.

In December 1925 another Anglo-Italian exchange of notes included British acknowledgement of Italian interests in Ethiopia, though the negative reaction of the Ethiopian government meant that nothing concrete came of this initiative.[69] Italy was greatly concerned about the arms trade in East Africa, backing several proposals to limit the transport and sale of arms to Ethiopia; the dream of one day returning to the assault there had not died. In the event, the completion of the 'pacification' of Libya in 1932 marked the beginning of Fascist planning for the

[66] Giampaolo Novati, 'L'annessione dell'Oltregiuba nella politica coloniale italiana', *Africa: Rivista trimestrale di studi e documentazione dell'Istituto italiano per l'Africa e l'Oriente* 40, no. 2 (1985): 225–8.
[67] Great Britain Treaty Series, Italy, No. 1 (1924). Although only formalized in 1924–5, the negotiations were undertaken in 1919–20. (For example, the 1921 *Statesman's Yearbook* announced a supposed Anglo-Italian Agreement of May 1920—pp. 1029–31.) In February 1924 debates in the British parliament suggested some elements were still unresolved and should be linked to a new settlement for the Dodecanese. See Lawrence Martin, ed., *The Treaties of Peace, 1919–1923...Maps Compiled Especially for This Edition and a Summary of the Legal Basis of the New Boundaries by Lt.-Col. Lawrence Martin* (New York: Carnegie endowment for international peace, 1924), vol. 1, xviii, fn.2. The Hansard debates over TransJuba in 1925 mention that these agreements 'were made in 1919–1920'.
[68] Novati, 'L'annessione dell'Oltregiuba'.
[69] Great Britain, *British and Foreign State Papers*, vol. 121 (1925), 805.

1935 invasion of Ethiopia. This war clearly followed the model already established in the liberal era, in which the projection of grandeur was paramount, as Laura Cerasi's analysis suggests:

> The seeming irrationality of the assault on Ethiopia is still striking. Putting out a force of half a million men, and committing most of the available military and material resources, in order to construct a belated, unstable and financially unprofitable empire, must have been rooted in a conception of power and strength that was inextricably linked to the imperial image.[70]

Liberal imperialism was also pursued in just such an 'irrational', 'belated, unstable and [...] unprofitable' way, and with similar underpinnings.

The arrival of the fascist regime is generally seen as marking a decisive shift in colonial policy. The new minister of the colonies, long-term nationalist leader Luigi Federzoni, promoted an approach which was based on direct rule explicitly underpinned by violence, and within which Italian prestige was defined in terms of both ethno-cultural and military superiority. But this apparent transformation of policy in fact conceals both the presence of ruthless repressive violence prior to 1922 and the continuity, at local levels, of many liberal-era governance practices well into the 1920s, including collaboration with, and reliance on, local power-brokers. Even after this supposed transformation of colonial style, the upper echelons of the fascist hierarchy were still concerned with the need to build a stronger culture of colonialism among settlers and officials well into the late 1920s.[71] As Eileen Ryan writes, 'it seems more useful to think of the Italian approach to colonial rule as shifting along a continuum of violence instead of switching from one mode to the other'.[72]

11.6 The Aftermath of War and Italy's Unfulfilled Desires

The mutilated victory was not only a national but an imperial affliction. Pre-war ambitions had grown more extensive during the war, boosting a sense of Italian entitlement to compete as a global colonial power in Africa and in Asia. Yet if Italy's colonial fantasies were so extensive, why did it not do more to put them into practice? In February 1919 Charles Hardinge, with all the lofty assurance of a former Viceroy of India, wrote that:

---

[70] Cerasi, 'Empires Ancient and Modern', 432.
[71] Eileen Ryan, 'Violence and the Politics of Prestige: The Fascist Turn in Colonial Libya', *Modern Italy* 20, no. 2 (3 April 2015): 123–35, 124, DOI: 10.1080/13532944.2015.1024214.
[72] Ryan, 'Violence and the Politics of Prestige', 131–2.

Their incapacity and vanity are extraordinary, and when one comes to think that they have never yet been able to administer or to finance any colony in their possession it really seems grotesque to add more to their undigested possessions. As it is they will have a considerable chunk of Anatolia but nevertheless they still want huge squares of Africa, and one asks oneself where is the money to come from, especially in view of the enormous debt which is hanging like a millstone round Italy's neck.[73]

Leaving aside the snarky commentary, his observation about the costs of colonial expansion was highly pertinent. Quite apart from the perennial problem of international rivalries, and what they did or did not permit Italy to contemplate, money was the eternal problem. Colonial organizations repeatedly requested state funding, highlighting opportunities abroad. In July 1919, for instance, the Camera di Commercio Italiana per l'Estremo Oriente (Italian Chamber of Commerce for the Far East) noted that China was really the only East Asian market left open to Italy, since British imperial preference blocked access to India; they established a direct shipping link to Shanghai and urged the creation of an Italian Bank for China, though their efforts to claim Austria-Hungary's concession in Tianjin were unsuccessful. The following year, the Società Coloniale per l'Africa Occidentale (Colonial Society for West Africa) wrote to Nitti seeking legislative and above all financial assistance to take up options in Portuguese Angola and to extend Italian shipping links with the south-western coast. What links these two cases was the urgent need for state investment; while individual and collective private investment did exist, it was insufficient. The Italian economy did not yet produce a sufficient surplus of capital to exploit all the opportunities which colonialists identified, and while the state played a major role—as in all late-entry colonizers—it too lacked the funds to really maximize the potential of these colonial endeavours. Both these pleas for investment went unfulfilled. Once again, we see that without the wealth of established empire, it was hard for an aspiring empire to compete in the early twentieth century.

---

[73] BOD Rennell Rodd Correspondence 20–1919: Hardinge to Rennell Rodd, 19 May 1919.

12

Conclusion

Alone of all the victorious Entente powers, the Italian state failed within just a few
years of the war. In certain respects—revolutionary activism of both left and right,
paramilitary violence, and extreme nationalism—the Italian post-war experience
more closely resembled that of the defeated empires of eastern and central Europe
than that of its allies France or Britain. Italy's experience of the war transformed
public life and paved the way for the failure of the Liberal State. But in many
regards, Italy's war experience shared key elements with its Entente partners: like
France and Britain, it fought as an empire, albeit a Liberal one, with all the
attendant racial and cultural beliefs which that entailed; imperial and colonial
concerns influenced its decision for and conduct of the war; and at the conflict's
end it sought to maximize its own territorial gains. Italy drew on the human and
economic resources of its overseas colonies, both formal and informal, and
engaged in military operations within its existing colonies and in pursuit of new
ones. Its global ambitions would be almost entirely unfulfilled, but it is nonetheless
essential to take seriously both the realities of Italian empire and the grandiose
schemes for its further expansion.

12.1 Rhetorics and Realities of Empire

The end of the Liberal regime marks an important turning point in the history of
Italian colonialism—the demise of the liberal emigrant model, in which diaspora
communities were still colonies, in favour of a more conventional vision based
solely on direct territorial control. From 1922 the Fascist regime would work to
discourage emigration and redirect surplus population towards colonial settlements under Italian rule. Ethiopia in particular was designed to complete the
creation of 'an *impero del lavoro* (an empire founded on labour), East Africa being
the (new) ideal destination for all those poor Italians who had been prevented
from emigrating to America'.[1] Settler colonies were also intended to proactively
Italianize lands and peoples to build a fascist future. What part did the First World
War play in this change? It is unarguable that the global diaspora made important
contributions to the Italian war effort, but it is equally clear that the value of these

---

[1] Srivastava, *Italian Colonialism and Resistances to Empire*, 29.

The Italian Empire and the Great War. Vanda Wilcox, Oxford University Press (2021). © Vanda Wilcox.
DOI: 10.1093/oso/9780198822943.003.0012

contributions was largely disappointing to many nationalists at home. The rhetoric of what Mark Choate terms the 'emigrant nation' had failed to fully convince Italians; when put to the test by the war, this model did not provide the kind of benefits which direct-rule colonies could offer. The strength which France and Britain gained from their vast empires was amply demonstrated during the conflict and at the peace conference, and from a nationalist perspective the lesson for future colonial development was clear.

Though Italians tended to blame the great powers, Italy's wartime imperial fantasies were to remain unrealized chiefly due to its own errors and weakness, and to the determination of their adversaries. One characteristic error was the failure to consider the reactions and agency of prospective colonial subjects. In 1911 the Italian army made serious strategic errors as a result of poor intelligence about the Libyan population during the invasion, and throughout the years that followed was unable to dominate the region as it had hoped. The anti-colonial resistance of Tripolitania and Cyrenaica was able to effectively ally with the Central Powers to fight against Italy throughout the war. Equally, the plan to colonize a portion of Anatolia failed to consider that this was not a remote periphery of the Ottoman Empire, waiting to be picked off, but a part of the Turkish imperial core (unlike French and British projects in Syria and Mesopotamia). The selection of this region as a prospect for Italian rule was doubly unrealistic—it relied on a false estimation of Italian means but also of Turkish sentiment and agency. Underpinning these miscalculations were deep-seated cultural scripts about Italian identity in terms of both nation and state: Italians perceived themselves as a racially superior white nation whose state embodied Risorgimento values of liberty and unity. The fact that in the late nineteenth and early twentieth century there was considerable anxiety about the validity of both assumptions did not prevent them from governing Italy's outlook through the era of the First World War. On the contrary, the war was welcomed as an opportunity to demonstrate and affirm these truths.

The failure to do so was often due to concrete practical problems, which underpinned the damaging impact of these false beliefs. In Italian there is an idiom which roughly translates to 'easier said than done': 'tra il dire e il fare c'è di mezzo il mare'—between saying and doing lies the sea. Between Italian rhetoric and the reality of colonial power there was indeed, quite literally, the sea, making life extremely difficult. Italy simply did not have the resources to compete financially, in real military and naval power, or in terms of social and political stability at home. Commenting on this phenomenon in 1928, the communist politician (and First World War veteran) Ruggiero Grieco called this 'the paradox of an artificial empire, an empire that does not give to the metropole but is sustained by the metropole'.[2] Even where the empire might have contributed more—as with the *ascari* soldiers who could have been sent to serve at the front—political anxieties and insecurities prevented Italy from acting as imperialists would have wished. The political system was too unstable, internal social tensions too high to be able to project power abroad as they wished to, to compete on a level playing field with France and Britain or even to fill the void which Austria's decline had left. Without the wealth of empire, it was no longer possible to acquire an empire.

Another paradox emerges in analysing the fate of Italy's Balkan aspirations: it might have been better for Italy had Austria-Hungary survived the war. Lands possessed by a defeated enemy might more readily have been transferred to them, whereas the newly independent 'national' kingdom of Yugoslavia was destined to prove an unsurmountable obstacle to Italian expansionist plans. The post-war occupations through which Italy endeavoured to pursue its dreams were a complete failure—in the words of Raoul Pupo, 'a deployment of men and means which was as burdensome as it was politically useless'.[3] Indeed there can be little doubt that just as the domestic political and social crisis contributed to the failure of these grandiose schemes, the persistent commitment of resources to these policies only worsened economic problems at home and thus the overall frailty of the liberal state.

The gulf between Italian ambitions and resources, between the rhetoric and reality of Italian empire, has long been regarded outside the country as either faintly comical or as a sign of chronic braggadocio. This tendency was acute at the Peace Conference, where Balfour remarked that 'The Italians must somehow be mollified, and the only question is how to mollify them at the smallest cost to mankind'; even the Italophile ambassador Rennell Rodd commented that they were both 'excessively reluctant to venture and nevertheless extremely grasping' and 'readily encouraged by a little success or flattery'.[4] Bismarck's infamous comment that Italy had 'a large appetite and rotten teeth' springs to mind. Italian politicians sometimes appear wilfully unrealistic in these judgements. But to treat the Italian empire as, at least in part, a rhetorical construct may offer a new insight: could rhetoric bring about reality? Might a discourse of colonialism eventually bring real colonies in its train? Even if the rhetoric were largely empty much of the time, it might have a generative power: many nationalists knew that it was impossible to achieve their goals immediately, but the discourse itself might help to produce the circumstances in which they one day could do so. Imperial(ist) rhetoric might increase respect for Italian great power status, from allies, enemies, and subject peoples alike. Being treated like a great power might, in

[2] Cited in Srivastava, *Italian Colonialism and Resistances to Empire*, 40.
[3] Pupo, *La Vittoria Senza Pace*.
[4] Balfour, Memorandum of 16 May 1919, reproduced in Albrecht-Carrié, *Italy at the Paris Peace Conference*; BOD Rennell Rodd Correspondence 20–1919: Rennell Rodd, letter to Secretary of State, 22 March 1919.

turn, make it easier to act like one. It is easy to dismiss such geopolitical magical thinking, but a serious examination of the relationship between rhetoric and reality in Fascist Italy suggests that it had a significant political force. Moreover, imperial habits of mind—including a racialized approach to military and civilian governance—strongly influenced wartime practices; even a fantasy empire could thus help shape reality.

Throughout the period 1911–24 Italy pursued an opportunistic approach to a consistent policy goal: territorial expansion. Whether in the form of supposedly national territories, direct-rule settler colonies, or an informal empire of 'spheres of influence', expansionism united multiple parties and actors. The myth of the 'mutilated victory' obscures the reality that some of these goals were indeed achieved; the grandiose scale of Italian imperial fantasy perhaps made a perception of failure almost inevitable. Liberal Italy's imperial dreams reached their climax in the First World War, but it ultimately proved better at building castles in the air than garrisons in the desert.

Bibliography

Archival Sources

Archivio Centrale dello Stato, Rome (ACS)
Archivio Antonio Salandra
Archivio Francesco Saverio Nitti
Fondo Giovanni Ameglio
Presidenza del Consiglio dei Ministri (PCM), Fondo Guerra Europea 1915–18 (GE)

Archivio Storico del Ministero degli Affari Esteri, Rome (ASMAE)
Consolato Generale di Gerusalemme
Rappresentanza Diplomatica in Egitto

Archivio Ufficio Storico Stato Maggiore dell'Esercito, Rome (AUSSME)
Fondo E1, E2, E3; F3; L8; Libia

Unione delle Comunità Ebraiche Italiane, Centro Bibliografico, Rome (UCEI)
Archivio Consorzio (AC)

Bodleian Library Special Collections, Oxford (BOD)
James Rennell Rodd, Private Papers
Milner Papers

Biblioteca di Storia Moderna e Contemporanea, Rome (BSMC)
Miscellaneous collections

Published Primary Sources

'A Letter from an Italian Reservist', *The Century Magazine* (December 1917).
Acquaviva, Savino. *L'avvenire coloniale d'Italia e la guerra*. Rome: Atheneum, 1917.
Adriacus. *Da Trieste a Valona: il problema adriatico e i diritti dell'Italia*. Milan: Alfieri & Lacroix, 1918.
Agreement between France, Russia, Great Britain and Italy. Signed in London April 26, 1915. London: His Majesty's Stationery Office, 1915.
Baccich, Icilio. *Fiume, il Quarnero e gli interessi d'Italia nel'Adriatico*. Turin: L'Ora presente, 1915.
Beer, George Louis. *African Questions at the Paris Peace Conference, with Papers on Egypt, Mesopotamia, and the Colonial Settlement*. New York: Macmillan, 1923.
Bottini, Ezio. 'La preparazione alla guerra e l'educazione militare della gioventù in Italia'. *Rivista Militare Italiana* 59, no. 2 (1914): 278–304.
Cadorna, Luigi. *La guerra alla fronte italiana (24 maggio 1915–9 novembre 1917)*. Milan: Fratelli Treves, 1921.

Campolieti, Nicola Maria. 'La disciplina militare e la disciplina del lavoro sociale'. *Nuova Rivista di Fanteria* VII, no. 5 (1914): 440–53.

Comitato Italo-Turco. *La pace con la Turchia al Congresso di San Remo*. Milan: Stab. Tip. Stucchi, Ceretti & C., 1920.

Consiglio, Placido. 'Medicina Sociale nell'esercito. Saggi di psicopatologia e di scienza criminale nei militari'. *Rivista Militare Italiana* 59, no. 10 (1914): 2906–20.

Consiglio, Placido. 'La rigenerazione fisica e morale della razza mediante l'esercito'. *Rivista Militare Italiana* 61, no. 1 (1916): 23–51.

'Convention Between the United States and Italy Providing for Reciprocal Military Service'. *The American Journal of International Law* 13, no. 2 (1 April 1919): 147–9.

Corradini, Enrico. *Sopra le vie del nuovo impero: dall'emigrazione di Tunisi alla guerra nell'Egeo*. Milan: Fratelli Treves, 1912.

Dainelli, Giotto. *La Dalmazia, sua italianità, suo valore per la libertà d'Italia nell'Adriatico*. Genoa: A.F. Formiggini, 1915.

D'Andrea, Giuseppe, ed. *Atti del convegno nazionale coloniale (Napoli 26–28 aprile 1917)*, Società africana d'Italia. Naples: A. Trani, 1917.

D'Annunzio, Gabriele. *Per la più grande Italia: Orazioni e messaggi*. Milan: Fratelli Treves, 1915.

D'Annunzio, Gabriele. *Contro uno e contro tutti*. Rome: Presso la Fionda, 1919.

Di Aichelburg, Errardo. 'Gli ascari d'Italia'. *Rivista Militare Italiana* 59, no. 4 (1914): 743–68.

Einaudi, Luigi. *Un principe mercante: studio sulla espansione coloniale italiana*. Turin: Fratelli Bocca, 1900.

Fidel, Camille. *Problèmes coloniaux italiens: le Congrès colonial de Naples, 26, 27 et 28 avril 1917: documents annexés*. Paris: Édition de la Société des études coloniales et maritimes, 1918.

Fileti, Vincenzo. *La concessione italiana di Tien-Tsin*. Genoa: Barabino e Graeve, 1921.

Fronte Macedone 1916–18. 'Tenente Raffaele Merendi', http://www.frontemacedone.com/tenente-raffaele-merendi.html (accessed 11 November 2019).

Gatti, Angelo. *Caporetto: Diario di Guerra*. Bologna: Il Mulino, 1964.

Giacone, Pietro. 'Educazione o istruzione militare?' *Rivista Militare Italiana* 59, no. 4 (1914): 792–801.

Great Britain. *British and Foreign State Papers*. Vol. 121 (1925).

Hailu, Gebreyesus. *The Conscript: A Novel of Libya's Anticolonial War*. Athens, OH: Ohio University Press, 2012.

Istituto Coloniale Italiano. *Atti del secondo congresso degli Italiani all'Estero (11–20 giugno 1911)*. Rome: Tip. Editrice Nazionale, 1911.

Istituto Coloniale Italiano. *Atti del Convegno nazionale coloniale per il dopo guerra delle colonie: Roma, 15–21 gennaio 1919; relazioni, comunicazioni e resoconti delle sedute*. Rome: Unione editrice, 1920.

Italia. *L'Emigrazione italiana...Relaziona presentata a S. E. il Ministro degli-affari esteri dal Commissario generale dell'emigrazione*. Rome: Commissariato generale dell'emigrazione, n.d.

Italia. Camera dei Deputati. *Atti Parlamentari*. Legislatura XXIV, 1913–1918. Rome: Tipografia della Camera dei deputati, 1918.

Italia. Camera dei Deputati. 'XXIV Legislatura Del Regno d'Italia / Lavori/Camera Dei Deputati – Portale Storico', https://storia.camera.it/lavori/regno-d-italia/leg-regno-XXIV/ (accessed 31 October 2019).

Italia. Ministero degli Affari Esteri. *I documenti diplomatici italiani*. [DDI] *Quinta Serie, 1914-1918*. XI vols. Rome: Istituto Poligrafico e Zecca dello Stato, n.d.

Italia. Ministero degli Affari Esteri. *I documenti diplomatici italiani*. [DDI] *Sesta Serie, 1919-1922*. IV vols. Rome: Istituto Poligrafico e Zecca dello Stato, n.d.

Italia. Ministero della Guerra. *Militari Caduti nella Guerra Nazionale 1915-1918: Albo d' Oro*. 28 vols. Rome: Istituto Poligrafico dello Stato Libreria, 1926.

Italia. Segretario per gli Affari Civili d'Albania. *Relazione sulla gestione dei servizi civili*. Vlorë: R. Officina Tip. Italiana, 1920.

Keynes, John Maynard. *The Economic Consequences of the Peace*. New York: Harcourt, Brace and Howe, 1920.

Lloyd George, David. *British War Aims. Statement by the Right Honourable David Lloyd George [. . .]. Authorized Version as published by the British Government*. New York: George H. Doran, 1918.

Lucatelli, Luigi. *Il volto della guerra*. Rome: M. Carra, 1913.

Moravec, Zdenko. *L'Italie et les Yougoslaves. Avec un exposé des relations Italo-Yougoslaves pendant la guerre et des documents à l'appui*. Paris: Imprimerie Lang, Blanchong et Cie, 1919.

Mortara, Giorgio. *Dati sulla giustizia e disciplina militare*. Rome: Provveditore generale dello stato, 1929.

Mussolini, Benito. *Il mio diario di guerra (1915-1917) con 10 illustrazioni fuori testo*. Milan: Imperia, 1923.

Mussolini, Benito. *The Doctrine of Fascism*. Florence: Vallecchi, 1935.

Mussolini, Benito. *Opera omnia di Benito Mussolini*. Edited by Edoardo Susmel and Duilio Susmel. 35 vols. Florence: La Fenice, 1951.

Orsini, Adolfo. 'Tripoli e Pentapoli'. *Rivista Militare Italiana* 56, no. 12 (1911): 2589-604.

Piazza, Giuseppe. *La nostra pace coloniale: l'Italia e l'alleanza in Oriente e in Africa*. Rome: Ausonia, 1917.

Plate, Federico. *Ricerche chimico-minerarie eseguite in Albania: relazione*. Vlorë: R. Officina Tip. Italiana, 1919.

'Primo esperimento d'impiego della manodopera libica in Italia'. *Bollettino del Comitato centrale di mobilitazione industriale*, no. 8-9 (febbraio–marzo 1918).

Salandra, Antonio. *I discorsi della guerra con alcune note*. Milan: Fratelli Treves, 1922.

Samama, Nissim. *Contributo allo studio della doppia cittadinanza nei riguardi del movimento migratorio*. Florence: Tip. E. Ariani, 1910.

Samama, Nissim. *Il problema della cittadinanza specialmente nei rapporti degli italiani all'estero: Tema primo (Istituto coloniale italiano. Secondo Congresso degli italiani all'estero (Roma, giugno 1911), sezione I, legislazione)*. Florence: Tip. E. Ariani, 1911.

'Statistica sulla leva della classe del 1891'. *Rivista Militare Italiana* 59, no. 7-8 (1914): 2290-300, 2468-78.

Tamaro, Attilio. *L'Adriatico, golfo d'Italia. L'Italianità di Trieste*. Milan: Fratelli Treves, 1915.

Ufficio Storico, Corpo di stato maggiore, ed. *L'esercito italiano nella Grande Guerra, 1915-1918* [IOH—Italian Official History]. *Vol. VII. Operazioni fuori del territorio nazionale. t.1: Il Corpo di Spedizione Italiano in Estremo Oriente*. Rome: Provveditorato generale dello stato libreria, 1934.

Ufficio Storico, Corpo di stato maggiore, ed. *L'esercito italiano nella Grande Guerra, 1915-1918. Vol. VII. Operazioni fuori del territorio nazionale. t.2: Soldati d'Italia in terra di Francia*. Rome: Provveditorato generale dello stato libreria, 1951.

Ufficio Storico, Corpo di stato maggiore, ed. *L'esercito italiano nella Grande Guerra, 1915–1918. Vol. VII. Operazioni fuori del territorio nazionale. t.3: Albania— Macedonia—Medio Oriente.* Rome: Provveditorato generale dello stato libreria, 1983.

Vaccarisi, Achille. 'Importanza dell'odierna espansione coloniale'. *Rivista Militare Italiana* 56, no. 8 (1911): 1685–702.

Secondary Sources

Acquarone, Alberto. 'Politica estera e organizzazione del consenso nell'età giolittiana: il Congresso dell'Asmara e la fondazione dell'Istituto coloniale italiano'. *Storia contemporanea* VIII (1977): 57–119.

Ahmida, Ali Abdullatif. *Forgotten Voices: Power and Agency in Colonial and Postcolonial Libya.* New York: Routledge, 2005.

Ahmida, Ali Abdullatif. 'When the Subaltern Speak: Memory of Genocide in Colonial Libya 1929 to 1933'. *Italian Studies* 61, no. 2 (2006): 175–90, DOI: https://doi.org/10.1179/007516306X142924.

Ahmida, Ali Abdullatif. *The Making of Modern Libya: State Formation, Colonization, and Resistance, Second Edition.* Albany, NY: SUNY Press, 2011.

Albanese, Giulia. *La marcia su Roma.* Rome: Laterza, 2006.

Albanese, Giulia. 'Demobilisation and Political Violence in Italy, 1918–1922'. In *Italy in the Era of the Great War,* edited by Vanda Wilcox, 232–52. Leiden: Brill, 2018. DOI: https://doi.org/10.1163/9789004363724_013.

Albrecht-Carrié, René. *Italy at the Paris Peace Conference.* New York: Columbia University Press, 1938.

Andall, Jacqueline, ed. *Italian Colonialism: Historical Perspectives.* Special Issue, *Journal of Modern Italian Studies* 8, no. 3 (2003), DOI: https://doi.org/10.1080/09585170320000113734.

Anderson, Lisa. 'The Tripoli Republic, 1918–1922'. In *Social & Economic Development of Libya,* edited by E. George H. Joffé and Keith Stanley McLachlan, 43–65. Wisbech: Middle East & North African Studies Press, 1982.

Andurain, Julie d', and Colette Zytnicki, eds. *Les Empires dans la Grande Guerre.* Special Issue. *Outre-Mers. Revue d'histoire* 390–91 (2016).

Arielli, Nir. *Fascist Italy and the Middle East, 1933–40.* Basingstoke and New York: Palgrave Macmillan, 2010.

Arielli, Nir. 'Hopes and Jealousies: Rome's Ambitions in the Middle East and the Italian Contingent in Palestine, 1915–1920'. In *Palestine and World War I: Grand Strategy, Military Tactics and Culture in War,* edited by Yigal Sheffy, Haim Goren, and Eran Dolev, 43–56. London: I. B. Tauris, 2014.

Atkinson, David. 'Geographical Imaginations, Public Education and the Everyday Worlds of Fascist Italy'. *Journal of Modern Italian Studies* 18, no. 5 (2013): 561–79, DOI: https://doi.org/10.1080/1354571X.2013.839487.

Azzi, Stephen Corrado. 'The Historiography of Fascist Foreign Policy'. *The Historical Journal* 36, no. 1 (1993): 187–203.

Balbirnie, Steven. 'Small War on a Violent Frontier: Colonial Warfare and British Intervention in Northern Russia, 1918–1919'. In *Small Nations and Colonial Peripheries in World War I,* edited by Gearóid Barry, Enrico Dal Lago, and Róisín Healy, 193–210. Leiden: Brill, 2016. DOI: https://doi.org/10.1163/9789004310018_013

Baldinetti, Anna. *The Origins of the Libyan Nation: Colonial Legacy, Exile and the Emergence of a New Nation-State*. London: Routledge, 2014.

Baldoli, Claudia. 'Catholic Neutralism and the Peasant Protest against War, 1914–1918'. In *Italy in the Era of the Great War*, edited by Vanda Wilcox, 210–31. Leiden: Brill, 2018. DOI: https://doi.org/10.1163/9789004363724_012.

Ballinger, Pamela. 'History's "Illegibles": National Indeterminacy in Istria'. *Austrian History Yearbook* 43 (2012): 116–37.

Banti, Alberto Mario. *La nazione del Risorgimento. Parentela, santità e onore alle origini dell'Italia unita*. Turin: Einaudi, 2011.

Barr, James. *A Line in the Sand: Britain, France and the Struggle That Shaped the Middle East*. London: Simon and Schuster, 2011.

Bartolini, Stefano. *Fascismo antislavo: il tentativo di bonifica etnica al confine nordorientale*. Pistoia: Istituto storico della Resistenza e della società contemporanea nella provincia di Pistoia, 2008.

Bassi, Gabriele, Nicola Labanca, and Enrico Sturani. *Libia. Una guerra coloniale italiana*. Rovereto (TN): Museo Storico Italiano della Guerra, 2011.

Battaglia, Antonello. *Da Suez Ad Aleppo: La campagna alleata e il distaccamento italiano in Siria e Palestina (1917–1921)*. Rome: Edizioni Nuova cultura, 2015.

Bechelloni, Antonio. 'De Petites Italies au service d'une Plus Grande Italie?' In *Les petites Italies dans le monde*, edited by Marie-Claude Blanc-Chaléard, Antonio Bechelloni, Bénédicte Deschamps, Michel Dreyfus, and Eric Vial, 339–51. Rennes: Presses Univ. de Rennes, 2007.

Becker, Jared. *Nationalism and Culture: Gabriele D'Annunzio and Italy After the Risorgimento*. New York: Peter Lang, 1994.

Bego, Fabio. 'The Vlora Conflict from a Trans-Adriatic Perspective'. In *Myths and Mythical Spaces: Conditions and Challenges for History Textbooks in Albania and South-Eastern Europe*, edited by Claudia Lichnofsky, Enriketa Pandelejmoni, and Darko Stojanov, 97–136. Göttingen: V&R unipress GmbH, 2017.

Belzer, Allison Scardino. *Women and the Great War: Femininity under Fire in Italy*. New York: Palgrave Macmillan, 2010.

Ben-Ghiat, Ruth. 'Modernity Is Just Over There'. *Interventions* 8, no. 3 (2006): 380–93, DOI: https://doi.org/10.1080/13698010600955883.

Ben-Ghiat, Ruth, and Mia Fuller, eds. *Italian Colonialism*. Basingstoke: Palgrave Macmillan, 2005.

Ben-Ghiat, Ruth, and Stephanie Malia Hom, eds. *Italian Mobilities*. London and New York: Routledge 2015.

Berhe, Simona. *Notabili libici e funzionari italiani: L'amministrazione coloniale in Tripolitania (1912–1919)*. Soveria Mannelli: Rubbettino, 2015.

Berhe, Simona. 'Neutralità in Italia e guerra in colonia: il primo conflitto mondiale in Libia (1914–1915)'. In *L'Italia neutrale 1914–1915*, edited by Giovanni Orsina and Andrea Ungari. Rome: Rodorigo editore, 2016.

Berhe, Simona. 'Il fronte meridionale della Grande guerra: la Libia come teatro del primo conflitto mondiale'. *Nuova Rivista Storica* 101, no. 3 (2017): 797–828.

Bernini, Simone. 'Documenti sulla repressione italiana in Libia agli inizi della colonizzazione (1911–1918)'. In *Un nodo: immagini e documenti sulla repressione coloniale italiana in Libia*, edited by Nicola Labanca. Manduria: Lacaita, 2002.

Bertagna, Federica. 'Nazionalismo da esportazione: la guerra di Libia sulla stampa italiana in Argentina e Brasile – A.S.E.I.' *A.S.E.I. ARCHIVIO STORICO DELL'EMIGRAZIONE*

ITALIANA (2012), https://www.asei.eu/it/2012/03/nazionalismo-da-esportazione-la-guerra-di-libia-sulla-stampa-italiana-in-argentina-e-brasile/.

Bianchi, Roberto. 'Social Conflict and Control, Protest and Repression (Italy)'. *1914–1918-Online International Encyclopedia of the First World War*, edited by Ute Daniel, Peter Gatrell, Oliver Janz, Heather Jones, Jennifer Keene, Alan Kramer, and Bill Nasson. Berlin: Freie Universität Berlin, 2014. https://encyclopedia.1914-1918-online.net/art icle/social_conflict_and_control_protest_and_repression_italy. DOI: https://doi.org/10. 15463/IE1418.10367.

Borgogni, Massimo. *Tra continuità e incertezza: Italia e Albania (1914–1939). La strategia politico-militare dell'Italia in Albania fino all'operazione 'Oltre Mare Tirana'*. Milan: FrancoAngeli, 2007.

Borutta, Manuel, and Sakis Gekas. 'A Colonial Sea: The Mediterranean, 1798–1956'. *European Review of History: Revue Européenne d'histoire* 19, no. 1 (2012): 1–13, DOI: https://doi.org/10.1080/13507486.2012.643609.

Bosworth, Richard J. B. *Italy, the Least of the Great Powers: Italian Foreign Policy before the First World War*. Cambridge: Cambridge University Press, 1979.

Bosworth, Richard J. B. *The Italian Dictatorship: Problems and Perspectives in the Interpretation of Mussolini and Fascism*. London: Bloomsbury Academic, 1998.

Bosworth, Richard J. B., and Giuseppe Finaldi. 'The Italian Empire'. In *Empires at War*, edited by Robert Gerwarth and Erez Manela, 34–51. Oxford: Oxford University Press, 2014. DOI: https://doi.org/10.1093/acprof:oso/9780198702511.003.0003.

Bosworth, Richard J. B., and Sergio Romano. *La politica estera italiana*. Bologna: Il Mulino, 1991.

Botchway, De-Valera N. Y. M., and Kwame Osei Kwarteng, eds. *Africa and the First World War: Remembrance, Memories and Representations after 100 Years*. Newcastle: Cambridge Scholars, 2018.

Brady, Sean. 'From Peacetime to Wartime: The Sicilian Province of Catania and Italian Intervention in the Great War, June 1914–September 1915'. In *Other Combatants, Other Fronts: Competing Histories of the First World War*, edited by Alisa Miller, Laura Rowe, and James Kitchen. Newcastle: Cambridge Scholars, 2011.

Bresciani, Marco. 'The Post-Imperial Space of the Upper Adriatic and the Post-War Ascent of Fascism'. In *Akteure der Neuordnung: Ostmitteleuropa und das Erbe der Imperien, 1917–1924*, edited by Tim Buchen and Frank Grelka, translated by Adam Peszke, 47–64. Berlin: epubli, 2016.

Burgio, Alberto, ed. *Nel nome della razza: Il razzismo nella storia d'Italia 1870–1945*. Bologna: Il Mulino, 1999.

Burgio, Alberto, and Luciano Casali, eds. *Studi sul razzismo italiano*. Bologna: CLUEB, 1996.

Caccamo, Francesco. *L'Italia e la «Nuova Europa». Il confronto sull'Europa orientale alla conferenza di pace di Parigi (1919–1920)*. Milan: Luni Editrice, 2000.

Caccamo, Francesco. 'Italy, the Adriatic and the Balkans: From the Great War to the Eve of the Peace Conference'. In *Italy in the Era of the Great War*, edited by Vanda Wilcox, 122–44. Leiden: Brill, 2018. DOI: https://doi.org/10.1163/9789004363724_008.

Cacciaguerra, Giuseppe. *Corpo di spedizione italiano in Murmania 1918–1919*. Rome: Stato maggiore dell'Esercito, Ufficio storico, 2014.

Cammarano, Fulvio, ed. *Abbasso la guerra!: neutralisti in piazza alla vigilia della Prima Guerra Mondiale in Italia*. Florence: Le Monnier, 2015.

Cappellano, Fabio. 'The Evolution of Tactical Regulations in the Italian Army in the Great War'. In *Italy in the Era of the Great War*, edited by Vanda Wilcox, 30–54. Leiden: Brill, 2018. DOI: https://doi.org/10.1163/9789004363724_004.

Capuzzo, Ester. 'Sudditanza e cittadinanza nell'esperienza coloniale italiana dell'età liberale'. *Clio* XXXI, no. 1 (1995): 65–95.

Capuzzo, Ester. 'In vista dell'annessione: i pieni poteri e la legislazione di guerra'. In *Dall'Austria all'Italia: aspetti istituzionali e problemi normativi nella storia di una frontiera*. Rome: La Fenice, 1996.

Caracciolo, Mario. *Le truppe italiane in Francia. Il II Corpo d'armata e le T.A.I.F.* Milan: Mondadori, 1929.

Carazzi, Maria. *La Società Geografica Italiana e l'esplorazione coloniale in Africa (1867–1900)*. Florence: La Nuova Italia, 1972

Carter, Nick. *Modern Italy in Historical Perspective*. London: Bloomsbury Academic, 2010.

Caselli Lapeschi, Alberto, and Giancarlo Militello, eds. *1918: Gli italiani sul fronte occidentale: nel diario del ten. Giacomo Tortora e in altri documenti inediti*. Buccinasco (MI): Società storica per la Guerra Bianca, 2007.

Cassels, Alan. 'Was There a Fascist Foreign Policy? Tradition and Novelty'. *The International History Review* 5, no. 2 (1983): 255–68.

Catalan, Tullia. 'Linguaggi e stereotipi dell'antislavismo irredentista dalla fine dell'Ottocento alla Grande Guerra'. In *Fratelli al massacro: linguaggi e narrazioni della Prima Guerra mondiale*, edited by Tullia Catalan, 39–68. Rome: Viella, 2015.

Cattaruzza, Marina. *L'Italia e il confine orientale: 1866–2006*. Bologna: Il Mulino, 2007.

Cecini, Giovanni. *Il Corpo di spedizione italiano in Anatolia: 1919–1922*. Rome: Stato Maggiore dell'Esercito, Ufficio Storico, 2010.

Cerasi, Laura. 'Empires Ancient and Modern: Strength, Modernity and Power in Imperial Ideology from the Liberal Period to Fascism'. *Modern Italy* 19, no. 4 (2014): 421–38, DOI: http://dx.doi.org/10.1080/13532944.2014.968116.

Chabod, Federico. *Storia della politica estera italiana: dal 1870 al 1896*. Bari: Laterza, 1962.

Chiti, Elena. 'Et si la Grande Guerre commençait en 1911? L'entrée en guerre vue d'Alexandrie'. *Revue des mondes musulmans et de la Méditerranée* no. 141 (15 June 2017): 153–71.

Choate, Mark I. 'From Territorial to Ethnographic Colonies and Back Again: The Politics of Italian Expansion, 1890–1912'. *Modern Italy* 8, no. 1 (2003): 65–75.

Choate, Mark I. *Emigrant Nation: The Making of Italy Abroad*. Cambridge, MA: Harvard University Press, 2008.

Cinel, Dino. *The National Integration of Italian Return Migration: 1870–1929*. Cambridge: Cambridge University Press, 2002.

Collotti, Enzo. 'Sul razzismo antislavo'. In *Nel nome della razza: il razzismo nella storia d'Italia 1870–1945*, edited by Alberto Burgio, 33–61. Bologna: Il Mulino, 1999.

Cresti, Federico. 'La prima emigrazione di lavoratori Maghrebini in Italia'. In *Conflitti, migrazioni e diritti dell'uomo: il Mezzogiorno laboratorio di un'identità mediterranea*, edited by Maurice Aymard and Fabrizio Barca, 47–59. Soveria Mannelli: Rubbettino, 2002.

Cresti, Federico. 'Quale futuro per la Libia italiana? Dal dibattito sulla politica coloniale del dopoguerra alla promulgazione degli statuti (1918–1920)'. In *Sudditi o Cittadini? L'evoluzione delle appartenenze imperiali nella Prima Guerra Mondiale*, edited by Sara Lorenzini and Simone Attilio Bellezza, 153–87. Rome: Viella, 2018.

Curli, Barbara. *Italiane al lavoro, 1914–1920*. Venice: Marsilio, 1998.

Daly, Selena. *Italian Futurism and the First World War*. Toronto: University of Toronto Press, 2016.

Daly, Selena. 'Emigrant Draft Evasion in the First World War: Decision-Making and Emotional Consequences in the Transatlantic Italian Family', *European History Quarterly*, 51, April 2021, forthcoming.

Das, Santanu. *Race, Empire and First World War Writing*. Cambridge: Cambridge University Press, 2011.

De Angeli, Aglaia. 'Italian Land Auctions in Tianjin: Italian Colonialism in Early Twentieth-Century China'. *Journal of Modern Italian Studies* 15, no. 4 (2010): 557–72, DOI: http://dx.doi.org/10.1080/1354571X.2010.501976.

De Felice, Renzo. *D'Annunzio Politico 1918–1938*. Rome; Bari: Laterza, 1978.

Del Boca, Angelo. *Dal fascismo a Gheddafi*. Vol. 2. 2 vols. Gli italiani in Libia: 2. Bari: Laterza, 1986.

Del Boca, Angelo. *Tripoli bel suol d'amore, 1860–1922*. Vol. 1. 2 vols. L'Italiani in Libia. Bari: Laterza, 1986.

Del Boca, Angelo. *Italiani, brava gente?* Vicenza: Neri Pozza, 2011.

Del Boca, Angelo. *Mohamed Fekini and the Fight to Free Libya*. New York: Palgrave Macmillan, 2011.

Del Boca, Angelo. *La disfatta di Gasr bu Hàdi*. Milan: Mondadori, 2014.

Del Negro, Piero. 'La leva militare dall'Unità alla Grande Guerra'. In *L'esercito italiano dall'unità alla Grande Guerra*, edited by Stato Maggiore dell'Esercito, 431–65. Rome: Ufficio Storico, Stato Maggiore dell'Esercito, 1980.

Dentoni, Maria Concetta. 'Food and Nutrition (Italy)'. *1914–1918-Online International Encyclopedia of the First World War*, edited by Ute Daniel, Peter Gatrell, Oliver Janz, Heather Jones, Jennifer Keene, Alan Kramer, and Bill Nasson. Berlin: Freie Universität Berlin, 2014. https://encyclopedia.1914-1918-online.net/article/food_and_nutrition_italy. DOI: https://doi.org/10.15463/ie1418.10511.

Dewhirst, Catherine. 'Colonising Italians: Italian Imperialism and Agricultural "Colonies" in Australia, 1881–1914'. *The Journal of Imperial and Commonwealth History* 44, no. 1 (2 January 2016): 23–47.

Di Michele, Andrea. 'L'Italia in Austria: Da Vienna a Trento'. In *La vittoria senza pace: le occupazioni militari italiane alla fine della Grande Guerra*, edited by Raoul Pupo, Prima edizione, 3–72. Rome: GLF editori Laterza, 2014.

Di Pasquale, Francesca. 'Libici per la patria Italia. Esperienze di lavoro e di vita nelle lettere degli operai coloniali durante la prima guerra mondiale'. *Zapruder. Storie in Movimento* 18 (2009): 50–63, http://storieinmovimento.org/wp-content/uploads/2017/07/Zap18_5-zoom4.pdf.

Di Pasquale, Francesca. 'The "Other" at Home: Deportation and Transportation of Libyans to Italy During the Colonial Era (1911–1943)'. *International Review of Social History* 63, no. Special Issue: Transportation, Deportation and Exile: Perspectives from the Colonies in the Nineteenth and Twentieth Centuries (2018): 211–31, DOI: https://doi.org/10.1017/S0020859018000299.

Di Scala, Spencer. *Vittorio Emanuele Orlando: Italy*. London: Haus Pub., 2010.

Di Scala, Spencer. 'Liberalism, Civil Rights, and Reform: Vittorio Emanuele Orlando and the Great War'. In *Italy in the Era of the Great War*, edited by Vanda Wilcox, 186–209. Leiden: Brill, 2018. DOI: https://doi.org/10.1163/9789004363724_011.

Dickie, John. *Darkest Italy: The Nation and Stereotypes of the Mezzogiorno, 1860–1900*. Basingstoke: Macmillan, 1999.

Dickinson, F. R. 'Toward a Global Perspective of the Great War: Japan and the Foundations of a Twentieth-Century World'. *The American Historical Review* 119, no. 4 (1 October 2014): 1154–83.

Donati, Sabina. *A Political History of National Citizenship and Identity in Italy, 1861–1950*. Palo Alto, CA: Stanford University Press, 2013.

Donati, Sabina. 'Citizenship and Identity Issues in the Italian Concession of Tientsin (1902–1922)'. In *Ideas and Identities. A Festschrift for Andre Liebich*, edited by Jaci Eisenberg and Davide Rodogno. Bern: Peter Lang, 2014.

Donati, Sabina. '"Cittadinanza", "sudditanza" e "nazionalità" in contesto imperiale': Riflessioni sul caso italiano tra guerra e dopoguerra, 1914–1925'. *Italian Culture* (2021), forthcoming.

Dorlhiac, Renaud, and Fabrice Jesné. 'Une alliance de circonstance: l'Italie et les musulmans d'Albanie (1912–1920)'. *Revue des mondes musulmans et de la Méditerranée* no. 141 (2017): 51–67.

Douki, Caroline. 'Les Italiens de Glasgow: identités et appartenances communautaires à l'épreuve de la Première guerre mondiale'. In *Les petites Italies dans le monde*, edited by Marie-Claude Blanc-Chaléard, Antonio Bechelloni, Bénédicte Deschamps, Michel Dreyfus, and Eric Vial, 243–60. Rennes: Presses Univ. de Rennes, 2007.

Duggan, Christopher. *Francesco Crispi, 1818–1901: From Nation to Nationalism*. Oxford: Oxford University Press, 2002.

Dumasy, François. 'La Libye, un laboratoire des variations de la relation coloniale pendant la Première Guerre mondiale?' *Revue des mondes musulmans et de la Méditerranée* no. 141 (2017): 67–85, DOI: https://doi.org/10.4000/remmm.9827.

Dunscomb, Paul. 'Siberian Intervention 1918–1922'. In *1914–1918 Online. International Encyclopedia of the First World War*, edited by Ute Daniel, Peter Gatrell, Oliver Janz, Heather Jones, Jennifer Keene, Alan Kramer, and Bill Nasson. Berlin: Freie Universität Berlin, 2018. https://encyclopedia.1914-1918-online.net/article/siberian_intervention_1918–1922.

El Houssi, Leila. 'Gli "italiani" dell'altra sponda. La collettività italiana di Tunisia fino all'avvento del fascismo'. In *Circolazioni Mediterranee*, edited by Valerio Giannattasio. Naples: Guida, 2017.

Ellero, Elpidio. *Le donne nella Prima Guerra mondiale: in Friuli e in Veneto*. Udine: Gaspari, 2016.

Ermacora, Matteo. 'Assistance and Surveillance: War Refugees in Italy, 1914–1918'. *Contemporary European History* 16, no. 4 (2007): 445–59.

Evans-Pritchard, E. E. *The Sanusi of Cyrenaica*. Oxford: Oxford University Press, 1949.

Faldella, Emilio. *Caporetto, le vere cause di una tragedia*. Bologna: Cappelli, 1967.

Fauri, Francesca. 'Italians in Africa (1870s–1914), or How to Escape Poverty and Become a Landowner'. *The International History Review* 27, no. 2 (2015): 325–41, DOI: https://doi.org/10.1080/07075332.2014.904811.

Fava, Andrea. 'D'Adamo, Agostino'. In *Dizionario Biografico Degli Italiani*. Vol. 31. Rome: Treccani, 1985.

Fava, Andrea. 'War, "National Education" and the Italian Primary School, 1915–1918'. In *State, Society and Mobilization in Europe during the First World War*, edited by John Horne, 53–69. Cambridge: Cambridge University Press, 1997.

Finaldi, Giuseppe. *Italian National Identity in the Scramble for Africa: Italy's African Wars in the Era of Nation-Building, 1870–1900*. New York: Peter Lang, 2009.

Finaldi, Giuseppe, and Daniela Baratieri. '"Without Flinching": Facing up to Race in Liberal Italy'. *Australian Journal of Politics & History* 65, no. 1 (2019): 1–16.

Finefrock, Michael M. 'Ataturk, Lloyd George and the Megali Idea: Cause and Consequence of the Greek Plan to Seize Constantinople from the Allies, June–August 1922'. *The Journal of Modern History* 52, no. 1 (1980): 1047–66, https://www.jstor.org/stable/1881129.

Fogarty, Richard S. 'La «Plus Grande Guerre». Les colonies, la race et l'armée française (1906–1916)'. *Mil neuf cent. Revue d'histoire intellectuelle* no. 33 (7 March 2016): 97–112.

Foppiani, Oreste. 'The Italian Navy in the Adriatic, 1918–1919. An Unknown Actor between Diplomatic Rivalry and International Competition'. *Nuova Rivista Storica* 101, no. 3 (2017): 969–90.

Ford, Nancy Gentile. '"Mindful of the Traditions of His Race": Dual Identity and Foreign-Born Soldiers in the First World War American Army'. *Journal of American Ethnic History* 16, no. 2 (1997): 35–57.

Ford, Nancy Gentile. *Americans All!: Foreign-Born Soldiers in World War I*. College Station: Texas A&M University Press, 2001.

Formigoni, Guido. 'Il neutralismo dei cattolici'. In *Abbasso la guerra!: neutralisti in piazza alla vigilia della prima guerra mondiale in Italia*, edited by Fulvio Cammarano. Florence: Le Monnier, 2015.

Forsyth, Douglas J. *The Crisis of Liberal Italy: Monetary and Financial Policy, 1914–1922*. Cambridge and New York: Cambridge University Press, 1993.

Forsyth, Douglas J. 'Monetary and Financial Policy and the Crisis of Liberal Italy, 1914–22'. In *Italy in the Era of the Great War*, edited by Vanda Wilcox, 287–308. Leiden: Brill, 2018. DOI: https://doi.org/10.1163/9789004363724_016.

Fox, Aimée. *Learning to Fight*. Cambridge: Cambridge University Press, 2018.

Franzina, Emilio. 'La guerra lontana. Il primo conflitto mondiale e gli italiani d'Argentina'. *Estudios Migratorios Latinoamericanos* 15, no. 44 (2000): 57–84.

Franzina, Emilio. 'Italiani del Brasile ed italobrasiliani durante il primo conflitto mondiale (1914–1918)'. *História. Debates e Tendências* 5, no. 1 (2004): 225–67.

Franzina, Emilio. 'Militari italiani e Grande Guerra'. *Zibaldone. Estudios italianos* 3, no. 1 (2015): 78–103.

Franzinelli, Mimmo. *Squadristi: Protagonisti e tecniche della violenza fascista*. Milan: Mondadori, 2004.

Frizzera, Francesco. *Cittadini dimezzati: I profughi trentini in Austria-Ungheria e in Italia (1914–1919)*. Bologna: Il Mulino, 2018.

Frizzera, Francesco. 'Dai pieni diritti all'esclusione dalla cittadinanza. I profughi di guerra nell'impero Asburgico e negli stati successori'. In *Sudditi o Cittadini? L'evoluzione delle appartenenze imperiali nella Prima Guerra Mondiale*, edited by Sara Lorenzini and Simone Attilio Bellezza. Rome: Viella, 2018.

Frizzera, Francesco. 'Refugees (Italy)'. In *International Encyclopedia of the First World War*, edited by Ute Daniel, Peter Gatrell, Oliver Janz, Heather Jones, Jennifer Keene, Alan Kramer, and Bill Nasson. Berlin: Freie Universität Berlin, 2018. https://encyclopedia. 1914-1918-online.net/article/refugees_italy.

Gabaccia, Donna. 'Italian History and gli italiani nel mondo, Part I'. *Journal of Modern Italian Studies* 2, no. 1 (1997): 45–66, DOI: https://doi.org/10.1080/13545719708454939

Gabaccia, Donna. 'Italian History and gli italiani nel mondo, Part II'. *Journal of Modern Italian Studies* 3, no. 1 (1998): 73–97, DOI: https://doi.org/10.1080/13545719808454967.

Gatti, Gian Luigi. *Dopo Caporetto. Gli Ufficiali P nella Grande guerra: propaganda, assistenza, vigilanza*. Gorizia: Libreria Editrice Goriziana, 2000.

Gemignani, Marco. 'Il bombardamento di Ancona del 24 maggio 1915'. *Bollettino d'Archivio dell'Ufficio Storico della Marina Militare* (December 2002).

Gentile, Emilio. *La grande Italia il mito della nazione nel XX secolo*. Rome: Laterza, 2011.

Gerwarth, Robert, and John Horne, eds. *War in Peace: Paramilitary Violence in Europe after the Great War*. Oxford: Oxford University Press, 2012.

Gerwarth, Robert, and Erez Manela, eds. *Empires at War: 1911–1923*. Oxford: Oxford University Press, 2014.

Gerwarth, Robert, and Erez Manela. 'The Great War as a Global War: Imperial Conflict and the Reconfiguration of World Order, 1911–1923'. *Diplomatic History* 38, no. 4 (30 July 2014): 786–800.

Ghazal, Amal. 'Counter-Currents: Mzabi Independence, Pan-Ottomanism and WWI in the Maghrib'. *First World War Studies* 7, no. 1 (May 2016): 81–96.

Ghisalberti, Carlo. 'Il mito della vittoria mutilata'. In *La Conferenza di pace di Parigi fra ieri e domani (1919–1920). Atti del Convegno Internazionale di Studi Portogruaro-Bibione. 31 maggio-4 giugno 2000*, edited by Antonio Scottà, 125–40. Soveria Mannelli: Rubbettino, 2003.

Ghosh, Durba. 'Whither India? 1919 and the Aftermath of the First World War'. *The Journal of Asian Studies* 78, no. 2 (2019): 389–97, DOI: https://doi.org/10.1017/S0021911819000044.

Gibelli, Antonio. *La Grande Guerra degli italiani, 1915–1918*. Milan: Sansoni, 1998.

Gillette, Aaron. *Racial Theories in Fascist Italy*. Abingdon: Routledge, 2003.

Giuliani, Gaia. *Race, Nation and Gender in Modern Italy: Intersectional Representations in Visual Culture*. London: Palgrave Macmillan, 2018.

Giuliani, Gaia, and Cristina Lombardi-Diop. *Bianco e nero: storia dell'identità razziale degli italiani*. Florence: Le Monnier, 2013.

Gooch, John. *Army, State and Society in Italy 1870–1915*. London: Macmillan, 1989.

Gooch, John. *The Italian Army and the First World War*. Cambridge University Press, 2014.

Gooch, John. 'Inevitable War, Improbable War? General Alberto Pollio and the Likelihood of War in 1914'. In *L'Italia neutrale 1914–1915*, edited by Andrea Ungari and Giovanni Orsina, 258–69. Rome: Rodorigo editore, 2016.

Gorgolini, Luca. *I dannati dell'Asinara: L'odissea dei prigionieri austro-ungarici nella Prima Guerra Mondiale*. Turin: UTET, 2011.

Guerrini, Irene and Marco Pluviano. 'L'area baltica tra il 1919 e il 1922 nelle fonti archivistiche diplomatiche e militari italiani', in *Da Versailles a Monaco. Vent'anni di guerre dimenticate*, edited by Davide Artico and Bruno Mantelli, 91–121. Turin: UTET, 2010.

Halpern, Paul G. *A Naval History of World War I*. Annapolis, MD: Naval Institute Press, 1994.

Halpern, Paul G. *The Battle of the Otranto Straits: Controlling the Gateway to the Adriatic in World War I*. Bloomington: Indiana University Press, 2004.

Hassiotis, Loukianos. 'Greece'. In *1914–1918-Online International Encyclopedia of the First World War*, edited by Ute Daniel, Peter Gatrell, Oliver Janz, Heather Jones, Jennifer Keene, Alan Kramer, and Bill Nasson. Berlin: Freie Universität Berlin, 2014. http://encyclopedia.1914-1918-online.net/article/greece/2014-10-08.

Hawthorne, Camilla. 'Making Italy: Afro-Italian Entrepreneurs and the Racial Boundaries of Citizenship'. *Social & Cultural Geography* (28 March 2019): 1–21, DOI: https://doi.org/10.1080/14649365.2019.1597151.

Helmreich, Paul C. 'Italy and the Anglo-French Repudiation of the 1917 St. Jean de Maurienne Agreement'. *The Journal of Modern History* 48, no. 2 (1976): 99–139, https://www.jstor.org/stable/1877819.

Hess, Robert L. 'Italy and Africa: Colonial Ambitions in the First World War'. *Journal of African History* 4, no. 1 (1963): 105–26, DOI: https://doi.org/10.1017/S0021853700003741.

Heyriès, Hubert. *Les travailleurs militaires italiens en France pendant la Grande Guerre: héros de la pelle et de la truelle au service de la victoire.* Montpellier: Presses universitaires de la Méditerranée, 2014.

Horne, John, and Alan Kramer. *German Atrocities, 1914: A History of Denial.* New Haven, CT: Yale University Press, 2001.

Hughes, Matthew. *Allenby in Palestine.* Stroud: The History Press Ltd, 2004.

Isnenghi, Mario. *Il mito della grande guerra.* 5th edn. Bologna: Il Mulino, 2002.

Isnenghi, Mario. *Le Guerre degli italiani: Parole, immagini, ricordi 1848-1945.* Bologna: Il Mulino, 2005.

Isnenghi, Mario. *Convertirsi alla guerra: liquidazioni, mobilitazioni e abiure nell'Italia tra il 1914 e il 1918.* Rome: Donzelli editore, 2015.

Jackson, Ashley, ed. *The British Empire and the First World War.* London: Routledge, 2016.

Jarboe, Andrew, and Richard Fogarty, eds. *Empires in World War I: Shifting Frontiers and Imperial Dynamics in a Global Conflict.* London: I. B. Tauris, 2013.

Johnson, Robert. *The Great War & the Middle East: A Strategic Study.* Oxford and New York: Oxford University Press, 2016.

Kallis, Aristotle. *Fascist Ideology: Territory and Expansionism in Italy and Germany, 1922-1945.* London: Routledge, 2000.

Kemény, Anna Milanini. *La Società d'esplorazione commerciale in Africa e la politica coloniale: (1879-1914).* Florence: La Nuova Italia, 1973.

Knox, MacGregor. *Mussolini Unleashed 1939-1941: Politics and Strategy in Fascist Italy's Last War.* Cambridge: Cambridge University Press, 1986.

Knox, MacGregor. 'The Fascist Regime, Its Foreign Policy and Its Wars: An "Anti-Anti-Fascist" Orthodoxy?' *Contemporary European History* 4, no. 3 (1995): 347-65, https://www.jstor.org/stable/20081559

Krause, Jonathan. 'Islam and Anti-Colonial Rebellions in North and West Africa, 1914-1918'. *The Historical Journal* (2020): 1-22, DOI: https://doi.org/10.1017/S0018246X20000357.

Labanca, Nicola. *In marcia verso Adua.* Turin: Einaudi, 1993.

Labanca, Nicola, ed. *Posti al sole. Diari e memorie di vita e di lavoro dalle colonie d'Africa.* Rovereto (TN): Museo Storico Italiano della Guerra, 2001.

Labanca, Nicola. 'Discorsi coloniali in uniforme militare, da Assab via Adua verso Tripoli'. In *Guerra e pace*, edited by Walter Barberis, I., 503-45. Storia d'Italia, Annali 18. Turin: Einaudi, 2002.

Labanca, Nicola. *Oltremare: storia dell'espansione coloniale italiana.* Bologna: Il Mulino, 2002.

Labanca, Nicola. *La guerra italiana per la Libia: 1911-1931.* Bologna: Il Mulino, 2012.

Labanca, Nicola. *Caporetto: storia e memoria di una disfatta.* Bologna: Il Mulino, 2017.

Latini, Carlotta. 'I pieni poteri in Italia durante la prima guerra mondiale'. In *Un paese in guerra: la mobilitazione civile in Italia, 1914-1918*, edited by Daniele Menozzi, Giovanna Procacci, and Simonetta Soldani, 87-104. Milan: Unicopli, 2010.

Ledeen, Michael Arthur. *The First Duce: D'Annunzio at Fiume.* Baltimore: Johns Hopkins University Press, 1977.

Lenci, Marco. 'Review of *La légende noire de la Sanusiyya. Une confrèrie musulmane saharienne sous le regard francais (1840-1930), 2 tomi,* by Jean-Louis Triaud'. *Africa: Rivista trimestrale di studi e documentazione dell'istituto italiano per l'Africa e l'Oriente* 51, no. 4 (1996): 607-9.

Lesti, Sante. *Riti di guerra. Religione e politica nell'Europa della Grande Guerra.* Bologna: Il Mulino, 2015.

Lohr, Eric. *Russian Citizenship: From Empire to Soviet Union*. Cambridge, MA: Harvard University Press, 2012.

Lombardi-Diop, Cristina and Caterina Romeo, eds. *Postcolonial Italy: Challenging National Homogeneity*. New York: Palgrave Macmillan, 2012.

Lorenzini, Sara, and Simone Attilio Bellezza, eds. *Sudditi o cittadini? L'evoluzione delle appartenenze imperiali nella Prima Guerra Mondiale*. Rome: Viella, 2018.

Lo Sardo, Eugenio, Anna De Pascale, Carlo M. Fiorentino, and Archivio centrale dello Stato. *La Grande Guerra: l'Italia e il Levante*. Rome: De Luca Editori d'Arte, 2017.

Lowe, Cedric J., and Frank Marzari. *Italian Foreign Policy, 1870–1940*. London and New York: Taylor & Francis, 2002.

McCollum, Jonathan. 'Reimagining Mediterranean Spaces: Libya and the Italo-Turkish War, 1911–1912', *Diacronie. Studi di Storia Contemporanea* 23, no. 3 (2015).

McCrae, Meighen. *Coalition Strategy and the End of the First World War: The Supreme War Council and War Planning, 1917–1918*. Cambridge and New York: Cambridge University Press, 2019.

McGuire, Valerie. 'An Imperial Education for Times of Transition: Italian Conquest, Occupation and Civil Administration of the Southeast Aegean, 1912–23'. In *Italy in the Era of the Great War*, edited by Vanda Wilcox, 145–63. Leiden: Brill, 2018. DOI: https://doi.org/10.1163/9789004363724_009.

McGuirk, Russell H. *The Sanusi's Little War: The Amazing Story of a Forgotten Conflict in the Western Desert, 1915–1917*. London: Arabian Publ., 2007.

Macmillan, Margaret. *Paris 1919: Six Months That Changed the World*. New York: Random House, 2002.

Malagodi, Olindo. *Conversazioni della Guerra*. Milan: Riccardo Ricciardi, 1960.

Malgeri, Francesco. *La guerra libica (1911–1912)*. Rome: Edizioni di storia e letteratura, 1970.

Mallett, Robert. *Mussolini in Ethiopia, 1919–1935: The Origins of Fascist Italy's African War*. New York: Cambridge University Press, 2015.

Manela, Erez. *The Wilsonian Moment: Self-Determination and the International Origins of Anticolonial Nationalism*. Oxford and New York: Oxford University Press, 2007.

Marcuzzi, Stefano. 'A Machiavellian Ally? Italy in the Entente (1914–1918)'. In *Italy in the Era of the Great War*, edited by Vanda Wilcox, 99–121. Leiden: Brill, 2018. DOI: https://doi.org/10.1163/9789004363724_007.

Marcuzzi, Stefano. 'Italy's "Parallel War" in Libya: A Forgotten Front of World War I (1914–1922)'. In *Africa and the First World War: Remembrance, Memories and Representations after 100 Years*, edited by De-Valera N. Y. M. Botchway and Kwame Osei Kwarteng, 164–87. Newcastle: Cambridge Scholars Publishing, 2018.

Marcuzzi, Stefano. *Britain and Italy in the Era of the First World War. Defending and Forging Empires*. Cambridge: Cambridge University Press, 2020.

Marinelli, Maurizio. 'The Genesis of the Italian Concession in Tianjin: A Combination of Wishful Thinking and Realpolitik'. *Journal of Modern Italian Studies* 15, no. 4 (2010): 536–56, DOI: http://dx.doi.org/10.1080/1354571X.2010.501975.

Martin, Lawrence, ed. *The Treaties of Peace, 1919–1923... Maps Compiled Especially for This Edition and a Summary of the Legal Basis of the New Boundaries by Lt.-Col. Lawrence Martin*. New York: Carnegie Endowment for International Peace, 1924.

Marzona, Alain. 'Les incidents franco-italiens de Fiume ou l'expression des frustrations italiennes (novembre 1918–juillet 1919)'. *Revue historique des armées* no. 254 (15 March 2009): 29–38, http://journals.openedition.org/rha/6383.

Mautone, Antonio. *Trentini e Italiani contro l'Armata Rossa: la storia del Corpo di Spedizione in Estremo Oriente e dei Battaglioni Neri, 1918–1920*. Trento: Temi, 2003.

Mazza, Roberto. 'Churches at War: The Impact of the First World War on the Christian Institutions of Jerusalem, 1914–20'. *Middle Eastern Studies* 45, no. 2 (2009): 207–27, DOI: https://doi.org/10.1080/00263200802383248.

Mazzetti, Massimo. 'I piani di guerra contro l'Austria dal 1866 alla Prima Guerra Mondiale'. In *L'esercito italiano dall'Unità alla Grande Guerra*, edited by Ufficio Storico, Stato Maggiore dell'Esercito. Rome: Stato Maggiore dell'Esercito, 1980.

Mellino, Miguel. 'De-Provincializing Italy'. In *Postcolonial Italy: Challenging National Homogeneity*, edited by Cristina Lombardi-Diop and Caterina Romeo, 83–102. New York: Palgrave Macmillan, 2012.

Melograni, Piero. *Storia politica della Grande Guerra*. Milan: Mondadori, 1965.

Mennasemay, Maimire. 'Adwa: A Dialogue between the Past and the Present'. *Northeast African Studies* 4, no. 2 (1997): 43–89, DOI: https://doi.org/10.1353/nas.1997.0008.

Menozzi, Daniele. *La Chiesa italiana nella Grande Guerra*. Brescia: Morcelliana, 2015.

Menozzi, Daniele, Giovanna Procacci, and Simonetta Soldani. *Un paese in guerra: la mobilitazione civile in italia (1914–1918)*. Milan: Unicopli, 2010.

Micheletta, Luca, and Andrea Ungari, eds. *L'Italia e la guerra di Libia cent'anni dopo*. Rome: Edizioni Studium, 2013.

Minerbi, Sergio. 'Angelo Levi-Bianchini in Levante (1918–1920)'. *Rivista di Studi Politici Internazionali* 34, no. 1 (1967): 45–108.

Mohammad Suliaman, Aesha. 'The Impact of the Italian Occupation of Cyrenaica with Reference to Benghazi, 1911–1942'. PhD Thesis, Bangor University, 2017.

Molony, John Neylon. *The Emergence of Political Catholicism in Italy: Partito Popolare 1919–1926*. London: C. Helm, 1977.

Mondini, Marco. *La guerra italiana. Partire, raccontare, tornare 1914–18*. Bologna: Il Mulino, 2014.

Mondini, Marco. 'L'historiographie italienne face à la Grande Guerre: saisons et ruptures'. *HISTOIRE@POLITIQUE* 22 (jan–avr 2014), http://www.histoire-politique.fr/index.php?numero=22&rub=dossier&item=208.

Mondini, Marco. *Il capo. La grande guerra del generale Cadorna*. Bologna: Il Mulino, 2017.

Mondini, Marco. *Fiume 1919. Una guerra civile italiana*. Rome: Salerno, 2019.

Monina, Giancarlo. *Il consenso coloniale: le società geografiche e l'Istituto Coloniale Italiano: 1896–1914*. Rome: Carocci, 2002.

Montalbano, Gabriele. 'The Italian Community of Tunisia: From Libyan Colonial Ambitions to the First World War'. In *The First World War from Tripoli to Addis Ababa (1911–1924)*, edited by Shiferaw Bekele, Uoldelul Chelati Dirar, Alessandro Volterra, and Massimo Zaccaria. Addis Abbeba: Centre français des études éthiopiennes, 2018. DOI: https://doi.org/10.4000/books.cfee.1532.

Montanari, Mario. *Le truppe italiane in Albania: (anni 1914–20 e 1939)*. Rome: Stato Maggiore Esercito, Ufficio Storico, 1978.

Montgomery, A. E. 'VIII. The Making of the Treaty of Sèvres of 10 August 1920'. *The Historical Journal* 15, no. 4 (December 1972): 775–87.

Monzali, Luciano. *Il colonialismo nella politica estera italiana 1878–1949: momenti e protagonisti*, Rome: Società Editrice Dante Alighieri, 2017.

Monzali, Luciano. 'La politica estera di Sidney Sonnino e i fini di guerra dell'Italia (1915–1917)'. In *La guerra di Cadorna 1915–1917*, edited by Pietro Neglie and Andrea Ungari, 315–25. Rome: Ufficio Storico, Stato Maggiore dell'Esercito, 2018.

Morrow, John. *The Great War: An Imperial History*. London and New York: Routledge, 2004.

Mosse, George L. 'The Poet and the Exercise of Political Power: Gabriele D'Annunzio'. In *Masses and Man: Nationalist and Fascist Perceptions of Reality*. Detroit: Wayne State University Press, 1987.

Moyd, Michelle R. *Violent Intermediaries: African Soldiers, Conquest, and Everyday Colonialism in German East Africa*. Athens, OH: Ohio University Press, 2014.

Moyd, Michelle R. 'Centring a Sideshow: Local Experiences of the First World War in Africa'. *First World War Studies* 7, no. 2 (2016): 111–30, DOI: https://doi.org/10.1080/19475020.2016.1174591.

Mulligan, William, Andreas Rose, and Dominik Geppert, eds. *The Wars before the Great War. Conflict and International Politics before the Outbreak of the First World War*. Cambridge: Cambridge University Press, 2015.

Nardi, Isabella, and Sandro Gentili, eds. *La grande illusione: opinione pubblica e mass media al tempo della guerra di Libia*. Perugia: Morlacchi, 2009.

Neiberg, Michael S. *Fighting the Great War: A Global History*. Cambridge, MA: Harvard University Press, 2005.

Neiberg, Michael S. *The Treaty of Versailles: A Concise History*. Oxford: Oxford University Press, 2017.

Newman, John Paul. 'Post-Imperial and Post-War Violence in the South Slav Lands, 1917–1923'. *Contemporary European History* 19, no. 3 (2010): 249–65, DOI: https://doi.org/10.1017/S0960777310000159.

Novati, Giampaolo Caichi. 'L'annessione dell'Oltregiuba nella politica coloniale italiana'. *Africa: Rivista trimestrale di studi e documentazione dell'Istituto italiano per l'Africa e l'Oriente* 40, no. 2 (1985): 221–54.

Novati, Giampaolo Caichi. 'Studi e politica ai convegni coloniali del primo e del secondo dopoguerra'. *Il Politico* 55, no. 3 (155) (1990): 487–514.

O'Halloran, Erin. '"A Tempest in a British Tea Pot": The Arab Question in Cairo and Delhi'. In *1916 in Global Context: An Anti-Imperial Moment*, edited by Enrico Dal Lago, Róisín Healy, and Gearóid Barry. Abingdon: Routledge, 2018.

Omodeo, Adolfo. *Momenti della vita di guerra. Dai diari e dalle lettere dei caduti, 1915–1918*. Turin: Einaudi, 1968.

Pack, Jason. 'The Antecedents and Implications of the So-Called Anglo-Sanussi War 1915–1917'. In *The First World War and Its Aftermath: The Shaping of the Middle East*, edited by T. G. Fraser, 41–62. London: Gingko, 2015.

Palabıyık, Mustafa Serdar. 'Contextualising the Ottoman Dynasty: Sultan Mehmed V Reşad and the Ottoman Princes in the Great War'. In *Monarchies and the Great War*, edited by Matthew Glencross and Judith Rowbotham, 121–51. Basingstoke: Palgrave Macmillan, 2018.

Paolini, Marcello. 'I fatti di Ancona e l'11° Bersaglieri (giugno 1920)'. *Quaderni di Resistenza Marche* 4 (1982): 95–119.

Patriarca, Silvana, and Valeria Deplano. 'Nation, "Race", and Racisms in Twentieth-Century Italy'. *Modern Italy* 23, no. 4 (2018): 349–53, DOI: https://doi.org/10.1017/mit.2018.38.

Payk, Marcus M., and Roberta Pergher, eds. *Beyond Versailles: Sovereignty, Legitimacy, and the Formation of New Polities after the Great War*. Bloomington: Indiana University Press, 2019.

Pedersen, Susan. *The Guardians: The League of Nations and the Crisis of Empire*. Oxford, New York: Oxford University Press, 2015.

Pelaggi, Stefano. *Il colonialismo popolare: L'emigrazione e la tentazione espansionistica italiana in America latina*. Rome: Nuova Cultura, 2015.

Pergher, Roberta. *Fascist Borderlands: Nation, Empire and Italy's Settlement Program, 1922-1943*. New York: Cambridge University Press, 2017.

Pergher, Roberta. 'An Italian War? War and Nation in the Italian Historiography of the First World War'. *Journal of Modern History* 90, no. 4 (December 2018): 863-99, DOI: https://doi.org/10.1086/700561.

Petricioli, Marta. *L'Italia in Asia Minore. Equilibrio mediterraneo e ambizioni imperialiste alla vigilia della prima guerra mondiale*. Florence: Sansoni, 1983.

Petricioli, Marta. *Oltre il mito: l'Egitto degli Italiani, 1917-1947*. Milan: Mondadori, 2007.

Petrignani, Rinaldo. *Neutralità e alleanza. Le scelte di politica estera dell'Italia dopo l'Unità*. Bologna: Il Mulino, 1987.

Pluviano, Marco, and Irene Guerrini. *Le fucilazioni sommarie nella prima guerra mondiale*. Udine: Gaspari, 2004.

Pollard, John F. *Money and the Rise of the Modern Papacy: Financing the Vatican, 1850-1950*. Cambridge: Cambridge University Press, 2009.

Procacci, Giovanna. *Soldati e prigionieri italiani nella Grande guerra*. Turin: Bollati Boringhieri, 2000.

Procacci, Giovanna. 'La società come una caserma: La svolta repressiva degli anni di guerra'. In *La violenza contro la popolazione civile nella Grande guerra: deportati, profughi, internati*, edited by Bruna Bianchi, 283-304. Milan: Unicopli, 2006.

Pupo, Raoul, ed. *La vittoria senza pace: le occupazioni militari italiane alla fine della grande guerra*. Rome: GLF editori Laterza, 2014.

Raza, Saima. 'Italian Colonisation & Libyan Resistance: the Al-Sanusi of Cyrenaica (1911-1922)'. *OGIRISI: A New Journal of African Studies* 9, no. 1 (2012): 1-43. http://dx.doi.org/10.4314/og.v9i1.1.

Re, Lucia. 'Italians and the Invention of Race: The Poetics and Politics of Difference in the Struggle over Libya, 1890-1913'. *California Italian Studies* 1, no. 1 (2010), https://escholarship.org/uc/item/96k3w5kn.

Renzi, William A. *In the Shadow of the Sword: Italy's Neutrality and Entrance into the Great War*. New York: Peter Lang, 1983.

Riccardi, Luca. *Alleati non amici. Le relazioni politiche tra l'Italia e l'Intesa durante la prima guerra mondiale*. Brescia: Morcelliana, 1992.

Rochat, Giorgio. *L'esercito italiano da Vittorio Veneto a Mussolini (1919-1925)*. Bari: Laterza, 1967.

Rochat, Giorgio. *Le guerre italiane 1935-1943*. Turin: G. Einaudi, 2005.

Romano, Ruggiero, and Corrado Vivanti, eds. *Storia d'Italia. Vol. 4, t. 3: Dall'Unità a oggi*. Turin: Einaudi, 1976.

Romano, Sergio. *Giuseppe Volpi et l'Italie moderne. Finance, industrie et État de l'ère giolitienne à la deuxième Guerre mondiale*. Vol. 65. Rome: École Française de Rome, 1982.

Rossi, Marina. *I prigionieri dello zar: soldati italiani dell'esercito austro-ungarico nei lager della Russia, 1914-1918*. Milan: Mursia, 1997.

Rovinello, Marco. *Fra servitù e servizio: storia della leva in Italia dall'Unità alla Grande Guerra*. Rome: Viella, 2020.

Ryan, Eileen. 'Violence and the Politics of Prestige: The Fascist Turn in Colonial Libya'. *Modern Italy* 20, no. 2 (3 April 2015): 123-35.

Ryan, Eileen. *Religion as Resistance: Negotiating Authority in Italian Libya*. New York: Oxford University Press, 2018.

Sala, Teodoro. '"Redenzione" e "conquista": la guerra del '15–'18 al confine orientale. I fucilati del 29 maggio 1915 a Villesse'. *Bollettino dell'Istituto regionale per la storia del Movimento di liberazione nel Friuli-Venezia Giulia* no. 1–2 (1975): 15–17.

Sala, Teodoro. 'Guerra e amministrazione in Jugoslavia, 1941–1943: un'ipotesi coloniale'. *Annali della Fondazione Micheletti* 5 (1991): 83–94.

Salata, Francesco. *Il Nodo di Gibuti: storia diplomatica su documenti inediti*. Milan: Istituto per gli Studi di Politica Internazionale, 1939.

Sale, Giovanni. *Libia 1911: I Cattolici, la Santa Sede e l'impresa Coloniale Italiana*. Milan: Jaca, 2011.

Salomone, A. William. *Italy in the Giolittian Era: Italian Democracy in the Making, 1900–1914*. Philadelphia: University of Pennsylvania Press, 1960.

Salvemini, Gaetano. *Come siamo andati in Libia e altri scritti dal 1900 al 1915*. Edited by Augusto Torre. Milan: Feltrinelli, 1973.

Salvemini, Gaetano. *The Origins of Fascism in Italy*. New York: Harper & Row, 1973.

Salvetti, Patrizia. 'Il movimento migratorio italiano durante la Prima Guerra Mondiale'. *Studi Emigrazione* 87 (1987): 282–95.

Saviano, Leonardo. 'Il Partito Socialista Italiano e la guerra di Libia (1911–1912). I.' *Aevum* 48, no. 1/2 (1974): 102–30, https://www.jstor.org/stable/25821263.

Scartabellati, Andrea. 'Un *Wanderer* dell'anormalità? Un Invito Allo Studio Di Placido Consiglio (1877–1959)'. *Rivista Sperimentale di Frenatria* 134 (2010): 89–112, DOI: https://doi.org/10.3280/RSF2010-003008.

Schiavulli, Antonio. *La guerra lirica: il dibattito dei letterati italiani sull'impresa di Libia (1911–1912)*. Ravenna: Fernandel, 2009.

Scolè, Pierluigi. 'War Losses (Italy)'. In *1914–1918-Online. International Encyclopedia of the First World War*, edited by Ute Daniel, Peter Gatrell, Oliver Janz, Heather Jones, Jennifer Keene, Alan Kramer, and Bill Nasson. Berlin: Freie Universität Berlin, 2015. https://encyclopedia.1914-1918-online.net/article/war_losses_italy.

Sieche, Erwin. 'La Guerra sottomarina tedesca nel Mediterraneo 1915–1918'. In *La Guerra Navale 1914–1918: Un contributo internazionale alle operazioni in Mediterraneo*, edited by Achille Rastelli, Alessandro Massignani, and Andrea Curami, 51–88. Novale, Vicenza: G. Rossato, 2002.

Simon, Rachel. *Libya between Ottomanism and Nationalism: The Ottoman Involvement in Libya during the War with Italy (1911–1919)*. Berlin: K. Schwarz, 1987.

Slight, John. 'British Understandings of the Sanussiyya Sufi Order's Jihad against Egypt, 1915–17'. *The Round Table* 103, no. 2 (2014): 233–42.

Smith, Leonard V. *Sovereignty at the Paris Peace Conference of 1919*. Oxford and New York: Oxford University Press, 2018.

Soldani, Simonetta, and Gabriele Turi. *Fare gli italiani: scuola e cultura nell'Italia contemporanea*. Bologna: Il Mulino, 1993.

Soresina, Marco. 'Italian Emigration Policy during the Great Migration Age, 1888–1919: The Interaction of Emigration and Foreign Policy'. *Journal of Modern Italian Studies* 21, no. 5 (2016): 723–46, DOI: https://doi.org/10.1080/1354571X.2016.1242260.

Sorgoni, Barbara. *Parole e corpi. Antropologia, discorso giuridico e politiche sessuali interrazziali nella colonia Eritrea*. Naples: Liguori, 1998.

Srivastava, Neelam Francesca Rashmi. *Italian Colonialism and Resistances to Empire, 1930–1970*. London: Palgrave Macmillan, 2018.

Stefani, Giulietta. *Colonia per Maschi: Italiani in Africa Orientale, Una Storia Di Genere*. Verona: Ombre corte, 2007.

Stein, Oliver. 'Scientists in Uniform: The German Military and the Investigation of the Ottoman Landscape'. In *Landscapes of the First World War*, edited by Selena Daly, Martina Salvante, and Vanda Wilcox, 139–56. London: Palgrave Macmillan, 2018.

Sterba, Christopher. *Good Americans: Italian and Jewish Immigrants during the First World War*. Oxford: Oxford University Press, 2003.

Stewart-Steinberg, Suzanne. *The Pinocchio Effect: On Making Italians 1860–1920*. Chicago: University of Chicago Press, 2007.

Stiaccini, Carlo. 'The Catholic Church and the War'. In *Italy in the Era of the Great War*, edited by Vanda Wilcox, 272–86. Leiden: Brill, 2018. DOI: https://doi.org/10.1163/9789004363724_015.

Storm, Eric, and Ali Al Tuma, eds. *Colonial Soldiers in Europe, 1914–1945: 'Aliens in Uniform' in Wartime Societies*. Abingdon: Routledge, 2015.

Stouraiti, Anastasia, and Alexander Kazamias. 'The Imaginary Topographies of the Megali Idea: National Territory as Utopia'. In *Spatial Conceptions of the Nation: Modernizing Geographies in Greece and Turkey*, edited by Nikiforos Diamandouros, Çağlar Keyder, and Thalia Dragonas. London: I.B. Tauris, 2014.

Strachan, Hew. *The First World War in Africa*. Oxford: Oxford University Press, 2004.

Strachan, Hew. 'The First World War as a Global War'. *First World War Studies* 1, no. 1 (March 2010): 3–14.

Streets-Salter, Heather. *World War One in Southeast Asia: Colonialism and Anticolonialism in an Era of Global Conflict*. Cambridge: Cambridge University Press, 2017.

Sury, Salaheddin Hasan and Giampaolo Malgeri, eds. *Gli esiliati libici nel periodo coloniale, 1911–1916: raccolta documentaria*. Rome: Istituto italiano per l'Africa e l'Oriente, 2005.

Svoljšak, Petra. 'La popolazione civile nella Slovenia occupata'. In *La violenza contro la popolazione civile nella Grande guerra: deportati, profughi, internati*, edited by Bruna Bianchi, 147–63. Milan: Unicopli, 2006.

Svoljšak, Petra. 'The Language Policy of the Italian Army in the Occupied Slovenian Territories, 1915–17'. In *Languages and the Military: Alliances, Occupation and Peace Building*, edited by Hilary Footitt and Michael Kelly, 70–85. London: Palgrave Macmillan UK, 2012.

Svoljšak, Petra, and Bojan Godeša. 'Italian interwar administration of Slovenian ethnic territory: Italian ethnic policy'. In *Frontwechsel: Österreich-Ungarns 'Grosser Krieg' im Vergleich*, edited by Wolfram Dornik, Julia Walleczek-Fritz, Stefan Wedrac, and Markus Wurzer. Vienna: Böhlau Verlag, 2014.

Tomassini, Luigi. 'Gli effetti sociali della mobilitazione industriale. Industriali, lavoratori, stato'. In *Un paese in guerra: la mobilitazione civile in Italia, 1914–1918*, edited by Daniele Menozzi, Giovanna Procacci, and Simonetta Soldani, 25–58. Milan: Unicopli, 2010.

Toscano, Mario. *Gli accordi di San Giovanni di Moriana; storia diplomatica dell'intervento italiano. II. (1916–1917)*. Milan: Dott. A. Giuffrè, 1936.

Troilo, Simona. '"A Gust of Cleansing Wind": Italian Archaeology on Rhodes and in Libya in the Early Years of Occupation (1911–1914)'. *Journal of Modern Italian Studies* 17, no. 1 (2012): 45–69, DOI: https://doi.org/10.1080/1354571X.2012.628103.

Trumpener, Ulrich. *Germany and the Ottoman Empire, 1914–1918*. Princeton, NJ: Princeton University Press, 1968.

Ungari, Andrea. 'The Official Inquiry into the Italian Defeat at the Battle of Caporetto (October 1917)'. *Journal of Military History* 76, no. 3 (2012): 695–725.

Ungari, Andrea, and Francesco Anghelone. *Addetti militari italiani alla vigilia della Grande Guerra 1914–1915*. Rome: Rodrigo Editore, 2015.

Vagnini, Alessandro. *L'Italia e i Balcani nella Grande Guerra: ambizioni e realtà dell'imperialismo italiano*. Rome: Carocci editore, 2016.

Valeri, Mauro. *Generale nero. Domenico Mondelli: bersagliere, aviatore e ardito*. Rome: Odradek, 2016.

Valiani, Leo. *Il Partito socialista italiano nel periodo della neutralità*. Milan: Feltrinelli, 1963.

Vandervort, Bruce. 'A Military History of the Turco-Italian War (1911–1912) for Libya and Its Impact on Italy's Entry into the First World War'. In *Italy in the Era of the Great War*, edited by Vanda Wilcox, 14–29. Leiden: Brill, 2018. DOI: https://doi.org/10.1163/9789004363724_003.

Vandewalle, Dirk. *A History of Modern Libya*. Cambridge: Cambridge University Press, 2006.

Ventresco, Fiorello B. 'Loyalty and Dissent: Italian Reservists in America During World War I'. *Italian Americana* 4, no. 1 (1978): 93–122.

Veracini, Lorenzo. 'Italian Colonialism through a Settler Colonial Studies Lens'. *Journal of Colonialism and Colonial History* 19, no. 3 (2018).

Vigezzi, Brunello. *I problemi della neutralità e della guerra nel Carteggio Salandra- Sonnino (1914–1917)*. Milan: Albrighi, Segati e C., 1962.

Vigezzi, Brunello. 'Un'inchiesta sullo stato pubblico alla vigilia dell'intervento'. In *Da Giolitti a Salandra*, edited by Brunello Vigezzi. Florence: Vallechi, 1969.

Vigezzi, Brunello. 'L'Italia del 1914–'15 e la crisi del sistema liberale'. In *L'Italia neutrale 1914–1915*, edited by Giovanni Orsina and Andrea Ungari, 11–26. Rome: Rodorigo editore, 2016.

Vigezzi, Brunello, ed. *Da Giolitti a Salandra*. Florence: Vallechi, 1969.

Visintin, Angelo. *L'Italia a Trieste: L'operato del governo militare italiano nella Venezia Giulia, 1918–1919*. Gorizia: LEG, 2000.

Vivarelli, Roberto. *Storia delle origini del fascismo*. 2 vols. Bologna: Il Mulino, 1991.

Volterra, Alessandro. *Progetto Ascari*. Rome: Libreria Efesto, 2014.

Volterra, Alessandro. 'Askaris and the Great War. Colonial Troops Recruited in Libya for the War but Never Sent to the Austrian Front'. In *The First World War from Tripoli to Addis Ababa (1911–1924)*, edited by Shiferaw Bekele, Uoldelul Chelati Dirar, and Massimo Zaccaria. Addis Abbeba: Centre français des études éthiopiennes, 2018. DOI: https://doi.org/10.4000/books.cfee.1400.

Walter, Dierk. *Colonial Violence: European Empires and the Use of Force*. Translated by Peter Lewis. London: Hurst & Company, 2017.

Webster, Richard A. *Industrial Imperialism in Italy, 1908–1915*. Berkeley: University of California Press, 1975.

Weitz, Eric D. 'Self-Determination: How a German Enlightenment Idea Became the Slogan of National Liberation and a Human Right'. *The American Historical Review* 120, no. 2 (2015): 462–96, DOI: https://doi.org/10.1093/ahr/120.2.462.

Welch, Rhiannon Noel. *Vital Subjects: Race and Biopolitics in Italy 1860–1920*. Liverpool: Liverpool University Press, 2016.

Wilcox, Vanda. 'Training, Morale and Battlefield Performance in the Italian Army, 1914–1917'. In *The Greater War: Other Combatants and Other Fronts, 1914–1918*, edited by Jonathan Krause, 177–94. London: Palgrave Macmillan, 2014.

Wilcox, Vanda. 'The Italian Soldiers' Experience in Libya, 1911–1912'. In *The Wars before the Great War*, edited by William Mulligan, Andreas Rose, and Dominik Geppert, 41–57. Cambridge: Cambridge University Press, 2015.

Wilcox, Vanda. *Morale and the Italian Army during the First World War*. Cambridge: Cambridge University Press, 2016.

Wilcox, Vanda, ed. *Italy in the Era of the Great War*. Leiden: Brill, 2018.

Wilcox, Vanda. 'Between Faith and Nation: Italian Jewish Soldiers in the Great War'. In *The Jewish Experience of the First World War*, edited by Edward Madigan and Gideon Reuveni, 183–206. London: Palgrave Macmillan, 2019. DOI: https://doi.org/10.1057/978-1-137-54896-2_9.

Wong, Aliza S. *Race and the Nation in Liberal Italy, 1861–1911: Meridionalism, Empire, and Diaspora*. New York: Palgrave Macmillan, 2006.

Zaccaria, Massimo. *Anch'io per la tua bandiera: il V Battaglione Ascari in missione sul fronte libico (1912)*. Ravenna: G. Pozzi, 2012.

Zaccaria, Massimo. 'Feeding the War: Canned Meat Production in the Horn of Africa and the Italian Front'. In *The First World War from Tripoli to Addis Ababa (1911–1924)*, edited by Shiferaw Bekele, Uoldelul Chelati Dirar, and Alessandro Volterra. Addis Abbeba: Centre français des études éthiopiennes, 2018. DOI: https://doi.org/10.4000/books.cfee.1619.

Index

For the benefit of digital users, indexed terms that span two pages (e.g., 52–53) may, on occasion, appear on only one of those pages